THE ENGLISH OFFICE BOOK

THE ENGLISH OFFICE BOOK

Revised Edition

All rights reserved. No part of this publication
may be reproduced, stored in a retrieval system, or
transmitted, in any form or by any means, electronic,
mechanical, photocopying or otherwise, without the
prior permission of the publisher, Canterbury Press

Text © Tufton Books 1956, 2006
Introduction © Julien Chilcott-Monk 2006

First published by Church Literature Association
This new edition published in 2006
by the Canterbury Press Norwich
St Mary's Works, St Mary's Plain
Norwich, Norfolk, NR3 3BH
by permission of the copyright holders,
Tufton Books (a Church Union imprint),
Tufton Street, London

British Library Cataloguing in Publication data

A catalogue record for this book is available
from the British Library

ISBN 1-85311-698-X
978 1-85311-698 8

INTRODUCTION

Once more I am privileged to write the Introduction to a long-awaited republication. *The English Office* – originally published in 1956 and subsequently revised – is now made uniform with *The English Ritual* (reissued by Canterbury Press in 2003) and, therefore, a second junior companion to *The English Missal* (reissued by Canterbury Press in 2001).

The English Office contains the daily offices of Mattins and Evensong whose recitation, for the Anglican priest, is obligatory, but whose recitation will benefit laymen and women enormously in their private prayer by providing a consistent structure for daily devotions. These offices are the essential parts of Morning and Evening Prayer found in *The Book of Common Prayer* but dressed here with antiphons for the psalms and canticles for both ferial and feast days from Sarum, Roman and, occasionally, other sources. A generous calendar of saints' days and other celebrations is given, accompanied by a treasury of fine collects. It is good to see, for example, the Feast of St. John Vianney, the Curé d'Ars, the patron of all parish priests. Psalms in Miles Coverdale's translation – in my view, quite the most beautiful translation ever made – are provided along with much neglected office hymns in the translations found in *The English Hymnal* and in *The Parish Supplementary Hymnal*. The Office of the Dead, a number of litanies, a wealth of general intercessions (some now quite unknown), prayers before and after mass, and anthems to Our Lady, are all here.

The original printing is preserved, but there are some minor imperfections in the text – for example: 'Praise ye the Lord. The Lord's name be praised.' is missing from the beginning of Evensong. In addition, the rubrics may, from time to time, have to be read twice before they become clear, but that is part of the charm of the book.

Up to a point, the editors and compilers of *The English Office* envisaged the use of the *Revised Lectionary*; nevertheless, the *Order for the Eucharist etc* (published annually by Canterbury Press for Tufton Books) will provide all the necessary information for the proper recitation of the Office throughout the year even though some of the saints' days will have to be searched for because the Calendar used in *The English Office* of course predates the modifications made after Vatican II.

Julien Chilcott-Monk
Epiphany 2006

CONTENTS

	Page
General Rubrics	vii
The Calendar	ix
The Order of Divine Service	1
Proper of Seasons	29
Proper of Saints	107
Common of Saints	194
Office of the Dead	215
The Litany	220
The Order of Commending a Soul	224
The Itinerary	226
Prayers before and after Mass	228
Appendix	238
Antiphons to the Psalms	243
The Psalter	

GENERAL RUBRICS

THE OFFICE. The Office of the day is either double or simple. Doubles of the First and Second Class have a first Evensong; other Offices begin at Mattins. The observance of simple feasts ends before Evensong.

COMMON OF SAINTS. On greater feasts, there are either proper antiphons to the Psalms and canticles, or else the rubric. **All as in the Common** shows that the antiphons are taken from the Common. On lesser feasts, the reference to the Common is given, but the antiphons to the Psalms are from the monthly course; the rest being taken from the Common, except as noted.

ANTIPHONS. On double feasts, the antiphon is said entire before and after each Psalm and Canticle. Otherwise only the first part of the antiphon (as far as the asterisk*) is said before it. When the words of the antiphon are identical with the opening words of the Psalm, they are not repeated in that verse. When the number of antiphons is less than the number of Psalms provided, the extra Psalms are said under the last antiphon.

PSALMS. When the 1923 list of Proper Psalms provides alternatives to those of the monthly course (or to the Proper Psalms in the Prayer Book list), the numbers of these are added in brackets: e.g. at Mattins on Advent I, **"Psalms of day (or 1, 7)"**.

HYMNS. When possible, the Hymns are (by permission) taken from **The English Hymnal** (to which the numbers under 800 refer); other hymns are from **The Parish Supplementary Hymnal** (to which numbers over 800 refer).

LESSONS. For a few occasions for which the Revised Lectionary makes no provision, proper lessons are suggested, e.g. Corpus Christi. These can always be found entire elsewhere in the Revised Lectionary, as noted.

COMMEMORATIONS. A feast is commemorated by the reciting of the antiphon appointed to the **Magnificat** or **Benedictus**, the proper ℣. & ℟., and the appointed Collect.

CALENDAR

JANUARY

1 CIRCUMCISION OF OUR LORD, D.II cl.
   (Sunday between Circumcision and Epiphany: HOLY NAME OF JESUS, D.II cl.)
2
3
4
5
6 EPIPHANY OF OUR LORD, D.I cl.
   Sunday in Octave: HOLY FAMILY, gr. d.
7
8 Com. St. Lucian.
9
10
11
12
13 Com. Baptism of our Lord, gr. d.
14 St Hilary, B.C.D., d.
15 St Paul, Hermit, C., d.
16
17 St Antony, Abbot, d.
18 St Peter's Chair at Rome, Gr.d. Com. St Prisca, V.M.
19 St Wulfstan. B.C., d.
20 SS Fabian and Sebastian, MM., d.
21 St Agnes, V.M., d.
22 SS Vincent and Anastasius, MM., s.
23
24 St Timothy, B.M., d.
25 CONVERSION OF ST PAUL, D.II cl.
26 St Polycarp, B.M., d.
27 St John Chrysostom, B.C.D., d.
28
29 St Francis de Sales, B.C.D., d.
30 King Charles, M. gr.d.
31 St John Bosco, C. d.

FEBRUARY

1 St Ignatius, B.M. d.
2 PURIFICATION OF OUR LADY, D.II cl.
3 Com. St Blaise, B.M.
4

5   St Agatha, V.M., d.
6   St Titus, B.C., d.
7
8
9   St Cyril of Alexandria, B.C.D., d.
10 St Scholastica, V., d.
11
12
13
14 Com. St Valentine, Priest, M.
15
16
17
18 Com. St Simeon, B.M.
19
20
21
22 Chair of St Peter at Antioch, gr.d.
23
24 ST MATTHIAS THE APOSTLE, D.II cl.
    (in Leap Year, on 25th).
25
26
27
28

MARCH

1   St David, B.C., d.
2   St Chad, B.C., d.
3
4
5
6   SS Perpetua and Felicity, MM., d.
7   St Thomas Aquinas, C.D., d.
8   St John of God, C., d.
9   St Frances of Rome, Widow, d.
10
11
12 St Gregory the Great, B.C.D., gr.d.
13
14
15
16
17 St Patrick, B.C., d.
18 St Cyril of Jerusalem, B.C.D., d.

THE CALENDAR xi

19 ST JOSEPH, SPOUSE OF OUR LADY, D.I cl.
20
21 St Benedict, Abbot, gr.d.
22
23
24 St Gabriel the Archangel, gr.d.
25 ANNUNCIATION OF OUR LADY, D.I cl.
26
27 St John Damascene, C.D., d.
28
29
30
31 Friday after Passion Sunday: Seven Sorrows of our Lady, gr.d.

APRIL

1
2
3 St Richard, B.C., d.
4 St Ambrose, B.C.D., d.
5
6
7
8
9
10
11 St Leo the Great, B.C.D., d.
12
13
14 St Justin, M., d.
15
16
17
18
19 St Alphege, B.M., d.
20
21 St Anselm, B.C.D., d.
22
23 ST GEORGE, M., D.I cl.
24
25 ST MARK THE EVANGELIST, D.II cl.
26
27
28
29

30 St Catherine of Siena, V. d.
ST JOSEPH THE WORKMAN, D.I cl.

MAY

1 SS PHILIP & JAMES, D.II cl.
2 St Athanasius, B.C.D., d.
3 FINDING OF THE HOLY CROSS, D.II cl.
4 St Monica, Widow, d.
5
6 St John before the Latin Gate, gr.d.
7
8
9 St Gregory of Nazianzus, B.C.D., d.
10
11
12 St Pancras & His Companions, s.
13
14
15
16
17
18
19 St Dunstan, B.C., d.
20
21
22
23
24
25 St Aldhelm, B.C., d.
26 ST AUGUSTINE, B.C., APOSTLE OF ENGLAND, D.II cl.
27 St Bede the Venerable, C.D., d.
28
29
30
31

JUNE

1 Com. St Nicomede, M.
2
3
4
5 St Boniface, B.M., d.
6
7

THE CALENDAR　　　　　　　　xiii

8　St William of York, B.C., d.
9　St Columba, Abbot, d.
10　St Margaret, Queen, Widow, s.
11　ST BARNABAS THE APOSTLE, D.II cl.
12
13　St Antony of Padua, C.D., d.
14　St Basil the Great, B.C.D., d.
15
16
17
18
19
20　Com. Translation of St Edward, K.M.
21
22　St Alban, M., gr.d.
23　Vigil
24　NATIVITY OF ST JOHN BAPTIST, D.I cl.
25
26
27
28　St Irenaeus, B.M., d.
29　SS PETER AND PAUL, APOSTLES, D.I cl.
30　Commemoration of St Paul, gr.d. Com. St Peter.

JULY

1　PRECIOUS BLOOD OF OUR LORD JESUS CHRIST D.I cl.
2　VISITATION OF OUR LADY D.II cl.
3
4　Translation of St Martin, d.
5
6
7
8
9
10
11
12
13
14
15　Translation of St Swithun, B.C., d.
16
17
18

THE CALENDAR

19 St Vincent de Paul, C., d.
20 Com. St Margaret, V.M.
21
22 St Mary Magdalene, gr.d.
23
24
25 ST JAMES THE APOSTLE, D.II cl.
26 ST ANNE, MOTHER OF B.V.M., D.II cl.
27
28
29 St Martha, V., s.
30
31 St Ignatius, C., gr.d.

AUGUST

1 St Peter's Chains, gr.d.
2
3
4 St Dominic, C., gr.d
5 Dedication of St Mary ("Of the Snows"), gr.d.
6 TRANSFIGURATION OF OUR LORD, D.II cl.
7 MOST HOLY NAME OF JESUS, D.II cl.
8
9 St John Mary Vianney, C., d.
10 ST LAWRENCE, M., D.II cl.
11
12 St Clare, V., d.
13
14 Vigil
15 ASSUMPTION OF OUR LADY, D.I cl.
16
17
18
19
20 St Bernard, Abbot, d.
21 St Jane Frances de Chantal, Widow, d.
22 SINLESS HEART OF OUR LADY, D.II cl.
23
24 ST BARTHOLOMEW THE APOSTLE, D.II cl.
25 St Louis, King, C., s.
26
27
28 St Augustine, B.C.D., d.
29 Beheading of St John Baptist, gr.d
30 St Aidan, B.C., d.
31

SEPTEMBER

1 Com. St. Giles, Abbot.
2
3
4
5
6
7 Com. St Evurtius, B.C.
8 NATIVITY OF OUR LADY, D.II cl.
9
10
11
12 Most Holy Name of Mary, gr.d.
13
14 Exaltation of the Holy Cross, gr.d.
15 VII SORROWS OF OUR LADY, D.II cl.
16 SS Cornelius & Cyprian, BB.MM., s.
17 Imprinting of Stigmata of St Francis, d.
18
19 St Theodore, B.C.
20 Vigil
21 ST MATTHEW THE APOSTLE, D.II cl.
22
23
24
25
26 Com. SS Cyprian & Justina, V., MM. Or: St Cyprian, B.M. s.
27
28
29 ST MICHAEL & ALL ANGELS, D.1 cl.
30 St Jerome, Priest, C.D., d.

OCTOBER

1 Com. St Remigius, B.C.
2 Holy Guardian Angels, gr.d.
3 St Teresa of the Child Jesus, V., d.
4 St Francis, C., gr.d.
5
6 Com. St Faith, V.M.
7 HOLY ROSARY OF THE B.V.M., D.II cl.
8
9 St Denys & His Companions, MM., s.

10 St Paulinus, B.C., d.
11 MOTHERHOOD OF OUR LADY, D.II cl.
12 St Wilfrid, B.C., d.
13 ST EDWARD, KING, C., D.II cl.
14
15 St Teresa, V., d.
16
17 St Etheldreda, V., d. St Margaret Mary, V., d.
18 ST LUKE THE EVANGELIST, D.II cl.
19 St Frideswide, V., d.
20
21
22
23
24 St Raphael the Archangel, gr.d.
25 Com. SS Crispin and Crispinian, MM.
Last Sunday in October: OUR LORD JESUS CHRIST THE KING, D.I cl.
26
27
28 SS SIMON & JUDE, APOSTLES, D.II cl.
29
30
31

NOVEMBER

1 ALL SAINTS, D.I cl.
2 Commemoration of All Souls, d.
3
4
5
6 Com. St Leonard, Abbot.
7
8
9
10
11 St Martin, B.C., d.
12
13 Com. St Britius, B.C.
14
15 St Albert the Great, B.C.D., d.
16 St Edmund, B.C., d.
17 St Hugh, B.C., d.
18

THE CALENDAR xvii

19 St Elisabeth, Widow, d.
20 St Edmund, K.M., d.
21
22 St Cecily, V.M., d.
23 St Clement, B.M., d.
24 St John of God, C.D., d.
25 St Catherine, V.M., d.
26
27
28
29
30 ST ANDREW THE APOSTLE, D.II cl.

DECEMBER

1
2
3 St Francis Xavier, C., gr.d.
4 St Peter Chrysologus, B.C.D., d.
5
6 St Nicholas, B.C., d.
7
8 CONCEPTION OF OUR LADY, D.I cl.
9
10
11 St Damasus, B.C., sd.
12
13 St Lucy, V.M., d.
14
15
16 St Eusebius, B.M., s.
17
18
19
20
21 ST THOMAS THE APOSTLE, D.II cl.
22
23
24 Vigil, d.
25 CHRISTMAS DAY, D.I cl.
26 ST STEPHEN, M., D.II cl.
27 ST JOHN THE APOSTLE, D.II cl.
28 HOLY INNOCENTS, D.II cl.
29 ST THOMAS OF CANTERBURY, B.M., D.II cl.
30 In Octave of Christmas, d.
31 St Silvester, B.C., d.

THE ORDER OF DIVINE SERVICE
BEFORE DIVINE SERVICE

OPEN thou my mouth, O Lord, to bless thy holy name; cleanse my heart from all vain, froward and wandering thoughts; enlighten my understanding, enkindle my affection, that I may say this Office worthily, attentively and devoutly, and may be counted worthy to be heard in the presence of thy divine majesty. Through Christ, our Lord. ℟. Amen.

O Lord, in union with that divine intention wherewith thou didst offer praise to God on earth, I offer this Service unto thee.

INTRODUCTION TO MATTINS AND EVENSONG

WHEN the wicked man turneth away from his wickedness that he hath committed, and doeth that which is lawful and right, he shall save his soul alive.

I acknowledge my transgressions, and my sin is ever before me.

Hide thy face from my sins, and blot out all mine iniquities.

The sacrifices of God are a broken spirit: a broken and a contrite heart, O God, thou wilt not despise.

Rend your heart, and not your garments, and turn unto the Lord your God: for he is gracious and merciful, slow to anger, and of great kindness, and repenteth him of the evil.

To the Lord our God belong mercies and forgivenesses, though we have rebelled against him: neither have we obeyed the voice of the Lord our God, to walk in his laws which he set before us.

O Lord, correct me, but with judgement; not in thine anger, lest thou bring me to nothing.

Repent ye; for the kingdom of heaven is at hand.

I will arise, and go to my father, and will say unto him: Father, I have sinned against heaven, and before thee, and am no more worthy to be called thy son.

Enter not into judgement with thy servant, O Lord; for in thy sight shall no man living be justified.

If we say that we have no sin, we deceive ourselves, and the truth is not in us: but, if we confess our sins, he is faithful and just to forgive us our sins, and to cleanse us from all unrighteousness.

DEARLY beloved brethren, the Scripture moveth us in sundry places to acknowledge and confess our manifold sins and wickedness; and that we should not dissemble nor cloke them before the face of almighty God our heavenly Father; but confess them with an humble, lowly, penitent, and obedient heart; to the end that we may obtain forgiveness of the same, by his infinite goodness and mercy. And although we ought at all times humbly to acknowledge our sins before God; yet ought we most chiefly so to do, when we assemble and meet together to render thanks for the great benefits that we have received at his hands, to set forth his most worthy praise, to hear his most holy Word, and to ask those things which are requisite and necessary, as well for the body as the soul. Wherefore I pray and beseech you, as many as are here present, to accompany me with a pure heart, and humble voice, unto the throne of the heavenly grace, saying after me:

ALMIGHTY and most merciful Father; We have erred and strayed from thy ways, like lost sheep. We have followed too much the devices and desires of our own hearts. We have offended against thy holy laws. We have left undone those things which we ought to have done; And we have done those things which we ought not to have done; And there is no health in us. But thou, O Lord, have mercy upon us, miserable offenders. Spare thou them, O God, which confess their faults. Restore thou them that are penitent; According to thy promises declared unto mankind in Christ Jesu our Lord. And grant, O most merciful Father, for his sake; That we may hereafter live a godly, righteous, and sober life. To the glory of thy holy name. Amen.

ALMIGHTY God, the Father of our Lord Jesus Christ, who desireth not the death of a sinner, but rather that he may turn from his wickedness and live; and hath given power, and commandment, to his ministers, to declare and pronounce to his people, being penitent, the absolution and remission of their sins; he pardoneth and absolveth all them that truly repent, and unfeignedly believe his holy Gospel. Wherefore let us beseech him to grant us true repentance, and his Holy Spirit, that those things may please him which we do at this present; and that the rest of our life hereafter may be pure and holy; so that at the last we may come to his eternal joy; through Jesus Christ our Lord. ℟. Amen.

OUR Father, which art in heaven, hallowed be thy name. Thy kingdom come. Thy will be done, in earth as it is in heaven. Give us this day our daily bread. And forgive us our trespasses, as we forgive them that trespass against us. And lead us not into temptation: but deliver us from evil. For thine is the kingdom, the power, and the glory, for ever and ever. Amen.

MATTINS

℣. O Lord, open thou our lips. ℟. And our mouth shall show forth thy praise.
℣. O God, make speed to save us. ℟. O Lord, make haste to help us.
℣. Glory be to the Father, and to the Son, and to the Holy Ghost. ℟. As it was in the beginning, is now, and ever shall be: world without end. Amen.
℣. Praise ye the Lord. ℟. The Lord's name be praised.

The Invitatory

Which may be said with the Psalm following (twice before the Psalm, and then the whole or the latter part alternately between the verses, as marked).

Through the year:

Sundays (after Epiphany, and from September 28 to Advent): Let us worship the Lord, * For he hath made us.

Sundays (after Trinity to September 27): The Lord who hath made us: * O come, let us worship him.

Mondays: O come, * Let us sing unto the Lord.

Tuesdays: Let us heartily rejoice * In the strength of our salvation.

Wednesdays: The Lord is a great God: * O come, let us worship him.

Thursdays: The Lord is a great King: * O come, let us worship him.

Fridays: The Lord is our God: * O come, let us worship him.

Saturdays: We are the people of the Lord, and the sheep of his pasture: * O come, let us worship him.

Ps. 95. Venite, exsultemus Domino

O COME, let us sing unto the Lord: let us heartily rejoice in the strength of our salvation. Let us come before his presence with thanksgiving: and shew ourselves glad in him with psalms.

For the Lord is a great God: and a great King above all gods.

In his hand are all the corners of the earth: and the strength of the hills is his also.

The sea is his, and he made it: and his hands prepared the dry land.

O come, let us worship, and fall down: and kneel before the Lord our Maker.

For he is the Lord our God: and we are the people of his pasture, and the sheep of his hand.

* *

To-day if ye will hear his voice, "Harden not your hearts: as in the provocation, and as in the day of temptation in the wilderness; When your fathers tempted me: proved me, and saw my works.

*

Forty years long was I grieved with this generation, and said: It is a people that do err in their hearts, for they have not known my ways.

Unto whom I sware in my wrath: that they should not enter into my rest."

* *

Glory be to the Father, and to the Son: and to the Holy Ghost. As it was in the beginning, is now, and ever shall be: world without end. Amen. *

* *

Then shall be said the Psalms (with their antiphons) as appointed.
Then shall be read the First Lesson.

Te Deum laudamus

WE praise thee, O God: * we acknowledge thee to be the Lord.

All the earth doth worship thee, * the Father everlasting.

To thee all Angels cry aloud, * the heavens and all the powers therein;

To thee Cherubin and Seraphins * continually do cry:

Holy, holy, holy, * Lord God of Sabaoth:

Heaven and earth are full of the majesty * of thy glory.

The glorious company of the Apostles * praise thee.

The goodly fellowship of the Prophets * praise thee.

The noble army of Martyrs * praise thee.

The holy Church throughout all the world * doth acknowledge thee:

The Father * of an infinite majesty;

Thine honourable, true * and only Son;

Also the Holy Ghost * the Comforter.

Thou art the King of glory * O Christ.

Thou art the everlasting Son * of the Father.

When thou tookest upon thee to deliver man, * thou didst not abhor the Virgin's womb.

When thou hadst overcome the sharpness of death, * thou didst open the kingdom of heaven to all believers.

Thou sittest at the right hand of God, * in the glory of the Father.

We believe that thou shalt come * to be our Judge.

The following verse is said kneeling.

We therefore pray thee, help thy servants, * whom thou hast redeemed with thy precious blood.

Make them to be numbered with thy Saints * in glory everlasting.

O Lord, save thy people, * and bless thine heritage.

Govern them, * and lift them up for ever.
Day by day * we magnify thee.
And we worship thy name * ever world without end.
Vouchsafe, O Lord, * to keep us this day without sin.
O Lord, have mercy upon us, * have mercy upon us.
O Lord, let thy mercy lighten upon us, * as our trust is in thee.
O Lord, in thee have I trusted: * let me never be confounded.

Or, Benedicite, omnia opera

The Prayer-book appoints the refrain Praise him and magnify him for ever after each half-verse, and the Gloria Patri instead of the final doxology.

O ALL ye works of the Lord, bless ye the Lord: * *praise him and magnify him for ever.*
O ye Angels of the Lord, bless ye the Lord: *
O ye heavens, bless ye the Lord.
O ye waters that be above the firmament, bless ye the Lord: *
O all ye powers of the Lord, bless ye the Lord.
O ye sun and moon, bless ye the Lord: *
O ye stars of heaven, bless ye the Lord.

O ye showers and dew, bless ye the Lord: *
O ye winds of God, bless ye the Lord.
O ye fire and heat, bless ye the Lord: *
O ye winter and summer, bless ye the Lord.
O ye dews and frosts, bless ye the Lord: *
O ye frost and cold, bless ye the Lord.
O ye ice and snow, bless ye the Lord: *
O ye nights and days, bless ye the Lord. *
O ye light and darkness, bless ye the Lord: *
O ye lightnings and clouds, bless ye the Lord.

O let the earth bless the Lord: * *yea, let it praise him, and magnify him for ever.*
O ye mountains and hills, bless ye the Lord. *
O all ye green things upon the earth, bless ye the Lord.
O ye wells, bless ye the Lord: *
O ye seas and floods, bless ye the Lord.
O ye whales and all that move in the waters, bless ye the Lord: *
O all ye fowls of the air, bless ye the Lord.
O all ye beasts and cattle, bless ye the Lord: *

O ye children of men, bless ye the Lord.
O let Israel bless the Lord: * *praise him and magnify him for ever.*
O ye priests of the Lord, bless ye the Lord: *
O ye servants of the Lord, bless ye the Lord.
O ye spirits and souls of the righteous, bless ye the Lord: *
O ye holy and humble men of heart, bless ye the Lord.
O Ananias, Azarias, and Misael, bless ye the Lord: * *praise him and magnify him for ever.*

Let us bless the Father, and the Son, with the Holy Ghost: * *let*

us praise him and magnify him for ever.
Blessed art thou, O Lord, in the firmament of heaven: * *and worthy to be praised, and glorious, and magnified for ever.*

Then shall follow the Second Lesson.

The Hymn follows, and then the ℣ *and* ℟*., and* **Benedictus** *with its antiphon, as below, except when otherwise appointed.*

Through the year:

Sundays
(after Epiphany, and from September 28 to Advent; 50*)*

THIS day the first of days was made,
When God in light the world arrayed,
Or when his Word arose again,
And conquering death, gave life to men,

Slumber and sloth drive far away;
Earlier arise to greet the day;
And ere the dawn in heaven unfold
The heart's desire to God be told:

Unto our prayer that he attend,
His all-creating power extend,
And still renew us, lest we miss
Through earthly stain our heavenly bliss.

That us, who here this day repair
To keep the Apostles' time of prayer,
And hymn the quiet hours o morn,
With blessèd gifts he may adorn.

For this, Redeemer, thee we pray
That thou wilt wash our sins away,
And of thy loving-kindness grant
What e'er of good our spirits want:

That, exiles here awhile in flesh,
Some earnest may our souls refresh
Of that pure life for which we long,
Some foretaste of the heavenly song.

* O Father, that we ask be done,
Through Jesus Christ, thine only Son,
Who, with the Holy Ghost, and thee,
Doth live and reign eternally. Amen.

℣. The Lord is King, and hath put on glorious apparel. ℟. The Lord hath put on his apparel, and girded himself with strength.

Proper antiphon.

Sundays
(after Trinity to September 27; 165*)*

FATHER, we praise thee, now the night is over,
Active and watchful, stand we all before thee;

Singing we offer prayer and meditation:
Thus we adore thee.

Monarch of all things, fit us for thy mansions;
Banish our weakness, health and wholeness sending;
Bring us to heaven, where thy Saints united
Joy without ending.

All-holy Father, Son and equal Spirit,
Trinity blessèd, send us thy salvation;
Thine is the glory, gleaming and resounding
Through all creation. Amen.

℣. The Lord is King, and hath put on glorious apparel. ℟. The Lord hath put on his apparel, and girded himself with strength.
Proper antiphon.

Mondays (52)

O SPLENDOUR of God's glory bright,
O thou that bringest light from light,
O Light of light, light's living spring,
O Day, all days illumining;

O thou true Sun, on us thy glance
Let fall in royal radiance,
The Spirit's sanctifying beam
Upon our earthly senses stream.

The Father, too, our prayers implore,
Father of glory evermore;
The Father of all grace and might,
To banish sin from our delight.

Our mind be in his keeping placed,
Our bodies true to him and chaste,
Where only faith her fire shall feed,
To burn the tares of Satan's seed.

And Christ to us for food shall be,
From him our drink that welleth free,
The Spirit's wine, that maketh whole,
And mocking not, exalts the soul.

Rejoicing may this day go hence,
Like virgin dawn our innocence,
Like fiery noon our faith appear,
Nor know the gloom of twilight drear.

Morn in her rosy car is borne,
Let him come forth, our perfect morn,
The Word in God the Father one,
The Father perfect in the Son.

* All laud to God the Father be,
All praise, eternal Son, to thee,
All glory, as is ever meet,
To God the holy Paraclete. Amen.

℣. O satisfy us early with thy mercy. ℟. That we may rejoice and be glad.

Ant. to Ben. Blessed * be the Lord God of Israel, for he hath visited and redeemed us.

Tuesdays (53)

THE wingèd herald of the day
Proclaims the morn's approaching ray:
And Christ the Lord our souls excites,
And so to endless life invites.

Take up thy bed, to each he cries,
Who sick or wrapt in slumber lies;
And chaste and just and sober stand,
And watch: my coming is at hand.

With earnest cry, with tearful care,
Call we the Lord to hear our prayer;
While supplication, pure and deep
Forbids each chastened heart to sleep.

Do thou, O Christ, our slumbers wake;
Do thou the chains of darkness break;
Purge thou our former sins away,
And in our souls new light display.

* All laud to God the Father be,
All praise, eternal Son, to thee;
All glory, as is ever meet,
To God the holy Paraclete. Amen.

℣. O satisfy us early with thy mercy. ℟. That we may rejoice and be glad.
Ant. to Ben. The Lord hath raised up * for us a mighty salvation in the house of his servant David.

Wednesdays (54)

YE clouds and darkness, hosts of night,
That breed confusion and affright,
Begone! o'erhead the dawn shines clear,
The light breaks in, and Christ is here.

Earth's gloom flees broken and dispersed,
By the sun's piercing shafts coerced,
The day-star's eyes rain influence bright,
And colours glimmer back to sight.

Thee, Christ, alone we know; to thee
We bend in pure simplicity;
Our songs with tears to thee arise,
Prove thou our hearts with thy clear eyes.

Though we be stained with blots within,
Thy quickening rays shall purge our sin;
Light of the Morning Star, thy grace
Shed on us from thy cloudless face.

* All laud to God the Father be,
All praise, eternal Son, to thee,
All glory, as is ever meet,
To God the holy Paraclete.
Amen.

℣. O satisfy us early with thy mercy. ℞. That we may rejoice and be glad.
Ant. to Ben. From the hand of all * that hate us hath the Lord delivered us.

Thursdays (55)

LO! golden light rekindles day:
Let paling darkness steal away,
Which all too long o'erwhelmed our gaze
And led our steps by winding ways.

We pray thee, rising light serene,
E'en as thyself our hearts make clean;
Let no deceit our lips defile,
Nor let our souls be vexed by guile.

O keep us, as the hours proceed,
From lying word and evil deed;
Our roving eyes from sin set free,
Our body from impurity.

For thou dost from above survey
The converse of each fleeting day;
Thou dost foresee from morning light
Our every deed, until the night.

* All laud to God the Father be,
All praise, eternal Son, to thee;
All glory, as is ever meet,
To God the holy Paraclete.
Amen.

℣. O satisfy us early with thy mercy. ℞. That we may rejoice and be glad.
Ant. to Ben. In holiness * let us serve the Lord, and he will deliver us from our enemies.

Fridays (56)

ETERNAL glory of the sky,
Blest hope of frail humanity,
The Father's sole-begotten One,
Yet born a spotless Virgin's Son!

Uplift us with thine arm of might,
And let our hearts rise pure and bright,
And, ardent in God's praises, pay
The thanks we owe him every day.

The day-star's rays are glittering clear,
And tell that day itself is near:
The shadows of the night depart,
Thou, holy light, illume the heart!

Within our senses ever dwell,
And worldly darkness thence expel;
Long as the days of life endure,
Preserve our souls devout and pure.

The faith that first must be possessed
Root deep within our inmost breast,
And joyous hope in second place,
Then charity, thy greatest grace.

* All laud to God the Father be,
All praise, eternal Son, to thee;
All glory, as is ever meet,
To God the holy Paraclete.
Amen.

℣. O satisfy us early with thy mercy. ℟. That we may rejoice and be glad.

Ant. to Ben. Through the tender mercy * of our God, the Day-spring from on high hath visited us.

Saturdays (57)

THE dawn is sprinkling in the east
Its golden shower, as day flows in:
Fast mount the pointed shafts of light,
Farewell to darkness and to sin!

Away, ye midnight phantoms all!
Away, despondence and despair!
Whatever guilt the night has brought,
Now let it vanish into air.

So, Lord, when that last morning breaks,
Looking to which we sigh and pray,
O may it to thy minstrels prove
The dawning of a better day.

* To God the Father glory be,
And to his sole-begotten Son;
Glory, O Holy Ghost, to thee,
While everlasting ages run.
Amen.

℣. O satisfy us early with thy mercy. ℟. That we may rejoice and be glad.

Ant. to Ben. Give light, O Lord, * to them that sit in darkness, and in the shadow of death; and guide thou our feet into the way of peace.

Benedictus

BLESSED be the Lord God of Israel, * for he hath visited, and redeemed his people;
And hath raised up a mighty salvation for us * in the house of his servant David;
As he spake by the mouth of his holy Prophets, * which have been since the world began:
That we should be saved from our enemies, * and from the hands of all that hate us.
To perform the mercy promised to our forefathers, * and to remember his holy covenant;
To perform the oath which he sware to our forefather Abraham, * that he would give us,
That we, being delivered out of the hands of our enemies, * might serve him without fear,

In holiness and righteousness before him * all the days of our life.

And thou, child, shalt be called the Prophet of the Highest: * for thou shalt go before the face of the Lord to prepare his ways,

To give knowledge of salvation unto his people * for the remission of their sins,

Through the tender mercy of our God, * whereby the Dayspring from on high hath visited us,

To give light to them that sit in darkness and in the shadow of death, * and to guide our feet into the way of peace.

Glory be to the Father.

The Apostles' Creed

I BELIEVE in God the Father almighty, Maker of heaven and earth.

And in Jesus Christ his only Son our Lord, who was conceived by the Holy Ghost, born of the Virgin Mary, suffered under Pontius Pilate, was crucified, dead, and buried; he descended into hell, the third day he rose again from the dead; he ascended into heaven; and sitteth on the right hand of God the Father almighty; from thence he shall come to judge the quick and the dead.

I believe in the Holy Ghost; the holy Catholic Church; the communion of Saints; the forgiveness of sins. ℣. The resurrection of the body. ℟. And the life everlasting. Amen.

But instead of the Apostles' Creed, the following is said on Christmas Day, the Epiphany, St Matthias' Day, Easter Day, Ascension Day, Whit-Sunday, Trinity Sunday, and the Feasts of St John Baptist, St James, St Bartholomew, St Matthew, SS Simon and Jude, and St Andrew

---

The Athanasian Creed

WHOSOEVER will be saved, * before all things it is necessary that he hold the catholic faith.

Which faith except every one do keep whole and undefiled, * without doubt he shall perish everlastingly.

And the catholic faith is this: * that we worship one God in Trinity, and Trinity in unity;

Neither confounding the Persons, * nor dividing the substance.

For there is one Person of the Father, another of the Son, * and another of the Holy Ghost;

But the Godhead of the Father, of the Son, and of the Holy Ghost, is all one, * the glory equal, the majesty co-eternal.

Such as the Father is, such is the Son, * and such is the Holy Ghost.

The Father uncreate, the Son uncreate, * and the Holy Ghost uncreate.

The Father incomprehensible, the Son incomprehensible, * and the Holy Ghost incomprehensible.

The Father eternal, the Son eternal, * and the Holy Ghost eternal.

And yet they are not three eternals, * but one eternal.

As also there are not three incomprehensibles, nor three uncreated, * but one uncreated, and one incomprehensible.

So likewise the Father is almighty, the Son almighty, * and the Holy Ghost almighty.

And yet they are not three almighties, * but one almighty.

So the Father is God, the Son is God, * and the Holy Ghost is God.

And yet not three Gods, * but one God.

So likewise the Father, is Lord, the Son Lord, * and the Holy Ghost Lord.

And yet not three Lords, * but one Lord.

For like as we are compelled by the Christian verity * to acknowledge every Person by himself to be God and Lord;

So are we forbidden by the catholic religion * to say, There be three Gods, or three Lords.

The Father is made of none: * neither created, nor begotten.

The Son is of the Father alone: * not made, nor created, but begotten.

The Holy Ghost is of the Father and of the Son: * neither made, nor created, nor begotten, but proceeding.

So there is one Father, not three Fathers, one Son, not three Sons; * one Holy Ghost, not three Holy Ghosts.

And in this Trinity none is afore, or after other: * none is greater, or less than another;

But the whole three Persons are co-eternal together ; and co-equal.

So that in all things, as is aforesaid, * the unity in Trinity, and the Trinity in unity is to be worshipped.

He therefore that will be saved * must thus think of the Trinity.

Furthermore, it is necessary to everlasting salvation, * that he also believe rightly the Incarnation of our Lord Jesus Christ.

For the right faith is, that we believe and confess, * that our Lord Jesus Christ, the Son of God, is God and man;

God, of the substance of the Father, begotten before the worlds: * and man, of the substance of his mother, born in the world.

Perfect God, and perfect man: * of a reasonable soul and human flesh subsisting.

Equal to the Father, as touching his Godhead: * and inferior to the Father, as touching his manhood.

Who although he be God and man, * yet he is not two, but one Christ.

One; not by conversion of the Godhead into flesh; * but by taking of the manhood into God.

One altogether; not by confusion of substance, * but by unity of Person.

For as the reasonable soul and flesh is one man: * so God and man is one Christ.

Who suffered for our salvation: * descended into hell; rose again the third day from the dead.

He ascended into heaven; he sitteth on the right hand of the Father, God almighty: * from whence he shall come to judge the quick and the dead.

At whose coming all men shall rise again with their bodies: * and shall give account for their own works.

And they that have done good shall go into life everlasting: * and they that have done evil into everlasting fire.

This is the catholic faith, * which except a man believe faithfully, he cannot be saved.

Glory be to the Father.

℣. The Lord be with you.
℟. And with thy spirit.
Let us pray.
Lord, have mercy upon us.
Christ, have mercy upon us.
Lord, have mercy upon us.

OUR Father, which art in heaven, hallowed be thy name. Thy kingdom come. Thy will be done, in earth as it is in heaven. Give us this day our daily bread. And forgive us our trespasses, as we forgive them that trespass against us.
℣. And lead us not into temptation. ℟. But deliver us from evil. Amen.

℣. O Lord, shew thy mercy upon us. ℟. And grant us thy salvation.
℣. O Lord, save the Queen.
℟. And mercifully hear us when we call upon thee.

℣. Endue thy ministers with righteousness. ℟. And make thy chosen people joyful.
℣. O Lord save thy people.
℟. And bless thine inheritance.
℣. Give peace in our time, O Lord. ℟. Because there is none other that fighteth for us, but only thou, O God.
℣. O God, make clean our hearts within us. ℟. And take not thy Holy Spirit from us.
℣. The Lord be with you.
℟. And with thy spirit.
Let us pray.

1. The Collect of the day; after which any commemoration that may occur.

2. For Peace

O GOD, who art the author of peace and lover of concord, in knowledge of whom standeth our eternal life, whose service is perfect freedom: defend us thy humble servants in all assaults of our enemies; that we, surely trusting in thy defence, may not fear the power of any adversaries. Through the might of Jesus Christ our Lord. ℟. Amen.

3. For Grace

O LORD, our heavenly Father, almighty and everlasting God, who hast safely brought us to the beginning of this day: defend us in the same with thy mighty power, and grant that this day we fall into no sin, neither run into any kind of danger; but that all our doings may be ordered by thy

governance, to do always that is righteous in thy sight. Through Jesus Christ our Lord. ℟. Amen.
℣. The Lord be with you.
℟. And with thy spirit.

℣. Let us bless the Lord.
℟. Thanks be to God.
℣. May the souls of the faithful, through the mercy of God, rest in peace.
℟. Amen.

PRAYERS AFTER MATTINS OR EVENSONG

For the Queen's Majesty

O LORD our heavenly Father, high and mighty, King of kings, Lord of lords, the only Ruler of princes, who dost from thy throne behold all the dwellers upon earth; most heartily we beseech thee with thy favour to behold our most gracious Sovereign Lady, Queen Elizabeth; and so replenish her with the grace of thy Holy Spirit, that she may alway incline to thy will, and walk in thy way; endue her plenteously with heavenly gifts; grant her in health and wealth long to live; strengthen her that she may vanquish and overcome all her enemies; and finally, after this life, she may attain everlasting joy and felicity. Through Jesus Christ our Lord. ℟. Amen.

For the Royal Family

ALMIGHTY God, the fountain of all goodness, we humbly beseech thee to bless Philip Duke of Edinburgh, Charles Prince of Wales, and all the Royal Family; endue them with thy Holy Spirit; enrich them with thy heavenly grace; prosper them with all happiness; and bring them to thine everlasting kingdom. Through Jesus Christ our Lord. ℟. Amen.

For the Clergy and People

ALMIGHTY and everlasting God, who alone workest great marvels; send down upon our bishops and curates, and all congregations committed to their charge, the healthful Spirit of thy grace; and that they may truly please thee, pour upon them the continual dew of thy blessing. Grant this, O Lord, for the honour of our Advocate and Mediator, Jesus Christ. ℟. Amen.

A Prayer of St Chrysostom

ALMIGHTY God, who hast given us grace at this time with one accord to make our common supplications unto thee; and dost promise, that when two or three are gathered together in thy name thou wilt grant their requests: fulfil now, O Lord, the desires and petitions of thy servants, as may be most expedient for them; granting us in this world knowledge

of thy truth, and in the world to come life everlasting. ℟. Amen.
The grace of our Lord Jesus Christ, and the love of God, and the fellowship of the Holy Ghost, be with us all evermore.

℟. Amen.

EVENSONG

℣. O Lord open thou our lips. ℟. And our mouth shall shew forth thy praise.
℣. O God, make speed to save us. ℟. O Lord, make haste to help us.
℣. Glory be to the Father, and to the Son, and to the Holy Ghost. ℟. As it was in the beginning, is now, and ever shall be, world without end. Amen.

Then shall be said the Psalms (with their antiphons) as appointed.

Then shall be read the First Lesson.

The Hymn follows, and then the ℣. & ℟. and **Magnificat** with its antiphon; as below, except when otherwise appointed.

Through the year:

Sundays (51)

O BLEST Creator of the light,
Who mak'st the day with radiance bright,
And o'er the forming world didst call
The light from chaos first of all;

Whose wisdom joined in meet array
The morn and eve, and named them day;
Night comes with all its darkling fears;
Regard thy people's prayers and tears;

Lest, sunk in sin and whelmed with strife,
They lose the gift of endless life;
While, thinking but the thoughts of time,
They weave new chains of woe and crime.

But grant them grace that they may strain
The heavenly gate and prize to gain:
Each harmful lure aside to cast,
And purge away each error past.

* O Father, that we ask be done,
Through Jesus Christ, thine only Son;
Who, with the Holy Ghost and thee,
Doth live and reign eternally. Amen.

℣. Let my prayer, O Lord, be set forth. ℟. In thy sight as the incense.
Proper antiphon.

Mondays (58)

O BOUNDLESS Wisdom, God most high,
O Maker of the earth and sky,
Who bidst the parted waters flow
In heaven above, on earth below;

The streams on earth, the clouds in heaven,
By thee their ordered bounds were given,
Lest 'neath the untempered fires of day
The parchèd soil should waste away.

E'en so on us who seek thy face
Pour forth the waters of thy grace;
Renew the fount of life within,
And quench the wasting fires of sin.

Let faith discern the eternal Light
Beyond the darkness of the night,
And through the mists of falsehood see
The path of truth revealed by thee.

* O Father, that we ask be done,
Through Jesus Christ, thine only Son;
Who, with the Holy Ghost and thee,
Doth live and reign eternally. Amen.

℣. Let my prayer, O Lord, be set forth. ℟. In thy sight as the incense.

Ant. to Magn. My soul * doth magnify the Lord, for he hath regarded my lowliness.

Tuesdays (59)

EARTH'S mighty Maker, whose command
Raised from the sea the solid land,
And drove each billowy heap away,
And bade the earth stand firm for aye;

That so, with flowers of golden hue,
The seeds of each it might renew;
And fruit-trees bearing fruit might yield,
And pleasant pastures of the field;

Our spirit's rankling wounds efface
With dewy freshness of thy grace:
That grief may cleanse each deed of ill,
And o'er each lust may triumph still.

Let every soul thy law obey,
And keep from every evil way;
Rejoice each promised good to win,
And flee from every mortal sin.

* O Father, that we ask be done,
Through Jesus Christ, thine only Son;
Who, with the Holy Ghost and thee,
Doth live and reign eternally. Amen.

℣. Let my prayer, O Lord, be set forth. ℟. In thy sight as the incense.

Ant. to Magn. My spirit * hath rejoiced in God my Saviour.

Wednesdays (60)

MOST holy Lord and God
  of heaven
Who to the glowing sky hast given
The fires that in the east are born
With gradual splendours of the morn;

Who, on the fourth day, didst reveal
The sun's enkindled flaming wheel,
Didst set the moon her ordered ways,
And stars their ever-winding maze;

That each in its appointed way
Might separate the night from day,
And of the seasons through the year
The well-remembered signs declare;

Illuminate our hearts within,
And cleanse our minds from stain of sin:
Unburdened of our guilty load
May we unfettered serve our God.

* O Father, that we ask be done,
Through Jesus Christ, thine only Son;
Who, with the Holy Ghost and thee,
Doth live and reign eternally. Amen.

℣. Let my prayer, O Lord, be set forth. ℟. In thy sight as the incense.

Ant. to Magn. The Lord hath regarded * my lowliness, and he that is mighty hath magnified me.

Thursdays (61)

ALMIGHTY God, who from
  the flood
Didst bring to light a twofold brood;
Part in the firmament to fly,
And part in ocean's depths to lie;

Appointing fishes in the sea,
And fowls in open air to be,
That each, by origin the same,
Its separate dwelling-place might claim;

Grant that thy servants, by the tide
Of Blood and water purified,
No guilty fall from thee may know,
Nor death eternal undergo.

Be none submerged in sin's distress,
None lifted up in boastfulness;
That contrite hearts be not dismayed,
Nor haughty souls in ruin laid.

* O Father, that we ask be done,
Through Jesus Christ, thine only Son;
Who, with the Holy Ghost and thee,
Doth live and reign eternally. Amen.

℣. Let my prayer, O Lord, be set forth. ℟. In thy sight as the incense.
Ant. to Magn. The Lord hath shewn * strength with his arm: he hath scattered the proud in the imagination of their heart.

Fridays (62)

MAKER of man, who from thy throne
Dost order all things, God alone;
By whose decree the teaming earth
To reptile and to beast gave birth;

The mighty forms that fill the land,
Instinct with life at thy command,
Are given subdued to humankind
For service in their rank assigned.

From all thy servants drive away
Whate'er of thought impure to-day
Hath been with open action blent.
Or mingled with the heart's intent.

In heaven thine endless joys bestow,
And grant thy gifts of grace below;
From chains of strife our souls release,
Bind fast the gentle bands of peace.

* O Father, that we ask be done,
Through Jesus Christ, thine only Son;
Who, with the Holy Ghost and thee,
Doth live and reign eternally. Amen.

℣. Let my prayer, O Lord, be set forth. ℟. In thy sight as the incense.
Ant. to Magn. The Lord hath put down * the mighty from their seat, and hath exalted the humble.

Saturdays (164)

O TRINITY of blessèd light,
O Unity of princely might,
The fiery sun now goes his way;
Shed thou within our hearts thy ray.

To thee our morning song of praise,
To thee our evening prayer we raise;
Thy glory suppliant we adore
For ever and for evermore.

* All laud to God the Father be;
All praise, eternal Son, to thee;
All glory, as is ever meet,
To God the Holy Paraclete. Amen.

℣. Let our evening prayer come up before thee, O Lord. ℟. And let thy mercy come down upon us.

On Saturdays before Epiphany II-VI:
Ant. to Magn. God hath holpen * his servant Israel: as he

Magnificat

MY soul doth magnify the Lord: * and my spirit hath rejoiced in God my Saviour;

For he hath regarded * the lowliness of his handmaiden.

For behold, from henceforth * all generations shall call me blessed.

For he that is mighty hath magnified me, * and holy is his name.

And his mercy is on them that fear him * throughout all generations.

He hath shewed strength with his arm: * he hath scattered the proud in the imagination of their hearts.

He hath put down the mighty from their seat, * and hath exalted the humble and meek.

He hath filled the hungry with good things, * and the rich he hath sent empty away.

He remembering his mercy hath helpen his servant Israel, * as he promised to our forefathers, Abraham and his seed for ever.

Glory be to the Father.

Then shall be read the Second Lesson.

Ant. Save us.

Nunc Dimittis

LORD, now lettest thou thy servant depart in peace * according to thy word.

For mine eyes have seen * thy salvation;

Which thou hast prepared * before the face of all people;

To be a light to lighten the Gentiles, * and to be the glory of thy people Israel.

Glory be to the Father.

Ant. Save us, O Lord, while waking, and guard us while sleeping; that awake we may be with Christ, and in peace may take our rest. (E.T. Alleluia.)

The Apostles' Creed

I BELIEVE in God the Father almighty, Maker of heaven and earth. And in Jesus Christ his only Son our Lord, who was conceived by the Holy Ghost, born of the Virgin Mary, suffered under Pontius Pilate, was crucified, dead, and buried; he descended into hell; the third day he rose again from the dead; he ascended into heaven; and sitteth on the right hand of God the Father almighty; from thence he shall come to judge the quick and the dead.

I believe in the Holy Ghost; the holy catholic Church; the communion of Saints; the forgiveness of sins. ℣. The resurrection of the body. ℟. And the life everlasting. Amen.

℣. The Lord be with you.
℟. And with thy spirit.
Let us pray.
Lord, have mercy upon us.
Christ, have mercy upon us.
Lord, have mercy upon us.

OUR Father, which art in heaven, hallowed be thy name. Thy kingdom come. Thy will be done, in earth as it is in

heaven. Give us this day our daily bread. And forgive us our trespasses, as we forgive them that trespass against us.
℣. And lead us not into temptation. ℟. But deliver us from evil. Amen.

℣. O Lord, shew thy mercy upon us. ℟. And grant us thy salvation.
℣. O Lord, save the Queen.
℟. And mercifully hear us when we call upon thee.
℣. Endue thy ministers with righteousness. ℟. And make thy chosen people joyful.
℣. O Lord, save thy people.
℟. And bless thine inheritance.
℣. Give peace in our time, O Lord. ℟. Because there is none other that fighteth for us, but only thou, O God.
℣. O God, make clean our hearts within us. ℟. And take not thy Holy Spirit from us.
℣. The Lord be with you.
℟. And with thy spirit.
Let us pray.

1. The Collect of the day; after which any commemoration that may occur.

2. For Peace

O GOD, from whom all holy desires, all good counsels, and all just works do proceed: give unto thy servants that peace which the world cannot give; that both our hearts may be set to obey thy commandments, and also that by thee, we being defended from the fear of our enemies, may pass our time in rest and quietness. Through the merits of Jesus Christ our Saviour. ℟. Amen.

3. For Aid against all Perils

LIGHTEN our darkness, we beseech thee, O Lord: and by thy great mercy defend us from all perils and dangers of this night; for the love of thy only Son, our Saviour Jesus Christ. ℟. Amen.

℣. The Lord be with you.
℟. And with thy spirit.
℣. Let us bless the Lord.
℟. Thanks be to God.
℣. May the souls of the faithful, through the mercy of God, rest in peace.
℟. Amen.

The Anthem of our Lady as follows, as below.
Lastly is said:
℣. May the divine assistance remain with us always. ℟. Amen.

FINAL ANTHEMS OF OUR LADY

From I Evensong of Advent I to II Evensong of the Purification:

MOTHER of Christ our Redeemer, O hear our entreaty, Thou who art call'd the portal of heaven, the star of the ocean; Still as we fall we struggle to rise; then help us, we pray thee; Nature in wonder stood when birth thou gavest thy Maker; Thou who, Virgin before thou didst bear, art a Virgin for ever, Heardest Gabriel's greeting, look down with pity on sinners.

In Advent

℣. The Angel of the Lord brought tidings unto Mary.
℟. And she conceived by the Holy Ghost.
Let us pray. *Prayer*

WE beseech thee, O Lord, pour thy grace into our hearts: that as we have known the Incarnation of thy Son Jesus Christ by the message of an Angel, so by his Cross and passion we may be brought unto the glory of his resurrection. Through the same Christ our Lord. ℟. Amen.

From I Evensong of Christmas onward

℣. After child-bearing thou didst remain a pure Virgin.
℟. Mother of God, intercede for us.
Let us pray. *Prayer*

O GOD, who through the fruitful virginity of blessed Mary hast bestowed upon mankind the rewards of eternal salvation: grant, we beseech thee; that we may ever perceive that she intercedeth for us, through whom we did receive the author of life, Jesus Christ thy Son our Lord. ℟. Amen.

After the Purification until the Wednesday in Holy Week:

HAIL, thou Queen of heavenly regions,
Mistress of angelic legions:
Root of Jesse, heaven's portal,
Whence hath risen the light immortal:

Joy be thine, O Virgin blessèd,
Fairest of our race confessèd,
Thee we hail, O glorious Maiden;
Plead to Christ for souls sin-laden.

℣. Vouchsafe to receive my praises, O hallowed Virgin.
℟. Strengthen me to resist all thine enemies.
Let us pray. *Prayer*

GRANT us, O merciful God, support in our weakness: that, as we keep the holy Mother of God in devout remembrance; so with the help of her intercession we may be raised up from all our iniquities. Through the same Christ our Lord. ℟. Amen.

In Eastertide:

JOY to thee, O Queen of heaven, alleluia;
He whom thou wast meet to bear, alleluia:

As he promised, hath arisen, alleluia:
Pour for us to God to prayer, alleluia.
℣. Rejoice and be glad, O Virgin Mary, alleluia. ℟. For the Lord hath arisen indeed, alleluia.
Let us pray. *Prayer*

O GOD, who by the resurrection of thy Son Jesus Christ hast vouchsafed to give joy to the whole world: grant we beseech thee; that through the help of his Mother, the Virgin Mary, we may obtain the joys of everlasting life. Through the same Christ our Lord. ℟. Amen.

From I Evensong of Trinity Sunday until Advent:

HAIL, holy Queen, Mother of mercy; hail our life, our sweetness, and our hope. To thee do we cry, poor banished children of Eve; to thee do we send up our sighs, mourning and weeping in this vale of tears. Turn then, most gracious advocate, thine eyes of mercy towards us; and after this our exile shew unto us the blessed fruit of thy womb, Jesus. O gentle, O loving, O sweet Virgin Mary.
℣. Pray for us, O holy Mother of God. ℟. That we may be made worthy of the promises of Christ.
Let us pray. *Prayer*

ALMIGHTY and everlasting God, who by the co-operation of the Holy Ghost didst prepare the body and soul of Mary, the glorious Virgin Mother, to be a dwelling-place meet for thy Son: grant, that as we rejoice to keep her in remembrance; so by her devout intercession we may be delivered from the evils that now beset us, and from eternal death. Through the same Christ our Lord. ℟. Amen.

AFTER DIVINE SERVICE

TO the most holy and undivided Trinity, to the Manhood of our crucified Lord, Jesus Christ, to the fruitful virginity of the most blessed and glorious ever-Virgin Mary, and to the whole company of the Saints, be everlasting praise, honour, might and glory from all things created, and unto us the remission of all our sins, for ever and ever. ℟. Amen.
℣. Blessed is the womb of the Virgin Mary, which bare the Son of the eternal Father. ℟. And blessed the breast that fed the Lord Christ.

Our Father. Hail Mary.

To which may be added:

O MOST gracious Jesu, I give thanks unto thee with my whole heart. Be merciful to me, a most wretched sinner. I offer this act of worship to thy divine

Heart, that thou wouldest correct whatever is amiss, and supply whatever is lacking, to the praise and glory of thy most holy Name, and to that of thy most blessed Mother; for the salvation of my soul and for that of all thy Church. Amen.

PRAYERS AND THANKSGIVINGS

PRAYERS

To be used before the two final prayers of the Litany, or of Morning and Evening Prayer.

For Rain

O GOD, heavenly Father, who by thy Son Jesus Christ hast promised to all them that seek thy kingdom, and the righteousness thereof, all things necessary to their bodily sustenance: send us, we beseech thee, in this our necessity, such moderate rain and showers, that we may receive the fruits of the earth to our comfort, and to thy honour; through Jesus Christ our Lord. ℟. Amen.

For Fair Weather

O ALMIGHTY Lord God, who for the sin of man didst once drown all the world, except eight persons, and afterward of thy great mercy didst promise never to destroy it so again; we humbly beseech thee, that although we for our iniquities have worthily deserved a plague of rain and waters, yet upon our true repentance thou wilt send us such weather, as that we may receive the fruits of the earth in due season; and learn both by thy punishment to amend our lives, and for thy clemency to give thee praise and glory; through Jesus Christ our Lord. ℟. Amen.

In time of Dearth and Famine

O GOD, heavenly Father, whose gift it is, that the rain doth fall, the earth is fruitful, beasts increase, and fishes do multiply; behold, we beseech thee, the afflictions of thy people; and grant that the scarcity and dearth, which we do now most justly suffer for our iniquity, may through thy goodness be mercifully turned into cheapness and plenty; for the love of Jesus Christ our Lord, to whom with thee and the Holy Ghost be all honour and glory now and for ever. ℟. Amen.

Or this

O GOD, merciful Father, who, in the time of Elisha the prophet, didst suddenly in Samaria turn great scarcity and dearth into plenty and cheapness; have mercy upon us, that we, who are now for our sins punished with like adversity, may likewise find a seasonable relief: increase the fruits of the earth by thy heavenly benediction; and grant that we, receiving thy bountiful liberality, may use the same to thy glory, the relief of those that are needy, and our own comfort; through Jesus Christ our Lord. ℟. Amen.

In time of War and Tumults

O ALMIGHTY God, King of all kings, and Governor of all things, whose power no creature is able to resist, to whom it belongeth justly to punish sinners, and to be merciful to them that truly repent; save and deliver us, we humbly beseech thee, from the hands of our enemies; abate their pride, assuage their malice, and confound their devices; that we, being armed with thy defence, may be preserved evermore from all perils, to glorify thee, who art the only giver of all victory; through the merits of thy only Son, Jesus Christ our Lord. ℟. Amen.

In time of any common Plague or Sickness

O ALMIGHTY God, who in thy wrath didst send a plague upon thine own people in the wilderness, for their obstinate rebellion against Moses and Aaron; and also, in the time of king David, didst slay with the plague of pestilence threescore and ten thousand, and yet remembering thy mercy didst save the rest; have pity upon us miserable sinners, who now are visited with great sickness and mortality; that like as thou didst then accept of an atonement, and didst command the destroying Angel to cease from punishing, so it may now please thee to withdraw from us this plague and grievous sickness; through Jesus Christ our Lord. ℟. Amen.

In the Ember Weeks, to be said every day, for those to be admitted into Holy Orders

ALMIGHTY God, our heavenly Father, who hast purchased to thyself an universal Church by the precious Blood of thy dear Son; mercifully look upon the same, and at this time so guide and govern the minds of thy servants the Bishops and Pastors of thy flock, that they may lay hands suddenly on no man, but faithfully and wisely make choice of fit persons to serve thee in the sacred Ministry of thy Church. And to those which shall be ordained to any holy function give thy grace and heavenly benediction; that both by their life and doctrine they may set forth thy glory, and set forward the salvation of all men; through Jesus Christ our Lord. ℟. Amen.

Or this

ALMIGHTY God, the giver of all good gifts, who of thy divine providence hast appointed divers Orders in thy Church; give thy grace, we humbly beseech thee, to all those who are to be called to any office and administration in the same; and so replenish them with the truth of thy doctrine, and endue them with innocency of life, that they may faithfully serve before thee, to the glory of thy great name, and the benefit of thy holy Church; through Jesus Christ our Lord. ℟. Amen.

A Prayer that may be said after any of the former

O GOD, whose nature and property is ever to have mercy and to forgive, receive our humble petitions; and though we be tied and bound with the chain of our sins, yet let the pitifulness of thy great mercy loose us; for the honour of Jesus Christ, our Mediator and Advocate. ℟. Amen.

A Prayer for the High Court of Parliament, to be read during their Session

MOST gracious God, we humbly beseech thee, as for this kingdom in general, so especially for the High Court of Parliament, under our most religious and gracious Queen at this time assembled; that thou wouldest be pleased to direct and prosper all their consultations to the advancement of thy glory, the good of thy Church, the safety, honour, and welfare of our Sovereign and her Dominions; that all things may be so ordered and settled by their endeavours upon the best and surest foundations, that peace and happiness, truth and justice, religion and piety, may be established among us for all generations. These and all other necessaries, for them, for us, and thy whole Church, we humbly beg in the name and mediation of Jesus Christ, our most blessed Lord and Saviour. ℟. Amen.

For all Conditions of Men (to be used at such times when the Litany is not appointed)

O GOD, the Creator and Preserver of all mankind, we humbly beseech thee for all sorts and conditions of men; that thou wouldest be pleased to make thy ways known unto them, thy saving health among all nations. More especially, we pray for the good estate of the catholic Church; that it may be so guided and governed by thy good Spirit, that all who profess and call themselves Christians may be led into the way of truth, and hold the faith in unity of spirit, in the bond of peace, and in righteousness of life. Finally, we commend to thy fatherly goodness all those who are any ways afflicted, or distressed, in mind, body, or estate; *(especially those for whom our prayers are desired;)* that it may please thee to comfort and relieve them, according to their several necessities, giving them patience under their sufferings, and a happy issue out of all their afflictions. And this we beg for Jesus Christ his sake. ℟. Amen.

For the Departed

O GOD, the Creator and Redeemer of all thy faithful people: grant unto the souls of thy servants and handmaids the forgiveness of all their sins; that as they have ever desired thy merciful pardon, so by the supplication of their brethren they may receive the same: who livest and reignest world without end. ℟. Amen.

THANKSGIVINGS

A General Thanksgiving

ALMIGHTY God, Father of all mercies, we thine unworthy servants do give thee most humble and hearty thanks for all thy goodness and lovingkindness to us, and to all men: (*particularly to those who desire now to offer up their praises and thanksgivings for thy mercies vouchsafed unto them.*) We bless thee for our creation, preservation, and all the blessings of this life; but above all, for thine inestimable love in the redemption of the world by our Lord Jesus Christ; for the means of grace, and for the hope of glory. And we beseech thee, give us that due sense of all thy mercies, that our hearts may be unfeignedly thankful, and that we shew forth thy praise, not only with our lips, but in our lives; by giving up ourselves to thy service, and by walking before thee in holiness and righteousness all our days; through Jesus Christ our Lord, to whom with thee and the Holy Ghost be all honour and glory, world without end. ℟. Amen.

For Rain

O GOD, our heavenly Father, who by thy gracious providence dost cause the former and the latter rain to descend upon the earth, that it may bring forth fruit for the use of man; we give thee humble thanks that it hath pleased thee, in our great necessity, to send us at the last a joyful rain upon thine inheritance, and to refresh it when it was dry, to the great comfort of us thy unworthy servants, and to the glory of thy holy name; through thy mercies in Jesus Christ our Lord. ℟. Amen.

For Fair Weather

O LORD God, who hast justly humbled us by thy late plague of immoderate rain and waters, and in thy mercy hast relieved and comforted our souls by this seasonable and blessed change of weather; we praise and glorify thy holy name for this thy mercy, and will always declare thy loving-kindness from generation to generation; through Jesus Christ our Lord. ℟. Amen.

For Plenty

O MOST merciful Father, who of thy gracious goodness hast heard the devout prayers of thy Church, and turned our dearth and scarcity into cheapness and plenty; we give thee humble thanks for this thy special bounty; beseeching thee to continue thy loving-kindness unto us, that our land may yield us her fruits of increase, to thy glory and our comfort; through Jesus Christ our Lord. ℟. Amen.

For Peace and Deliverance from our Enemies

O ALMIGHTY God, who art a strong tower of defence unto thy servants against the face of their enemies; we yield thee praise and thanksgiving for our deliverance from those great and apparent dangers wherewith we were compassed; we acknowledge it thy goodness that we were not delivered over as a prey unto them; beseeching thee still to continue thy mercies towards us; that all the world may know that thou art our Saviour and mighty Deliverer; through Jesus Christ our Lord. ℟. Amen.

For restoring public Peace at Home

O ETERNAL God, our heavenly Father, who alone makest men to be of one mind in a house, and stillest the outrage of a violent and unruly people; we bless thy holy name, that it hath pleased thee to appease the seditious tumults which have been lately raised up amongst us; most humbly beseeching thee to grant to all of us grace, that we may henceforth obediently walk in thy commandments; and leading a quiet and peaceable life in all godliness and honesty, may continually offer unto thee our sacrifice of praise and thanksgiving for these thy mercies towards us; through Jesus Christ our Lord. ℟. Amen.

For Deliverance from the Plague, or other common Sickness

O LORD God, who hast wounded us for our sins, and consumed us for our transgressions, by thy late heavy and dreadful visitation; and now, in the midst of judgement remembering mercy, hast redeemed our souls from the jaws of death; we offer unto thy fatherly goodness ourselves, our souls and bodies which thou hast delivered, to be a living sacrifice unto thee, always praising and magnifying thy mercies in the midst of thy Church; through Jesus Christ our Lord. ℟. Amen.

Or this

WE humbly acknowledge before thee, O most merciful Father, that all the punishments which are threatened in thy law might justly have fallen upon us, by reason of our manifold transgressions and hardness of heart: yet seeing it hath pleased thee of thy tender mercy, upon our weak and unworthy humiliation, to assuage the contagious sickness wherewith we lately have been sore afflicted, and to restore the voice of joy and health into our dwellings; we offer unto thy divine majesty the sacrifice of praise and thanksgiving, lauding and magnifying thy glorious name for such thy preservation and providence over us; through Jesus Christ our Lord. ℟. Amen.

PROPER OF SEASONS
ADVENT I
1 EVENSONG

Ant. 1 In that day * the mountains shall drop down new wine, and the hills shall flow with milk and honey, alleluia.

2 Rejoice greatly, * O daughter of Sion; shout aloud, O daughter of Jerusalem, alleluia.

3 Behold, the Lord cometh, * and all his Saints with him; and there shall be in that day a great light, alleluia.

4 Ho, every one that thirsteth, * come ye to the waters: seek ye the Lord while he may be found, alleluia.

5 Lo, there cometh * a mighty prophet, and he shall build again Jerusalem, alleluia.

Hymn(1)

CREATOR of the stars of night,
Thy people's everlasting light,
Jesu, Redeemer, save us all,
And hear thy servants when they call.

Thou, grieving that the ancient curse
Should doom to death a universe,
Hast found the medicine, full of grace,
To save and heal a ruined race.

Thou cam'st, the Bridegroom of the bride,
As drew the world to eventide;
Proceeding from a virgin-shrine,
The spotless Victim, all-divine;

At whose dread name, majestic now,
All knees must bend, all hearts must bow;
And things celestial thee shall own,
And things terrestrial, Lord alone.

O thou, whose coming is with dread
To judge and doom the quick and dead,
Preserve us, while we dwell below,
From every insult of the foe.

To God the Father, God the Son,
And God the Spirit; Three in One:
Laud, honour, might and glory be
From age to age eternally. Amen.

℣. Drop down, ye heavens, from above, and let the skies pour down righteousness.

℟. Let the earth open, and let it bring forth salvation.

Ant. to Magn. Behold, the name of the Lord * cometh from afar, and his glory filleth all the earth.

Collect

ALMIGHTY God, give us grace that we may cast away the works of darkness, and put upon us the armour of light; now in the time of this mortal life, in which thy Son Jesus Christ came to visit us in great humility; that in the last day, when he shall come again in his glorious majesty to judge both the quick and the dead, we may rise to the life immortal; through him who liveth and reigneth with thee and the Holy Ghost, now and ever.

MATTINS

Invit. The Lord, the King that draweth nigh,* O come, let us worship him.

Psalms of day (or 1, 7), with antiphons as at Evensong. Benedicite is said on Sundays and ferias of Advent.

Hymn (2)

HIGH Word of God, who once didst come,
Leaving thy Father and thy home,
To succour with thy birth our kind,
When, towards thine Advent, time declined.

Pour light upon us from above,
And fire our hearts with thy strong love,
That, as we hear thy Gospel read,
All fond desires may flee in dread;

That when thou comest from the skies,
Great Judge, to open thine assize,
To give each hidden sin its smart,
And crown as kings the pure in heart;

We be not set at thy left hand,
Where sentence due would bid us stand,
But with thy Saints thy face may see,
For ever wholly loving thee.

Praise to the Father and the Son,
Through all the ages as they run,
And to the Holy Paraclete
Be praise with them and worship meet. Amen.

℣. The voice of one crying in the wilderness: Prepare ye the way of the Lord.
℟. Make straight the paths of our God.

Ant. to Ben. The Holy Ghost * shall come down upon thee, Mary: fear not, thou shalt conceive in thy womb the Son of God, alleluia.

II EVENSONG

As at I Evensong, except: Psalms of day (or 46, 48).
Ant. to Magn. Fear not, Mary, * thou hast found favour with the Lord; behold, thou shalt concieve and bear a Son, alleluia.

On ferias in Advent, the Invitatory, Hymn, ℣. & ℟. as on the previous Sunday. Except on ferias of 1st week, commem. of Advent I after Collect of day.

ANTIPHONS TO CANTICLES

MONDAY
Ben. The Angel of the Lord * brought the tidings to Mary, and she conceived by the Holy Ghost, alleluia.
Magn. Lift up thine eyes, * O Jerusalem, and see the King in his power; lo, thy Redeemer cometh to release thee from thy chain.

TUESDAY
Ben. Before they came together, * Mary was found with child of the Holy Ghost.
Magn. Seek ye the Lord * while he may be found: call ye upon him while he is near, alleluia.

WEDNESDAY
Ben. Out of Sion * shall go forth the law: and the word of the Lord from Jerusalem.
Magn. There shall come * after me one that is mightier than I; the latchet of whose shoes I am not worthy to unloose.

THURSDAY
Ben. Blessed art thou * among women, and blessed is the fruit of thy womb.
Magn. I will wait * upon the Lord my Saviour, and I will look for him when he is near, alleluia.

FRIDAY
Ben. Lo, there cometh * one that is both God and man, of the house of David, to sit upon the throne, alleluia.
Magn. Out of Egypt * have I called my Son: he shall come to save his people.

SATURDAY
Ben. Sion, be not dismayed, * for behold, thy God cometh, alleluia.

ADVENT II

As on Advent I, except:

I EVENSONG

Ant. 1 Behold, the Lord shall appear * in the clouds of heaven with power and great glory, alleluia.
2 Sion is our strong city, * a Saviour will God appoint within her for walls and bulwarks: open ye the gates, for God is with us, alleluia.
3 Behold, our Lord * shall come with power, to enlighten the eyes of his servants, alleluia.
Ant. to Magn. Come, O Lord, * and visit us in peace, that we may rejoice before thee with a perfect heart.

Collect
BLESSED Lord, who hast caused all holy scriptures to be written for our learning: grant that we may in such wise hear them, read, mark, learn and inwardly digest them; that by patience and comfort of thy holy word, we may embrace and ever hold fast the blessed hope of everlasting life, which thou hast given us in our Saviour Jesus Christ: Who liveth.

MATTINS

Psalms of day (or 9, 11), with antiphons as at Evensong.
Ant. to Ben. Now when John * had heard in the prison the works of Christ, he sent two of his disciples, and asked him, saying: Art thou he that should come, or look we for another?

II EVENSONG

Psalms of day (or 50, 67), with antiphons as at I Evensong.
Ant. to Magn. Art thou he that should come, * or look we for another? Tell John the things which ye have seen: the blind receive their sight, the dead are raised up, the poor have the gospel preached unto them, alleluia.

ANTIPHONS TO CANTICLES

MONDAY
Ben. From heaven there cometh * the Lord the Ruler, and in his hand are honour and dominion.
Magn. Behold the King cometh, * the Lord of the earth, and he shall take away the yoke of our captivity.

TUESDAY
Ben. The Lord shall arise * upon thee, O Jerusalem, and his glory shall be seen upon thee.
Magn. The voice of one crying * in the wilderness: Prepare ye the way of the Lord: make straight a highway for our God.

WEDNESDAY
Ben. Behold, I send * my messenger, and he shall prepare thy way before thy face.
Magn. Sion, thou shalt be renewed, * and shalt see thy Righteousness, that is come unto thee.

THURSDAY
Ben. Thou, O Lord, * art he that should come, for whom we look, to save thy people.
Magn. He that cometh after me * is preferred before me: the latchet of whose shoes I am not worthy to unloose.

FRIDAY
Ben. Say to them * that are of a fearful heart: Be strong, for behold, the Lord our God shall come.
Magn. O sing unto the Lord * a new song: and his praise to the ends of the earth.

SATURDAY
Ben. The Lord shall set up an ensign * for the nations, and shall assemble the outcasts of Israel.

GREATER ANTIPHONS

To be said in full before and after **Magnificat**; or, on Feasts, with ℣. & ℟. and Advent Collect after the Collect of the Feast.

Dec. 16. O Wisdom, * which camest out of the mouth of the most High, and reachest from one end to another, mightily and sweetly ordering all things: come and teach us the way of prudence.

Dec. 17. O Adonai, * and Leader of the house of Israel, who appearedst in the bush to Moses in a flame of fire, and gavest him the law in Sinai: come and deliver us with an outstretched arm.

Dec. 18. O Root of Jesse, * which standest for an ensign of the people, at whom kings shall shut their mouths, to whom the Gentiles shall seek: come and deliver us, and tarry not.

Dec. 19. O Key of David, * and Sceptre of the house of Israel, that openest, and no man shutteth, and shuttest and no man openeth: come and bring the prisoner out of the prison-house, and him that sitteth in darkness and the shadow of death.

Dec. 20. O Day-spring, * brightness of light everlasting, and Sun of righteousness: come and enlighten him that sitteth in darkness and the shadow of death.

Dec. 21. O King of the nations, * and their desire: the Cornerstone, who makest both one: come and save mankind, whom thou formedst of clay.

Dec. 22. O Emmanuel, * our King and law-giver, the desire of all nations, and their salvation: come and save us, O Lord our God.

Dec. 23. O Virgin of virgins, * how shall this be? For neither before thee was any like thee, nor shall there be after. Daughters of Jerusalem, why marvel ye at me? The thing which ye behold is a divine mystery.

ADVENT III

I EVENSONG

Ant. 1 The Lord will surely come * and will not tarry: and will bring to light the hidden things of darkness, and will manifest himself to all nations, alleluia.

2 Rejoice, O Jerusalem, * with great rejoicing, for thy Saviour cometh unto thee, alleluia.

3 I will place salvation * in Sion, and in Jerusalem my glory, alleluia.

4 Let us live righteously, * and godly, looking for that blessed hope, and the coming of the Lord.

Hymn, ℣. & ℟. as on Advent I.

Ant. to Magn. (unless Gr. Ant.). Before me * there was no God formed, nor shall there be after me: for to me shall every knee be bowed, and me shall every tongue confess.

Collect

O LORD Jesu Christ, who at thy first coming didst send thy messenger to prepare thy way before thee: grant that the ministers and stewards of thy mysteries may likewise so prepare and make ready thy way, by turning the hearts of the disobedient to the wisdom of the just; that at thy second coming to judge the world we may be found an acceptable people in thy sight: Who livest.

MATTINS

Invit. The Lord is now nigh at hand: * O come, let us worship him.
Psalms of day (or 73), with antiphons as at Evensong.

Hymn, ℣. & ℟. as on Advent I.
Ant. to Ben. On the throne * of David, and over his kingdom, shall he reign for ever, alleluia.

II EVENSONG

As at I Evensong, except:
Psalms of day (or 75, 76, 82).
Ant. to Magn. (unless Gr. Ant.).
Blessed art thou, Mary * who hast believed: there shall be performed in thee the things which were told thee from the Lord, alleluia.

ANTIPHONS TO CANTICLES

Except on Dec. 21 and 23 at Mattins, and when the Greater Antiphons are appointed at Evensong, the following are used.

Magn. Awake, awake, * arise, O Jerusalem: loose the bands from off the neck, O captive daughter of Sion.

MONDAY

Ben. There shall come forth * a Rod from the stem of Jesse, and all the earth shall be filled with his glory: and all flesh shall see the salvation of God.
Magn. All generations * shall call me blessed, for God hath regarded his lowly handmaiden.

EMBER WEDNESDAY

Ben. The Angel Gabriel * was sent to Mary, a Virgin espoused to Joseph.
Magn. Behold the handmaid of the Lord: * be it unto me according to thy word.

THURSDAY

Ben. Watch ye therefore * in your hearts: for the Lord our God is nigh at hand.
Magn. Rejoice ye * with Jerusalem, and be glad with her, all ye that love her, for ever.

TUESDAY

Ben. Thou, Bethlehem, * in the land of Judah, shalt not be the least; for out of thee shall come a Governor, that shall rule my people Israel.

EMBER FRIDAY

Ben. As soon as the voice * of thy salutation sounded in mine ears, the babe leaped in my womb for joy, alleluia.

EMBER SATURDAY

Ben. How shall this be, * Angel of God, seeing I know not a man? Hearken, O Virgin Mary: the Holy Ghost shall come upon thee, and the power of the Highest shall overshadow thee.

The Ant. to Ben. on Dec. 21 & 23 are as follows:

Dec. 21. Be not afraid, * for on the fifth day our Lord will come unto you.

Dec. 23. Behold, all things are fulfilled * which were spoken by the Angel of the Virgin Mary.

ADVENT IV
I EVENSONG

Ant. 1 Blow ye the trumpet * in Sion, for the day of the Lord is nigh at hand: behold, he cometh to save us, alleluia, alleluia.
2 Behold, he cometh, * the Desire of all nations; and the house of the Lord shall be filled with glory, alleluia.
3 The crooked * shall be made straight, and the rough places plain: come, O Lord, and tarry not, alleluia.
4 Thine almighty Word, * O Lord, shall proceed from heaven out of thy royal throne, alleluia.

Hymn, ℣. & ℟. as on Advent I.
Greater Antiphon to Magn.

Collect

O LORD, raise up (we pray thee) thy power and come among us, and with great might succour us; that whereas through our sins and wickedness we are sore let and hindered in running the race that is set before us, thy bountiful grace and mercy may speedily help and deliver us; through the satisfaction of thy Son our Lord, to whom with thee and the Holy Ghost be honour and glory, world without end.

MATTINS

Invit. The Lord is now nigh at hand: * O come, let us worship him.
Psalms of day (or 94), with antiphons as at Evensong.

Hymn, ℣. & ℟. as on Advent I.
Ant. to Ben. Hail, Mary, * full of grace: the Lord is with thee, blessed art thou among women, alleluia.

II EVENSONG

As at I. Evensong, except: Psalms of day (or, 96, 97, 98).

MATTINS DURING WEEK

(Ant. to Ben. on Dec. 21 & 23 as on p. 35.)

MONDAY

Ant. 1 Behold, the Lord shall come, * the Prince of the kings of the earth: blessed are they who are prepared to meet him.
2 When the Son of man * shall come, thinkest thou he shall find faith upon the earth?
3 Behold, now is come * the fulness of time, in which God sent his own Son on the earth.
4 The Lord shall go forth * from his holy place: he shall come to save his people.
Ant. to Ben. Thus saith the Lord: * Repent ye and turn again, because the kingdom of heaven is at hand, alleluia.

TUESDAY

Ant. 1 Drop down, ye heavens, from above, * and let the skies pour down righteousness: let the earth open, and let it bring forth salvation.
2 Send forth, O Lord, the Lamb, * the Ruler of the earth from the rock of the desert, to the mountain of the daughter of Sion.
3 That thy way, O Lord, may be known upon earth, and thy saving health among all nations.
4 The law was given by Moses, * grace and truth came by Jesus Christ.
Ant. to Ben. Awake, awake, * put on strength, O arm of the Lord.

WEDNESDAY

Ant. 1 The Prophets foretold * that a Saviour would be born of the Virgin Mary.
2 The Spirit of the Lord * is upon me: because he hath anointed me to preach the gospel to the poor.
3 For Sion's sake * will I not hold my peace, until the Righteous One come forth as brightness.
4 Declare this * among the people, and say: Behold, God our Saviour shall come.
Ant. to Ben. I will place salvation * in Sion, and my glory in Jerusalem, alleluia.

THURSDAY

Ant. 1 The Lord almighty * shall come from Sion, that he may save his people.
2 Turn thee again, * O Lord, at the last, and tarry not to come unto thy servants.
3 Out of Sion * the Lord shall come to be our King: Emmanuel is his great name.
4 The Lord is our Law-giver, * the Lord is our King: he shall come and save us.
Ant. to Ben. Comfort ye, comfort ye, * my people, saith the Lord your God.

FRIDAY

Ant. 1 Be ye stedfast, * and ye shall see the help of the Lord upon you.
2 Unto thee, O Lord, * do I lift up my soul: come and deliver me, O Lord: in thee have I made my place of refuge.

3 Come, O Lord, * and tarry not: purge the transgressions of thy people Israel.

4 Yet will I look * unto the Lord: I will await God my Saviour.

December 24
CHRISTMAS EVE
Double
MATTINS

Invit. To-day ye shall know that the Lord will come: * And in the morning ye shall see his glory.

Ant. 1 O Judah and Jerusalem, * be ye not dismayed: to-morrow go ye forth, and the Lord himself will be with you.

2 Ye shall know * this day that the Lord will come: and in the morning ye shall see his glory.

3 To-morrow * ye shall have deliverance, saith the Lord of hosts.

Hymn as on Advent I.

℣. To-morrow the iniquity of the earth shall be done away.

℟. And the Saviour of the world shall reign over us.

Ant. to Ben. The Saviour of the world * shall arise as the sun: and shall come down into the Virgin's womb as the showers upon the grass.

Collect

O GOD, who makest us glad with the yearly expectation of our redemption: grant that as we joyfully receive thine only-begotten Son as our Redeemer; so we may with sure confidence behold him, when he shall come to be our Judge, even Jesus Christ our Lord: Who liveth.

December 25
CHRISTMAS DAY
Double of I class
I EVENSONG

Psalms of day (or 89, vv. 1-36).

Ant. 1 The King of peace * is highly exalted, and the whole earth seeketh to his presence.

2 The King of peace * is highly exalted, over all the kings of the whole earth.

3 The days of Mary * are fulfilled, that she should bring forth her first-born Son.

4 Lift up your heads: * behold, your redemption draweth nigh.

Hymn (17)

JESU, the Father's only Son,
Whose death for all redemption won;
Before the worlds, of God most high
Begotten all ineffably.

The Father's light and splendour thou;
Their endless hope to thee that bow;

Accept the prayers and praise to-day
That through the world thy servants pay.

Salvation's author, call to mind
How, taking form of humankind,
Born of a Virgin undefiled,
Thou in man's flesh becam'st a child.

Thus testifies this present day,
Through every year in long array,
That thou, salvation's source alone,
Proceededst from the Father's throne.

Whence sky, and stars, and sea's abyss,
And earth, and all that therein is,
Shall still, with laud and carol meet
The Author of thine advent greet.

And we, who, by thy precious blood
From sin redeemed, are marked for God,
On this the day that saw thy birth,
Sing the new song of ransomed earth;

For that thine advent glory be,
O Jesu, Virgin-born, to thee;
With Father and with Holy Ghost,
From men and from the heavenly host. Amen.

℣. To-morrow the iniquity of the earth shall be done away.
℟. And the Saviour of the world shall reign over us.
Ant. to Magn. Or ever the sun * be risen in the heavens, ye shall see the King of kings proceeding from the Father, as a bridegroom out of his chamber.

Collect

ALMIGHTY God, who hast given us thy only-begotten Son to take our nature upon him, and as at this time to be born of a pure Virgin: grant that we being regenerate, and made thy children by adoption and grace, may daily be renewed by thy Holy Spirit. Through the same our Lord Jesus Christ, who liveth and reigneth with thee and the same Spirit, ever one God, world without end.

MATTINS

Invit. Unto us the Christ is born: * O come, let us worship.
Psalms 19, 45, 85 (or 19, 85).
Ant. 1 Whom beheld ye, * O shepherds, tell us; declare to us the tidings: on earth who hath appeared? We beheld an Infant, the new-born Lord and Saviour, amidst a choir of Angels, alleluia, alleluia.
2 Lo, a Maiden, * hath borne the Monarch, whose name is everlasting: she hath the joy of a Mother, with the honour of virginity: before her none hath been seen like her, nor

PROPER OF SEASONS 39

shall there be after, alleluia.
3 The Angel * said unto the shepherds: Behold, I bring you good tidings of great joy: for unto you is born this day the Saviour of the world, alleluia.

Hymn (18)

FROM east to west, from shore to shore,
Let every heart awake and sing
The holy Child whom Mary bore,
The Christ, the everlasting King.

Behold, the world's Creator wears
The form and fashion of a slave;
Our very flesh our Maker shares,
His fallen creature, man, to save.

For this how wondrously he wrought!
A maiden, in her lowly place,
Became in ways beyond all thought
The chosen vessel of his grace.

She bowed her to the Angel's word
Declaring what the Father willed,
And suddenly the promised Lord
That pure and hallowed temple filled.

He shrank not from the oxen's stall,
He lay within the manger-bed,
And he, whose bounty feedeth all,
At Mary's breast himself was fed.

And while the Angels in the sky
Sang praise above the silent field,
To shepherds poor the Lord most high,
The one great Shepherd, was revealed.

All glory for this blessèd morn
To God the Father ever be;
All praise to thee, O Virgin-born;
All praise, O Holy Ghost, to thee. Amen.

℣. The Lord hath made known, alleluia. ℟. His salvation, alleluia.
Ant. to Ben. Glory to God in the highest, * and on earth peace, goodwill toward men, alleluia, alleluia.

Athanasian Creed, to-day only.

II EVENSONG

Psalms 89, 110, 132 (or 132).
Ant. 1 He shall call * me, alleluia: Thou art my Father, alleluia. Ps 89.
2 In the day of thy power * shall the people offer thee free-will offerings with an holy worship: the dew of thy birth is of the womb of the morning. Ps. 110.

3 Of the fruit of thy body * shall I set upon thy seat. Ps. 132.
Hymn as at I Evensong.
℣. The Lord hath made known, alleluia. ℟. His salvation, alleluia.
Ant. to Magn. To-day * the Christ is born: to-day hath a Saviour appeared: to-day on earth Angels are singing, Archangels rejoicing: to-day the righteous exult and say: Glory to God in the highest, alleluia.

COMMEMORATION OF CHRISTMAS
MATTINS

Ant. Glory to God in the highest, and on earth peace, goodwill toward men, alleluia, alleluia.
℣. The Lord hath made known, alleluia. ℟. His salvation, alleluia.

Collect

ALMIGHTY God, who hast given us thy only-begotten Son to take our nature upon him, and as at this time to be born of a pure Virgin: grant that we being regenerate, and made thy children by adoption and grace, may daily be renewed by thy Holy Spirit. Through the same our Lord Jesus Christ, who liveth and reigneth with thee and the same Spirit, ever one God, world without end.

EVENSONG

Antiphons to Psalms until Dec. 30 inclusive.
1 In the day of thy power * shall the people offer thee freewill offerings with an holy worship: the dew of thy birth is of the womb of the morning.
2 The Lord hath sent * redemption unto his people: he hath commanded his covenant for ever and ever.
3 Unto the godly * there ariseth up light in the darkness: the Lord is merciful, loving and righteous.
4 With the Lord * there is mercy, and with him is plenteous redemption.
5 Of the fruit * of thy body shall I set upon thy seat.
Ant. To-day the Christ is born: to-day hath a Saviour appeared: to-day on earth Angels are singing, Archangels rejoicing: to-day the righteous exult and say: Glory to God in the highest, alleluia.
℣., ℟. and Collect as at Mattins.

December 26
ST STEPHEN THE FIRST MARTYR
Double of II class
MATTINS

Invit. The new-born Christ, who on this day crowned blessed Stephen: * O come, let us worship him.

Ant. 1 They stoned Stephen * calling upon the Lord, and saying: Lord lay not this sin to their charge.

2 The stones of the brook * were sweet unto him: him doth every soul of the righteous follow.

3 My soul hangeth upon thee: * for thy sake hath my body been stoned, O my God.

4 Stephen saw * the heavens opened; he saw and entered: how blessed is the man unto whom heaven stood open.

5 Behold, I see * heaven opened, and Jesus standing on the right hand of the power of God.

Hymn from Common, p. 198.

℣. Devout men carried Stephen to his burial. ℟. And made great lamentation over him.

Ant. to Ben. But Stephen, * full of grace and power, did great wonders among the people.

Collect

GRANT, O Lord, that in all our sufferings here upon earth for the testimony of thy truth, we may stedfastly look up to heaven, and by faith behold the glory that shall be revealed: and being filled with the Holy Ghost, may learn to love and bless our persecutors, by the example of thy first Martyr Saint Stephen, who prayed for his murderers to thee, O blessed Jesus, who standest at the right hand of God, to succour all those that suffer for thee, our only Mediator and Advocate.

Commem. of Christmas

EVENSONG

Christmas antiphons; Hymn from Common, p. 197.
℣. Stephen saw the heavens opened. ℟. He saw and entered: how blessed is the man unto whom heaven stood open.

Ant. to Magn. Devout men carried Stephen * to his burial, and made great lamentation over him.

Commem. of Christmas

December 27
ST JOHN, APOSTLE AND EVANGELIST
Double of II class
MATTINS

Invit. The Lord, the King of Apostles: * O come, let us worship him.

Ant. 1 Right worthy of honour * is blessed John, who leaned on the Lord's bosom at supper.

2 This is the disciple * which did testify: and we know that his testimony is true.

3 This is my disciple: * if I will that he tarry till I come, what is that to thee?

4 There be some standing here, * which shall not see death, until they see the Son of man in his kingdom.

5 Behold mine elect servant, * whom I have chosen: I have set my Spirit upon him.

Hymn from Common, p. 194.

℣. This is the disciple which testifieth of these things. ℟. And we know that his testimony is true.

Ant. to Ben. This is that John * which leaned on the Lord's bosom at supper; the blessed Apostle, unto whom were revealed the secrets of heaven.

Collect

MERCIFUL Lord, we beseech thee to cast thy bright beams of light upon thy Church: that it being enlightened by the doctrine of thy blessed Apostle and Evangelist Saint John may so walk in the light of thy truth; that it may at length attain to the light of everlasting life. Through.

Commem. of Christmas

EVENSONG

Christmas antiphons; Hymn from Common, p. 194.

℣. Right worthy of honour is blessed John the Apostle. ℟. Who leaned on the Lord's bosom at supper.

Ant. to Magn. This saying * went out among the brethren, that that disciple should not die; yet Jesus said not: He shall not die; but: If I will that he tarry till I come, what is that to thee?

Commem. of Christmas

December 28
THE HOLY INNOCENTS, MM.
Double of II class
MATTINS

Invit. The Lord, the King of Martyrs: * O come, let us worship him.

Ant. 1 Herod, being exceeding wroth, * slew many children in Bethlehem of Judaea, the city of David.

2 From two years old * and under, did Herod slay many children for the Lord's sake.

3 In Ramah * there was heard a voice, lamentation and bitter weeping: Rachel weeping for her children.

4 Under the throne of God * all the Saints cry out: Avenge our blood, O our God.

Hymn (34)

ALL hail, ye little Martyr flowers,
Sweet rosebuds cut in dawning hours!
When Herod sought the Christ to find
Ye fell as bloom before the wind.

First victims of the Martyr bands,
With crowns and palms in tender hands,
Around the very altar, gay
And innocent ye seem to play.

What profited this great offence?
What use was Herod's violence?
A Babe survives that dreadful day,
And Christ is safely borne away.

All honour, laud, and glory be,
O Jesu, Virgin-born, to thee;
All glory, as is ever meet,
To Father and to Paraclete.
Amen.

℣. Herod was exceeding wroth, and slew many children. ℟. In Bethlehem of Judaea, the city of David.

Ant. These are they * which were not defiled with women, for they are virgins: and they follow the Lamb whithersoever he goeth.

Collect

O ALMIGHTY God, who out of the mouths of very babes and sucklings hast ordained strength, and madest infants to glorify thee by their deaths: mortify and kill all vices in us, and so strengthen us by thy grace, that by the innocency of our lives, and constancy of our faith even unto death, we may glorify thy holy name. Through.

Commem. of Christmas, p. 40.

EVENSONG

Christmas antiphons; Hymn as at Mattins.

℣. Under the throne of God all the Saints cry out. ℟. Avenge our blood, O Lord our God.

Ant. to Magn. **Many innocent children * were slain in Christ's behalf; by a ruthless tyrant were sucklings put to death; pure and unspotted, they follow the Lamb himself, and say without ceasing: Glory be to thee, O Lord.**

Commem. of Christmas, p. 40.

December 29
ST THOMAS, B.M.
Double of II class

As in Common, p. 197; with Collect as below, and commem. of Christmas, and at Evensong Christmas antiphons to Psalms.

Collect

O GOD, on behalf of whose Church the glorious Bishop Thomas fell by the swords of wicked men: grant, we beseech thee; that all they who implore his help may obtain the wholesome benefits after which they seek. Through.

SUNDAY IN OCTAVE OF CHRISTMAS

As on Christmas Day, with Psalms occurring (or, at Mattins 2, 8; at Evensong, 45, 110, 113).

December 30
WITHIN THE OCTAVE
Double

As on Christmas Day, with Psalms occurring.

December 31
ST SILVESTER, B.C.
Double

At Mattins, from Common, p. 203; with commem. of Christmas. Evensong of morrow, without commem.

January 1
CIRCUMCISION OF OUR LORD
Double of II class
I EVENSONG

Psalms of day (or 90, 133, 134).
Ant. 1 O wondrous trafficking: * the Creator of mankind, taking upon him a living body, vouchsafed to be born of a Virgin; and begotten in no carnal wise, hath made us partakers of his Godhead.
2 When thou wast born * all ineffably of a Virgin, then were the scriptures fulfilled: thou didst come down as showers upon the mown grass, to bring salvation unto all mankind: we praise thee, O our God.
3 In the bush * which Moses saw unconsumed, we acknowledge the preservation of thy glorious virginity: holy Mother of God, intercede for thy children.
4 The root of Jesse * hath budded, the Star hath come out of Jacob, a Virgin hath borne the Saviour: we praise thee, O our God.
5 Lo, Mary hath borne * to us the Saviour, of whom, when John beheld him, he cried, saying: Behold the Lamb of God, behold him that taketh away the sins of the world, alleluia.
Hymn as on Christmas Day, p. 37.
℣. The Word was made flesh, alleluia. ℟. And dwelt among us, alleluia.
Ant. to Magn. For his great love * wherewith God loved us, he sent his Son in the likeness of sinful flesh, alleluia.

Collect

ALMIGHTY God, who madest thy blessed Son to be circumcised, and obedient to the law for men: grant us the true circumcision of the Spirit; that our hearts, and all our members, being mortified from all worldly and carnal lusts, we may in all things obey thy blessed will. Through the same.

MATTINS

Invitatory as on Christmas Day.
Psalms of day (or 119, vv. 1-32), with antiphons as at I Evensong.
Hymn as on Christmas Day.
℣. The Word was made flesh, alleluia. ℟. And dwelt among us, alleluia.
Ant. to Ben. A great and wondrous mystery * is made known to us this day: a new thing is wrought in nature; God is made man; that which he was he remaineth, and that which he was not he assumeth, suffering neither confusion nor yet division.

II EVENSONG

As at I Evensong, except: Psalms of day (or 9, 121), with antiphons as at I. Evensong.
℣. The Lord hath made known, alleluia. ℟. His salvation, alleluia.
Ant. to Magn. **Heirs are we** * of a great mystery: the womb of her that knew not man is become the temple of the Godhead: he, of a Virgin incarnate, suffereth no defilement: all the nations shall gather, saying: Glory be to thee, O Lord.

Sunday between Circumcision and Epiphany
MOST HOLY NAME OF JESUS

See August 7.

January 2 to 5

As on Jan. 1, with Psalms and antiphons as in the monthly course.

January 6
EPIPHANY OF OUR LORD

Double of I class

I EVENSONG

Psalms of day (or 19, 87).
Ant. 1 **Before the morning star begotten,** * and Lord from everlasting, our Saviour is made manifest to-day unto the world.
2 **Thy light is come,** * O Jerusalem, and the glory of the Lord is risen upon thee, and the Gentiles shall walk in thy light, alleluia.
3 **When they had opened their treasures,** * the Sages offered gifts unto the Lord, incense, gold and myrrh, alleluia.

Hymn (38)

WHY, impious Herod, shouldst thou fear
Because the Christ is come so near?
He who doth heavenly kingdoms grant
Thine earthly realm can never want.

Lo, Sages from the east are gone
To where the star hath newly shone;
And on by light to Light they press,
And by their gifts their God confess.

The Lamb of God is manifest
Again in Jordan's water blest,
And he who sin had never known
By washing hath our sins undone.

Yet he that ruleth everything
Can change the nature of the spring,
And gives at Cana this for sign:
The water reddens into wine.

Then glory, Lord, to thee we pay
For thine Epiphany to-day;
All glory through eternity
To Father, Son and Spirit be. Amen.

℣. The kings of Tharsis and of the isles shall give presents.
℟. The kings of Arabia and Saba shall bring gifts.

Ant. to Magn. The Sages, * beholding the star, said one to another: This is the sign of a mighty King; let us go forth and seek him, and let us offer him gifts, gold, incense, and myrrh.

Collect

O GOD, who by the leading of a star didst manifest thy only-begotten Son to the Gentiles: mercifully grant; that we, which know thee now by faith, may after this life have the fruition of thy glorious Godhead. Through the same.

MATTINS

Invit. The Christ hath been manifested unto us: * O come, let us worship him.
Psalms of day (or 72) with antiphons as above. Hymn as at I Evensong.
℣. O worship the Lord, alleluia.
℟. All ye Angels of his, alleluia.
Ant. to Ben. To-day * to her heavenly Bridegroom is the Church espoused, forasmuch as in Jordan Christ hath washed away her iniquities; Sages with their offerings hasten to the royal marriage; and with water turned to wine the guests are regaled, alleluia.

Athanasian Creed, to-day only.

II EVENSONG

Psalms of day (or 96, 97, 117), with antiphons as above.
Hymn, ℣. ℟., as at I Evensong.
Ant. to Magn. We celebrate a holy day * adorned with three wonders: to-day the star led the Sages to the crib; to-day did water become wine at the marriage-feast; to-day Christ willed to be baptized by John in Jordan, for our salvation, alleluia.

Within the Octave, Psalms with their antiphons as in the monthly course, the rest as on the Feast, except as below.

ANTIPHONS DURING OCTAVE

Jan. 7. Ben. From the east * there came Sages to Bethlehem for to worship the Lord: and when they had opened their treasures, they presented unto him precious gifts: gold as to a mighty monarch, incense as to the true God, and myrrh

to foreshew his burial, alleluia.
Magn. Seeing the star, the Sages * rejoiced with great rejoicing: and entering into the house, they presented to the Lord incense, gold and myrrh.
Jan. 8. *Ben.* Three are the offerings * which the Sages brought unto the Lord: gold and myrrh and incense, to the Son of God, the mighty King, alleluia.
At Mattins, Commem. of St Lucian & his Companions, MM., from Common, p. 199.
Magn. Light of light, * thou, O Christ, hast appeared, unto whom the Wise Men present their gifts, alleluia, alleluia, alleluia.
Jan. 9. *Ben.* We have seen his star * in the east, and are come with gifts to worship the Lord.
Magn. Herod inquired * of the Sages: What sign did ye see over the new-born King? We have seen a star gleaming, the brightness of which lighteneth the world.

Jan. 10. *Ben.* Many nations * shall come from afar, bearing their gifts, alleluia.
Magn. All they from Saba * shall come, bearing gold and incense, alleluia, alleluia.
Jan. 11. *Ben.* They that despised thee * shall come unto thee, and shall bow themselves before thy feet.
Magn. The Sages, being warned * in dreams by an Angel, departed into their own country another way.
Jan. 12. *Ben.* Great is the mystery * of godliness: God manifest in the flesh, seen of Angels, preached unto the Gentiles, and believed on in the world.
Magn. The Sages, * beholding the star, said one to another: This is the sign of a mighty King let us go forth and seek him, and let us offer him gifts, gold, incense and myrrh.

Sunday in Octave of Epiphany

(1) EPIPHANY I

Psalms, with their antiphons as in the monthly course, the rest as on the Epiphany, except:

I EVENSONG

℣. All they from Sheba shall come, alleluia. ℟. They shall bring gold and incense, alleluia.
Ant. to Magn. The Child Jesus * tarried behind in Jerusalem, and his parents knew not of it, supposing him to have been in the company: and they sought him among their kinsfolk and acquaintance.

Collect

O LORD, we beseech thee mercifully to receive the prayers of thy people which call upon thee: and grant that they may both perceive and know what things they ought to do, and also may have grace and power faithfully to fulfil the same. Through.

MATTINS

Psalms of day (or 46, 47, 67). ℣., ℟. and Ant. as at I Evensong.

II EVENSONG

Psalms of day (or 18), with antiphons of Epiphany.
℣. & ℟. as at I Evensong.
Ant. to Magn. Son, * why hast thou thus dealt with us? Thy father and I have sought thee sorrowing. How is it that ye sought me? Wist ye not that I must be about my Father's business?

(2) FEAST OF THE HOLY FAMILY
Greater double

MATTINS

Invit. Christ the Son of God, who was made subject to Mary and Joseph: * O come, let us worship him.
Psalms of day (or 46, 47, 67).
Ant. 1 Jesus went down * with them, and came to Nazareth, and was subject unto them.
2 And Jesus increased * in wisdom and stature, and in favour with God and man.
3 And they said: * Whence hath this man this wisdom, and these mighty powers? Is not this the carpenter's son?

Hymn (808)

A BLESSING rests on Nazareth,
Whose walls to Christ their shelter lent,
Where in the holy Family
The Church's Lord his childhood spent.

The sun that in its daily course
Bathes all the lands with golden light
Never had fairer home than this
Nor holier dwelling in its sight.

And hither from the heavenly courts
Angelic messengers descend;
Full eagerly and oft they come
This shrine of virtue to defend.

Obedient both in thought and deed,
Here Jesus bows to Joseph's will;
And here the Virgin's heart exults
A Mother's office to fulfil.

Saint Joseph shares the life and cares
Of Mary in this hallowed place,
Bound to her by a thousand bonds
Of virtue by the God of grace.

Each loves the other, and their love
Commingles, and to Jesus flows;

On each of them in sweet return
Jesus abounding love bestows.

So be it; may such holy love
Unite us everlastingly,
Preserve our homes in lasting peace
And from life's evils keep us free.

To parents once obedient made,
Jesu, all glory be to thee,
Whom with the Father we adore
And Holy Ghost, eternally.
Amen.

℣. All thy children shall be taught of the Lord. ℟. And great shall be the peace of thy children.

Ant. to Ben. Enlighten us, O Lord, * by the example of thy Family, and guide our feet into the way of peace.

Collect

O LORD Jesu Christ, who didst become subject unto Mary and Joseph, and thereby didst hallow the life of the home with virtues beyond our telling: grant that aided by them both, we may be taught by the example of thy holy Family, and at length come unto its eternal fellowship: Who livest and reignest.

Commem. of Sunday.

EVENSONG

Psalms of day (or 18), with antiphons as at Mattins.

Hymn (809)

O JESU, light of hosts above,
And hope supreme of sons of earth,
The love that hallows homes below
Shone on thee through thy human birth;

And Mary, rich in grace divine,
In thee alone did God invest
The right to give a Mother's kiss
To Jesus, nourished at thy breast;

And thou, the Virgin's Guardian true,
Elect of all the patriarch line,
Upon the lips of Mary's Child
A father's title oft was thine.

From Jesse's noble stock ye came,
That ransom might for sin be paid;
O hear us, who with reverent prayers
Before your altars seek your aid.

The evening sun sinks in the west,
Its splendour from the land departs;
Yet we would here abide, to pour
Our prayers from out our inmost hearts.

Where'er has been your dwelling-place
There grace and virtue ever stay,
O may that grace be ours to bless

Our lives and homes from day to day.

To parents once obedient made,
Jesu, all glory be to thee,
Whom with the Father we adore,
And Holy Ghost, eternally.
Amen.

℣. All thy children shall be taught of the Lord. ℟. And great shall be the peace of thy children.

Ant. to Magn. But Mary * kept all these things, and pondered them in her heart.

Commem. of Sunday.

January 13
COMMEMORATION OF BAPTISM OF OUR LORD
Greater double

As on Epiphany, except:

Collect

O GOD, whose only-begotten Son hath been made manifest in the substance of our flesh: grant, we beseech thee; that like as we have known him after the fashion of our outward likeness, so we may inwardly be made regenerate in him: Who liveth.

EPIPHANY II

Collect

ALMIGHTY and everlasting God, who dost govern all things in heaven and earth: mercifully hear the supplications of thy people, and grant us thy peace all the days of our life. Through.

MATTINS

Psalms of day (or 27, 36).
Ben. Now there was a marriage * in Cana of Galilee and Jesus himself was there, with Mary his Mother.

II EVENSONG

Psalms of day (or 68).
Magn. And when they wanted wine, * Jesus commanded them to fill the water-pots with water: and it was turned into wine, alleluia.

EPIPHANY III

Collect

ALMIGHTY and everlasting God, mercifully look upon our infirmities; and in all our dangers and necessities stretch forth thy right hand to help and defend us. Through.

MATTINS

Psalms of day (or 42, 43).
Ben. And when Jesus was come down * from the mountain, behold, there came a leper and worshipped him, saying: Lord, if thou wilt thou canst make me clean: and he put forth his hand and touched him, saying: I will, be thou clean.

II EVENSONG

Psalms of day (or 33, 34).
Magn. Lord, * if thou wilt, thou canst make me clean; and Jesus said: I will, be thou clean.

EPIPHANY IV

Collect

O GOD, who seest us to be set in the midst of so many and great dangers, that by reason of the frailty of our nature we cannot always stand upright: grant to us such strength and protection, as may support us in all dangers, and carry us through all temptations. Through.

MATTINS

Psalms of day (or 60, 63).
Ben. And when Jesus was entered * into a ship, behold, there arose a great tempest in the sea: and his disciples came and awoke him, saying unto him: Master, save us, we perish.

II EVENSONG

Psalms of day (or 74).
Magn. Master, * save us, we perish: speak the word, O God, and make the storm to cease.

EPIPHANY V

Collect

O LORD, we beseech thee to keep thy Church and household continually in thy true religion: that they who do lean only upon the hope of thy heavenly grace may evermore be defended by thy mighty power. Through.

MATTINS

Psalms of day (or 99, 112).
Ben. Master, * sowedst thou not good seed in thy field? Whence then hath it tares? And he said: An enemy hath done this.

II EVENSONG

Psalms of day (or 106).
Magn. Gather ye together * first the tares, and bind them in bundles to burn them: but gather the wheat into my barn.

EPIPHANY VI

Collect

O GOD, whose blessed Son was manifested that he might destroy the works of the devil, and make us the sons of God, and heirs of eternal life: grant us, we beseech thee; that, having this hope, we may purify ourselves, even as he is pure; that when he shall appear again with power and great glory, we may be made like unto him in his eternal and glorious kingdom; where with thee, O Father, and thee, O Holy Ghost, he liveth and reigneth.

MATTINS

Psalms of day (or 80, 81).
Ben. As the lightning * cometh out of the east, and shineth even to the west: so shall also the coming of the Son of man be.

II EVENSONG

Psalms of day (or 78).
Magn. Wheresoever the carcase is, * there will the eagles be gathered together.

SEPTUAGESIMA

I EVENSONG

Magn. The Lord said unto Adam: * Of the tree which is in the midst of the garden thou shalt not eat: in the day wherein thou eatest thereof, thou shalt surely die.

Collect

O LORD, we beseech thee favourably to hear the prayers of thy people: that we, who are justly punished for our offences, may be mercifully delivered by thy goodness, for the glory of thy name. Through Jesus Christ our Saviour, who liveth.

℣. Let us bless the Lord, alleluia, alleluia. ℟. Thanks be to God, alleluia, alleluia.

MATTINS

Invit. Let us come before the presence of the Lord: * And shew ourselves glad in him with Psalms.

Psalms of day (or 104).
Benedicite is said on Sundays and ferias until Easter.
℣. O Lord, thou hast been our

refuge. ℟. From one generation to another.
Ant. to Ben. The kingdom of heaven * is likened unto a man that is an householder, which went out early in the morning to hire labourers into his vineyard, saith the Lord.

II EVENSONG

Psalms of day (or 147, 148).
Ant. to Magn. The householder said * unto the labourers: Why stand ye here all the day idle? And they answering said: Because no man hath hired us. Go ye also into the vineyard; and whatsoever is right, that will I give you.

ANTIPHONS TO MAGNIFICAT

Mon. These last * have wrought but one hour, and thou hast made them equal unto us, which have borne the burden and heat of the day.
Tues. But the householder said: * Friend, I do thee no wrong; didst thou not agree with me for a penny? Take that thine is, and go thy way.
Wed. Take that thine is, * and go thy way: for I am righteous, saith the Lord.
Thurs. Is it not lawful * for me to do what I will? Is thine eye evil? For I am righteous, saith the Lord.
Fri. So the last shall be first, * and the first last: for many are called, but few are chosen.

SEXAGESIMA

I EVENSONG

Ant. to Magn. The Lord spake * unto Noah: The end of all flesh is come before me: make thee an ark of gopher wood: that the seed of all may be saved therein.

Collect

O LORD God, who seest that we put not our trust in any thing that we do: mercifully grant; that by thy power we may be defended against all adversities. Through.

MATTINS

Invitatory as on Septuagesima.
Psalms of day (or 139).
Ant. to Ben. When much people * were gathered together to Jesus, and were come to him out of every city, he spake by a parable: A sower went out to sow his seed.

II EVENSONG

Psalms of day (or 25, 26).
Ant. to Magn. Unto you it is given * to know the mystery of the kingdom of God, but to others in parables, saith Jesus to his disciples.

ANTIPHONS TO MAGNIFICAT

Mon. If ye seek * the summit of true honour, hasten to your heavenly country with what speed ye may.
Tues. The seed is the word * of God, and Christ is the sower: every one that heareth him, abideth for ever.
Wed. But that which fell * on the good ground are they which in an honest and good heart receive the word, and bring forth fruit with patience.
Thurs. If then, brethren, * ye would be truly rich, set your affection on the true riches.
Fri. They which keep the word of God * in an honest and good heart, bring forth fruit with patience.

QUINQUAGESIMA
I EVENSONG

Ant. to Magn. The great Abraham * is our father in the faith, who on the altar sacrificed a burnt-offering for his son.

Collect

O LORD, who hast taught us that all our doings without charity are nothing worth: send thy Holy Ghost, and pour into our hearts that most excellent gift of charity, the very bond of peace and of all virtues, without which whosoever liveth is counted dead before thee: grant this for thine only Son Jesus Christ's sake, who with thee and the same Holy Ghost liveth.

MATTINS

Invit. as on Septuagesima.
Psalms of day (or 15, 20, 23).
Ant. to Ben. Behold, we go up * to Jerusalem, and all things shall be accomplished which were written concerning the Son of man: for he shall be delivered unto the Gentiles, and shall be mocked and spitted upon: and after they have scourged him, they shall kill him; and the third day he shall rise again.

II EVENSONG

Psalms of day (or 30, 31)
Ant. to Magn. And Jesus, standing, * commanded him to be brought unto him, and asked him, saying: What wilt thou that I should do unto thee? Lord, that I may receive my sight. And Jesus said unto him: Receive thy sight, thy faith hath saved thee. And straightway he received his sight, and followed, glorifying God.

ANTIPHONS TO MAGNIFICAT

Mon. And they which went before * rebuked him, that he should hold his peace: but he cried so much the more: Have mercy on me, thou Son of David.

Tues. Have mercy upon me, * thou Son of David. What wilt thou that I should do unto thee? Lord, that I may receive my sight.

ASH WEDNESDAY

MATTINS

Ant. 1 Save me, * O Lord, for thy mercy's sake. Ps. 6.
2 Be glad, O ye righteous, * and rejoice in the Lord: and be joyful, all ye that are true of heart. Ps. 32.
3 Chasten me not, * O Lord, in thy heavy displeasure. Ps. 38.
℣. O satisfy us early with thy mercy. ℟. That we may rejoice and be glad.
Ant. to Ben. When ye fast, * be not like the hypocrites, of a sad countenance.

Collect

ALMIGHTY and everlasting God, who hatest nothing that thou hast made, and dost forgive the sins of all them that are penitent: create and make in us new and contrite hearts; that we, worthily lamenting our sins, and acknowledging our wretchedness, may obtain of thee, the God of all mercy, perfect remission and forgiveness. Through.

EVENSONG

Ant. 1 Let my crying * come unto thee, O Lord: turn not away thy face from me. Ps. 102.
2 Out of the deep * have I called unto thee, O Lord, Ps. 130.
3 Quicken me, O Lord, * for thy name's sake, and for thy righteousness. Ps. 143.
℣. Let my prayer, O Lord, be set forth. ℟. In thy sight as the incense.
Ant. to Magn. Lay not up for yourselves * treasures in heaven, where neither moth nor rust doth corrupt.

The Ash Wed. antiphon, ℣., ℟. and collect are used daily through Lent after the collect of the day, except on Feasts, when the antiphon, ℣. & ℟. are of the feria occurring.

THURSDAY
Ben. Lord, my servant * lieth at home, sick of the palsy, grievously tormented. Verily I say unto thee: I will come and heal him.
Magn. Lord, I am not worthy * that thou shouldest come under my roof: but speak the word only, and my servant shall be healed.

FRIDAY
Ben. When thou doest thine alms, * let not thy left hand know what thy right hand doeth.
Magn. But thou, when thou prayest, * enter into thy closet: and when thou hast shut thy door, pray to thy Father.

SATURDAY
Ben. From day to day * they seek me therefore, and would know my ways.

LENT I

I EVENSONG

Hymn (66)

O KIND Creator, bow thine ear
To mark the cry, to know the tear
Before thy throne of mercy spent
In this thy holy fast of Lent.

Our hearts are open, Lord, to thee;
Thou knowest our infirmity;
Pour out on all who seek thy face
Abundance of thy pardoning grace.

Our sins are many, this we know;
Spare us, good Lord, thy mercy show;
And for the honour of thy name
Our fainting souls to life reclaim.

Give us the self-control that springs
From discipline of outward things,
That fasting inward secretly
The soul may purely dwell with thee.

We pray thee, Holy Trinity,
One God, unchanging Unity,
That we from this our abstinence
May reap the fruits of penitence.
Amen.

℣. God shall give his Angels charge over thee. ℟. To keep thee in all thy ways.
Ant. to Magn. Then thou shalt call, * and the Lord shall hear thee: thou shalt cry out, and he shall say: Behold, here I am.

Collect

O LORD, who for our sake didst fast forty days and forty nights: give us grace to use such abstinence; that our flesh being subdued to the Spirit, we may ever obey thy godly motions in righteousness and true holiness, to thy honour and glory: Who livest.

MATTINS

Invit. Think it not lost labour that ye haste to rise up early before the light: * For the Lord hath promised a crown unto them that watch.

Psalms of day (or 51).

Hymn (65)

THE fast, as taught by holy lore,
We keep in solemn course once more;
The fast to all men known, and bound
In forty days of yearly round.

The law and seers that were of old
In divers ways this Lent foretold,
Which Christ, all seasons' King and guide,
In after ages sanctified.

More sparing therefore let us make
The words we speak, the food we take,
Our sleep and mirth; and closer barred
Be every sense in holy guard.

In prayer together let us fall,
And cry for mercy, one and all
And weep before the Judge's feet,
And his avenging wrath entreat.

Thy grace have we offended sore,
By sins, O God, which we deplore:
But pour upon us from on high,
O pardoning one, thy clemency.

Remember thou, though frail we be,
That yet thine handiwork are we;
Nor let the honour of thy name
Be by another put to shame.

Forgive the sin that we have wrought;
Increase the good that we have sought;
That we at length, our wanderings o'er,
May please thee here and evermore.

We pray thee, Holy Trinity,
One God, unchanging Unity,
That we from this our abstinence
May reap the fruits of penitence. Amen.

℣. God shall give his Angels charge over thee. ℟. To keep thee in all thy ways.

Ant. to Ben. Jesus was led up * of the Spirit into the wilderness, to be tempted of the devil: and when he had fasted forty days and forty nights, he was afterward an hungred.

II EVENSONG

As at I Evensong, except:
Psalms of day (or 6, 32, 143).
Ant. to Magn. Behold, now is the accepted time, * now is the day of salvation; let us therefore in these days approve ourselves as the servants of God, in much patience, in watchings, in fastings, and by love unfeigned.

On ferias in Lent, the Invitatory, Hymn, ℣. & ℟. and collect as on previous Sunday.

ANTIPHONS TO CANTICLES

MONDAY
Ben. O come, ye blessed * children of my Father: inherit the kingdom prepared for you from the foundation of the world.
Magn. Inasmuch * as ye have done it unto the least of these, ye have done it unto me, saith the Lord.

TUESDAY
Ben. And Jesus went * into the temple of God, and began to cast out all them that sold and bought in the temple: and overthrew the tables of the moneychangers, and the seats of them that sold doves.
Magn. For it is written, * that my house is a house a prayer for all nations: but ye have made it a den of thieves: and he was teaching daily in the temple.

EMBER WEDNESDAY
Ben. This generation * being perverse and crooked, seeketh a sign from me: and no sign shall be given to it, but the sign of Jonah the prophet.
Magn. For as Jonah * was three days and three nights in the whale's belly, so shall the Son of man be in the heart of the earth.

THURSDAY
Ben. And Jesus went thence * and departed into the coasts of Tyre and Sidon: and behold, a woman of Canaan came out of the same coasts, and cried unto him, saying: Have mercy on me, thou Son of David.
Magn. O woman, * great is thy faith: be it unto thee, even as thou wilt.

EMBER FRIDAY
Ben. An Angel of the Lord * descended from heaven, and troubled the water: and one was made whole.
Magn. He that made me whole, * the same said unto me: Take up thy bed, and go in peace.

EMBER SATURDAY
Ben. And Jesus taketh * his disciples, and goeth up into a mountain, and was transfigured before them.

LENT II

As on Lent I, except:

I EVENSONG

Ant. to Magn. Tell the vision which ye have seen * to no man, until the Son of man be risen from the dead.

Collect
ALMIGHTY God, who seest that we have no power of ourselves to help ourselves;

keep us both outwardly in our bodies, and inwardly in our souls; that we may be defended from all adversities which may happen to the body, and from all evil thoughts which may assault and hurt the soul. Through.

MATTINS

Psalms of day (or 119, vv. 1-33). Ant. to Ben. And Jesus went thence * and departed into the coasts of Tyre and Sidon: and behold, a woman of Canaan came out of the same coasts, and cried unto him, saying: Have mercy on me, thou Son of David.

II EVENSONG

Psalms of day (or 119, vv. 33-72). Ant. to Magn. O woman, * great is thy faith: be it unto thee, even as thou wilt.

ANTIPHONS TO CANTICLES

MONDAY

Ben. I am the Beginning: * even I that speak unto you.

Magn. He that sent me * is with me, and he hath not left me alone: for I do always those things that please him.

TUESDAY

Ben. One is your Master, * which is in heaven, even Christ the Lord.

Magn. All ye are brethren; * and call no man your father upon earth; for one is your Father, which is in heaven: neither be ye called masters, for one is your Master, even Christ.

WEDNESDAY

Ben. Behold, we go up * to Jerusalem; and the Son of man shall be betrayed to be crucified.

Magn. He shall be delivered * to the Gentiles, to mock, and to scourge, and to crucify him.

THURSDAY

Ben. Son, remember * that thou in thy lifetime receivedst thy good things, and likewise Lazarus evil things.

Magn. The same rich man * begged a drop of water, who had denied crumbs of bread to Lazarus.

FRIDAY

Ben. He will miserably destroy * those miserable men; and will let out his vineyard unto other husbandmen, which shall render him the fruits in their seasons.

Magn. When they sought to take him, * they feared the people; because they counted him as a prophet.

SATURDAY

Ben. I will go unto my father, * and will say unto him: Father, make me as one of thy hired servants.

LENT III

As on Lent I, except:

I EVENSONG

Ant. to Magn. But the father said * unto his servants: Bring forth quickly the best robe and put it on him, and put a ring on his finger, and shoes on his feet.

Collect

WE beseech thee, almighty God, look upon the hearty desires of thy humble servants, and stretch forth the right hand of thy majesty to be our defence against all our enemies. Through.

MATTINS

Psalms of day (or 119, vv. 73-104).
Ant. to Ben. When a strong man armed * keepeth his palace, his goods are in peace.

II EVENSONG

Psalms of day (or 119, vv. 105-144).
Ant. to Magn. A certain woman * of the company lift up her voice, and cried: Blessed is the womb that bare thee, and the paps which thou hast sucked. But Jesus answered: Yea, rather blessed are they that hear the word of God, and keep it.

ANTIPHONS TO CANTICLES

MONDAY
Ben. Verily, I say unto you: * that no prophet is accepted in his own country.
Magn. But Jesus, passing * through the midst of them, went his way.

TUESDAY
Ben. If two of you shall agree * on earth as touching aught for which they shall make request, it shall be done for them of my Father which is in heaven, saith the Lord.
Magn. Where two or three * are gathered together in my name, there am I in the midst of them, saith the Lord.

WEDNESDAY
Ben. Hearken and understand ye: * the traditions which the Lord hath given you.
Magn. To eat with unwashen hands * defileth not a man.

THURSDAY
Ben. And devils also came out of many, * crying out and saying: Thou art Christ, the Son of God: and he rebuking them suffered them not to speak, for they knew that he was Christ.

Magn. All they that had any sick * brought them to Jesus, and they were healed.

FRIDAY
Ben. If any man drink * of the water that I shall give, he shall never thirst.
Magn. Sir, I perceive * that thou art a prophet: our fathers worshipped in this mountain.

SATURDAY
Ben. And Jesus stooped down, * and wrote upon the ground: he that is without sin, let him cast a stone at her.

LENT IV

As on Lent I, except:

I EVENSONG

Ant. to Magn. Woman, hath no man condemned thee? * No man, Lord. Neither do I condemn thee: go and sin no more.

Collect

GRANT, we beseech thee, almighty God, that we, who for our evil deeds do worthily deserve to be punished, by the comfort of thy grace may mercifully be relieved. Through our Lord and Saviour Jesus Christ.

MATTINS

Psalms of day (or 119, vv. 145-176).
Ant. to Ben. When Jesus lift up his eyes, * and saw a great company come unto him, he said unto Philip: Whence shall we buy bread, that these may eat? And this he said to prove him, for he himself knew what he would do.

II EVENSONG

Psalms of day (or 39, 40).
Ant. to Magn. Jesus went up * into a mountain, and there he sat with his disciples.

ANTIPHONS TO CANTICLES

MONDAY
Ben. Take these things hence, * saith the Lord: and make not my Father's house a house of merchandise.
Magn. Destroy this temple, * saith the Lord: and in three days I will raise it up; but this he said of the temple of his body.

TUESDAY
Ben. Wherefore do ye seek * to kill me, a man that hath told you the truth?

Magn. No man laid hands on him, * because his hour was not yet come.

WEDNESDAY

Ben. Master, who hath sinned, * this man or his parents, that he was born blind? And Jesus answered, saying: Neither hath this man sinned, nor his parents: but that the works of God should be manifested in him.
Magn. A man that is called Jesus * made clay out of spittle, and anointed mine eyes, and now I see.

THURSDAY

Ben. Jesus went * into a city called Nain: and behold, there was a dead man carried out, the only son of his mother.
Magn. A great prophet * is risen up amongst us, and God hath visited his people.

FRIDAY

Ben. Our friend Lazarus * sleepeth: let us go, that we may awake him out of sleep.
Magn. Lord, if thou hadst been here, * Lazarus would not have died: lo, by this time he stinketh, being in the sepulchre four days already.

SATURDAY

Ben. He that followeth me * shall not walk in darkness: but shall have the light of life, saith the Lord.

PASSION SUNDAY

I EVENSONG

Hymn (94)

THE royal banners forward go;
The Cross shines forth in mystic glow;
Where he in flesh, our flesh who made,
Our sentence bore, our ransom paid:

Where deep for us the spear was dyed,
Life's torrent rushing from his side,
To wash us in that precious flood,
Where mingled water flowed, and blood.

Fulfilled is all that David told
In true prophetic song of old;
Amidst the nations, God, saith he,
Hath reigned and triumphed from the tree.

O tree of beauty, tree of light!
O tree with royal purple dight!
Elect on whose triumphal breast
Those holy limbs should find their rest:

On whose dear arms, so widely flung,
The weight of this world's ransom hung:
The price of humankind to pay,
And spoil the spoiler of his prey.

The next verse is sung kneeling.

O Cross, our one reliance, hail!
So may thy power with us avail
To give new virtue to the saint,
And pardon to the penitent.

To thee, eternal Three in One,
Let homage meet by all be done:
Whom by the Cross thou dost restore
Preserve and govern evermore. Amen.

℣. Deliver me, O Lord, from the evil man. ℟. And preserve me from the wicked man.

Ant. to Magn. I am one, * that bear witness of myself, and the Father that sent me beareth witness of me.

Collect

WE beseech thee, almighty God, mercifully to look upon thy people: that by thy great goodness they may be governed and preserved evermore, both in body and soul. Through.

MATTINS

Invit. To-day, if ye will hear the voice of the Lord, * Harden not your hearts.
Glory be is omitted from Venite until Easter.
Psalms of day (or 22).
Ant. 1 Behold, O Lord,* and look upon mine afflictions: for the enemy hath magnified himself.
2 In my tribulation * I called upon the Lord: and he heard me, and hath brought me into a place of liberty.
3 O Lord, thou hast pleaded * the causes of my soul: thou hast redeemed my life, O Lord my God.
4 O my people, * what have I done unto thee, and wherein have I wearied thee? Testify against me.
5 Shall evil * be recompensed for good? for they have digged a pit for my soul.

Hymn (95)

On Sunday, Tuesday, Thursday, and Saturday.

SING, my tongue, the glorious battle,
Sing the ending of the fray;
Now above the Cross, the trophy,
Sound the loud triumphant lay;
Tell how Christ, the world's Redeemer,
As a victim won the day.

God in pity saw man fallen,
Shamed and sunk in misery,
When he fell of death by tasting
Fruit of the forbidden tree;
Then another tree was chosen,
Which the world from sin should free.

Thus the scheme of our salvation
Was of old in order laid,
That the manifold deceiver's
Art by art might be outweighed,
And the lure the foe put forward
Into means of healing made.

Therefore when the appointed fulness
Of the holy time was come,
He was sent who maketh all things

Forth from God's eternal home;
Thus he came to earth, incarnate,
Offspring of a maiden's womb.

To the Trinity be glory
Everlasting, as is meet;
Equal to the Father, equal
To the Son and Paraclete:
Trinal Unity, whose praises
All created things repeat. Amen.

Or, on Monday, Wednesday, and Friday:

(96)

THIRTY years among us dwelling,
His appointed time fulfilled,
Born for this, he meets his passion,
For that this he freely willed,
On the Cross the Lamb is lifted
Where his life-blood shall be spilled.

He endured the nails, the spitting,
Vinegar, and spear, and reed;
From that holy Body broken
Blood and water forth proceed:
Earth and stars and sky and ocean
By that Blood from stain are freed.

Faithful Cross, above all other
One and only noble tree!
None in foliage, none in blossom,
None in fruit thy peer may be:
Sweetest wood and sweetest iron!
Sweetest weight is hung on thee.

Bend thy boughs, O tree of glory!
Thy relaxing sinews bend;
For awhile the ancient rigour
That thy birth bestowed, suspend;
And the King of heavenly beauty
On thy bosom gently tend!

Thou alone wast counted worthy
This world's ransom to uphold;
For a shipwrecked race preparing
Harbour like the Ark of old;
With the sacred Blood anointed
From the smitten Lamb that rolled.

To the Trinity be glory
Everlasting, as is meet;
Equal to the Father, equal
To the Son and Paraclete:
Trinal Unity, whose praises
All created things repeat. Amen.

℣. Deliver me from mine enemies, O God. ℟. Defend me from them that rise up against me.

Ant. to Ben. Jesus said * unto the multitudes of the Jews, and to the chief priests: He that is of God, heareth my words; ye therefore hear them not, because ye are not of God.

II EVENSONG

Psalms of day (or 51), with antiphons as in monthly course.
Ant. to Magn. Your father Abraham * rejoiced to see my day: he saw it, and was glad.

ANTIPHONS TO CANTICLES

MONDAY

Ben. In the last day * of the feast, Jesus stood and cried, saying: If any man thirst, let him come unto me and drink.
Magn. If any man thirst, * let him come and drink: and out of his belly shall flow rivers of living water, saith the Lord.

TUESDAY

Ben. My time * is not yet come: but your time is alway ready.
Magn. Go ye up * unto this feast: I go not up yet, for my time is not yet fully come.

WEDNESDAY

Ben. My sheep * hear my voice: and I the Lord do know them.
Magn. Many good works * have I wrought among you: for which of those works do ye seek to kill me?

THURSDAY

Ben. The Master saith: * My time is at hand: I will keep the Passover at thy house with my disciples.
Magn. With desire have I desired * to eat this Passover with you, before I suffer.

FRIDAY

Ben. Now the feast-day * was nigh at hand, and the chief priests and elders sought for occasion to slay Jesus: but they feared the multitude.
Magn. The chief priests and elders * took counsel together how they might destroy him: but they spake and said: Not on the feast-day, lest there be an uproar among the people.

SATURDAY

Ben. Glorify me, O Father, * with thine own self, with the glory which I had before the world was.

PALM SUNDAY

As on Passion Sunday, except:

I EVENSONG

Ant. to Magn. Righteous Father, * the world hath not known thee: but I have known that thou didst send me.

Collect

ALMIGHTY and everlasting God, who of thy tender love towards mankind, hast sent thy Son, our Saviour Jesus Christ, to take upon him our flesh, and to suffer death upon the Cross, that all mankind should follow the example of his great humility: mercifully grant; that we may both follow the example of his patience, and also be made partakers of his resurrection. Through the same.

MATTINS

Psalms of day (or 61, 62).
Ant. 1 The Lord my God * will be my helper: and so shall I not be confounded.
2 They compassed me * together round about: but in the name of the Lord will I destroy them.
3 Judge thou my cause: * be thou my defence, for thou art mighty, O Lord.
4 With the Angels * and with the children let us be found faithful, crying out to the conqueror of death: Hosanna in the highest.
5 Let them be confounded * that persecute me, and let me not be confounded, O Lord my God.
Ant. to Ben. Much people, * which was come together on the feast-day, cried out and said: Blessed is he that cometh in the name of the Lord: Hosanna in the highest.

II EVENSONG

Psalms of the day (or 86, 130) with their antiphons.
Ant. to Magn. For it is written: * I will smite the shepherd, and the sheep of the flock shall be scattered: but after I am risen, I will go before you into Galilee: there shall ye see me, saith the Lord.

MONDAY IN HOLY WEEK
MATTINS

Psalms of day (or 13, 25).
Ant. 1 I hid not my face * from shame and spitting.
2 Awake, O sword, * against them that disperse and scatter my flock.
3 They have weighed * for my price thirty pieces of silver, that I was priced at of them.
4 The waters have come in * over my soul: I have said, I perish; but I will call upon thy name, O Lord.
5 Behold the lips of them * that rise up against me, and their devices, O Lord.
Ant. to Ben. Glorify me, O Father, * with thine own self, with the glory which I had before the world was.

EVENSONG

Psalms of day (or 26, 27, 28), with their antiphons.
Ant. to Magn. Thou couldest have no power * at all against me, except it were given thee from above.

TUESDAY IN HOLY WEEK
MATTINS

Ant. 1 See, O Lord, * and consider, for I am in trouble: O haste thee, and hear me.
2 Defend thou my cause, * O Lord my God: O deliver me from the deceitful and wicked man.
3 When I was in trouble * I cried unto the Lord from the belly of hell: and he heard my complaint.
4 O Lord, I suffer wrong, * answer thou for me: for I know not what to say unto mine enemies.
5 The ungodly said: * Let us oppress the righteous man, for he is clean contrary to our doings.
Ant. to Ben. Before the day of the feast * of the Passover, Jesus, knowing that his hour was come, when he loved his own, he loved them unto the end.

EVENSONG

Psalms of day (or 88), with their antiphons.
Ant. to Magn. I have power * to lay down my life, and I have power to take it up again.

WEDNESDAY IN HOLY WEEK
MATTINS

Psalms of day (or 41, 42, 43).
Ant. 1 Deliver me * from bloodguiltiness, O God, my God: and my tongue shall sing of thy righteousness.
2 Reproaches and terrors * have I suffered of them: but the Lord is with me as a mighty warrior.
3 But thou, O Lord, * knowest all their plotting against me, to put me to death.
4 All mine enemies * have heard of my evil: O Lord, they have rejoiced that thou hast done it.
5 Do justice, O Lord, * to them that suffer wrong: and bring the ways of sinners to confusion.
Ant. to Ben. Simon, sleepest thou? * Couldest thou not watch with me one hour?

EVENSONG

Psalms of day (or 54, 55) with their antiphons.
Ant. to Magn. A maid said * unto Peter: Verily thou art one of them; and thy speech betrayeth thee.

MAUNDY THURSDAY
Double of I class

On this and the two days next following, the Invitatory, the Psalm **Venite**, Hymns, ℣℣. & ℟℟. are omitted; and the Psalms and Canticles are said without **Gloria**.

MATTINS

Psalms of day (or 56, 64).
Ant. 1 Thou shalt be justified, O Lord, * in thy saying, and clear when thou art judged.
2 The Lord * was led as a lamb to the slaughter, and he opened not his mouth.
3 My heart in the midst of me * is broken; all my bones shake.
4 Thou hast comforted us, * O Lord, in thy strength: and refreshed us in thine holiness.
5 He was offered up * because that he himself willed it: and he bare our sins.
Ant. to Ben. Now he that betrayed him * gave them a sign, saying: Whomsoever I shall kiss, that same is he; hold him fast.

Conclusion

The Office anciently concluded as follows, everything else after the Benedictus (or Nunc Dimittis at Evensong) being omitted.
Ant. Christ for us became obedient unto death.
Our Father, said silently; then Psalm 51, in a low voice; and the Good Friday Collect, as below, the ending being said silently.

Collect

ALMIGHTY God, we beseech thee graciously to behold this thy family, for which our Lord Jesus Christ was contented to be betrayed, and given up into the hands of wicked men, and to suffer death upon the Cross: Who now liveth and reigneth with thee and the Holy Ghost, ever one God, world without end, Amen.

EVENSONG

Psalms of day (or 23, 109), with their antiphons.
Ant. to Magn. And as they were eating, * Jesus took bread, and blessed it, and brake it, and gave it to his disciples.
The ancient conclusion is as above.

GOOD FRIDAY
Double of I class
MATTINS

Psalms 22, 40, 54 (or 22).
Ant. 1 They parted my garments * among them, and cast lots upon my vesture. Ps. 22.
2 Let them be ashamed * and confounded together that seek after my soul to destroy it. Ps. 40.
3 Strangers also * are risen up against me, and tyrants seek after my soul. Ps. 54.

Ant. to Ben. And they set up * over his head his accusation written: Jesus of Nazareth, the King of the Jews.
For the conclusion:
Ant. Christ for us became obedient unto death, even the death of the Cross.
And the rest as on Maundy Thursday.

EVENSONG

Psalms 69, 88 (or 40, 69), with their usual antiphons.
Ant. to Magn. When he had received the vinegar, * he said: It is finished; and he bowed his head, and gave up the ghost.
The conclusion as at Mattins.

HOLY SATURDAY
Double of I class

Psalms of day (or 23, 30, 142).
Ant. 1 O death, * I will be thy plagues: O grave, I will be thy destruction.
2 They shall mourn for him * as one mourneth for his only son: for the Lord, who is without sin, is slain.
3 All ye my people, * behold and see my sorrow.
4 From the gate of hell, * O Lord, deliver my soul.
5 All ye that pass by, * behold and see, if there be any sorrow like unto my sorrow.
Ant. to Ben. The women also, * sitting at the sepulchre, made lamentation, weeping for the Lord.
For the conclusion:
Ant. Christ for us became obedient unto death, even the death of the Cross: wherefore God also hath highly exalted him, and given him a name which is above every name.
Our Father, said silently, and the rest as on Maundy Thursday; but after Our Father is said immediately:

Collect

GRANT, O Lord, that as we are baptized into the death of thy blessed Son our Saviour Jesus Christ: so by continual mortifying our corrupt affections we may be buried with him, and that through the grave, and gate of death, we may pass to our joyful resurrection; for his merits, who died, and was buried, and rose again for us, thy Son Jesus Christ our Lord. And in silence is added: Who liveth and reigneth.

EVENSONG

Psalms of day (or 115, 116, 117), with their antiphons.

Ant. to Magn. The chief priests * and Pharisees guarded the sepulchre, sealing the stone, and setting a watch.

The Office is concluded in the usual way, with the collect as above.

EASTER DAY
Double of I class
MATTINS

Instead of the Venite, the following anthems are said.

CHRIST our passover is sacrificed for us: * therefore let us keep the feast.

Not with the old leaven, nor with the leaven of malice and wickedness: * but with the unleavened bread of sincerity and truth.

Christ being raised from the dead dieth no more: * death hath no more dominion over him.

For in that he died, he died unto sin once: * but in that he liveth, he liveth unto God.

Likewise reckon ye also yourselves to be dead indeed unto sin, * but alive unto God through Jesus Christ our Lord.

Christ is risen from the dead, * and become the first-fruits of them that slept.

For since by man came death, * by man came also the resurrection of the dead.

For as in Adam all die, * even so in Christ shall all be made alive.

Glory be. As it was.

Psalms 2, 57, 111 (or 2, 16, 111).

Ant. 1 The Angel of the Lord * descended from heaven, and came and rolled back the stone, and sat upon it, alleluia, alleluia.

2 And behold, * there was a great earthquake: for the Angel of the Lord descended from heaven, alleluia.

3 His countenance * was like lightning, and his raiment white as snow, alleluia, alleluia.

4 For fear of him * the keepers did shake, and became as dead men, alleluia.

5 And the Angel answered * and said unto the women: Be not affrighted, for I know that ye seek Jesus, alleluia.

Ant. (instead of hymn): This is the day * which the Lord hath made: we will rejoice and be glad in it.

Ant. to Ben. And very early in the morning, * the first day of the week, they came to the sepulchre at the rising of the sun, alleluia.

Athanasian Creed, to-day only.

Collect

ALMIGHTY God, who through thine only-begotten Son Jesus Christ hast overcome death, and opened unto us the gate of everlasting life: we humbly beseech thee, that, as by thy special grace preventing us thou dost put into our minds good desires, so by the continual help we may bring the same to good effect. Through Jesus Christ our Lord, who liveth and reigneth with thee and the Holy Ghost, ever one God, world without end.

At the end: ℣. The Lord be with you. ℟. And with thy spirit.

℣. Let us bless the Lord, alleluia, alleluia. ℟. Thanks be to God, alleluia, alleluia.

EVENSONG

Psalms 113, 114, 118, with antiphons as at Mattins. Ant. (instead of hymn) This is the day, as above.

Ant. to Magn. And when they looked, * they saw that the stone was rolled away; for it was very great, alleluia.

Conclusion as at Mattins.

WITHIN THE OCTAVE

Psalms of day, with antiphons as above; Ant. This is the day, and conclusion as on Easter Day. The Invitatory The Lord is risen indeed, * Alleluia.

MONDAY

Ben. Jesus joined himself * to his disciples in the way, and went with them; but their eyes were holden that they knew him not; and he rebuked them, saying: O fools and slow of heart to believe all that the Prophets have spoken, alleluia.

Magn. What manner of communications * are these that ye have one to another, as ye walk, and are sad? alleluia.

TUESDAY

Ben. Jesus stood * in the midst of his disciples, and said unto them: Peace be unto you, alleluia, alleluia.

Magn. Behold my hands * and my feet, that it is I myself, alleluia, alleluia.

WEDNESDAY

Ben. Cast the net * on the right side of the ship, and ye shall find, alleluia.

Magn. Jesus said * to his disciples: Take of the fish which ye have now caught. But Simon Peter went up, and drew the net to land, full of great fishes, alleluia.

THURSDAY

Ben. Mary stood * at the sepulchre weeping, and seeth two Angels in white sitting, and the napkin that was about the head of Jesus, alleluia.

Magn. They have taken away

my Lord * and I know not where they have laid him; if thou have borne him hence, tell me, alleluia, and I will take him away, alleluia.

FRIDAY

Ben. The eleven disciples * when they saw the Lord in Galilee, worshipped him, alleluia.

Magn. All power is given * unto me in heaven and in earth, alleluia.

SATURDAY

Ben. They ran both together, * and the other disciple did outrun Peter, and came first to the sepulchre, alleluia.

LOW SUNDAY

I EVENSONG

Psalms of day, under one antiphon Alleluia, * alleluia, alleluia.

Hymn (125)

THE Lamb's high banquet we await
In snow-white robes of royal state;
And now, the Red Sea's channel past,
To Christ, our Prince, we sing at last.

Upon the altar of the Cross
His Body hath redeemed our loss;
And tasting of his roseate Blood
Our life is hid with him in God.

That Paschal eve God's arm was bared;
The devastating angel spared;
By strength of hand our hosts went free
From Pharoah's ruthless tyranny.

Now Christ our Paschal Lamb is slain,
The Lamb of God that knows no stain;
The true Oblation offered here,
Our own unleavened Bread sincere.

O thou from whom hell's monarch flies,
O great, O very sacrifice,
Thy captive people are set free,
And endless life restored in thee.

For Christ, arising from the dead,
From conquered hell victorious sped;
He thrusts the tyrant down to chains,
And Paradise for man regains.

Maker of all, to thee we pray,
Fulfil in us thy joy to-day;
When death assails, grant, Lord, that we
May share thy Paschal victory.

To thee, who, dead, again dost live,
All glory, Lord, thy people give;
All glory, as is ever meet,
To Father and to Paraclete.
Amen.

℣. Abide with us, O Lord,

alleluia. ℟. For it is toward evening, alleluia.
Ant. to Magn. The same day at evening, * being the first day of the week, when the doors were shut where the disciples were assembled, Jesus stood in the midst of them, and said unto them: Peace be unto you, alleluia.

Collect

ALMIGHTY Father, who hast given thine only Son to die for our sins, and to rise again for our justification: grant us so to put away the leaven of malice and wickedness that we may alway serve thee in pureness of living and truth. Through the merits of the same thy Son Jesus Christ our Lord.

MATTINS

Invit. The Lord is risen indeed, * Alleluia.
Psalms of day (or 3, 57), under one antiphon Alleluia, * alleluia, alleluia.

Hymn (123)

THE day draws on with golden light,
Glad songs go echoing through the height,
The broad earth lifts an answering cheer,
The deep makes moan with wailing fear.

For lo, he comes, the mighty King,
To take from death his power and sting,
To trample down his gloomy reign
And break the weary prisoner's chain.

Enclosed he lay in rocky cell,
With guard of armèd sentinel;
But thence returning, strong and free,
He comes with pomp of jubilee.

The sad Apostles mourn him slain,
Nor hope to see their Lord again;
Their Lord, whom rebel thralls defy,
Arraign, accuse, and doom to die.

But now they put their grief away,
The pains of hell are loosed to-day;
For by the grave, with flashing eyes,
'Your Lord is risen', the Angel cries.

Maker of all, to thee we pray,
Fulfil in us thy joy to-day;
When death assails, grant, Lord, that we
May share thy Paschal victory.

To thee who, dead, again dost live,
All glory, Lord, thy people give;
All glory, as is ever meet
To Father and to Paraclete. Amen.

℣. In thy resurrection, O Christ, alleluia. ℟. Let heaven and earth rejoice, alleluia.
Ant. to Ben.: as to Magn. at I Evensong.

II EVENSONG

As at I. Evensong, except:
Psalms of day (or 103).
Ant. to Magn. After eight days, * when the doors were shut, the Lord entered, and said unto them: Peace be unto you; alleluia, alleluia.
Throughout Eastertide the Office is said (with the Psalms appointed) as on this Sunday, except as below.

MONDAY

Ben. When Jesus was risen * early the first day of the week, he appeared first to Mary Magdalene, out of whom he had cast seven devils, alleluia.
Magn. Peace be unto you* it is I: be not afraid, alleluia.

TUESDAY

Ben. I go before you * into Galilee: there shall ye see me, as I said unto you, alleluia, alleluia.
Magn. Reach hither thy hand * and thrust it into my side, alleluia: and be not faithless but believing, alleluia.

WEDNESDAY

Ben. I am the true vine, * and ye are the branches, alleluia.
Magn. Because thou hast seen me, * Thomas, thou hast believed: blessed are they that have not seen, and yet have believed, alleluia.

THURSDAY

Ben. My heart burneth, * I long to behold my Lord: I seek him, and I find him not where they laid him, alleluia, alleluia.
Magn. I put my finger * into the prints of the nails, and my hands into his side; and I said: My Lord and my God, alleluia.

FRIDAY

Ben. There came unto the tomb * Mary Magdalene and the other Mary, to see the sepulchre, alleluia.
Magn.: Ant. as on Sunday.

EASTER II

I EVENSONG

Ant. to Magn. I am the Shepherd of the sheep: * I am the way, the truth and the life; I am the good Shepherd, and know my sheep and am known of mine, alleluia, alleluia.

Collect

ALMIGHTY God, who hast given thine only Son to be unto us both a sacrifice for sin, and also an example of godly life: give us grace that we may always most thankfully receive that his inestimable benefit, and also daily endeavour ourselves to follow the blessed steps of his most holy life. Through the same Jesus Christ our Lord.

MATTINS

Psalms of day (or 120, 121, 122, 123).

Ant. to Ben. I am the Shepherd, as above at Evensong.

II EVENSONG

Psalms of day (or 65, 66).
Ant. to Magn. I am the good Shepherd, * and I feed my sheep; and I lay down my life for the sheep, alleluia.

MONDAY
Ben. Go ye into all the world * and teach all nations, alleluia.
Magn. The good Shepherd * layeth down his life for the sheep, alleluia.

TUESDAY
Ben. Go ye into all the world, * and teach all nations, baptizing them in the name of the Father, and of the Son, and of the Holy Ghost, alleluia.
Magn. He that is an hireling, * whose own the sheep are not, seeth the wolf coming, and leaveth the sheep, and fleeth: and the wolf catcheth them, and scattereth the sheep, alleluia.

WEDNESDAY
Ben. Go unto my brethren, * and say unto them, alleluia, that they go into Galilee, alleluia: there shall they see me, alleluia, alleluia, alleluia.
Magn. As the Father knoweth me, * even so know I the Father: and I lay down my life for the sheep, alleluia.

THURSDAY
Ben. Art thou only a stranger * and hast not heard concerning Jesus, how they delivered him to be condemned to death, alleluia.
Magn. Other sheep I have, * which are not of this fold: them also I must bring, and they shall hear my voice: and there shall be one fold and one Shepherd, alleluia.

FRIDAY
Ben. Ought not Christ to have suffered * these things, and to enter into his glory? alleluia.
Magn.: Ant. as on Sunday.

EASTER III

I EVENSONG

Ant. to Magn. A little while * and ye shall not see me, saith the Lord: and again a little while, and ye shall see me, because I go to the Father, alleluia.

Collect

ALMIGHTY God, who shewest to them that be in error the light of thy truth, to the intent that they may return into the way of righteousness: grant unto all them that are admitted into the fellowship of Christ's religion; that they may eschew those things that are contrary to their profession, and follow all such things as are agreeable to the same. Through.

MATTINS

Psalms of day (or 124, 125, 126, 127).

Ant. to Ben. A little while, as above.

II EVENSONG

Psalms of day (or 81, 85).
Ant. to Magn. Verily I say unto you, * that ye shall weep and lament; and the world shall rejoice; and ye shall be sorrowful, but your sorrow shall be turned into joy, alleluia.

MONDAY

Ben. And beginning at Moses * and all the Prophets, he expounded unto them the scriptures concerning himself, alleluia.
Magn. Your sorrow * shall be turned into joy, alleluia: and your joy no man taketh from you, alleluia, alleluia.

TUESDAY

Ben And they constrained him, * saying: Abide with us, for it is toward evening, alleluia.
Magn. Sorrow hath filled * your heart: but your joy no man taketh from you, alleluia, alleluia.

WEDNESDAY

Ben. Abide with us, * for it is toward evening, and the day is far spent, alleluia.
Magn. Your sorrow, * alleluia, shall be turned into joy, alleluia.

THURSDAY

Ben. And he went in * to tarry with them; and it came to pass, as he sat at meat with them, he took bread, and blessed it, and brake, and gave it to them, alleluia.
Magn. Verily, verily, * I say unto you: I will see you again, and your heart shall rejoice, and your joy no man taketh from you, alleluia.

FRIDAY

Ben. They knew the Lord * Jesus, alleluia, in breaking of bread, alleluia.
Magn.: Ant. as on Sunday.

EASTER IV
I EVENSONG

Ant. to Magn. I go my way to him * that sent me; and none of you asketh me: Whither goest thou? alleluia, alleluia.

Collect

O ALMIGHTY God, who alone canst order the unruly wills and affections of sinful men: grant unto thy people; that they may love the thing which thou commandest, and desire that which thou dost promise; that so, among the sundry and manifold changes of the world, our hearts may surely there be fixed, where true joys are to be found. Through.

MATTINS

Psalms of day (or 128, 129, 130, 131).

Ant, to Ben. I go my way, as above.

II EVENSONG

Psalms of day (or 145, 146).
Ant. to Magn. I go my way * to him that sent me; but because I have said these things unto you, sorrow hath filled your heart, alleluia.

MONDAY

Ben. Did not our heart burn * within us concerning Jesus, while he talked with us in the way? alleluia.

Magn. I tell you the truth: * it is expedient for you that I go away; for if I go not away, the Comforter will not come unto you, alleluia.

TUESDAY

Ben. Peace be unto you, * it is I, alleluia; be not afraid, alleluia.

Magn. When the Comforter shall come, * even the Spirit of truth, he shall reprove the world of sin, and of righteousness, and of judgement, alleluia.

WEDNESDAY

Ben. A spirit hath not flesh * and bones, as ye see me have; therefore believe, alleluia.

Magn. I have yet many things * to say into you, but ye cannot bear them now; howbeit, when he, the Spirit of truth, shall come, he will guide you into all truth, alleluia.

THURSDAY

Ben. The disciples * set before the Lord a piece of broiled fish, and of an honeycomb, alleluia, alleluia.

Magn. He shall not speak * of himself, but whatsoever he shall hear, that shall he speak; and he will shew you things to come, alleluia.

FRIDAY

Ben These are the words * which I spake unto you, while I was yet with you, alleluia, alleluia.

Magn.: Ant. as on Sunday.

EASTER V
I EVENSONG

Ant. to Magn. Hitherto * have ye asked nothing in my name; ask, and ye shall receive, alleluia.

Collect

O LORD, from whom all good things do come: grant unto us thy humble servants, that by thy holy inspiration we may think those things that be good, and by thy merciful guiding may perform the same. Through our Lord Jesus Christ, who liveth.

MATTINS

Psalms of day (or 132, 133, 134).

Ant. to Ben. Hitherto, as at I Evensong.

II EVENSONG

Psalms of day (or 107).
Ant. to Magn. Ask ye, * and ye shall receive, that your joy may be fulfilled; for the Father himself loveth you, because ye have loved me, and have believed, alleluia.

ROGATION MONDAY

Benedicite is said to-day.
Ben. Ask, and it shall be given you; * seek, and ye shall find; knock, and it shall be opened unto you, alleluia.

To-day and the two following days, the Litany is said.
Magn. The Father himself loveth * you, because ye have loved me, and have believed, alleluia.

ROGATION TUESDAY

Ben. It behoved * Christ to suffer, and to rise again from the dead, alleluia.
Magn. I came forth * from the Father, and am come into the world; again, I leave the world, and go to the Father, alleluia.

ROGATION WEDNESDAY (VIGIL)

Ben. Father, the hour is come, * glorify thy Son with the glory which I had with thee before the world was, alleluia.

ASCENSION DAY
Double of I class
I EVENSONG

Psalms of day (or 15, 97, 99).
Ant. 1 Ye men of Galilee, * why stand ye gazing up into heaven? This same Jesus, which is taken up from you into heaven, shall so come, alleluia.
2 And they looked stedfastly * toward heaven, as he went up, alleluia.
3 Lifting up his hands, * he was taken up into heaven; and he blessed them, alleluia.
4 Exalt ye the King of kings, * and unto God make melody, alleluia.
5 While they behold, * he was taken up, and a cloud received him into heaven, alleluia.

Hymn (814)

SAVIOUR of men, who dost impart
Pure joys to every faithful heart;
Creator of a world redeemed,
Whose light on loving souls hath beamed;

What wondrous pity thee o'ercame,
To make thee bear our load of shame.
And, guiltless, to resign thy breath,
To win our guilty souls from death.

The realms of death are forced by thee,
The captives from their chains set free;
And thou, amidst thy ransomed train,
At God's right hand again dost reign.

May pity still with thee prevail
To cure the ills we now bewail,
And raise us to the blessèd place
Where Saints in glory see thy face.

Be thou our heavenly guide and way,
The Leader, whom our hearts obey;
Be thou the solace of our tears,
Our crown of life beyond the spheres. Amen.

℣. God is gone up with a merry noise, alleluia. ℟. And the Lord with the sound of the trump, alleluia.
Ant. to Magn. Father, * I have manifested thy name unto the men whom thou hast given me; and now I pray for them, not for the world, because I come to thee, alleluia.

Collect

GRANT, we beseech thee, almighty God, that like as we do believe thy only-begotten Son our Lord Jesus Christ to have ascended into the heavens; so we may also in heart and mind thither ascend, and with him, continually dwell: Who liveth and reigneth with thee and the Holy Ghost, one God, world without end.

MATTINS

Invit. Alleluia, Christ the Lord ascendeth into heaven: * O come, let us worship him, alleluia.

Psalms 8, 15, 21 (or 8, 21), with antiphons as at I Evensong. Hymn as at I Evensong.

℣. The Lord hath prepared, alleluia. ℟. His throne in heaven, alleluia.

Ant. to Ben. I ascend to my Father, * and your Father; and to my God, and your God, alleluia.

Athanasian Creed, to-day only.

II EVENSONG

As at I. Evensong, except: Psalms 24, 47, 108 (or 24, 47, 110).
℣. God is gone up with a merry noise, alleluia. ℟. And the Lord with the sound of the trump, alleluia. Ant. to Magn. O King of glory, * Lord of Sabaoth, who on this day ascendest with exceeding triumph far above all heavens: we pray thee, leave us not comfortless, but send the promise of the Father on us, even the Spirit of truth, alleluia.

Within the Octave, and on the two following days as on the Feast, with Psalms and antiphons as in the monthly course.

SUNDAY AFTER ASCENSION DAY

As on the Feast, except:

I EVENSONG

Psalms of day with antiphons of Feast.
℣. The Lord hath prepared, alleluia. ℟. His throne in heaven, alleluia.

Ant. to Magn. When the Comforter is come, * whom I will send unto you, even the Spirit of truth, which proceedeth from the Father, he shall testify of me, alleluia.

Collect

O GOD the King of glory, who hast exalted thine only Son Jesus Christ with great triumph unto thy kingdom in heaven: we beseech thee, leave us not comfortless, but send to us thine Holy Ghost to comfort us, and exalt us unto the same place whither our Saviour Christ is gone before: Who liveth and reigneth with thee and the same Holy Ghost, one God, world without end.

MATTINS

Psalms of day (or 93, 96), with antiphons as on Feast.
℣. God is gone up with a merry noise, alleluia. ℟. And the Lord with the sound of the trump, alleluia.

Ant. to Ben. When the Comforter is come, * whom I will send unto you, even the Spirit of truth, which proceedeth from the Father, he shall testify of me, alleluia.

II EVENSONG

Psalms of day (or 148, 149, 150), with antiphons as on Feast.
℣. The Lord hath prepared, alleluia. ℟. His throne on heaven, alleluia.

Ant. to Magn. These things have I told you, * that when the hour cometh, ye may remember that I told you of them, alleluia.

WHITSUNDAY

Double of I class
I EVENSONG

Psalms of day (or 48, 145).
Ant. 1 When the day of Pentecost * was fully come, they were all with one accord in one place, alleluia.
2 The Spirit of the Lord * filleth the world, alleluia.
3 They were all filled * with the Holy Ghost, and began to speak, alleluia.
4 O ye wells and all * that move in the waters, sing praise to God, alleluia.
5 The Apostles * did speak with other tongues the wonderful works of God, alleluia, alleluia, alleluia.

The first verse of the following hymn is sung kneeling.

Hymn (154)

COME, O Creator Spirit, come,
And make within our hearts thy home;
To us thy grace celestial give,
Who of thy breathing move and live.

O Comforter, that name is thine,
Of God most high the gift divine,
The well of life, the fire of love,
Our souls' anointing from above.

Thou dost appear in sevenfold dower,
The sign of God's almighty power;
The Father's Promise, making rich
With saving truth our earthly speech.

Our senses with thy light inflame,
Our hearts to heavenly love reclaim;
Our bodies poor infirmity
With strength perpetual fortify.

Our mortal foe afar repel,
Grant us henceforth in peace to dwell,
And so to us, with thee for guide,
No ill shall come, no harm betide.

May we by thee the Father learn,
And know the Son, and thee discern,
Who art of both; and thus adore
In perfect faith for evermore. Amen.

℣. They were all filled with the Holy Ghost, alleluia. ℟. And began to speak, alleluia.

Ant. to Magn. I will not leave you * comfortless, alleluia; I go away, and come again unto you, alleluia; and your heart shall rejoice, alleluia.

Collect

GOD, who as at this time didst teach the hearts of thy faithful people by the sending to them the light of thy Holy Spirit: grant us by the same Spirit to have a right judgement in all things, and evermore to rejoice in his holy comfort. Through the merits of Christ Jesus our Saviour, who liveth and reigneth with thee in the unity of the same Spirit, one God, world without end.

MATTINS

Invit. Alleluia, the Spirit of the Lord filleth the world: * O come, let us worship him, alleluia.

Psalms 48, 68 (or 68), with antiphons as at I Evensong.

Hymn (151)

REJOICE, the year upon its way
Has brought again that blessed day
When on the chosen of the Lord
The Holy Spirit was outpoured.

On each the fire, descending, stood
In quivering tongues' similitude.
Tongues, that their words might ready prove,
And fire, to make them flame with love.

To all in every tongue they spoke;
Amazement in the crowd awoke,
Who mocked, as overcome with wine,
Those who were filled with power divine.

These things were done in type that day,
When Eastertide had passed away,
The number told which once set free
The captive at the jubilee.

And now, O holy God, this day
Regard us as we humbly pray,
And send us, from thy heavenly seat,
The blessings of the Paraclete.

To God the Father, God the Son,
And God the Spirit, praise be done;
May Christ the Lord upon us pour
The Spirit's gift for evermore. Amen.

℣. They were all filled with the Holy Ghost, alleluia. ℟. And began to speak, alleluia.

Ant. to Ben. Receive ye * the Holy Ghost; whosoever sins ye remit, they are remitted unto them, alleluia.

Athanasian Creed, to-day only.

II EVENSONG

Psalms 104, 105 (or 104), with antiphons as at I Evensong.
Hymn as at I Evensong.
℣. The Apostles did speak with other tongues, alleluia. ℟. The wonderful works of God, alleluia.
Ant. to Magn. To-day * are fulfilled the days of Pentecost, alleluia; to-day the Holy Spirit appeared in fire to the disciples, and bestowed upon them his manifold graces, sending them into all the world, to preach and to testify: He that believeth and is baptized shall be saved, alleluia.
Within the Octave, as on the Feast (with Psalms of day), except as below.

WHITSUN MONDAY
Double of I class

Ben. God so loved the world * that he gave his only-begotten Son: that whosoever believeth in him should not perish, but have everlasting life, alleluia.
Magn. If a man love me, * he will keep my word: and my Father will love him, and we will come unto him, and make our abode with him, alleluia.

WHITSUN TUESDAY
Double of I class

Ben. I am the door, * saith the Lord: by me if any man enter in, he shall be saved, and shall find pasture, alleluia.
Magn. Peace I leave * with you, my peace I give unto you: not as the world giveth, give I unto you, alleluia.

EMBER WEDNESDAY
Double

Ben. I am the living bread, * saith the Lord, which came down from heaven, alleluia.
Magn. I am the living bread, * which came down from heaven: if any man eat of this bread, he shall live for ever; and the bread that I will give is my flesh, for the life of the world, alleluia.

THURSDAY
Double

Ben. Jesus called the twelve * disciples together, and gave them power and authority over unclean spirits, and to cure diseases: and he sent them to preach the kingdom of God, and to heal the sick, alleluia.

Magn. The Spirit, * which proceedeth from the Father, alleluia: he shall glorify me, alleluia, alleluia.

EMBER FRIDAY
Double

Ben. Jesus said: * But that ye know that the Son of man hath power on earth to forgive sins (he saith unto the sick of the palsy): I say unto thee: Arise, take up thy bed, and go thy way into thine house, alleluia.

Magn. But the Comforter, * which is the Holy Ghost, whom the Father will send in my name, he shall teach you all things, and bring all things to your remembrance, whatsoever I have said unto you, alleluia.

EMBER SATURDAY
Double

Ben. The love of God * is shed abroad in our hearts by his Spirit which dwelleth in us, alleluia.

TRINITY SUNDAY
Double of I class
I EVENSONG

Psalms of day.
Ant. 1 Glory be to thee, O Trinity * co-equal, one Godhead, even before all ages, and now, and for evermore.
2 Praise and everlasting glory * to God the Father, and to the Son, and to the Holy Comforter, through endless ages.
3 Glory and praise * resound from the lips of all, to the Father, and to his only-begotten Son, and like praise for ever be to the Holy Ghost.
4 Praise to God the Father, * and likewise to his Son, and to thee, O Spirit, in everlasting devotion, resound from our lips through every age.
5 Of whom are all things, * through whom are all things, in whom are all things: to him be glory for ever.

Hymn (164)

O TRINITY of blessed light,
O Unity of princely might,
The fiery sun now goes his way;
Shed thou within our hearts thy ray.

To thee our morning song of praise,
To thee our evening prayer we raise;
Thy glory suppliant we adore
For ever and for evermore.

All laud to God the Father be;
All praise, eternal Son, to thee;
All glory, as is ever meet,
To God the holy Paraclete.
Amen.

℣. Let us bless the Father and the Son with the Holy Ghost.
℟. Let us praise him and magnify him for ever.
Ant. to Magn. Thanks, O God,

* be unto thee, thanks be unto thee: one and very Trinity, one and supreme Deity, holy and perfect Unity.

Collect

ALMIGHTY and everlasting God, who hast given unto us thy servants grace by the confession of a true faith to acknowledge the glory of the eternal Trinity, and in the power of the divine majesty to worship the Unity: we beseech thee; that thou wouldest keep us stedfast in this faith, and evermore defend us from all adversities: Who livest and reignest, one God, world without end.

MATTINS

Invit. The very God, one in Trinity, and Trinity in Unity: * O come, let us worship him.
Psalms of day (or 29, 33), with antiphons as at I Evensong.

Hymn (815)

O THREE in One, and One in Three,
Who rulest all things mightily,
Accept this canticle of praise,
Which in our morning watch we raise.

The star of dawn fades in the sky,
The sun shines forth, the shadows fly;
So may the dawn of inward light
Chase from our souls the shades of night.

All laud to God the Father be,
All praise, eternal Son, to thee;
All glory, as is ever meet,
To God the holy Paraclete. Amen.

℣. Let us bless the Father and the Son with the Holy Ghost.
℟. Let us praise him and magnify him for ever.
Ant. to Ben. Blessed be the Creator * and Ruler of all things, the holy and undivided Trinity, both now and throughout all ages, world without end.

Athanasian Creed.

II EVENSONG

As at I Evensong, except:
Psalms of day (or 93, 99, 115), with antiphons as at I Evensong.
℣. Blessed art thou, O Lord, in the firmament of heaven. ℟. Above all to be praised and glorified for ever.
Ant. to Magn. Thee, O God, * the Father unbegotten; thee, the only-begotten Son; thee, O Holy Spirit, the Paraclete; holy and undivided Trinity, with our whole heart and voice we acknowledge thee, we praise thee, we bless thee; to thee be glory for ever and ever.

On the following days, the Office of the Season, with Collect as above.

CORPUS CHRISTI
Double of I class

Ant. 1 Christ the Lord, * a Priest for ever after the order of Melchisedech, offered bread and wine. Ps. 110.
2 The merciful and gracious Lord * hath given meat unto them that fear him, in remembrance of his marvellous works. Ps. 111.
3 I will receive * the cup of salvation, and I will offer the sacrifice of praise. Ps. 116, vv. 10-end.
4 Like the olive-branches * may the children of the Church be round about the table of the Lord. Ps. 128.
5 The Lord, that maketh peace * in the borders of the Church filleth us with the flour of wheat. Ps. 147, vv. 12-end.

I Lesson Exodus 16.2-15. (As at Evensong of Maundy Thursday)

Hymn (326)

OF the glorious Body telling,
O my tongue, its mysteries sing,
And the Blood, all price excelling,
Which the world's eternal King,
In a noble womb once dwelling,
Shed for this world's ransoming.

Given for us, for us descending
Of a Virgin to proceed,
Man with man in converse blending,
Scattered he the Gospel seed,
Till his sojourn drew to ending,
Which he closed in wondrous deed.

At the last great supper lying
Circled by his brethren's band,
Meekly with the law complying,
First he finished its command,
Then, immortal food supplying,
Gave himself with his own hand.

Word made flesh, by word he maketh
Very bread his Flesh to be;
Man in wine Christ's Blood partaketh:
And, if senses fail to see,
Faith alone the true heart waketh
To behold the mystery.

Therefore we, before him bending,
This great Sacrament revere;
Types and shadows have their ending,
For the newer rite is here;
Faith, our outward sense befriending,
Makes the inward vision clear.

Glory let us give, and blessing,
To the Father and the Son,
Honour, might and praise addressing
While eternal ages run:
Ever to his love confessing,
Who, from both, with both is one. Amen.

℣. Thou gavest them Bread from heaven, alleluia. ℟. Containing in itself all sweetness, alleluia.

Ant. to Magn. O how sweet, * O Lord, is thy spirit, who, to shew forth thy loving-kindness to thy children, feedest them with the most sweet Bread, which came from heaven; filling the hungry with good things, and sending the disdainful rich empty away.

II Lesson St John 6.22-40
(As at Evensong on Epiphany III)

Collect

O GOD, who in a wonderful Sacrament hast left unto us the memorial of thy passion: grant us, we beseech thee; so to venerate the sacred mysteries of thy Body and Blood, that we may ever perceive within ourselves the fruit of thy redemption: Who livest.

MATTINS

Invit. Let us worship Christ the King, the Lord of all the world: * Who giveth health of spirit to them that feed on him.
Psalms 20, 23, 42.
Ant. 1 Wisdom hath builded * her house: she hath mingled her wine and furnished her table, alleluia. Ps. 20.
2 Thou feddest thine own people * with Angels' food: and didst give them Bread from heaven to eat, alleluia. Ps. 23.
3 Rich is the Bread * of Christ, providing a royal banquet, alleluia. Ps. 42.
4 It pertaineth unto priests * of the Lord to offer incense and bread unto God, alleluia.
5 To him that overcometh * will I give the hidden manna, and a new name, alleluia.

I Lesson Exodus 24.1-11.
(As at Mattins on Maundy Thursday)
II Lesson St John 6.47-69.
(As at Evensong on Easter V)

Hymn (330)

THE Word of God, proceeding forth
Yet leaving not his Father's side,
And going to his work on earth,
Had reached at length life's eventide.

By false disciple to be given
To foemen for his blood athirst,
Himself, the living Bread from heaven,
He gave to his disciples first.

In twofold form of sacrament,
He gave his Flesh, he gave his Blood,
That man, of twofold substance blent,
Might wholly feed on mystic food.

In birth man's fellow-man was he,
His meat while sitting at the board;
He died, his ransomer to be,
He reigns to be his great reward.

O saving Victim, opening wide
The gate of heaven to man below,
Our foes press hard on every side,
Thine aid supply, thy strength bestow.

All praise and thanks to thee ascend
For evermore, blest One in Three;
O grant us life that shall not end,
In our true native land with thee. Amen.

℣. He maketh peace in thy borders, alleluia. ℟. And filleth thee with the flour of wheat, alleluia.

Ant. to Ben. I am the living Bread * which came down from heaven; if any man eat of this Bread, he shall live for ever, alleluia.

II EVENSONG

As at I Evensong, except:
Psalms 43, 81, 84, with antiphons as at I Evensong.

I Lesson Joel 2.21-7.
(As at Mattins on Wednesday after Easter V).

II Lesson Hebrews 4.14-5.10.
(As at Evensong on Saturday after Ascension Day).

℣. Thou gavest them Bread from heaven, alleluia. ℟. Containing in itself all sweetness, alleluia.

Ant. to Magn. O sacred banquet, * in which Christ is received, the memory of his passion renewed, the mind filled with grace, and a pledge of future glory given unto us, alleluia.

TRINITY I

As on Corpus Christi, except:

I EVENSONG

Psalms of day, with antiphons as on Feast; Lessons occurring.
℣. He fed them with the finest wheat flour, alleluia. ℟. And with honey out of the stony rock hath he satisfied them, alleluia.
Ant. to Magn. The child Samuel * ministered before the Lord in the presence of Eli; and the word of the Lord was precious unto him.

Collect

O GOD, the strength of all them that put their trust in thee: mercifully accept our prayers, and because through the weakness of our mortal nature we can do no good thing without thee, grant us the help of thy grace, that in keeping of thy commandments we may please thee both in will and deed. Through.

MATTINS

Psalms of day (or 1, 3, 5), with antiphons as on Feast.
℣. Thou gavest them Bread from heaven, alleluia. ℟. Containing in itself all sweetness, alleluia.

Ant. to Ben. **Father Abraham,** * have mercy upon me, and send Lazarus that he may dip the tip of his finger in water, and cool my tongue.

II EVENSONG

Psalms of day (or 4, 7, 8), with antiphons as on Feast.
℣. He fed them with the finest wheat flour, alleluia. ℟. And with honey out of the stony rock hath he satisfied them, alleluia.

Ant. to Magn. **Son, remember** * that thou in thy lifetime receivedst thy good things, and likewise Lazarus evil things.

THE SACRED HEART OF JESUS
Double of I class

I EVENSONG

Psalms of day, with antiphons as below.
Ant. 1 **With thine easy yoke,** * O Lord, be thou ruler in the midst of thine enemies.
2 **Merciful** * and gracious is the Lord: he hath given meat unto them that fear him.
3 **There is sprung up** * a light for the righteous: merciful and gracious is the Lord.
4 **What reward shall I give** * unto the Lord, for all the benefits that he hath done unto me?
5 **With the Lord** * there is mercy, and with him is plenteous redemption.

Hymn (820)

WHAT proud attack our sins have launched
In furious waves, like warriors fierce,
To wound the sinless Heart divine,
The sacred Heart of Christ to pierce!

Ours was the hand that aimed the spear
Against our Saviour crucified;
Ours was the sin, the mortal guilt,
That thrust it deep into his side.

From out that riven Heart, the Church,
The Bride of Christ, received her birth;
Salvation through this portal came
To all the nations of the earth.

Hence issuing in a sevenfold stream
The grace divine shall ever flow;

Here in the precious Blood of Christ
Our robes are washed as white as snow.

To sins that wound this blessed Heart
Shame were it now to turn anew;
In our own hearts light we instead
The flame of love, its symbol true.

All glory, Jesu, be to thee,
Who from thy Heart all grace dost pour;
To Father and to Spirit blest
Be praise and glory evermore. Amen.

℣. Take my yoke upon you, and learn of me. ℟. For I am meek and lowly of Heart.

Ant. to Magn. I am come * to send fire on the earth: and what will I if it be already kindled?

Collect

O GOD. who, forasmuch as the Heart of thy Son was wounded by our sins, hast therein bestowed upon us the abundant treasures of thy love: grant, we beseech thee, that as we give him the devout service of our hearts, so we may duly bring forth fruits of penance. Through the same.

MATTINS

Invit. The Heart of Jesus was wounded for love of us: * O come, let us worship him.

Psalms of the day.

Ant. 1 One of the soldiers * with a spear pierced his side, and forthwith came there out blood and water.

2 Jesus stood, * and cried, saying: If any man thirst, let him come unto me, and drink.

3 God hath loved us * with an everlasting love; and therefore, being lifted up from the earth, he hath drawn us unto his Heart, having mercy on us.

4 Come unto me, * all ye that labour and are heavy laden, and I will refresh you.

5 My son, * give me thine heart, and let thine eyes keep my ways.

Hymn (821)

O HEART of Jesus, ark of God,
Where rests, as in a hallowed shrine
A law not now to bondmen given,
But gracious, merciful, benign.

O Heart of Jesus, temple blest
For God's new covenant of grace;
To thee, its veil now rent in twain
The older temple yields its place.

O Heart of Jesus, Heart of love,
Which by a spear hast opened been,
That we in reverent awe may gaze
On wounds, the signs of love unseen.

Of his great love, who suffering bore,
Thou art the sign for ever blest;
Of Christ's great sacrifice for man
Thou art the symbol manifest.

Who would not render love for love,
Redemption's price by love repay?
Who to this Heart would not resort,
Content for ever here to stay?

All glory, Jesu, be to thee,
Who from thy Heart all grace dost pour;
To Father and to Spirit blest
Be praise and glory evermore.
Amen.

℣. With joy shall ye draw water. ℟. From the wells of salvation.
Ant. to Ben. Now these things * were done, that the Scripture should be fulfilled which saith: They shall look on him whom they pierced.

II EVENSONG

Psalms of day, with antiphons as at Mattins.
Hymn as at I Evensong.
℣. With joy shall ye draw water. ℟. From the wells of salvation.
Ant. to Magn. But when they came to Jesus, * and saw that he was dead already, they brake not his legs; but one of the soldiers with a spear pierced his side, and forthwith came there out blood and water.

TRINITY II

Where the Feast of the Sacred Heart is not observed, the antiphons to the Psalms, and the Hymn, with ℣. & ℟. are of the Season. When the Feast is observed, as on the Feast, except as below.

I EVENSONG

Psalms of day, with antiphons as on I Evensong of Feast.
Hymn as on I Evensong of Feast.
℣. Take my yoke upon you, and learn of me. ℟. For I am meek and lowly of heart.
Ant. to Magn. And all Israel knew * from Dan even to Beersheba, that Samuel was ordained a prophet of the Lord.

Collect

O LORD, who never failest to help and govern them whom thou dost bring up in thy stedfast fear and love: keep us, we beseech thee, under the protection of thy good providence, and make us to have a perpetual fear and love of thy holy name. Through.

MATTINS

Psalms of day (or 10, 12, 13), with antiphons as on Feast.
℣. Take my yoke upon you, and learn of me. ℟. For I am meek and lowly of heart.
Ant. to Ben. A certain man * made a great supper, and bade many; and he sent his servants at supper time to say to them that were bidden: Come, for all things are now ready, alleluia.

II EVENSONG

Psalms of day (or 15, 16, 17), with antiphons as on Feast.
℣. The gracious Lord hath made his marvellous works to be had in remembrance. ℟. He hath given meat unto them that fear him.
Ant. to Ben. Go out quickly * into the streets and lanes of the city; and compel the poor and the maimed, the halt and the blind, to come in, that my house may be filled, alleluia.

TRINITY III
I EVENSONG

Ant. to Magn. Ye mountains of Gilboa, * let there be neither rain nor dew upon you; for there the shield of the mighty is vilely cast away, the shield of Saul, as though he had not been anointed with oil. How are the mighty fallen in the midst of the battle! Jonathan was slain upon your high places. Saul and Jonathan were lovely and pleasant in their lives, and in their death they were not divided.

Collect

O LORD, we beseech thee mercifully to hear us: and grant that we, to whom thou hast given an hearty desire to pray, may by thy mighty aid be defended and comforted in all dangers and adversities. Through.

MATTINS

Psalms of day (or 18).
Ant. to Ben. What man among you * having an hundred sheep, if he lose one of them, doth not leave the ninety and nine in the wilderness, and go after that which is lost, until he find it? alleluia.

II EVENSONG

Psalms of day (or 19, 20, 21).
Ant. to Magn. What woman * having ten pieces of silver, if she lose one piece, doth not light a candle, and sweep the house, and seek diligently, until she find it?

TRINITY IV
I EVENSONG

Ant. to Magn. And David said * unto the Lord, when he saw the Angel that smote the people: It is I that have sinned, I that have done perversely; but these which are the sheep, what have they done?

Collect

O GOD, the protector of all that trust in thee, without whom nothing is strong, nothing is holy: increase and multiply upon us thy mercy; that, thou being our ruler and guide, we may so pass through things temporal, that we finally lose not the things eternal. Grant this, O heavenly Father, for Jesus Christ's sake, our Lord: Who liveth.

MATTINS

Psalms of day (or 24, 25).
Ant. to Ben. Be ye therefore merciful, * even as your Father also is merciful, saith the Lord.

II EVENSONG

Psalms of day (or 22, 23).
Ant. to Magn. Judge not, that ye be not judged: for with what judgement ye judge, ye shall be judged, saith the Lord.

TRINITY V
I EVENSONG

Ant. to Magn. So David prevailed * over the Philistine with a sling and a stone, in the name of the Lord.

Collect

GRANT, O Lord, we beseech thee, that the course of this world may be so peaceably ordered by thy governance, that thy Church may joyfully serve thee in all godly quietness. Through.

MATTINS

Psalms of day (or 26, 28).
Ant. to Ben. And Jesus entered * into a ship and sat down and taught the people.

II EVENSONG

Psalms of day (or 27, 29, 30).
Ant. to Magn. Master, * we have toiled all the night, and have taken nothing; nevertheless, at thy word I will let down the net.

TRINITY VI
I EVENSONG

Ant. to Magn. I am distressed * for thee, my brother Jonathan; thy love to me was wonderful, passing the love of women; as a mother loveth her only son, so have I loved thee. The bow of Jonathan was never turned back, neither swerved his shield from the battle, and his spear returned not empty.

Collect

O GOD, who hast prepared for them that love thee such good things as pass man's understanding: pour into our hearts such love toward thee, that we, loving thee above all things, may obtain thy promises, which exceed all that we can desire. Through.

MATTINS

Psalms of day (or 31, 32).
Ant. to Ben. Ye have heard * that it was said by them of old time: Thou shalt not kill, and whosoever shall kill shall be in danger of the judgement.

II EVENSONG

Psalms of day (or 33, 36).
Ant. to Magn. If thou bring thy gift * to the altar, and rememberest that thy brother hath ought against thee, leave there thy gift before the altar, and go thy way; first be reconciled to thy brother, and then come and offer thy gift, alleluia.

TRINITY VII
I EVENSONG

Ant. to Magn. But King David * covered his head, and mourned for Absalom, saying: O my son Absalom, O my son Absalom; would God I had died for thee, O my son Absalom!

Collect

LORD of all power and might, who art the author and giver of all good things: graft in our hearts the love of thy name, increase in us true religion, nourish us with all goodness, and of thy great mercy keep us in the same. Through.

MATTINS

Psalms of day (or 34).
Ant. to Ben. When a great multitude * was with Jesus, and had nothing to eat, he called his disciples and said unto them: I have compassion on the multitude, because they have now been with me three days, and have nothing to eat, alleluia.

II EVENSONG

Psalms of day (or 37).
Ant. to Magn. I have compassion * on the multitude, because they have now been with me three days, and have nothing to eat; and if I send them away fasting, they will faint by the way, alleluia.

TRINITY VIII
I EVENSONG

Ant. to Magn. Wisdom crieth aloud * in the broad places: Whosoever loveth wisdom, let him turn in hither, and he shall find her; and when he hath found her, happy is he if he hold her fast.

Collect

O GOD, whose never-failing providence ordereth all things both in heaven and earth: we humbly beseech thee to put away from us all hurtful things, and to give us those things which be profitable for us. Through.

MATTINS

Psalms of day (or 39, 40).
Ant. to Ben. Beware ye * of false prophets, which come unto you in sheep's clothing, but inwardly they are ravening wolves; ye shall know them by their fruits.

II EVENSONG

Psalms of day (or 41, 42, 43).
Ant. to Magn. A good tree * cannot bring forth evil fruit, neither can a corrupt tree bring forth good fruit. Every tree which bringeth not forth good fruit is hewn down, and cast into the fire, alleluia.

TRINITY IX
I EVENSONG

Ant. to Magn. I beseech thee, O Lord, * remember now how I have walked before thee in truth and with a perfect heart, and have done that which is good in thy sight.

Collect

GRANT to us, Lord, we beseech thee, the spirit to think and do always such things as be rightful: that we, who cannot do any thing that is good without thee, may by thee be enabled to live according to thy will. Through.

MATTINS

Psalms of day (or 46, 47, 48).
Ant. to Ben. The lord said unto his steward: * What is this I hear of thee? Give an account of thy stewardship, alleluia.

II EVENSONG

Psalms of day (or 44, 45).
Ant. to Magn. What shall I do, * seeing my master taketh from me the stewardship? I cannot dig, to beg I am ashamed; I am resolved what to do, that when I am removed from the stewardship, they may receive me into their houses.

TRINITY X

I EVENSONG

Ant. to Magn. Go not * after other gods to serve them.

Collect

LET thy merciful ears, O Lord, be open to the prayers of thy humble servants: and that they may obtain their petitions, make them to ask such things as shall please thee. Through.

MATTINS

Psalms of day (or 50, 53).
Ant. to Ben. When Jesus drew nigh * to Jerusalem, he beheld the city and wept over it, saying: O that thou hadst known, even thou; for the days shall come unto thee, when they shall compass thee about, and shall keep thee in on every side, and shall lay thee even with the ground; forasmuch as thou knewest not the time of thy visitation, alleluia.

II EVENSONG

Psalms of day (or 51, 54).
Ant. to Magn. It is written: * My house shall be called the house of prayer for all nations; but ye have made it a den of thieves. And he was daily with them, teaching in the temple.

TRINITY XI

I EVENSONG

Ant. to Magn. Son of man, * I send thee to the children of Israel, to a rebellious nation.

Collect

O GOD, who declarest thy almighty power most chiefly

in shewing mercy and pity: mercifully grant unto us such a measure of thy grace; that we, running the way of thy commandments, may obtain thy gracious promises, and be made partakers of thy heavenly treasure. Through.

MATTINS

Psalms of day (or 56, 57).
Ant. to Ben. Standing afar off, * the publican would not so much as lift up his eyes unto heaven; but smote upon his breast, saying: God be merciful to me a sinner.

II EVENSONG

Psalms of day (or 61, 62, 63).
Ant. to Magn. This man went down * justified rather than the other; for every one that exalteth himself shall be abased, and he that humbleth himself shall be exalted.

TRINITY XII
I EVENSONG

Ant. to Magn. I will shake the heavens * and the earth; and I will destroy the strength of the kingdom of the heathen.

Collect

ALMIGHTY and everlasting God, who art always more ready to hear than we to pray, and art wont to give more than either we desire or deserve: pour down upon us the abundance of thy mercy; forgiving us those things whereof our conscience is afraid, and giving us those good things which we are not worthy to ask, but through the merits and mediation of Jesus Christ thy Son our Lord: Who liveth.

MATTINS

Psalms of day (or 65, 66).
Ant. to Ben. When the Lord had passed * through the coasts of Tyre, he made the deaf to hear, and the dumb to speak.

II EVENSONG

Psalms of day (or 68).
Ant. to Magn. He hath done all things well; * he maketh the deaf to hear, and the dumb to speak.

TRINITY XIII
I EVENSONG

Ant. to Magn. I will stand * upon my watch, and set me upon my tower.

Collect

ALMIGHTY and merciful God, of whose only gift it cometh that thy faithful people do unto thee true and laudable service: grant we beseech thee; that we may so faithfully serve thee in this life, that we fail not finally to attain thy heavenly promises, through the merits of Jesus Christ our Lord: Who liveth.

MATTINS

Psalms of day (or 71).
Ant. to Ben. Master, * what shall I do to inherit eternal life? He said unto him: What is written in the law? Thou shalt love the Lord thy God with all thy heart, alleluia.

II EVENSONG

Psalms of day (or 67, 72).
Ant. to Magn. A certain man * went down from Jerusalem to Jericho, and fell among thieves, which stripped him of his raiment, and wounded him, and departed, leaving him half dead.

TRINITY XIV
I EVENSONG

Ant. to Magn. Blessed be the name * of God for ever; for wisdom and might are his.

Collect

ALMIGHTY and everlasting God, give unto us the increase of faith, hope, and charity: and that we may obtain that which thou dost promise, make us to love that which thou dost command. Through.

MATTINS

Psalms of day (or 75, 76).
Ant. to Ben. As Jesus entered * into a certain village, there went out to meet him ten men that were lepers; and they stood afar off, and lifted up their voices, saying: Jesus, Master, have mercy upon us.

II EVENSONG

Psalms of day (or 73, 77).
Ant. to Magn. But one of them, * when he saw that he was cleansed, turned back, and with a loud voice glorified God, alleluia.

TRINITY XV
I EVENSONG

Ant. to Magn. Blessed be the God * of Shadrach, Meshach and Abed-nego, who hath delivered his servants that trusted in him.

Collect

KEEP, we beseech thee, O Lord, thy Church with thy perpetual mercy: and because the fraility of man without thee cannot but fall, keep us ever by thy help from all things hurtful, lead us to all things profitable to our salvation. Through

MATTINS

Psalms of day (or 84, 85).
Ant. to Ben. Take no thought for your life, * saying: What shall we eat, or what shall we drink? for your Father knoweth that ye have need of all these things, alleluia.

II EVENSONG

Psalms of day (or 89).
Ant. to Magn. But seek ye first * the kingdom of God, and his righteousness, and all these things shall be added unto you, alleluia.

TRINITY XVI
I EVENSONG

Ant. to Magn. The sun shone * upon the shields of gold, and the mountains glistened therewith; and yet the forces of the heathen were discomfited.

Collect

O LORD, we beseech thee, let thy continual pity cleanse and defend thy Church: and because it cannot continue in safety without thy succour, preserve it evermore by thy help and goodness. Through.

MATTINS

Psalms of day (or 86, 87).
Ant. to Ben. Jesus entered * into a city which was called Nain; and behold there was a dead man carried out, the only son of his mother.

II EVENSONG

Psalms of day (or 90, 91).
Ant. to Magn. A great Prophet * is risen up among us, and God hath visited his people.

TRINITY XVII
I EVENSONG

Ant. to Magn. Now when Job had heard * the words of the messengers, he endured with patience, saying: Shall we receive good at the Lord's hand, and shall we not receive evil also? In all this Job sinned not with his lips, neither charged God in any thing foolishly.

Collect
LORD, we pray thee that thy grace may always prevent and follow us, and make us continually to be given to all good works. Through.

MATTINS

Psalms of day (or 92, 93).
Ant. to Ben. As Jesus went * into the house of one of the chief Pharisees to eat bread on the sabbath day, behold there was a certain man before him which had the dropsy; and he took him, and healed him, and let him go.

II EVENSONG

Psalms of day (or 100, 101, 102).
Ant. to Magn. When thou art bidden * to a wedding, sit down in the lowest room; that he that bade thee may say: Friend, go up higher. Then shalt thou have worship in the presence of them that sit at meat with thee, alleluia.

TRINITY XVIII
I EVENSONG

Ant. to Magn. Dominion and fear * are with him: he maketh peace in his high places.

Collect
LORD, we beseech thee, grant thy people grace to withstand the temptations of the world, the flesh and the devil, and with pure hearts and minds to follow thee the only God. Through.

MATTINS

Psalms of day (or 103).
Ant. to Ben. Master * which is the great commandment of the law? And Jesus answered: Thou shalt love the Lord thy God with all thy heart, alleluia.

II EVENSONG

Psalms of day (or 107).
Ant. to Magn. What think ye * of Christ? whose son is he? They say unto him: The Son of David. Jesus saith unto them: How then doth David in spirit call him Lord, saying: The Lord said unto my Lord, Sit thou on my right hand?

TRINITY XIX

I EVENSONG

Ant. to Magn. Where shall wisdom be found, * and where is the place of understanding?

Collect

O GOD, forasmuch as without thee we are not able to please thee: mercifully grant that thy Holy Spirit may in all things direct and rule our hearts. Through . . . in the unity of the same Holy Spirit.

MATTINS

Psalms of day (or 111, 112, 113).
Ant. to Ben. Jesus said * to the sick of the palsy: Son, be of good cheer, thy sins are forgiven thee.

II EVENSONG

Psalms of day (or 120, 121, 122, 123).
Ant. to Magn. The sick of the palsy therefore * took up his bed, on which he lay, and glorified God: and all the people, when they saw it, gave praise to God.

TRINITY XX

I EVENSONG

Ant. to Magn. Wisdom hath builded her house, * she hath hewn out her seven pillars, she hath subdued the nations, and hath trodden on the necks of the haughty in the might of her own strength.

Collect

O ALMIGHTY and most merciful God, of thy bountiful goodness keep us, we beseech thee, from all things that may hurt us: that we, being ready both in body and soul, may cheerfully accomplish those things that thou wouldest have done. Through.

MATTINS

Psalms of day (or 114, 115).
Ant. to Ben. Tell them which are bidden: * Behold, I have prepared my dinner, come unto the marriage, alleluia.

II EVENSONG

Psalms of day (or 124, 125, 126, 127).
Ant. to Magn. But when the king came in * to see the guests, he saw there a man not having a wedding garment, and said unto him: Friend, how camest thou in hither, not having a wedding garment?

TRINITY XXI

I EVENSONG

Ant. to Magn. In the way of righteousness * is life, and in the pathway thereof there is no death.

Collect

GRANT, we beseech thee, merciful Lord, to thy faithful people pardon and peace: that they may be cleansed from all their sins, and serve thee with a quiet mind. Through.

MATTINS

Psalms of day (or 116, 117).
Ant. to Ben. There was a certain nobleman * whose son was sick at Capernaum; who, when he heard that Jesus was come into Galilee, went and besought him that he would come down and heal his son.

II EVENSONG

Psalms of day (or 128, 129, 130, 131).
Ant. to Magn. So the father knew * that it was at the selfsame hour in the which Jesus said: Thy son liveth; and himself believed, and his whole house.

TRINITY XXII

I EVENSONG

Ant. to Magn. All wisdom * proceedeth from the Lord, and was with him for all time, and is before the ages.

Collect

LORD, we beseech thee to keep thy household the Church in continual godliness:

that through thy protection it may be free from all adversities, and devoutly given to serve thee in good works, to the glory of thy name. Through.

MATTINS

Psalms of day (or 118).
Ant. to Ben. The lord said unto his servant: * Pay that thou owest. But that servant fell down and besought him, saying: Have patience with me, and I will pay thee all.

II EVENSONG

Psalms of day (or 132, 133, 134).
Ant. to Magn. Thou wicked servant, * I forgave thee all that debt, because thou desiredst me; shouldest not thou also have had compassion on thy fellow-servant, even as I had pity on thee? alleluia.

TRINITY XXIII
I EVENSONG

Ant. to Magn. Arm yourselves * and be ye men of valour, and be in readiness for the conflict; for it is better for us to perish in battle than to look upon the evils of our nation and our altars. As the will of God is in heaven, even so let him do.

Collect

O GOD, our refuge and strength, who art the author of all godliness: be ready, we beseech thee, to hear the devout prayers of thy Church; and grant that those things which we ask faithfully we may obtain effectually. Through.

MATTINS

Psalms of day (or 110, 135).
Ant. to Ben. Master, * we know that thou art true, and teachest the way of God in truth, alleluia.

II EVENSONG

Psalms of day (or 137, 138, 139).
Ant. to Magn. Render therefore * unto Caesar the things which are Caesar's; and unto God the things that are God's, alleluia.

TRINITY XXIV

I EVENSONG

Ant. to Magn. I dwell * in the height above, and my throne is set in a cloudy pillar.

Collect

O LORD, we beseech thee, absolve thy people from their offences: that through thy bountiful goodness we may all be delivered from the bands of those sins, which by our frailty we have committed. Grant this, O heavenly Father, for Jesus Christ's sake, our blessed Lord and Saviour: Who liveth.

MATTINS

Psalms of day (or 136).
Ant. to Ben. For she said * within herself: If I may but touch the hem of his garment, I shall be whole.

II EVENSONG

Psalms of day (or 140, 141, 142).
Ant. to Magn. But Jesus turned him about, * and when he saw her, he said: Daughter, be of good comfort, thy faith hath made thee whole, alleluia.

When there are more than twenty-five Sundays after Trinity, the omitted service of Epiphany VI, or of Epiphany V and VI, shall be said, except as below.

TRINITY XXV

I EVENSONG

Ant. to Magn. Give peace, O Lord, * in this our time; because there is none other that fighteth for us, but only thou, our God.

MATTINS

Psalms of day (or 25, 49).

II EVENSONG

Psalms of day (or 79, 83).

TRINITY XXVI

I EVENSONG

Ant. to Magn. Let your song rejoice * in his mercy, and be not ashamed of his peace.

MATTINS

Psalms of day (or 84, 144).

II EVENSONG

Psalms of day (or 105).

SUNDAY NEXT BEFORE ADVENT
I EVENSONG

Ant. to Magn. The Lord give ear * unto your prayers, and be reconciled with you; and may the Lord our God never forsake you in time of trouble, alleluia.

Collect

STIR up, we beseech thee, O Lord, the wills of thy faithful people: that they, plenteously bringing forth the fruit of good works, may of thee be plenteously rewarded. Through.

MATTINS

Psalms of day (or 145, 146).
Ant. to Ben. When Jesus lift up his eyes, * and saw a great company come unto him, he said unto Philip: Whence shall we buy bread, that these may eat? And this he said to prove him, for he himself knew what he would do.

II EVENSONG

Psalms of day (or 147, 148, 149, 150).
Ant. to Magn. Then those men, * beholding the miracle that Jesus did, glorified God, and said: Of a truth, this is the Saviour of the world.

THE PROPER OF SAINTS

The Psalms with their antiphons are from the monthly course, except when otherwise noted.

November 30
ST ANDREW THE APOSTLE
Double of II class
I EVENSONG

Ant. 1 The Lord beheld * Peter and Andrew, and he called them.

2 Come ye after me, * saith the Lord, and I will make you fishers of men.

3 Leaving their nets, * they followed the Lord, the Redeemer.

4 Hail, O cross most precious, * receive the disciple of him who hung upon thee, even Christ my master.

Hymn, ℣. & ℟., from Common, p. 194.

Ant. to Magn. One of the two * which followed the Lord was Andrew, Simon Peter's brother, alleluia.

Collect

ALMIGHTY God, who didst give such grace unto thy holy Apostle Andrew, that he readily obeyed the calling of thy Son Jesus Christ and followed him without delay: grant unto us all; that we, being called by thy holy word, may forthwith give up ourselves obediently to fulfil thy holy commandments. Through the same.

MATTINS

Antiphons to Psalms and Collect, as above; the rest from the Common, p. 194. Athanasian Creed.

II EVENSONG

Antiphons to Psalms as above; the rest from Common.

December 3
ST FRANCIS XAVIER, C.
Greater double

Common, p. 201.

Collect

O GOD, who by the preaching and wondrous works of blessed Francis didst unite unto thy Church the peoples of India: mercifully grant; that we who venerate his glorious merits may likewise follow the example of his virtuous life. Through.

December 4
ST PETER CHRYSOLOGUS, B.C.D.
Double

Common, p. 201.

Collect

O GOD, who by divine foreshewing wast pleased to summon thy great teacher Saint Peter Chrysologus to be a ruler and doctor of thy Church: grant, we beseech thee; that as we have learned of him the doctrine of life on earth, so we may be found worthy to have for our advocate in heaven. Through.

December 6
ST NICHOLAS, B.C.
Double

Common, p. 201.

Collect

O GOD, who didst adorn thy blessed Bishop Nicholas with power to work many and great miracles: grant, we beseech thee; that by his merits we may be delivered from the fires of everlasting torment. Through.

December 7

(For St Ambrose, see April 4).

December 8
THE CONCEPTION OF THE BLESSED VIRGIN MARY
Double of I class

As in Common, p. 211, except:

I EVENSONG

Ant. 1 Thou art the exaltation of Jerusalem, * thou art the great glory of Israel, thou art the great rejoicing of our nation.
2 Blessed art thou, * O Virgin Mary, of the Lord, the most high God, above all the women on the earth.
3 Draw us, * O sinless Virgin; we will run after thee, because of the savour of thy good ointments.

Ant. to Magn. All generations * shall call me blessed, for he that is mighty hath done to me great things, alleluia.

PROPER OF SAINTS 109

Collect

Either as in the Common, or:

GOD, who by the immaculate Conception of the blessed Virgin didst hallow a dwelling-place meet for thy Son: mercifully grant; that as in the fore-knowledge of his death thou didst preserve her from all defilement, so she may evermore pray for us, until we finally attain unto thee in purity of heart. Through the same.

MATTINS

Invit. Let us celebrate the Conception of the Virgin Mary: * Let us worship her Son Christ our Lord.
Antiphons to Psalms as above.
Ant. to Ben. To-day let us celebrate * with due solemnity the Conception of the most holy Mother of God, the ever-Virgin Mary; of whom the King of kings was born, alleluia.

II EVENSONG

As at I Evensong, except:

Ant. to Magn. Let us celebrate * the worshipful Conception of the blessed and glorious Virgin Mary; whose lowliness the Lord regarded, when at the word of an Angel she conceived the world's Redeemer, alleluia.

December 11
ST DAMASUS, B.C.
Simple

Common, p. 201.

Collect

O LORD, we beseech thee mercifully to hear our prayers: and at the intercession of blessed Damasus thy Confessor and Bishop, of thine abundant mercy grant to us pardon and peace. Through.

December 13
ST LUCY, V.M.
Double

Common, p. 205, with Collect 3.

December 16
ST EUSEBIUS, B.M.
Simple

Common, p. 197, with Collect 2.

December 21
ST THOMAS THE APOSTLE
Double of II class

All as in Common, p. 194, except as below.

Ant. to Magn. and Ben. Because thou hast seen me, * Thomas, thou hast believed: blessed are they that have not seen, and yet have believed.

Collect

ALMIGHTY and everlasting God, who for the more confirmation of the faith didst suffer thy holy Apostle Thomas to be doubtful in thy Son's resurrection: grant us so perfectly and without all doubt to believe in thy Son Jesus Christ; that our faith in thy sight may never be reproved. Hear us, O Lord, through the same Jesus Christ, to whom, with thee and the Holy Ghost, be all honour and glory, now and for evermore.

January 14
ST HILARY, B.C.D.
Double

Common, p. 201.

January 15
ST PAUL, HERMIT, C.
Double

Common, p. 201, with Collect 4.

January 17
ST ANTONY, ABBOT
Double

Common, p. 201, with Collect 6.

January 18
(1) ST PETER'S CHAIR AT ROME
Greater double

As on February 22, with commem. of St Prisca at Mattins.

(2) ST PRISCA, V.M.
Commemoration

Ant. The kingdom of heaven is likened unto a merchant-man seeking goodly pearls: who, when he had found one pearl of great price, went and sold all that he had, and bought it.
℣. Full of grace are thy lips.
℟. Because God hath blessed thee for ever.

Collect

GRANT, we beseech thee, almighty God; that we who this day observe the heavenly birthday of blessed Prisca thy Virgin and Martyr, may in such wise rejoice in her yearly festival; that we may learn to follow rightly the pattern of her faith. Through.

January 19
ST WULFSTAN, B.C.
Double

Common, p. 201.

Collect

WE beseech thee, O Lord: pour into our hearts the spirit of charity; that at the intercession of thy blessed Confessor and Bishop Saint Wulfstan we may be counted worthy to taste of thy sweetness in everlasting felicity. Through.

January 20
SS FABIAN AND SEBASTIAN, MM.
Double

Common, p. 199.

Collect

ALMIGHTY God, mercifully look upon our infirmities: that whereas we are sore afflicted by the burden of our sins, the effectual prayers of blessed Fabian and Sebastian thy Martyrs may be our succour and defence. Through.

January 21
ST AGNES, V.M.
Double

Common, p. 205.

MATTINS

Ant. to Ps. I bless thee, * O Father of my Lord Jesus Christ, because through thy Son the fire is quenched from beside me.
Ant. to Ben. Lo, that which I desired, * now I see; that for which I hoped, I now possess; I am united in heaven unto him, whom on earth I loved with all my heart.

Collect

ALMIGHTY and everlasting God, who dost choose the weak things of the world to confound those things that are mighty: mercifully grant; that we who keep the feast of blessed Agnes thy Virgin and Martyr may feel the succour of her intercession in thy sight. Through.

EVENSONG

Ant. to Ps., as above.
Ant. to Magn. Blessed Agnes, standing * in the midst of the flames, stretched out her hands and prayed to the Lord: Almighty, to be adored, worshipped and feared, I bless thee, and I glorify thy name for evermore.

January 22
SS VINCENT AND ANASTASIUS, MM.
Simple

Common, p. 199.

Collect

ASSIST us, mercifully, O Lord, in these our supplications: that whereas we are tied and bound by the chain of our sins, the intercession of thy blessed Martyrs Vincent and Anastasius may speedily help and deliver us.

January 24
ST TIMOTHY, B.M.
Double

Common, p. 197 with Collect 1.

January 25
CONVERSION OF ST PAUL
Double of II class
I EVENSONG

Ant. 1 I have planted, * Apollos watered, but God gave the increase. (Alleluia.)
2 Most gladly will I glory * in mine infirmities, that the power of Christ may rest upon me.
3 The grace of God * in me was not in vain, but his grace ever abideth with me.
4 In Damascus the governor * under Aretas the king was desirous to apprehend me: and in a basket was I let down by the wall by the disciples, and thus I escaped his hands in the name of the Lord.
5 Thrice was I beaten * with rods, once was I stoned, thrice I suffered ship-wreck for the name of Christ.

Hymn (226, vv. 4, 6)

O NOBLE Teacher, Paul, we trust to learn of thee
Both earthly converse and the flight of ecstasy;
Till from the fading truths that now we know in part
We pass to fulness of delight for mind and heart.

Now to the glorious Trinity be duly paid
Worship and honour, praise and service unafraid,
Who in unchanging Unity, one Lord sublime,
Hath ever lived as now and to unending time. Amen.

℣. Thou art a chosen vessel, holy Apostle Paul. ℞. A preacher of the truth throughout the world.

Ant. to Magn. Go forth, Ananias, * and seek out Saul; for behold, he prayeth: for he is a chosen vessel unto me, to carry my name before the Gentiles and kings and the children of Israel.

Collect

O GOD, who, through the preaching of the blessed Apostle Saint Paul, hast caused the light of the Gospel to shine throughout the world: grant, we beseech thee; that we, having his wonderful conversion in remembrance, may shew forth our thankfulness for the same, by following the holy doctrine which he taught. Through.

Commem. of St Peter.

Ant. Thou art the Shepherd of the sheep, the Prince of the Apostles; to thee were given the keys of the kingdom of heaven.
℣. Thou art Peter. ℞. And upon this rock I will build my Church.

Collect

O GOD, who didst bestow upon thy blessed Apostle Saint Peter the keys of the kingdom of heaven, and didst appoint unto him the priesthood for the binding and loosing of sin: grant, we beseech thee; that by the help of his intercession we may be delivered from the bonds of all our iniquities.(Who livest.)

MATTINS

Invit. For the conversion of the Teacher of the Gentiles: * Let us praise our God.
Antiphons to Psalms as above. Hymn from Common, p. 194.
℣. Thou art a chosen vessel, holy Apostle Paul. ℟. A preacher of the truth throughout the world.
Ant. to Ben. Ye which have followed me * shall sit upon twelve thrones, judging the twelve tribes of Israel, saith the Lord.
Commem. of St Peter, as above.

II. EVENSONG

As at I. Evensong, except:
Ant. to Magn. Holy Apostle Paul, * preacher of the truth and Teacher of the Gentiles, intercede for us unto God who chose thee.
Commem. of St Peter as above.

January 26
ST POLYCARP, B.M.
Double

Common, p. 197, with Collect 2.

January 27
ST JOHN CHRYSOSTOM, B.C.D.
Double

Common, p. 201.

Collect

O LORD, who didst illumine thy Church with the wondrous righteousness and doctrine of thy blessed Confessor and Bishop Saint John Chrysostom: grant, we beseech thee; that the bounty of thy heavenly grace may evermore increase and multiply the same. Through.

January 29
ST FRANCIS DE SALES, B.C.D.
Double

Common, p. 201.

Collect

O GOD, who for the salvation of souls didst cause thy blessed Confessor Saint Francis to become all things to all men: pour into our hearts, we pray thee, the sweetness of thy charity; that by the direction of his counsels and the succour of his merits we may attain to the joys of life everlasting. Through.

January 30
KING CHARLES, M.
Greater double

Common, p. 197.

Collect

BLESSED Lord, in whose sight the death of thy Saints is precious: we magnify thy name for thine abundant grace bestowed upon our martyred Sovereign; by which he was enabled so cheerfully to follow the steps of his blessed Master and Saviour, in a constant meek suffering of all barbarous indignities, and at last resisting unto blood; and even then, according to the same pattern, praying for his murderers; let his memory, O Lord, be ever blessed among us, that we may follow the example of his courage and constancy, his meekness and patience, and great charity. And grant that this our land be freed from the vengeance of his righteous blood, and thy mercy glorified in the forgiveness of our sins: and all for Jesus Christ his sake, our only Mediator and Advocate: Who liveth.

Or Collect 3 from Common.

January 31
ST JOHN BOSCO, C.
Double

Common, p. 201.

Collect

O GOD, who didst raise up blessed John thy Confessor to be a father and teacher of thy children, and through him didst enrich thy Church with homes of true religion: grant, we beseech thee; that our hearts being enkindled with the same fire of love, we may seek for souls and serve thee alone. Through.

February 1
ST IGNATIUS, B.M.
Double

Common, p. 197, with Collect 1. of preceding. Evensong of morrow, commem.

February 2
THE PURIFICATION OF THE BLESSED VIRGIN MARY
Double of II class
I EVENSONG

Antiphons to Psalms as on January 1, p. 45. Hymn as in Common, p. 211.

℣. It was revealed unto Simeon by the Holy Ghost. ℟. That he should not see death before he had seen the Lord's Christ.

Ant. to Magn. The elder * took up the Child in his arms, yet was the Child the elder's Lord: whom a Virgin bare, after child-birth remaining a Virgin; he was her Child, and him she worshipped.

Collect

ALMIGHTY and everliving God, we humbly beseech thy majesty: that as thy only-begotten Son was this day presented in the temple in substance of our flesh; so we may be presented unto thee with pure and clean hearts, by the same thy Son Jesus Christ our Lord: Who liveth.

MATTINS

Invit. Behold, the Lord, the Ruler, cometh into his holy temple: * Rejoice and be glad, O Sion, and go forth to meet thy God.

Ant. 1 Simeon was righteous * and devout, and awaiting the consolation of Israel, and the Holy Ghost was upon him.

2 It was revealed * unto Simeon by the Holy Ghost that he should not see death before he had seen the Lord.

3 Simeon took the Child * up in his arms, and giving thanks, he blessed the Lord.

Hymn, ℣. & ℟. from Common, p. 212.

Ant. to Ben. And when his parents * brought in the Child Jesus, then Simeon took him up in his arms, and blessed God, saying: Lord, now lettest thou thy servant depart in peace.

II EVENSONG

Antiphons to Psalms as at Mattins; the rest as at I Evensong, except:
Ant. to Magn. To-day * the blessed Virgin Mary presented the Child Jesus in the temple, and Simeon being full of the Holy Ghost took him up in his arms, and blessed God for ever.

February 3
ST BLAISE, B.M.
Commemoration

Ant. He that hateth his life in this world, shall keep it unto life eternal.
℣. The righteous shall flourish like a palm tree. ℟. And shall spread abroad like a cedar in Libanus.

Collect

O GOD, who makest us glad with the yearly festival of Saint Blaise thy Martyr and Bishop: mercifully grant; that as we now observe his heavenly birthday, so we may likewise rejoice in his protection. Through.

February 5
ST AGATHA, V.M.
Double

Common, p. 205, with Collect 1.

February 6
ST TITUS, B.C.
Double

Common, p. 201.

Collect

O GOD, who didst adorn thy blessed Confessor Saint Titus with apostolic virtues: grant, we beseech thee; that by his merits and intercession we may so live righteously and soberly in this present world, that we may finally attain unto our country in heaven. Through.

February 9
ST CYRIL OF ALEXANDRIA, B.C.D.
Double

Common, p. 201.

Collect

O GOD, who didst strengthen thy blessed Confessor and Bishop Saint Cyril, invincibly to maintain the divine motherhood of the blessed Virgin Mary: vouchsafe that at his intercession we, believing her to be indeed the Mother of God, may as her children rejoice in her protection. Through the same.

February 10
ST SCHOLASTICA, V.
Double

Common, p. 205.

Collect

O GOD, who for a testimony unto the path of innocency didst cause the soul of thy blessed Virgin Scholastica to enter heaven in the appearance of a dove: grant unto us by her merits and intercession so to walk in innocency of life that we may attain to everlasting felicity. Through.

February 14
ST VALENTINE, PRIEST, M.
Commemoration

Ant. He that hateth his life in this world, shall keep it unto life eternal.

℣. The righteous shall flourish like a palm tree. ℟. And shall spread abroad like a cedar in Libanus.

Collect

GRANT, we beseech thee, almighty God: that we, who observe the heavenly birthday of blessed Valentine thy Martyr, may by his intercession be delivered from all the evils that beset us. Through.

February 18
ST SIMEON, B.M.
Commemoration

Ant., ℣. & ℟. as above for St Valentine; Collect 1 on p. 198.

February 22
THE CHAIR OF ST PETER AT ANTIOCH
Greater double
MATTINS

Invit. Thou art the Shepherd of the sheep, the Prince of the Apostles: * To thee were given the keys of the kingdom of heaven.

Ant. 1 Behold a great priest * who in his days pleased God, and was found righteous.

2 There was none found * like unto him, to keep the law of the most High.

3 Therefore with an oath * the Lord made him to increase among the people.

Hymn Good Shepherd Peter (p. 152).

℣. Let them exalt him in the congregation of the people. ℟. And praise him in the seat of the elders.

Ant. to Ben. Whatsoever * thou shalt bind on earth shall be bound in heaven; and whatsoever thou shalt loose on earth shall be loosed in heaven: saith the Lord to Simon Peter.

Collect

O GOD, who didst bestow upon thy blessed Apostle Saint Peter the keys of the kingdom of heaven, and didst appoint unto him the priesthood for the binding and loosing of sin: grant, we beseech thee; that by the help of his intercession we may be delivered from the bonds of all our iniquities: Who livest.

Commem. of St Paul, p. 153.

EVENSONG

Antiphons to Psalms as a Mattins.

Hymn (863)

WHATE'ER on earth below,
 thy word, O Peter, chained,
Beyond the stars in heaven above fast bound remained;
And whatsoe'er on earth was rightly loosed by thee,
Was in the heavenly courts by power divine set free;
Thou at the day of doom a judge of men shalt be.

Now to the Father be eternal glory done;
Our songs we raise to thee, O everlasting Son;
O Spirit from on high, thy throne we bow before;
To thee be honour, praise and glory evermore;
The Holy Trinity we worship and adore. Amen.

℣. The Lord chose him for a priest unto himself. ℟. To offer unto him the sacrifice of praise.

Ant. to Magn. Being a high priest, * he feared not the things of earth, but attained in glory unto the heavenly realms.

February 24 (25 in Leap Year)
ST MATTHIAS THE APOSTLE
Double of II class

All as in Common, p. 194, except:

Collect

O ALMIGHTY God, who into the place of the traitor Judas didst choose thy faithful servant Matthias to be of the number of the twelve Apostles: grant that thy Church, being alway preserved from false Apostles, may be ordered and guided by faithful and true pastors. Through.

Athanasian Creed

March 1
ST DAVID, B.C.
Double

Common, p. 201.

Collect

GRANT, we beseech thee, almighty God: that the devout prayers of blessed David thy Confessor and Bishop may in such wise succour and defend us; that we who on this day observe his festival, may follow his constancy in the defence of the catholic faith. Through.

March 2
ST CHAD, B.C.
Double

Common, p. 201.

Collect

ALMIGHTY and everlasting God, who on this day dost gladden us with the feast of blessed Chad thy Confessor and Bishop: we humbly beseech thy mercy; that we, who here do honour him with our devout observance, may by his intercession obtain thy healing unto life eternal. Through.

March 6
SS PERPETUA AND FELICITY, MM.
Double
Common, p. 207, with Collect 3, p. 208.

March 7
ST THOMAS AQUINAS, C.D.
Double

Common, p. 201.

Collect

O GOD, who hast enlightened thy Church with the wondrous learning of thy blessed Confessor Saint Thomas, and enriched it with his holiness of life: grant, we beseech thee; that we may both understand the doctrine that he taught, and also follow in all things the pattern of his conversation. Through.

March 8
ST JOHN OF GOD, C.
Double

Common, p. 201.

Collect

O GOD, who didst enkindle with thy love the heart of thy blessed servant Saint John, that he was thereby enabled to walk unhurt amid the flames of fire, and hast through him enriched thy Church with a new offspring: grant that by the help of his merits our sins may be purged with the fire of thy charity, and our souls healed to the attainment of everlasting salvation. Through.

March 9
ST FRANCES OF ROME, WIDOW
Double

Common, p. 207.

Collect

O GOD, who amidst the manifold gifts of thy grace didst endue thy blessed servant Frances with the familiar converse of an Angel: grant, we beseech thee; that at her intercession we may be found worthy to be admitted to the company of the Angels in thy heavenly kingdom. Through.

March 12
ST GREGORY THE GREAT, B.C.D.
Greater double

Common, p. 201.

Collect

O GOD, who on the soul of thy servant Gregory didst bestow the rewards of everlasting felicity: mercifully grant; that we, who are sore oppressed by the burden of our sins, by the succour of his intercession may be relieved. Through.

March 17
ST PATRICK, B.C.
Double

Common, p. 201.

Collect

O GOD, who didst send forth blessed Patrick thy Confessor and Bishop, to preach among the Gentiles the glory of thy name: grant that by his merits and intercession we may of thy mercy be enabled to perform such things as thou dost command. Through.

March 18
ST CYRIL OF JERUSALEM, B.C.D.
Double

Common, p. 201.

Collect

GRANT, we beseech thee, almighty God: that at the intercession of thy blessed Bishop Saint Cyril we may learn to know thee, the only true God, and Jesus Christ whom thou hast sent; that we may be found worthy to be numbered for ever among the sheep that hear his voice. Through the same.

At Mattins, Commem. of St Edward, K.M., as on June 20, p. 156.
Evensong of morrow, without commem. of preceding.

March 19
ST JOSEPH, SPOUSE OF OUR LADY
Double of I class

In Eastertide, Alleluia is added to Antt., Invit., ℣℣. & ℟℟.

PROPER OF SAINTS

I EVENSONG

Ant. 1 And Jacob * begat Joseph, the husband of Mary, of whom was born Jesus, which is called Christ.
2 When as Mary the Mother of Jesus * was espoused to Joseph, before they came together, she was found with child of the Holy Ghost.

Hymn as on p. 131.

℣. He made him lord also of his house. ℞. And ruler of all his substance.
Ant. to Magn. Then Joseph, * being raised from sleep, did as the Angel of the Lord had bidden him, and took unto him his wife.

Collect

GRANT, O Lord, we beseech thee, that we may be assisted by the merits of the Spouse of thy most holy Mother: and those things which by our own power we cannot obtain, do thou, at his intercession, vouchsafe to give us: Who livest.

MATTINS

Invit. Christ, the Son of God, deigned to be thought the son of Joseph: * O come, let us worship him.
Ant. 1 The parents of Jesus * went to Jerusalem every year at the feast of the Passover.
2 When they returned, * the child Jesus tarried behind in Jerusalem, and his parents knew not of it.
3 When they could not find * Jesus, they returned to Jerusalem, seeking him; and after three days they found him in the temple, sitting in the midst of the doctors, both hearing them and asking them questions.
4 Jesus went down * with them, and came to Nazareth, and was subject unto them.

Hymn (858)

HE whom the faithful praise to-day, rejoicing,
Singing of Joseph and his heavenly triumph,
This day hath entered on the endless glories
Of life immortal.

Great were his blessings, deep his soul's contentment,
When by his death-bed, as they prayed together,
Christ and his Mother watched with loving patience
Over his passing.

So, as a victor, freed from earthly perils,
Peacefully resting, through death's gate he passeth,
And with the blessèd in the heavenly mansions
Life's crown receiveth.

Therefore together let us now entreat him
That at his pleading God our sins may pardon,
Strengthen our weakness, and the peace of heaven
Shower upon us.

Thine be all honour, thine all adoration,
Trinity blessèd, who for ever reigning
Crownest with glory every faithful servant
Through all the ages. Amen.

℣. The mouth of the righteous is exercised in wisdom. ℟. And his tongue will be talking of judgement.

Ant. to Ben. Jesus himself * began to be about thirty years of age, being, as was supposed, the son of Joseph.

II EVENSONG

Antiphons as at Mattins; the rest as at I Evensong, except:
℣. Riches and plenteousness shall be in his house. ℟. And his righteousness remaineth for ever.

Ant. to Magn. Behold a faithful and wise steward, * whom his Lord hath made ruler over his household.

March 21
ST BENEDICT, ABBOT

Greater double

Common, p. 201, with Collect 6.

March 24
ST GABRIEL THE ARCHANGEL

Greater double

MATTINS

Invit. The Lord the King of Archangels: * O come, let us worship him. (E.T. Alleluia.)

Ant. 1 When Zacharias entered * into the temple of the Lord, the Angel Gabriel appeared unto him, standing at the right side of the altar of incense. (E.T. Alleluia.)

2 I am Gabriel * the Angel, who stand before God, and am sent to speak unto thee. (E.T. Alleluia.)

3 The Angel Gabriel * spake unto Mary, saying: Behold, thou shalt conceive in thy womb, and bear a Son, and thou shalt call his name Jesus. (E.T. Alleluia.)

Hymn (859)

THE Father's pardon from above,
O Christ, bestow, thy servants spare;
And, bending from thy throne of love,
Regard the blessèd Virgin's prayer.

Be ever nigh, Archangel pure
Whose name proclaims God's mighty power;
Therewith do thou our sickness cure,
And comfort us in sorrow's hour.

Bright Angels, happy evermore,
Who in your circles nine ascend,
As ye have guarded us before,
So may ye still our steps defend.

So may the realms of faith be blest,
So unbelief be chased away,
Till all within one fold find rest,
Secure beneath one Shepherd's sway.

To God the Father glory be,
Praise to the Saviour, Christ our Lord,
Praise, Holy Spirit, unto thee;
And may God's Angels be our ward. Amen.

℣. An Angel stood by the altar of the temple. (E.T. Alleluia.)
℟. Having a golden censer in his hand. (E.T. Alleluia.)

Ant. to Ben. The Angel Gabriel * came down to Zacharias, and said unto him: Thy wife shall bear thee a son, and thou shalt call his name John, and many shall rejoice in his birth: for he shall go before the face of the Lord to prepare his ways. (E.T. Alleluia.)

Collect

O GOD, whom from among the number of thy holy Angels didst choose the Archangel Gabriel to make known the mystery of thine Incarnation: mercifully grant; that we, who celebrate his festival on earth, may find him a patron in the heavens: Who livest.

Evensong of morrow, commem. of Lent only.

March 25

THE ANNUNCIATION OF THE BLESSED VIRGIN MARY

Double of I class

I EVENSONG

Ant. 1 The Angel Gabriel * was sent unto Mary, a Virgin espoused unto Joseph. (E.T. Alleluia.)

2 Hail, Mary, * full of grace; the Lord is with thee; blessed art thou among women. (E.T. Alleluia.)

3 Fear not, Mary, * for thou hast found favour with the Lord: behold, thou shalt conceive and bear a Son. (E.T. Alleluia.)

4 The Lord shall give unto him * the throne of his father David, and he shall reign for ever. (E.T. Alleluia.)

5 Behold the handmaid of the Lord: * be it unto me according to thy word.

Hymn as in Common, p. 211.
℣. Hail, Mary, full of grace. (E.T. Alleluia.) ℟. Be it unto me according to thy word. (E.T. Alleluia.)

Ant. to Magn. The Holy Ghost * shall come upon thee, and the power of the Highest shall overshadow thee. (E.T. Alleluia.)

Collect

WE beseech thee, O Lord, pour thy grace into our hearts: that as we have known the Incarnation of thy Son Jesus Christ by the message of an Angel, so by his Cross and passion we may be brought unto the glory of his resurrection. Through the same.

MATTINS

Invit. Hail, Mary, full of grace;* The Lord is with thee. (E.T. Alleluia)
Antiphons to Psalms as at Evensong.
Hymn as in Common, p. 212.
V. Hail, Mary, full of grace. (E.T. Alleluia) R̸. The Lord is with thee. (E.T. Alleluia)
Ant. to Ben. How shall this be, * O Angel of God, seeing I know not a man? Hearken, O Virgin Mary: the Holy Ghost shall come upon thee, and the power of the Highest shall overshadow thee. (E.T. Alleluia)

II EVENSONG

As at I Evensong, except:
Ant. to Magn. The Angel Gabriel * spake unto Mary, saying: Hail, full of grace; the Lord is with thee: blessed art thou among women. (E.T. Alleluia)

March 27
ST JOHN DAMASCENE, C.D.
Double

Common, p. 201.

Collect

ALMIGHTY and everlasting God, who didst endue thy blessed Saint John with heavenly learning and wondrous strength of spirit for the defence of the honour of holy images: grant unto us, we pray thee; that by his intercession and example we may so honour the images of thy Saints, that we may follow them in all true godliness, and feel the effectual succour of their advocacy. Through.

Friday after Passion Sunday
THE SEVEN SORROWS OF THE BLESSED VIRGIN MARY
Greater double

MATTINS

Invit. Remembering the sorrows of the glorious Virgin at the sufferings of the Lord for us:* O come, let us worship him.

Ant. 1 I will get me to the mountain * of myrrh, and to the hill of frankincense.
2 My Beloved * is white and ruddy: the hair of his head is like the purple of a king, bound with bands.
3 Whither is thy Beloved gone, * O thou fairest among women, whither is thy Beloved turned aside?
4 A bundle of myrrh * is my Well-beloved unto me; he shall lie all night betwixt my breasts.
5 Stay me with flagons, * comfort me with apples; for I am sick of love.

Hymn (848, ii)

MOTHER blest, may this be granted,
That the wounds of Christ be planted
In my heart, and there remain.
Since for me in tribulation
Jesus deigned to win salvation,
Let me share with him his pain.

May I still thy tears be sharing,
Through my life all sorrows bearing
With my Lord, the Crucified.
By the Cross my station keeping,
As thou standest, Mother, weeping,
Let me stand there by thy side.

Maid of maidens, from my pleading
Turn thee not away unheeding,
Let me stand and weep with thee.
Teach me on Christ's death to ponder,
On his passion gaze in wonder,
Hold his wounds in memory.

May Christ's wounds be borne within me,
May his Blood a new life win me,
Be his Cross my strength and stay.
Lest in flames of hell I perish,
Guard me, Virgin blest, and cherish
In the dreadful judgement-day.

When death's bonds no more enthral me,
Christ, at Mary's prayers, then call me
To the palm of victory.
When my body lies forsaken
May my soul to glory waken,
In thy paradise with thee. Amen.

℣. Pray for us, O Virgin most sorrowful. ℟. That we may be made worthy of the promises of Christ.

Ant. to Magn. When Jesus saw * his Mother standing by the Cross, and the disciple whom he loved, he saith unto his Mother: Woman, behold thy son. Then saith he to the disciple: Behold thy Mother.

Collect

O GOD, in whose passion, as Simeon foretold, the sword of grief did pierce the gentle soul of the glorious Virgin Mary thy Mother: mercifully grant; that we who here do call to mind her sorrows may by the glorious merits and prayers of all the Saints that have faithfully stood beneath the Cross, obtain the blessed fruit of that passion: Who livest.

EVENSONG

Antiphons to Psalms as at Mattins.

Hymn (115, vv. 1-5)

AT the Cross her station keeping,
Stood the mournful Mother, weeping,
Close to Jesus at the last,
Through her soul, of joy bereavèd,
Bowed with anguish, deeply grievèd,
Now at length the sword hath passed.

O that blessèd one, grief-laden,
Blessèd Mother, blessèd Maiden
Mother of the all-holy One;
O that silent, ceaseless mourning,
O those dim eyes, never turning
From that wondrous, suffering Son.

Who on Christ's dear Mother gazing,
In her trouble so amazing,
Born of woman, would not weep,
Who on Christ's dear Mother thinking?
Such a cup of sorrow drinking,
Would not share her sorrow deep?

For his people's sins, in anguish,
There she saw the Victim languish,
Bleed in torments, bleed and die;
Saw the Lord's Anointed taken,
Saw her Child in death forsaken;
Heard his last expiring cry.

In the passion of my Maker
Be my sinful soul partaker,
May I bear with her my part;
Of his passion bear the token
In a spirit bowed and broken,
Bear his death within my heart. Amen.

℣. & ℟. and Ant. to Magn. *When Jesus saw* as at Mattins.

April 3
ST RICHARD, B.C.
Double

Common, p. 201.

Collect

O GOD, who by the merits of blessed Richard thy Confessor and Bishop didst adorn thy Church with wondrous miracles: grant we beseech thee; that by his intercession thy servants may attain to the glory of everlasting felicity. Through.

April 4
ST AMBROSE, B.C.D.
Double

Common, p. 201, with Collect 3.

April 11
ST LEO THE GREAT, B.C.D.
Double

Common, p. 201, with Collect 2.

April 14
ST JUSTIN, M.
Double

Common, pp. 195 or 197.

Collect

O GOD, who by the foolishness of the Cross didst wondrously teach thy blessed Martyr Saint Justin the excellent knowledge of Christ Jesus: grant that by his intercession, we, being delivered from the deceitfulness of all false doctrine, may be firmly grounded in thy true religion. Through.

April 19
ST ALPHEGE, B.M.
Double

Common, pp. 195 or 197.

Collect

O GOD, who didst adorn blessed Alphege, devoutly confessing thy most holy name, with the dignity of priesthood and the palm of martydom: mercifully grant; that by his intercession we may find such succour in thy sight, that we may be found worthy to rejoice with him in everlasting felicity. Through.

April 21
ST ANSELM, B.C.D.
Double

Common, p. 201, with Collect 3.

April 23
ST GEORGE, M.
Double of I class

All as in Common, p. 195, except:
At I and II Evensong, and at Mattins:
℣. With thy loving kindness, alleluia. ℟. Thou hast defended him as with a shield, alleluia.
Ant. The Saints through faith * subdued kingdoms, wrought righteousness, obtained promises, alleluia.

Collect

O GOD, who makest us glad with the merits and intercession of blessed George thy Martyr: mercifully grant; that we who implore thy bounty by his aid, may receive it by the gift of thy grace. Through.

April 25
ST MARK THE EVANGELIST
Double of II class

All as in Common, p. 195, except:

Collect

O ALMIGHTY God, who hast instructed thy holy Church with the heavenly doctrine of thy Evangelist Saint Mark: give us grace; that being not like children carried away with every blast of vain doctrine, we may be established in the truth of thy holy Gospel. Through.

The Litany is said after Mattins.

April 30
ST CATHERINE OF SIENA, V.
Double

Common, p. 205.

Collect

GRANT, we beseech thee, almighty God, that we who here observe the heavenly birthday of thy blessed Virgin Catherine, may so rejoice in her yearly festival, that we may learn to follow rightly the pattern of her godliness. Through.
Evensong of SS Philip and James, with commem. of preceding.

ST JOSEPH THE WORKMAN
Double of I class
I EVENSONG

Ant. 1 And Jacob * begat Joseph, the husband of Mary, of whom was born Jesus, which is called Christ, alleluia.

2 The Angel Gabriel * was sent from God to a city of Galilee named Nazareth, to a Virgin espoused to a man whose name was Joseph, alleluia.

3 And Joseph * went up from Galilee, out of the city of Nazareth, into Judaea, unto the city of David, which is called Bethlehem, alleluia.

4 And they came with haste, * and found Mary, and Joseph, and the Babe lying in a manger, alleluia.

5 And Jesus himself * began to be about thirty years of age, being, as was supposed, the son of Joseph, alleluia.

Hymn (856)

LET Angels chant thy praise,
  pure Spouse of purest Maid,
While Christendom's sweet choirs the gladsome strains repeat,
To tell thy wondrous fame, to raise the pealing hymn,
Wherewith we all thy glory greet.

When doubts and bitter fears thy heavy heart oppressed,
And filled thy righteous soul with sorrow and dismay,
An Angel swiftly sped, the wondrous secret told,
And drove thy anxious griefs away.

Thy arms thy new-born Lord with tender joy embrace,
Him then to Egypt's land thy watchful care doth bring;
Him in the temple's courts once lost thou dost regain,
And 'mid thy tears dost greet thy King.

Not till death's pangs are o'er do others gain their crown,
But, Joseph, unto thee the blessèd lot was given
While life did yet endure, thy God to see and know,
As do the Saints above in heaven.

Grant us, great Trinity, who sing thy praise below,
In highest bliss and love, above the stars to reign,
That we in joy with him may praise our loving God,
And raise our glad eternal strain. Amen.

℣. He made him lord also of his house, alleluia. ℟. And ruler of all his substance, alleluia.

Ant. to Magn. When as Mary the Mother of Jesus * was espoused to Joseph, before they came together, she was found with child of the Holy Ghost alleluia.

Collect

O GOD, who of thine unspeakable providence didst choose thy blessed Saint Joseph to be the Spouse of thy most holy Mother: grant, we pray thee; that we may so venerate him as our protector on earth, that we may be worthy to have him for our advocate in heaven: Who livest.

MATTINS

Invit. Let us praise our God * In veneration of blessed Joseph our protector, alleluia.
Antiphons to Psalms as at Evensong.

Hymn (857)

JOSEPH, thou splendour of the heavenly mansions,
Prince of all nations, hope of all men living,
Graciously hear the praises that we offer,
Joyously singing.

Thee the Creator chose for spouse most blessèd
Of the pure Virgin, thee the Word incarnate
Loved as a father, who for our salvation
Ever art pleading.

When the Redeemer was in manger lying,
He for whose advent prophet-choirs had waited,
With joy beholding, lowly didst thou worship
God born an Infant.

He who rules all things, King o'er all kings reigning,
At whose will tremble all the realms infernal,
Who by the prostrate hosts of heaven is worshipped,
To thee was subject.

Praises eternal to the Triune Godhead,
From whom great honour thou in heaven receivest,
O may he grant us, through thy wondrous merits,
Life everlasting. Amen.

℣. Thou hast given me the defence of thy salvation, alleluia. ℟. Thy right hand also hath held me up, alleluia.
Ant. to Ben. Joseph, thou son of David, * fear not to take unto thee Mary thy wife; for that which is conceived in her is of the Holy Ghost, alleluia.

II EVENSONG

As at I Evensong, except:
℣. I sat down under his shadow with great delight, alleluia. ℟. And his fruit was sweet to my taste, alleluia.

Ant. to Magn. Son, why hast thou thus dealt * with us? Behold, thy father and I have sought thee sorrowing, alleluia.

May 1
SS PHILIP AND JAMES, APOSTLES
Double of II class
I EVENSONG

Ant. 1 Lord, * shew us the Father, and it sufficeth us, alleluia.

2 Philip, * he that hath seen me hath seen my Father, also, alleluia.

3 Have I been so long time * with you, and yet ye have not known me? Philip, he that hath seen me hath seen my Father also, alleluia.

4 If ye had known me, * ye should have known my Father also, and now ye hath both known him and have seen him, alleluia, alleluia, alleluia.

5 If ye love me, * keep my commandments, alleluia, alleluia, alleluia.

Hymn as on p. 195.

℣. O ye Saints and righteous, rejoice in the Lord, alleluia. ℟. God hath chosen you for his own inheritance, alleluia.

Ant. to Magn. Let not your heart * be troubled, neither let it be afraid; ye believe in God, believe also in me; in my Father's house are many mansions, alleluia, alleluia.

Collect

O ALMIGHTY God, whom truly to know is everlasting life: grant us perfectly to know thy Son Jesus Christ to be the way, the truth and the life; that following the steps of thy holy Apostles Saint Philip and Saint James, we may stedfastly walk in the way that leadeth to eternal life. Through the same.

Commem. of St Catherine, p. 130.

MATTINS

Invit. The Lord the King of Apostles: * O come, let us worship him, alleluia.

Antiphons to Psalms as above.

Hymn, ℣. & ℟. as in Common, p. 196.

Ant. to Ben. I am the way, * the truth and the life; no man cometh unto the Father, but by me, alleluia.

II EVENSONG

As at I Evensong, except:
℣. Right dear in the sight of the Lord, alleluia. ℟. Is the death of his Saints, alleluia.

May 2
ST ATHANASIUS, B.C.D.
Double
Common, p. 201, with Collect 2.

May 3
THE FINDING OF THE HOLY CROSS
Double of II class

I EVENSONG

Ant. 1 O mighty work of mercy: * death then died, when life died upon the tree. (E.T. Alleluia.)

2 Behold the Cross of the Lord * displayed; flee away, ye that oppose yourselves; the lion of the tribe of Judah, the root of David, hath prevailed. (E.T. Alleluia.)

3 By the sign of the Cross * deliver us from our enemies, O our God. (E.T. Alleluia.)

Hymn as on p. 63.

℣. This sign of the Cross shall be in heaven. (E.T. Alleluia.)
℟. When the Lord shall come to judgement. (E.T. Alleluia.)

Ant. to Magn. O Cross, * surpassing all the stars in splendour, world-renowned, justly dear to all Christian people, holiest of earth's treasures; which only wast counted worthy to bear the price of our redemption; sweetest wood and sweetest iron, sweetest weight is hung on thee; bring aid to this congregation, who are here assembled to celebrate thy praises. (E.T. Alleluia, alleluia.)

Collect

O GOD, who in the finding of the Cross of our salvation didst renew the wonders of thy passion: vouchsafe to grant; that through the ransom once paid upon that tree of life, we may attain unto life eternal: Who livest.

MATTINS

Invit. Christ crucified is our King: * O come, let us worship him (E.T. Alleluia.)

Antiphons to Psalms as above.

Hymn as on p. 65.

℣. We adore thee, O Christ, and we bless thee. (E.T. Alleluia.) ℟. Because by thy Cross thou hast redeemed the world. (E.T. Alleluia.)

Ant. to Ben. Above all cedar-trees * art thou noble. O tree on which the life of the world hung, on which Christ triumphed, and death overcame death for evermore. (E.T. Alleluia.)

II EVENSONG

As at I Evensong, except:
Ant. to Magn. He the holy Cross endured, * who destroyed the power of hell; he with strength did gird himself, on the third day to rise again, alleluia.

May 4
ST MONICA, WIDOW
Double

Common, p. 207.

Collect

O GOD, the comforter of them that mourn, and the hope of them that put their trust in thee, who didst favourably accept the tears of thy blessed Saint Monica for the conversion of Augustine her son: grant, we pray thee; that at the intercession of these thy servants, we may so bewail the sins that we have committed, that we may be worthy to obtain the abundant pardon of thy grace. Through.

May 6
ST JOHN BEFORE THE LATIN GATE
Greater double

All from Common, p. 195, except as below.

Collect

O GOD, who seest the evils that by reason of our sins do beset us: grant, we beseech thee; that the glorious intercession of thine Apostle and Evangelist Saint John may be our succour and defence. Through.

EVENSONG

Ant. to Magn. John the Apostle, * being cast into a cauldron of boiling oil, by grace protected came forth unharmed, alleluia.

May 9
ST GREGORY OF NAZIANZUS, B.C.D.
Double

Common, p. 201, with Collect 3.

May 12
ST PANCRAS AND HIS COMPANIONS, MM.
Commemoration

Ant. Daughters of Jerusalem, come forth, and behold the Martyrs with the diadems wherewith the Lord hath crowned them in the day of solemnity and rejoicing, alleluia, alleluia. ℣. Right dear in the sight of the Lord, alleluia. ℟. Is the death of his Saints, alleluia.

Collect

GRANT, O Lord that this holy festival of thy blessed Martyrs Neeeus, Achilles, Domitilla and Pancras, may ever assist us in thy service: and that we may thereby be rendered worthy to walk after thy commandments. Through.

May 19
ST DUNSTAN, B.C.
Double

Common, p. 201.

Collect

O GOD, who didst exalt blessed Dunstan thy Bishop to thy heavenly kingdom: grant, we beseech thee; that by his glorious merits we may attain to everlasting felicity. Through.

May 25
ST ALDHELM, B.C.
Double

Common, p. 201.

Collect

O GOD, who on this day didst exalt thy blessed Bishop Saint Aldhelm to everlasting felicity: we pray thee; that by his merits and intercession thy mercy may bring us unto the same. Through. Evensong of morrow, commem. of preceding.

May 26
ST AUGUSTINE, B.C., APOSTLE OF ENGLAND
Double of II class

All as in Common, p. 201, except:

Collect

O GOD, who didst bestow on the people of England the blessed Bishop Augustine to be their first teacher: grant, we beseech thee; that as on earth we do proclaim his merits, so we may know the benefit of his prayers in heaven. Through.

May 27
ST BEDE THE VENERABLE, C.D.
Double

Common, p. 201.

Collect

O GOD, who dost enlighten thy Church with the wondrous learning of blessed Bede thy Confessor and Doctor: mercifully grant unto us thy servants; that we, being in all things enlightened by his wisdom, may at all times feel the effectual succour of his righteousness. Through.

June 1
ST NICOMEDE, M.
Commemoration

In Eastertide:
Ant. Daughters of Jerusalem, come forth, and behold the Martyrs with the diadems wherewith the Lord hath crowned them in the day of solemnity and rejoicing, alleluia, alleluia.
℣. Right dear in the sight of the Lord, alleluia. ℟. Is the death of his Saints, alleluia.
Outside Eastertide:
Ant. He that hateth his life in this world, shall keep it unto life eternal.

℣. The righteous shall flourish like a palm tree. ℟. And shall spread abroad like a cedar in Libanus.

Collect

WE beseech thee, O Lord, mercifully to assist thy people: that like as we do venerate the singular merits of thy blessed Martyr Saint Nicomede; so his advocacy may at all times succour us to the obtaining of thy mercy. Through.

June 5
ST BONIFACE, B.M.
Double

Common, pp. 195 or 197.

Collect

O GOD, who by the labours of blessed Boniface thy Martyr and Bishop didst vouchsafe to call many nations to the knowledge of thy name: mercifully grant; that we who this day keep his feast may by his advocacy be holpen in thy sight. Through.

June 8
ST WILLIAM OF YORK, B.C.
Double

Common, p. 201.

Collect

O GOD, who makest us glad with the merits and intercession of blessed William thy Confessor and Bishop: mercifully grant; that we, who by his aid implore thy bounty, may by the abundance of thy grace receive the same. Through.

June 9
ST COLUMBA, ABBOT
Double

Common, p. 201.

June 10
ST MARGARET, QUEEN, WIDOW
Simple

Common, p. 207.

Collect

O GOD, who didst render thy blessed Saint, Queen Margaret, glorious by reason of her singular charity to the poor: grant that by her intercession and example thy charity may continually increase within our hearts. Through.

Evensong of morrow.

June 11
ST BARNABAS, APOSTLE
Double of II class

All as in Common, pp. 194 or 195, except:

Collect

O LORD God almighty, who didst endue thy holy Apostle Barnabas with singular gifts of the Holy Ghost: leave us not, we beseech thee, destitute of thy manifold gifts, nor yet of grace to use them alway for thy honour and glory. Through.

June 13
ST ANTONY OF PADUA, C.D.
Double

Common, p. 201.

Collect

GRANT, O God, that the solemn festival of thy holy Confessor and Doctor Saint Antony may bring gladness to thy Church: that being defended by thy succour in all things spiritual, we may be found worthy to attain to everlasting felicity. Through.

June 14
ST BASIL THE GREAT, B.C.D.
Double

Common, p. 201, with Collect 2.

June 20
TRANSLATION OF ST EDWARD, K.M.
Commemoration

Ant. He that hateth his life in this world, shall keep it unto life eternal.

℣. The righteous shall flourish like a palm tree. ℟. And shall spread abroad like a cedar in Libanus.

Collect

O GOD, who reignest in glory over an everlasting kingdom, we beseech thee mercifully to behold thy family, who on this day call to remembrance blessed Edward thy King and Martyr: and grant that by his merits and intercession they which now rejoice in his triumph may likewise attain to his reward in heaven. Through.

June 22
ST ALBAN, M.
Greater double

Common, p. 197.

Collect

O LORD, who hast sanctified this day to thy blessed Saint Alban by his glorious martyrdom: grant, we beseech thee; that as year by year we do rejoice to pay him honour, so we may ever be defended by his continual help. Through.

June 23
VIGIL

Collect

GRANT, we beseech thee, O Lord, that we thy family may ever walk in the way of salvation: that following the teachings of thy holy forerunner Saint John, we may attain unto him whom he foretold, even Jesus Christ thy Son our Lord: Who liveth.

June 24
THE NATIVITY OF ST JOHN BAPTIST
Double of I class
I EVENSONG

Ant. 1 He shall go before * him in the spirit and power of Elias, to prepare for the Lord a perfect people.

2 This child * shall be great in the sight of the Lord: for the hand of the Lord is with him.

Hymn (223)

LET thine example, holy John remind us,
Ere we can meetly sing thy deeds of wonder,
Hearts must be chastened, and the bonds that bind us
Broken asunder.

Lo! a swift Angel, from the skies descending,
Tells to thy father what shall be thy naming;
All thy life's greatness to its bitter ending
Duly proclaiming.

But when he doubted what the Angel told him,
Came to him dumbness to confirm the story;
At thine appearing, healed again behold him,
Chanting thy glory.

Oh! what a splendour and a revelation
Came to each mother, at thy joyful leaping,
Greeting thy Monarch, King of every nation,
In the womb sleeping.

Angels in orders everlasting praise thee,
God, in thy triune majesty tremendous;
Hark to the prayers we, penitents, upraise thee,
Save and defend us. Amen.

℣. There was a man sent from God. ℟. Whose name was John.

Ant. to Magn. When Zacharias * went into the temple, there appeared unto him the Angel Gabriel, standing on the right side of the altar of incense.

Collect

ALMIGHTY God, by whose providence thy servant John Baptist was wonderfully born, and sent to prepare the way of thy Son our Saviour, by preaching of repentance: make us so to follow his doctrine and holy life; that we may truly repent according to his preaching, and after his example constantly speak the truth, boldly rebuke vice, and patiently suffer for the truth's sake. Through the same.

MATTINS

Invit. The Lord, the King of the Forerunner: * O come, let us worship him.

Ant. 1 Elisabeth bare to Zacharias * a mighty son, John the Baptist, the Forerunner of the Lord.

2 They made signs * to his father, how he would have him called; and he wrote, saying: His name is John.

3 His name shall be called John, * and many shall rejoice at his birth.

4 Thou, child, * shalt be called the Prophet of the Highest; thou shalt go before the face of the Lord to prepare his ways.

Hymn (224)

E'EN in thy childhood, 'mid the desert places,
Thou hadst a refuge from the city gainèd,
Far from all slander and its bitter traces
Living unstainèd.

Often had prophets in the distant ages
Sung to announce the Daystar and to name him;
But as the Saviour, last of all the sages,
Thou didst proclaim him.

Than John the Baptist, none of all Eve's daughters
E'er bore a greater, whether high or lowly:
He was thought worthy, washing in the waters
Jesus the holy.

Angels in orders everlasting praise thee,
God, in thy triune majesty tremendous;
Hark to the prayers we, penitents, upraise thee:
Save and defend us. Amen.

℣. This child shall be great in the sight of the Lord. ℟. For the hand of the Lord is with him.

Ant. to Ben. The mouth of Zacharias * was opened, and he prophesied, saying: Blessed be the God of Israel.

Athanasian Creed.

II EVENSONG

Antiphons to Psalms as at Mattins: hymn as at I Evensong.
℣. This child shall be great in the sight of the Lord. ℟. For the hand of the Lord is with him.

Ant. to Magn. The child * who is born unto us, is more than a Prophet; for this is he of whom the Saviour saith: Among all those born of women there hath not arisen a greater than John the Baptist.

June 28
ST IRENAEUS, B.M.
Double

Common, p. 197.

Collect

O GOD, who didst bestow upon blessed Irenaeus thy Martyr and Bishop grace to overcome false doctrine by the teaching of the truth, and to establish thy Church in peace and prosperity: we beseech thee; that thou wouldest give thy people constancy in thy true religion, and grant us thy peace all the days of our life. Through. Evensong of morrow only.

June 29
SS PETER AND PAUL, APOSTLES
Double of I class

I EVENSONG

Antiphons to Psalms as at Mattins.

Hymn (226, vv. 1,2,5,6)

WITH golden splendour and with roseate hues of morn,
O gracious Saviour, Light of Light, this day adorn;
Which brings to ransomed sinners hopes of that far home
Where Saints and Angels sing the praise of martyrdom.

Lo, the Key-bearer, lo, the Teacher of mankind,
Lights of the world and judges sent to loose and bind,

Alike triumphant or by cross or sword-stroke found,
In life's high senate stand with victor's laurel crowned.

Twin olive branches, pouring oil of gladness forth,
Your prayers shall aid us, that for all our little worth,
Believing, hoping, loving, we for whom ye plead,
This body dying, may attain to life indeed.

Now to the glorious Trinity be duly paid
Worship and honour, praise and service unafraid,

Who in unchanging Unity, one Lord sublime,
Hath ever lived as now and to unending time. Amen.

℣. Their sound is gone out into all lands. ℟. And their words into the ends of the world.

Ant. to Magn. Thou art the Shepherd of the sheep, * the Prince of the Apostles; to thee were given the keys of the kingdom of heaven.

Collect

O ALMIGHTY God, who by thy Son Jesus Christ didst give to thy Apostle Saint Peter many excellent gifts, and commandedst him earnestly to feed thy flock: make, we beseech thee, all bishops and pastors diligently to preach thy holy Word, and the people obediently to follow the same, that they may receive the crown of everlasting glory. Through the same.

Or:

GOD, who on this day dost recall to us the martyrdom of thine Apostles Peter and Paul: grant, we beseech thee, unto thy Church ever to walk stedfastly in the commandment of those from whom the true faith was first received. Through.

MATTINS

Invit. The Lord, the King of Apostles: * O come, let us worship him.

Ant. 1 Peter and John * went up into the temple at the hour of prayer, being the ninth hour.
2 Silver and gold * have I none: but such as I have give I thee.
3 The Angel said unto Peter: * Cast thy garment about thee, and follow me.
4 Thou art Peter, * and upon this rock I will build my Church.

Hymn (226, vv. 3-6)

GOOD Shepherd Peter, unto whom the charge was given
To close or open ways of pilgrimage to heaven,
In sin's hard bondage held may we have grace to know
The full remission thou hast granted to bestow.

O noble Teacher, Paul, we trust to learn of thee
Both earthly converse and the flight of ecstasy;
Till from the fading truths that now we know in part
We pass to fulness of delight for mind and heart.

Now to the glorious Trinity be duly paid
Worship and honour, praise and service unafraid,
Who in unchanging Unity, one Lord sublime,
Hath ever lived as now and to unending time. Amen.

℣. They declared the work of God. ℟. And wisely considered of his doings.

Ant. to Ben. Whatsoever thou shalt bind * on earth shall be bound in heaven; and whatsoever thou shalt loose on earth shall be loosed in heaven: saith the Lord unto Simon Peter.

II EVENSONG

Antiphons to Psalms as in Common, p. 194; hymn as at I Evensong.
℣. They declared the work of God. ℟. And wisely considered of his doings.
Ant. to Magn. To-day * Simon Peter ascended the scaffold of the cross, alleluia; to-day the key-bearer of heaven went with joy unto Christ; to-day the Apostle Paul, the light of the world, bowed his head, and for the name of Christ was crowned with martyrdom, alleluia.

June 30
COMMEMORATION OF ST PAUL
Greater double

At Mattins as on January 25 p. 114, except:
Invit. The Lord, the King of Apostles: * O come, let us worship him.

Collect

O GOD, who through the preaching of thy blessed Apostle Saint Paul hast caused the light of the Gospel to shine forth upon the Gentiles: grant, we beseech thee; that we who this day call him to remembrance may feel the effectual succour of his intercession. Through.

Commem. of St Peter, as on p. 113.
Evensong of morrow, without commem.

July 1
THE PRECIOUS BLOOD OF OUR LORD JESUS CHRIST
Double of I class
I EVENSONG

Ant. 1 Who is this * that cometh from Edom, with dyed garments from Bozrah, this that is glorious in his apparel?
2 I that speak * in righteousness, mighty to save.
3 He was clothed * with a vesture dipped in blood; and his name is called the Word of God.
4 Wherefore art thou * red in thine apparel, and thy garments like him that treadeth in the wine-fat?

Hymn (825)

NOW let our paths resound with song and melody,
Now let God's people join in high festivity,
The young and old go forth in glad procession now,
With tapers borne right joyfully.

Yet even in our joy lay we not grief aside,
For still we bear in mind our Saviour crucified,
The precious Blood outpoured, the cause of all our joy,
The wounds in hands and feet and side.

Once through his wilfulness Adam's iniquity
Fearsome disaster wrought for all his progeny;
Then the new Adam came new life for men to win,
And gained o'er sin the victory.

And since from dying lips, rending the very sky,
From Christ on Calvary broke forth the last strong cry,
The debt of sin now paid, forgiveness has been won,
And pardon from our God on high.

Whoso his wedding-robe, defiled by sinful stains,
Unto this laver bring, fair purity regains,
And bright as Angels clad, well-pleasing to the King,
The wedding-banquet he attains.

So forward on our way let us, once purified,
Still press, nor ever turn with wandering steps aside,
Till God the prize shall give, who on our path below
Is even now our strength and guide.

We pray thee, Father blest, whose power surpasses thought,
Have mercy on the souls the Blood of Christ once bought,
And as thy Spirit still renews us with his grace,
In heaven perfect what he has wrought. Amen.

℣. Thou hast redeemed us, O Lord, by thy Blood. ℟. And hast made us a kingdom unto our God.

Ant. to Magn. Ye are come * unto mount Sion, and unto the city of the living God, the heavenly Jerusalem, and to Jesus the mediator of the new covenant, and to the blood of sprinkling, that speaketh better things than that of Abel.

Collect

ALMIGHTY and everlasting God, who didst appoint that thine only-begotten Son should be the Redeemer of the world, and hast vouchsafed to accept his Blood for the propitiation for our sins: mercifully grant that we who here rejoice to honour that Blood, the price of our salvation, may be defended by its power in this present world; and rejoice in the everlasting fruits thereof in the world to come. Through the same.

MATTINS

Invit. Christ, the Son of God, who hath redeemed us by his Blood: ✶ O come, let us worship him.

Ant. 1 These that are clothed ✶ in white robes, who are they, and whence came they?

2 These are they ✶ which came out of great tribulation, and have washed their robes in the blood of the Lamb.

3 Therefore are they ✶ before the throne of God, and serve him day and night.

4 And they overcame ✶ the dragon through the blood of the Lamb, and by the word of their testimony.

5 Blessed ✶ are they who wash their robes in the blood of the Lamb.

Hymn (826)

THE Saviour's holy wounds we hail,
The sacred wounds from which there ran
The precious Blood, the token true
Of Christ's undying love for man.

We hail them, brighter than the stars,
Richer than gems of Orient,
Far sweeter than the honeycomb,
Fragrant beyond the rose's scent.

Thy wounds, O Christ, our stronghold are,
Defence for every soul distressed,
A rampart no assault can breach,
A refuge where no foes molest.

How oft on Jesus' shoulders bare
The cruel scourging strokes have rained!
How oft the stones of Pilate's hall
With that redeeming Blood are stained!

Behold the crown about his brow,
Dread circlet of the sharpest thorn!
The iron pierces through his hands;
See, where the nails his feet have torn!

And when his trusting prayers his soul
Into his Father's hand commend,
A double stream flows from his side,
Water and blood together blend.

Our Saviour thus the winepress trod,
Redemption for our souls to win;
And, for our sakes withholding nought,
He paid the price of all our sin.

Though deep, O sinner, be thy guilt,
Cleansed shalt thou be, when on thee poured
The saving waters lave thy soul,
The Blood of the redeeming Lord.

To Christ, who reigns, enthroned on high
At God's right hand, our thanks we pay,
Who by his Blood redemption won,
Whose Holy Spirit is our stay. Amen.

II EVENSONG

As at I Evensong, except:
℣. We therefore pray thee, help thy servants. ℟. Whom thou hast redeemed with thy precious blood.

Ant. to Magn. And this day * shall be unto you for a memorial: and ye shall keep it a feast to the Lord throughout your generations by an ordinance for ever.

Commem. of morrow.

July 2
THE VISITATION OF THE BLESSED VIRGIN MARY
Double of II class

When I Evensong is said fully, all as at II Evensong, except for the Ant. to Magn. as noted below.

I EVENSONG

Ant. to Magn. Blessed art thou, * O Mary, who hast believed: for there shall be a performance of those things which were told thee from the Lord, alleluia.
℣. Blessed art thou among women. ℟. And blessed is the fruit of thy womb.

Collect

WE beseech thee, O Lord, pour into our hearts the abundance of thy heavenly grace: that like as the childbearing of the Virgin Mary was unto us thy servants the beginning of salvation, so the devout observance of her Visitation may avail for the increasing of our peace. Through.

MATTINS

Invit. Let us celebrate the Visitation of the Virgin Mary: * Let us worship her Son, Christ the Lord.

Ant. 1 Mary arose, * and went into the hill country with haste, into a city of Judah.

2 Mary entered * into the house of Zacharias, and saluted Elisabeth.

3 Blessed art thou * among women, and blessed is the fruit of thy womb.

Hymn as on p. 212.
℣. Blessed art thou among women. ℟. And blessed is the fruit of thy womb.

Ant. to Ben. When Elisabeth * heard the salutation of Mary, she cried with a loud voice, saying: Whence is this to me, that the Mother of my Lord should come to me? alleluia.

II EVENSONG

Antiphons to Psalms as at Mattins; hymn as on p. 211. ℣. Blessed art thou among women. ℟. And blessed is the fruit of thy womb.

Ant. to Magn. All generations * shall call me blessed, for God hath regarded the lowliness of his handmaiden, alleluia.

July 4
TRANSLATION OF ST MARTIN, B.C.
Double

Common, p. 201, with Collect as on p. 190.

July 15
TRANSLATION OF ST SWITHUN, B.C.
Double

Common, p. 201.

Collect

ALMIGHTY and everlasting God, who hast made this day honourable unto us by reason of the festival of blessed Swithun thy Confessor and Bishop: grant we beseech thee; that thy Church may so rejoice in this observance; that we who on this day do honour him in this solemnity on earth, may obtain thy succour by his intercession in heaven. Through.

July 19
ST VINCENT DE PAUL, C.
Double

Common, p. 201.

Collect

O GOD, who didst endue thy blessed Saint Vincent with apostolic virtue, to the intent that he should preach thy Gospel to the poor and establish the honour of the holy orders of thy Church: grant, we beseech thee; that we may so hold in reverence his works of righteousness, that we may learn to follow the pattern of his godly conversation. Through.

July 20
ST MARGARET, V.M.
Commemoration

Ant. The kingdom of heaven is likened unto a merchant-man seeking goodly pearls: who, when he had found one pearl of great price, went and sold all that he had, and bought it.
℣. Full of grace are thy lips.
℟. Because God hath blessed thee for ever.

Collect

GRANT, O Lord, that as thy blessed Virgin and Martyr Saint Margaret by the merits of her chastity and godliness of conversation did ever walk acceptably in thy sight: so she may at all times effectually intercede for our forgiveness. Through.

July 22
ST MARY MAGDALENE
Double of II class
I EVENSONG

Antiphons to Psalms as in monthly course.

Hymn (864)

FATHER of lights, one glance of thine,
Whose eyes the universe control,
Fills Magdalene with holy love,
And melts the ice within her soul.

Her precious ointment forth she brings
Upon those sacred feet to pour;
She washes them with burning tears,
And with her hair she wipes them o'er.

Impassioned to the Cross she clings,
Nor fears beside the tomb to stay,
Nor dreads the soldiers' savage mien,
For love doth cast all fear away.

O Christ, O very charity,
By thee be all our sins forgiven;
Do thou our hearts with grace fulfil,
And grant us the rewards of heaven.

* To God the Father glory be,
And to his sole-begotten Son;
And glory, Holy Ghost, to thee,
While everlasting ages run. Amen.

℣. Full of grace are thy lips.
℟. Because God hath blessed thee for ever.

Ant. to Magn. A woman * in the city, which was a sinner, when she knew that Jesus sat at meat in the house of Simon the leper, brought an alabaster box of ointment, and stood behind at the feet of Jesus, and began to wash his feet with tears, and did wipe them with the hairs of her head; and kissed his feet, and anointed them with the ointment.

Or:

MERCIFUL Father, give us grace that we never presume to sin through the example of any creature: but if it shall chance us at any time to offend thy divine majesty, that then we may truly repent, and lament the same, after the example of Mary Magdalene; and by lively faith obtain remission of all our sins. Through the only merits of thy Son our Saviour Christ: Who liveth.

Collect

Either:

O LORD, forasmuch as thou didst answer the entreaties of blessed Mary Magdalene, and raise her brother Lazarus to life when he had been four days dead: we beseech thee; that we may know the succour of her intercession: Who livest.

MATTINS

Invit. For the conversion of Mary Magdalene: * Let us praise our God.

Hymn (865)

LOOK on us, Son of God most high,
With gracious mien and pitying eye;
Who didst such blessed joys impart
To Magdalene's repentant heart.

Safe in the coffers of the Lord
The long-lost coin is now restored;
Freed from the mire, the jewel bright
Now glitters as the stars of night.

O Jesus, good physician, sent
For healing of the penitent,
Remember Mary's tears and grief,
And grant us from our sins relief.

And may thy Mother's prayers avail
To help our human nature frail,
Until we reach, from stormy sea,
That haven dear where we would be.

God's glory ever be extolled,
And all his mercies manifold,
For pardon to the sinner given
And everlasting bliss of heaven. Amen.

℣. God hath chosen and forechosen her. ℟. He hath made her to dwell in his tabernacle.

Ant. to Ben. Mary * anointed the feet of Jesus and wiped them with her hair, and the house was filled with the fragrance of the ointment.

II EVENSONG

As at I Evensong, except:
℣. God hath chosen and forechosen her. ℟. He hath made her to dwell in his tabernacle.
Ant. to Magn. A woman* in the city, which was a sinner, brought an alabaster box of ointment, and stood behind at the Lord's feet, and began to wash his feet with her tears, and wiped them with the hair of her head.

July 25
ST JAMES THE APOSTLE
Double of II class

All as in Common, p. 194.

Collect

GRANT, O merciful God, that as thine holy Apostle Saint James, leaving his father and all that he had, without delay was obedient unto the calling of thy Son Jesus Christ, and followed him; so we, forsaking all worldly and carnal affections, may be evermore ready to follow thy holy commandments. Through the same.
Athanasian Creed.
At Evensong, commem. of morrow.

July 26
ST ANNE, MOTHER OF THE BLESSED VIRGIN MARY
Double of II class

All from Common, p. 207, except:

Collect

O GOD, who didst vouchsafe to give grace to blessed Anne that she might be worthy to bear the Mother of thine only-begotten Son: mercifully grant; that we who rejoice in the observance of her festival may be aided by her pleading before thee. Through the same.

July 29
ST MARTHA, V.
Simple

Common, p. 205, with Collect 3.

July 31
ST IGNATIUS, C.
Greater double

Common, p. 201.

Collect

O GOD, who for the propagation of the greater glory of thy name didst through thy blessed Saint Ignatius stablish thy Church militant with a new defence: grant, we pray thee; that by the succour of his intercession and by the following of his example we may so fight manfully in this life on earth, that we may be found worthy to share the glory of his crown in heaven. Through.

August 1
ST PETER'S CHAINS
Greater double

MATTINS

Invit. The Lord, the King of Apostles: * O come, let us worship him.

Ant. 1 Herod the King * proceeded to take Peter also; and when he had apprehended him, he put him in prison, intending after Easter to bring him forth to the people.

2 Peter therefore * was kept in prison; but prayer was made without ceasing of the Church unto God for him.

3 The Angel said * unto Peter, Cast thy garment about thee, and follow me.

4 The Lord hath sent * his Angel, and hath delivered me out of the hand of Herod, alleluia.

5 Thou art Peter, * and upon this rock I will build my Church.

Hymn (226, vv. 3, 6)

GOOD Shepherd, Peter, unto whom the charge was given
To close and open ways of pilgrimage to heaven;
In sin's hard bondage held may we have grace to know
The full remission thou wast granted to bestow.

Now to the glorious Trinity be duly paid
Worship and honour, praise and service unafraid,
Who in unchanging Unity, one Lord sublime,
Hath ever lived as now and to unending time. Amen.

℣. Thou art Peter. ℟. And upon this rock I will build my Church.

Ant. to Ben. Whatsoever * thou shalt bind on earth shall be bound in heaven; and whatsoever thou shalt loose on earth shall be loosed in heaven: saith the Lord to Simon Peter.

PROPER OF SAINTS

Collect

O GOD, who didst deliver thy holy Apostle Saint Peter from his bonds and suffer him to depart unhurt: vouchsafe, we pray thee; to deliver us from the bonds of our sins, and of thy mercy preserve us from all evil. Through.

Commem. of St Paul
Ant. Holy Apostle Paul, preacher of the truth and Teacher of the Gentiles, intercede for us unto God who chose thee.

℣. Thou art a chosen vessel, holy Apostle Paul. ℟. A preacher of the truth throughout the world.

Collect

O GOD, who through the preaching of the blessed Apostle Paul hast caused the light of the Gospel to shine forth upon the Gentiles: grant, we beseech thee; that we who this day call him to remembrance may feel the effectual benefit of his intercession. Through.

EVENSONG

Antiphons to Psalms as at Mattins.

Hymn (867)

RIGHT wondrously released, see, Peter freedom gains, And at the Lord's command casts off his iron chains; As shepherd and as guide, the sheepfold owns his sway, He shows to fields of life and sacred springs the way, And from his Master's flock drives guileful wolves away.

Now to the Father be eternal glory done; Our songs we raise to thee, O everlasting Son; O Spirit from on high, thy throne we bow before, To thee be honour, praise and glory evermore; The Holy Trinity we worship and adore. Amen.

℣. Thou art Peter. ℟. And upon this rock I will build my Church.
Ant. to Magn. Free us, * as God doth ordain, O Peter, on earth from our fetters; who to the blessed above dost open the heavenly portals.
Commem. of St Paul as at Mattins.

August 4
ST DOMINIC, C.
Greater double

Common, p. 201.

Collect

O GOD, who hast vouchsafed to enlighten thy Church with the merits and teaching of blessed Dominic thy Confessor: grant, we pray thee; that by his intercession we may never be destitute of thy succour in things temporal, but may continually prosper in all spiritual advancement. Through.

August 5
DEDICATION OF OUR LADY (OF THE SNOWS)
Greater double
Common, p. 211. Evensong of morrow, commem. of preceding.

August 6
THE TRANSFIGURATION OF OUR LORD
Double of II class
I EVENSONG

Ant. 1 Jesus taketh * Peter and James, and John his brother, and bringeth them up into an high mountain apart, and was transfigured before them.
2 His face did shine * as the sun, and his raiment was white as snow, alleluia.
3 And behold, * there appeared unto them Moses and Elias talking with Jesus.

Hymn (868)

ALL ye who seek, in hope and love,
For your dear Lord, look up above:
There may your faith discern the rays
Of glory bright, which Christ displays.

Behold his form all brightly glow,
Who end of days can never know;
Immortal, infinite, sublime,
Older than earth, and space, and time.

This is the Gentiles' mighty Lord,
The Prince of Judah's race adored;
To father Abraham of old,
And his posterity, foretold.

To him the Prophets witness bear,
And his divinity declare,
And this the Father's own decree:
'Hear my beloved Son,' saith he.

To Jesus, from the proud concealed,
But evermore to babes revealed,
All glory with the Father be,
And Holy Ghost, eternally. Amen.

℣. Glorious didst thou appear in the sight of the Lord. ℟. Because the Lord hath clothed thee with majesty.

Ant. to Magn. Christ Jesus, * the brightness of the Father and the express image of his substance, upholding all things by the word of his power, making atonement for our sins, to-day on the lofty mountain deigned to appear in his glory.

Collect

O GOD, who in the glorious Transfiguration of thine only begotten Son didst confirm the mysteries of the faith by the testimony of the fathers, and in the voice proceeding from the shining cloud didst wondrously foreshow the perfect adoption of all thy sons: mercifully grant; that as thou hast vouchsafed to make us fellow-heirs of the same thy Son the King of glory, so we may also be glorified together with him: Who liveth.

MATTINS

Invit. Christ, the most high King of glory: * O come, let us worship him.
Antiphons to Psalms as at I Evensong.

Hymn (869)

LIGHT of the soul, thou Saviour blest,
Soon as thy Spirit fills each breast
Away earth's clouds and darkness roll,
And sweetness overflows the soul.

How happy he who feels thee nigh,
Son of the Father, Lord most high;
Thy light in heaven doth sweetly glow,
Denied to earthly sight below.

Thou brightness of the Father's throne,
Thou love that never can be known,
Possess our souls, and bid them be
Fulfilled with love for heaven and thee.

To Jesus, from the proud concealed,
But evermore to babes revealed,
All glory with the Father be,
And Holy Ghost, eternally. Amen.

V. A crown of gold is set upon his head. R. Wherein is engraved holiness, glory and honour.
Ant. to Ben. And behold, * a voice out of the cloud, which said: This is my beloved Son, in whom I am well pleased; hear ye him, alleluia.

II EVENSONG

As at I Evensong, except:
Ant. to Magn. And when the disciples * heard it, they fell on their faces, and were sore afraid; and Jesus came and touched them, and said: Arise, and be not afraid, alleluia.

August 7
THE MOST HOLY NAME OF JESUS
Double of II class

If I Evensong is said in full, all as in II Evensong, except as below.

Ant. to Magn. He that is mighty * hath done to me great things, and holy is his name, alleluia.

℣. Blessed be the name of the Lord, alleluia. ℟. From this time forth for evermore, alleluia.

MATTINS

Invit. How excellent is the name of Jesus, which is above every name: * O come, let us worship him.

Ant. 1 Thy name * is as ointment poured forth, therefore do the virgins love thee.

2 Be ye sure * that the Lord he is God, whose name is for everlasting.

3 Young men and maidens, * old men and children, praise the name of the Lord: for his name only is excellent.

Hymn (816)

JESU, delight of heavenly host,
The song that charmest us the most,
Pure honey to the mouth thou art,
And heavenly nectar to the heart.

We taste, and for thee hunger still,
We drink, and thirst to drink our fill;
Desiring nought below, above,
Save Jesus, whom our spirits love.

O Jesu, most desired and dear,
Hope of the longing spirit here;
To thee with earnest tears we turn,
For thee our hearts impatient yearn.

Abide with us, O Lord, to-day,
In every soul thy light display;
Disperse the gloomy shades of ill,
And all things with thy sweetness fill.

Jesu, the Virgin Mother's flower,
O love supreme of gracious power;
All honour to thy name shall be
Both now and through eternity.
Amen.

℣. Our help standeth in the name of the Lord. ℟. Who hath made heaven and earth.

Ant. to Ben. He gave himself * that he might deliver his people, and obtain for himself an everlasting name, alleluia.

Collect

O GOD, who didst appoint thine only-begotten Son to be the Saviour of mankind, and didst command that his Name should be called Jesus: mercifully grant; that we who rejoice to worship his holy Name on earth many likewise attain to the fruition of beholding him in heaven. Through the same.

II EVENSONG

Ant. 1 Whosoever * shall call upon the name of the Lord shall be saved.
2 Holy and reverend * is his name; the fear of the Lord is the beginning of wisdom.
3 I will offer * the sacrifice of praise, and I will call upon the name of the Lord.

Hymn (238, i)

JESU, the very thought is sweet!
In that dear name all heart-joys meet;
But sweeter than the honey far
The glimpses of his presence are.

No word is sung more sweet than this,
No name is heard more full of bliss,
No thought brings sweeter comfort nigh,
Than Jesus, Son of God most high.

Jesu, the hope of souls forlorn,
How good to them for sin that mourn!
To them that seek thee, O how kind!
But what art thou to them that find?

No tongue of mortal can express
No letters write its blessedness:
Alone who hath thee in his heart
Knows, love of Jesus, what thou art.

Jesu, our only joy to-day,
As thou wilt be our prize for aye;
In thee may all our glory be
Both now and through eternity. Amen.

℣. Blessed be the name of the Lord, alleluia. ℟. From this time forth for evermore, alleluia.
Ant. Thou shalt call * his Name Jesus; for he shall save his people from their sins, alleluia.

August 9
ST JOHN MARY VIANNEY, C.
Double

Common, p. 201.

Collect

ALMIGHTY and merciful God, who didst wonderfully endue Saint John Mary with pastoral zeal and with a continual desire for prayer and repentance: grant, we beseech thee; that by his example and intercession we may win the souls of our brethren for Christ, and with them attain glory everlasting. Through the same.

At Mattins, commem. of Vigil of St Lawrence: Ant., ℣. & ℟. of feria.

Collect

ASSIST us mercifully, O Lord, in these our supplications, and at the intercession of thy blessed Martyr Saint Lawrence, whose festival we now approach; mercifully bestow upon us the continual succour of thy mercy. Through.

Evensong of morrow, commem. of preceding.

August 10
ST LAWRENCE, M.
Double of II class
I EVENSONG

Ant. 1 Lawrence * hath gone forth to martyrdom, and hath confessed the name of the Lord Jesus Christ.
2 Lawrence * hath wrought a good work, who by the sign of the cross hath given sight to the blind.
3 My soul * hath longed for thee, for my flesh is consumed in the fire for thee, O my God.
Hymn, ℣. & ℟. as in Common, p. 197.
Ant. to Magn. The Levite Lawrence * hath wrought a good work, who by the sign the cross hath given sight to the blind, and bestowed the treasures of the Church on the poor.

Collect

GRANT us, we beseech thee, almighty God: to quench the flames of our temptations; even as thou didst enable thy blessed servant Lawrence to overcome the fires of his torments. Through.

MATTINS

Invit. Blessed Lawrence, Christ's Martyr, is crowned in triumph in heaven: * O come, let us worship the Lord.
Antiphons to Psalms as at I Evensong; hymn from the Common, p. 198.
℣. He hath dispersed abroad, and given to the poor. ℟. His righteousness remaineth for ever.

Ant. to Ben. On the iron grate, * O God, I denied thee not; and when the fire was kindled beneath me, O Christ, I confessed thee: thou hast proved my heart and hast visited me in the night-season; thou hast tried me with fire, and hast found no wickedness in me.

II EVENSONG

As at I Evensong, except:
℣. The Levite Lawrence hath wrought a good work. ℟. Who by the sign of the cross hath given sight to the blind.
Ant. to Magn. Blessed Lawrence, * when laid and burning on the iron grating, spake to the impious tyrant, saying: The feast is ready, turn and eat; for the Church's treasures, which thou claimest, have been garnered up in heaven by the hands of the poor and needy.

August 12
ST CLARE, V.

Double

Common, p. 205, with Collect 3.

August 14
VIGIL

Collect

O GOD, who didst vouchsafe to choose the virgin womb of blessed Mary wherein to make thy dwelling-place: grant, we beseech thee; that we, being defended by her protection, may of thee be enabled joyfully to celebrate her coming festival: Who livest.

August 15
THE ASSUMPTION OF THE BLESSED VIRGIN MARY

Double of I class
I EVENSONG

Ant. 1 Mary is taken up * into heaven: the Angels rejoice, exalting and blessing the Lord.
2 Mary the Virgin * is taken up to her heavenly resting-place, where the King of kings is seated on his starry throne.
3 Thou art blessed * of the Lord, O Mary, for through thee are we partakers of the fruit of life.

I Lesson   Prov. 8.1, 22-end.
(As on Trin. XXIV at Mattins)

Hymn (840)

BLEST Maid, to highest dignity
Ordained by God eternally,
Forechosen by decree divine
To bear his Son, to call him thine.

The devil's ancient enmity
Won no dominion over thee;
With sin thy soul was never stained,
God's grace alone therein has reigned.

That Adam's loss he might retrieve
Thou didst our very Life conceive:
Flesh of thy flesh, he came to give
Himself that we through him might live.

Now death, our sinful race's dower,
No more can hold thee in its power;
Thou to the heavenly courts dost fly
To join thy gracious Son on high.

Such wondrous glories on thee rest,
Nature itself with thee is blest;
Thy holy calling was its own,
It shares with thee thine honoured throne.

Then to us exiles turn thine eyes,
Fair Queen, triumphant in the skies;
Till, aided by thy prayers, we see
Our blessed fatherland with thee.

All honour, laud and glory be,
O Jesu, Virgin-born, to thee,
Whom with the Father we adore,
And Holy Ghost, for evermore. Amen.

℣. Thou art exalted, O holy Mother of God. ℟. Above the choirs of Angels, unto the heavenly kingdom.

Ant. to Magn. O Virgin most prudent, * whither goest thou, shining forth like the dawn? O daughter of Sion, thou art all fair and gracious, fair as the moon, clear as the sun.

II Lesson   Luke 1.26-45.
(As on Advent IV at Mattins)

Collect

ALMIGHTY and everlasting God, who hast taken the Virgin Mary, the sinless Mother of thy Son, to be (in body and soul) in heavenly glory: grant us, we beseech thee; ever to reach after the things that are above, that we may be made partakers of that glory hereafter. Through the same thy Son.

MATTINS

Invit. O come, let us worship the King of kings: * To-day hath he taken his Virgin Mother to heaven above.

Antiphons to Psalms as at I Evensong.

I Lesson Gen. 3.1-15.
(As on Lady Day at Mattins)

II Lesson Matt. 1.18-23.
(As on Lady Day at II Evensong)

Hymn (841)

VIRGIN most holy, robed in
  golden sunlight,
Queen for whose crowning
  twelve bright stars were garnered,
Lady, enthronèd, with the moon
  thy footstool,
Great is thy glory.

There in the presence of thy
  Son and Saviour,
Where death is vanquished, hell
  hath no dominion,
Looking upon us, Queen of
  earth and heaven,
For us thou prayest.

We are thy children, to thy care
  entrusted:
Still are we threatened by the
  ancient serpent,
Still then, O Mother, may thy
  intercession
Aid and defend us.

Pray that the faithful find
  divine protection,
Pray that the erring to the fold
  be gathered,
Pray that the heathen, freed
  from death's dark shadow,
Come to salvation.

May thy entreaty win for
  sinners pardon,
Comfort for mourners, strength
  for all the needy;
Lighten our pathway, star of
  hope above us,
Still as we struggle.

God who hath crowned thee
  with a crown of glory,
One in three Persons, him we
  praise for ever,
Who in his mercy chose thee
  for our Mother,
Virgin most blessèd. Amen.

℣. Thou art exalted, O holy Mother of God. ℟. Above the choirs of Angels unto the heavenly kingdom.
Ant. to Ben. Who is she * that ascendeth as the dawning of the morning, fair as the moon, clear as the sun, and terrible as an army of banners?

II EVENSONG

Antiphons to Psalms as at I Evensong.
I Lesson Cant. 2.8-end.
(As on Wednesday in Easter Week at Evensong)

Hymn as in Common, p. 211.
℣. Thou art exalted, O holy Mother of God. ℟. Above the choirs of Angels unto the heavenly kingdom.

Ant. to Magn. To-day * Mary the Virgin is taken up into heaven: rejoice, for with Christ she reigneth for ever.

II Lesson   Luke 2.1-10.
(As on Christmas Day at Mattins)

August 20
ST BERNARD, ABBOT, D.
Double
Common, p. 201, with Collect 3.

August 21
ST JANE FRANCES DE CHANTAL, WIDOW
Double

Common, p. 207.

Collect

ALMIGHTY and most merciful God, who didst enkindle blessed Jane Frances with the fire of thy love, and endue her with wondrous constancy to walk stedfastly in all the paths of her life in the way of perfection, and who through her didst vouchsafe to glorify thy Church with a new offspring: grant, we pray thee, by her merits and intercession; that we who, knowing the frailty of our mortal nature do put our trust and confidence in thy mighty power, may by the help of thy heavenly grace overcome all things that are contrary to our salvation. Through.

Evensong of morrow, commem. of preceding.

August 22
THE SINLESS HEART OF THE BLESSED VIRGIN MARY
Double of II class
All as in Common, p. 211, except:

I & II EVENSONG

Ant. to Magn. My heart rejoiceth * in the Lord, mine horn is exalted in the Lord, because I rejoice in thy salvation.

Collect

ALMIGHTY and everlasting God, who in the Heart of the blessed Virgin Mary hast prepared an habitation meet for the indwelling of thy Holy Spirit: mercifully grant, that we may keep the feast of that immaculate Heart with inward devotion, and ever live after thine own heart. Through.

MATTINS

Ant. to Ben. O blessed Virgin * Mary: thou art the Mother of grace, thou art the world's hope; hearken unto us thy children that cry unto thee.

August 24
ST BARTHOLOMEW THE APOSTLE
Double of II class

All from Common, p. 194, except:

Collect

O ALMIGHTY and everlasting God, who didst give to thine Apostle Bartholomew grace truly to believe and to preach thy word: grant, we beseech thee, unto thy Church to love that word which he believed, and both to preach and receive the same. Through. Athanasian Creed at Mattins.

August 25
ST LOUIS, KING, C.
Simple

Common, p. 201.

Collect

O GOD, who didst exalt blessed Louis thy Confessor from an earthly realm to the glory of thy heavenly kingdom: grant, we pray thee; that by his merits and intercession we may be made heirs of the King of kings, even Jesus Christ thy Son: Who liveth.

August 28
ST AUGUSTINE, B.C.D.
Double

Common, p. 201.

Collect

ASSIST us mercifully, O Lord, in these our supplications: that we, whom thou dost suffer to put our trust and confidence in thy mercy, may at the intercession of blessed Augustine thy Confessor and Bishop obtain of thy goodness the wonted effects of thy compassion. Through.

August 29
THE BEHEADING OF ST JOHN BAPTIST
Greater double

MATTINS

All as in Common, p. 197, except:

Ant. 1 Now Herod had laid hold * on John, and bound him, and put him in prison for Herodias' sake.

2 When the damsel had danced, * her mother bade her: Ask for nothing else but the head of John the Baptist.

3 Give me in a charger * the head of John the Baptist. And the king was exceeding sorry because of his oath.

Ant. to Ben. Herod sent an executioner * and commanded the head of John to be cut off in the prison. And when his disciples heard it, they came and took up his corpse, and laid it in a tomb.

Collect

WE pray thee, O Lord, that this solemn festival of John Baptist thy blessed Forerunner and Martyr may effectually bestow upon us thy succour, to the attainment of everlasting salvation: Who livest.

EVENSONG

Ant. to Magn. The unbelieving king * sent his wicked servants, and commanded that the head of John the Baptist be cut off.

August 30
ST AIDAN, B.C.
Double

Common, p. 201, with Collect 1.

September 1
ST GILES, ABBOT
Commemoration

Ant. Well done, good and faithful servant, because thou hast been faithful over a few things, I will make thee ruler over many things, saith the Lord.

℣. The Lord guided the righteous in right paths. ℟. And shewed him the kingdom of God.

Collect

GRANT, we beseech thee, O Lord, that the prayers of thy holy Abbot Saint Giles may commend us unto thee: that we, who have no power of ourselves to help ourselves, may by his advocacy be aided in thy sight. Through.

September 7
ST EVURTIUS, B.C.
Commemoration

Ant., ℣. & ℟. as above for St Giles.

Collect

GRANT, we beseech thee, almighty God, that we devoutly observing the festival of blessed Evurtius thy Confessor and Bishop, may advance in true godliness, and attain unto everlasting salvation. Through.

September 8
THE NATIVITY OF THE BLESSED VIRGIN MARY
Double of II class

I EVENSONG

Ant. 1 The Nativity of the glorious Virgin * Mary, of the seed of Abraham, sprung from the tribe of Judah, of the noble stem of David.
2 From royal lineage descended * is Mary illustrious; and with deepest devotion both of soul and spirit we implore the help of her prayers.
3 With joy and gladness * let us celebrate the Nativity of blessed Mary, that she may plead for us to Jesus Christ our Lord.
Hymn as on p. 211.
℣. To-day is the Nativity of the holy Virgin Mary. ℟. Whose glorious life illumineth all the churches.

Ant. to Magn. Let us celebrate * the most honourable birth of the glorious Virgin Mary, who both attained to the dignity of motherhood, and suffered no loss of virgin modesty.

Collect

WE beseech thee, O Lord, pour into our hearts the abundance of thy heavenly grace: that like as the childbearing of the blessed Virgin Mary was unto us thy servants the beginning of salvation, so the devout observance of her Nativity may avail for the increasing of our peace. Through.

MATTINS

Invit. Let us celebrate the Nativity of the Virgin Mary: * Let us worship her Son, Christ the Lord.

Antiphons to Psalms as at I Evensong. Hymn from Common, p. 212.
℣. To-day is the Nativity of the

holy Virgin Mary. ℟. Whose glorious life illumineth all the churches.

Ant. to Magn. To-day let us devoutly celebrate * the Nativity of God's most holy Mother, the ever-Virgin Mary; from whom the Son of the Highest proceeded, alleluia.

II EVENSONG

As at I Evensong, except:

Ant. to Magn. Thy Nativity, * O Virgin Mother of God, hath proclaimed joyful tidings unto all the world; for from thee arose the Sun of righteousness, even Christ our God; who, taking away the curse, hath bestowed a blessing and despoiling death, hath given unto us life everlasting.

September 12
THE MOST HOLY NAME OF MARY
Greater double

Common, p. 211.

Collect

GRANT, we beseech thee, almighty God: that we thy faithful people, who rejoice in the Name and in the advocacy of the most holy Virgin Mary; may by her loving intercession be delivered upon earth from all evil, and attain in heaven to everlasting felicity. Through.

September 14
THE EXALTATION OF THE HOLY CROSS
Greater double

As on May 3 (p. 134), except:

Collect

O GOD, who dost gladden us upon this day by the festival of the Exaltation of the holy Cross: grant that we who have acknowledged the mystery of redemption here on earth, may finally rejoice in the fruits thereof in heaven. Through.

Evensong of morrow, commem. of preceding.

September 15
THE SEVEN SORROWS OF THE BLESSED VIRGIN MARY
Double of II class
I EVENSONG

Ant. 1 Whither is thy beloved gone, * O thou fairest among women? whither is thy beloved turned aside? that we may seek him with thee.

2 Look away from me, * I will

weep bitterly, labour not to comfort me.
3 He hath no form * nor comeliness; and when we shall see him, there is no beauty that we should desire him.

Hymn (849)

ACROSS the landscape now fall shades of eventide,
Now let the sun be veiled, the daylight banished be;
For now I bear in mind my Saviour crucified,
His woes I keep in memory.

O Mother, thou wast there sharing his suffering,
Beside that bed of death watching so patiently,
Standing beside the Cross, with heart unwavering,
Where thy Son hung on Calvary.

Before thine eyes he hung, transfixed in agony;
To that torn frame remained nor form nor comeliness;
His every wound was then a sword of misery
To pierce thy soul with new distress.

The spitting and the shame, the blows and buffetting,
The thorn-crown and the thirst, the vinegar and gall,
The nailing and the spear: in thy Son's suffering
Thy heart was wounded by them all.

While yet beside the Cross, Virgin, thou stoodest nigh,
Beyond the Martyrs brave, this wonder new arose:
Though mortal were thy wounds, Mother, thou didst not die,
Enduring all these bitter woes.

All honour and all praise to the blest Trinity,
Whom humbly I adore, and for this blessing pray
That strength like Mary's strength to me may granted be
When hard my lot and rough my way. Amen.

℣. Pray for us, O Queen of Martyrs. ℟. Who didst stand by the Cross of Jesus.
Ant. to Magn. Look not * upon me because I am swarthy, because the sun hath looked upon me; my mother's children were angry with me.

Collect

O GOD, in whose passion the sword of grief did pierce the gentle soul of the glorious Virgin Mary thy Mother, fulfilling the word of thy prophet Simeon: mercifully grant; that we who here do call to mind her sorrows may be filled with the blessed fruits of thy passion: Who livest.

Commem. of preceding.
Ant. O Cross, exceeding blessed, * which alone wast counted worthy to bear the Lord, the King of heaven, alleluia.
℣. This sign of the Cross shall be in heaven. ℟. When the Lord shall come to judgement.
Collect as above, p. 166.

MATTINS

Invit. Let us stand by the Cross with Mary the Mother of Jesus: * Through whose soul a sword of sorrow passed.

Antiphons to Psalms as at I Evensong.

Hymn (850)

O GOD, the merciful and true,
This grace be ours, with reverence due
To share the Virgin's sorrows seven,
To mourn the wounds to Jesus given.

In the sad vigil Mary kept,
How often for her Son she wept!
Lord, by her many tears, we pray
Take thou the sins of men away.

Christ's wounds our shelter here shall prove,
Our blessedness in heaven above
And all the Virgin's sorrows be
Our glory to eternity.

Jesu, all praise to thee on high,
Who for thy servants once didst die;
Whom with the Father we adore,
And Holy Ghost, for evermore. Amen.

℣. O Virgin Mary, by the virtue of so many sorrows.
℟. Make us to rejoice in the heavenly kingdom.

Ant. to Ben. O come ye, * and let us go up to the hill of the Lord; and behold ye if there be any sorrow like unto my sorrow.

II EVENSONG

As at I Evensong, except:
Ant. to Magn. Sorrow hath weighed me down, * and my face is swollen with weeping, and on mine eye-lids is the shadow of death.

September 16

SS CORNELIUS AND CYPRIAN, BB.MM.

Simple

Common, p. 199, with Collect 1.

September 17

IMPRINTING OF STIGMATA OF ST FRANCIS

Double

Common, p. 201, except:

MATTINS

Hymn, p. 202, with the third verse as follows:

Again the circling year hath brought
The blessèd day, with gladness fraught,
When in thy servant's flesh were shown
The wounds thou barest in thine own.

Collect

O LORD Jesu Christ, who when the world was waxing cold, that thou mightest inflame our hearts with the fire of thy love didst renew in the flesh of thy blessed Saint Francis the sacred marks of thy passion: mercifully grant; that by his merits and intercession we may be enabled ever to bear our cross, and bring forth fruits worthy of repentance: Who livest.

Commem. of St Lambert, from Common, p. 197, with Collect 2.

September 19
ST THEODORE, B.C.
Double

Common, p. 201, with Collect 1.

September 21
ST MATTHEW THE APOSTLE
Double of II class

All as in Common, p. 194, except:

Collect

O ALMIGHTY God, who by thy blessed Son didst call Matthew from the receipt of custom to be an Apostle and Evangelist: grant us grace to forsake all covetous desires, and inordinate love of riches, and to follow the same thy Son Jesus Christ: Who liveth.

Athanasian Creed at Mattins.

September 26
ST CYPRIAN, B.M.
Simple

Common, p. 197.   Or:

SS CYPRIAN AND JUSTINA, V., MM.
Commemoration

Ant. The hairs of your head are all numbered: fear not, ye are of more value than many sparrows.

℣. Let the Saints be joyful in glory. ℟. Let them rejoice in their beds.

Collect

O LORD, who never failest to look down in mercy on them on whom thou bestowest the succour of thy Saints: grant, we pray thee; that the intercession of thy blessed Martyrs Cyprian and Justina may evermore avail to comfort and defend us. Through.

September 29
ST MICHAEL AND ALL ANGELS
Double of I class
I EVENSONG

Ant. 1 An Angel stood * at the altar of the temple, having a golden censer in his hand.
2 While the Archangel * Michael contended with the dragon, a voice was heard of them that said: Salvation to our God, alleluia.
3 Angels and Archangels, * Thrones and Dominions, Principalities and Powers, heavenly Virtues, sing praises to the Lord of heaven, alleluia.

Hymn (241)

THEE, O Christ, the Father's splendour,
Life and virtue of the heart,
In the presence of the Angels
Sing we now with tuneful art,
Meetly in alternate chorus
Bearing our responsive part.

Thus we praise with veneration
All the armies of the sky;
Chiefly him, the warrior Primate
Of celestial chivalry,
Michael, who in princely virtue
Cast Abaddon from on high.

By whose watchful care repelling—
King of everlasting grace—
Every ghostly adversary,
All things evil, all things base,
Grant us, of thine only goodness
In thy paradise a place.

Laud and honour to the Father,
Laud and honour to the Son,
Laud and honour to the Spirit,
Ever Three, and ever One,
Consubstantial, co-eternal,
While unending ages run. Amen.

℣. An Angel stood at the altar of the temple. ℟. Having a golden censer in his hand.

Ant. to Magn. While John beheld * the sacred mystery, the Archangel Michael sounded the trumpet: Forgive us, O Lord our God, that openest the book, and loosest the seals thereof, alleluia.

Collect

O EVERLASTING God, who hast ordained and constituted the services of Angels and men in a wonderful order: mercifully grant; that as thy holy Angels alway do thee service in heaven, so by the appointment they may succour and defend us on earth. Through.

MATTINS

Invit. The Lord, the King of Archangels: * O come, let us worship him.
Antiphons to Psalms as at I Evensong.

Hymn (242)

CHRIST, the fair glory of the holy Angels,
Thou who hast made us, thou who o'er us rulest,
Grant of thy mercy unto us thy servants
Steps up to heaven.

Send thy Archangel, Michael, to our succour;
Peacemaker blessèd, may he banish from us
Striving and hatred, so that for the peaceful
All things may prosper.

Send thy Archangel, Gabriel, the mighty,
Herald of heaven, may he from us mortals
Spurn the old serpent, watching o'er the temples
Where thou art worshipped.

Send thy Archangel, Raphael, the restorer
Of the misguided ways of men who wander,
Who at thy bidding strengthens soul and body
With thine anointing.

May the blest Mother of our God and Saviour,
May the assembly of the Saints in glory,
May the celestial companies of Angels
Ever assist us.

Father almighty, Son and Holy Spirit,
God ever blessèd, be thou our preserver;
Thine is the glory which the Angels worship
Veiling their faces. Amen.

℣. An Angel stood at the altar of the temple. ℟. Having a golden censer in his hand.
Ant. to Ben. Silence was kept * in heaven, when the dragon went forth to battle; and Michael contended with him, and gained the victory, alleluia.

II EVENSONG

As at I Evensong, except:
℣. Even before the Angels will I sing praise unto thee, O my God. ℟. I will worship toward thy holy temple, and praise thy name.

Ant. to Magn. O prince most glorious, * Archangel Michael, be mindful of us: ever pray for us, here and everywhere, unto the Son of God, alleluia, alleluia.

September 30
ST JEROME, PRIEST, C.D.
Double

Common, p. 201.

Collect

O GOD, who for the exposition of thy holy Scriptures didst bestow upon thy Church the wondrous teaching of blessed Jerome thy Confessor and Doctor: grant, we beseech thee; that by the intercession of his merits we may of thee be enabled to perform those things which he taught both by word and deed. Through.

October 1
ST REMIGIUS, B.C.
Commemoration

Ant. Well done, good and faithful servant, because thou hast been faithful over a few things, I will make thee ruler over many things, saith the Lord.
℣. The Lord guided the righteous in right paths. ℟. And shewed him the kingdom of God.

Collect

GRANT, we beseech thee, almighty God: that we devoutly observing the festival of blessed Remigius, thy Confessor and Bishop, may advance in true godliness, and attain unto everlasting salvation. Through.

October 2
THE HOLY GUARDIAN ANGELS
Greater double

MATTINS

Invit. The Lord, the King of Angels: * O come, let us worship him.
Ant. 1 God shall give * his Angels charge over thee to keep thee in all thy ways.
2 Their Angels * do alway behold the face of my Father which is in heaven.
3 Praise God, * all ye Angels of his: praise him, all his hosts.

Hymn (870)

ETERNAL Ruler of the sky,
All things thou hast created lie
Within thy hand, nor pass they thence,
God of eternal providence.

So, sinful though thy people be,
Be with them, as they pray to thee,

PROPER OF SAINTS

And as the shades of night depart,
Shed thy new light in every heart.

Thy holy Angel still be near,
Chosen for our protection here;
And may his ever-watchful care
Preserve us from each sinful snare.

May he our Guardian ever be
Against the devil's trickery,
Lest we should, with unheeding mind
Be in those crafty toils entwined.

He from our fatherland drive far
The fear of foes, the dread of war;
May he preserve our civic peace,
And cause all pestilence to cease.

To God the Father praise be done;
He, who redeemed us by his Son
And poured on us the Holy Ghost,
Preserve us with his Angel-host. Amen.

℣. Even before the Angels will I sing praise unto thee, O my God. ℟. I will worship toward thy holy temple, and praise thy name.

Ant. to Ben. The Angel that talked with me * came again, and waked me, as a man that is awakened out of sleep.

Collect

O GOD, who in thine ineffable providence dost vouchsafe to send thy holy Angels to be our Guardians: grant to us thy humble servants; that we may in this life ever be defended by their protection, and in heaven rejoice in their everlasting company. Through.

EVENSONG

Antiphons to Psalms as at Mattins.

Hymn (871)

ANGELIC Guardians blest, in your high praise we sing,
And hymn the mighty aid ye from our Father bring,
To help our nature frail, lest we in danger's hour
Fall by our foes' deceiving power.

For as through woeful sin the angel traitor fell,
To lose the bliss of heaven in endless night of hell,
With burning envy still he seeks to draw astray
The souls God calls to endless day.

Then with thy sleepless watch, O Guardian true, be near,
To whom the Lord entrusts this land for ever dear,
Keep from our souls all ills, make thou all harm to cease,
Preserve our people still in peace.

All honour be to God, one holy Trinity,
The threefold world is ruled by his divinity,
Who throned in glory reigns, and shall throughout all days:
To him be everlasting praise. Amen.

℣. Even before the Angels will I sing praise unto thee, O God.
℟. I will worship toward thy holy temple, and praise thy name.

Ant. to Magn. Holy Angels, * our Guardians, defend us in the day of battle, that we perish not in the fearful judgement.

October 3
ST TERESA OF THE CHILD JESUS, V.
Double

Common, p. 205.

Collect

O LORD, who hast said, Except ye become as little children ye shall not enter into the kingdom of heaven: grant us, we beseech thee; so to follow in the footsteps of Saint Teresa thy Virgin, that in all humility and singleness of heart we may attain unto the rewards of everlasting life: Who livest.

October 4
ST FRANCIS, C.
Greater double

Common, p. 201.

Collect

O GOD, who by the merits of blessed Francis dost increase thy Church with a new offspring: grant, we beseech thee; that after his pattern we may learn to despise all things earthly, and ever to rejoice in the partaking of thy heavenly bounty. Through.

October 6
ST FAITH, V.M.
Commemoration

Ant. The kingdom of heaven is likened unto a merchant-man seeking goodly pearls: who, when he has found one pearl of great price, went and sold all that he had, and bought it.
℣. Full of grace are thy lips.
℟. Because God hath blessed thee for ever.

Collect

O GOD, who hast made this day to be honourable by the martyrdom of thy blessed Virgin

Saint Faith: grant, we pray thee; that like as thy Church doth glory in her merits, so it may at all times feel the succour of her intercession. Through.

October 7

THE HOLY ROSARY OF THE BLESSED VIRGIN MARY

Double of II class

I EVENSONG

Ant. 1 Who is she, * fair as a dove, and like a rose-tree planted beside the rivers of waters?
2 Hail, Mary, * full of grace; the Lord is with thee: blessed art thou among women.
3 The daughters of Sion * beheld her, blossoming with rose-flowers, and called her most blessed.

Hymn (851)

THE herald of the heavenly court
Prepares the shrine for Godhead's rest,
Saluting Mary, full of grace,
Mother of God, and Virgin blest.

Then to her aged cousin's home
She fares unto the hills with speed,
And lo, the prophet from his shrine
Proclaims that Christ is come indeed.

Proceeding from the Father's mind
Before the world to being came,
The Word now from a Virgin's womb
Is born a babe of mortal frame.

So to the temple comes the Child,
The Lawgiver the law obeys,
And with the price the poor must pay
The great Redeemer ransom pays.

The Mother, having mourned him lost,
With joy beholds her Son once more,
Where he among the doctors stands,
Proclaiming truths unheard before.

All praise and glory evermore
Be, Jesu, Virgin-born, to thee,
All glory, as is ever meet,
To Father and to Spirit be. Amen.

℣. Queen of the most holy Rosary, pray for us. ℟. That we may be made worthy of the promises of Christ.

Ant. to Magn. Blessed art thou, * O Virgin Mary, Mother of God, who hast believed the Lord; the things are performed in thee which were spoken unto thee; intercede for us unto the Lord, our God.

Collect

O GOD, whose only-begotten Son by his life, death and resurrection hath procured for us the rewards of everlasting salvation: grant, we beseech thee; that we, recalling these mysteries in the holy Rosary of the blessed Virgin Mary, may imitate what is shewn forth therein, and obtain what is promised. Through the same.

MATTINS

Invit. Let us celebrate the solemnity of the Rosary of the Virgin Mary: * Let us worship her Son, Christ the Lord.

Ant. 1 Rejoice, * O Virgin Mary; Christ hath risen from the tomb.

2 The Virgin Mary * is exalted above the choirs of the Angels; and on her head is a crown of twelve stars.

Hymn (852)

BENEATH the olives on the mount
The Saviour bowed in prayer is found;
He mourns, exceeding sorrowful,
While sweat of blood falls to the ground.

Through traitor's kiss to foes betrayed,
The very God, to torment borne,
Is held fast in the cruel bonds,
With scourging thongs his flesh is torn.

Twined round with bitter piercing points
The crown of shame, the crown of thorn,
Encircles now his royal head,
Who wears a robe,—the robe of scorn.

A cross of threefold weight he bears,
With streaming sweat, with gasping breath,
And falling to the ground, perforce
He drags it to the hill of death.

'Mid sinners hangs the Innocent,
Upon the cross his arms flung wide,
For those who kill him first he pleads,
Then pours his life-blood from his side.

All praise and glory evermore
Be, Jesu, Virgin-born, to thee;
All glory, as it ever meet,
To Father and to Spirit be. Amen.

℣. God hath chosen and forechosen her. ℟. He hath made her to dwell in his tabernacle.

Ant. to Ben. This day's solemnity * of the most holy Rosary of Mary the Mother of God let us celebrate with devotion, that she may intercede for us unto the Lord Jesus Christ.

II EVENSONG

As at I Evensong, except:

Hymn (853)

THE victor Christ from vanquished hell
To life returns, for death is slain;
The chains of guilt asunder burst;
The gates of heaven are wide again.

Awhile beheld by mortal eyes,
Now to the heavenly realm he goes,
And there, enthroned at God's right hand,
Like glory for his own he knows.

He sends the Holy Ghost to man,
Fulfilling what his promise said:
In sign of love the Spirit rests
In tongues of flame on every head.

Freed from the bonds of flesh at length,
His Mother enters heaven's gate
While Angels sing in jubilee
Receiving her with royal state.

A circlet of twelve stars is set
Around that gentle Mother's brow,
Next to the throne of Christ she sits,
The Queen of all creation now.

All praise and glory evermore
Be, Jesu, Virgin-born, to thee;
All glory, as is ever meet,
To Father and to Spirit be. Amen.

Ant. to Magn. O blessed Mother * and purest Virgin, glorious Queen of the world, may all perceive thine aid who celebrate thy solemnity of the most holy Rosary.

October 9

ST DENYS AND HIS COMPANIONS, MM.

Simple

Common, p. 199.

Collect

O GOD, who as on this day didst endow thy blessed Martyr and Bishop Saint Denys with strength to suffer stedfastly for thy sake, and didst join unto him Rusticus and Eleutherius for the preaching of thy glory to the Gentiles: grant us, we beseech thee; so to follow their good example, that for the love of thee we may despise all worldly prosperity and be afraid of no manner of worldly adversity. Through.

PROPER OF SAINTS

October 10
ST PAULINUS, B.C.
Double

Common, p. 201, with Collect 1. of preceding.
Evensong of morrow, commem.

October 11
THE MOTHERHOOD OF THE BLESSED VIRGIN MARY
Double of II class

I EVENSONG

Ant. 1 Blessed art thou, * O Virgin Mary, who hast borne the Creator of all things.
2 Thou hast brought forth * him who made thee, and for ever remainest a Virgin.
3 The daughters of Sion * beheld her, and called her blessed, and queens have praised her.
Hymn from Common, p. 211.
℣. Blessed art thou among women. ℟. And blessed is the fruit of thy womb.
Ant. to Magn. With joyfulness * let us celebrate the Motherhood of blessed Mary ever Virgin.

Collect

O GOD, who didst vouchsafe that thy Word should be made flesh in the womb of the blessed Virgin Mary at the message of an Angel: grant to us thy humble servants; that we, believing her to be indeed the Mother of God, may by her intercession be holpen in thy sight. Through the same.
Commem. of preceding.

MATTINS

Invit. Let us celebrate the Motherhood of the blessed Virgin Mary: * Let us worship her Son, Christ the Lord.
Antiphons to Psalms as at I Evensong.

Hymn (842)

MOST gracious Mother of the Lord,
To thee we plead with one accord:
O may thy prayers our shelter be
Against the devil's treachery.

In gracious purpose to reclaim
Our fallen race from sin and shame,
The King of all elected thee
To Motherhood's high dignity.

O look with tender pity then
On all the sinful race of men,
And to thy Son our Saviour plead,
And for our pardon intercede.

All honour, laud and glory be,
O Jesu, Virgin-born, to thee;

Whom with the Father we adore,
And Holy Ghost, for evermore. Amen.

℣. The root of Jesse hath blossomed; a star is risen out of Jacob. ℟. A Virgin hath brought forth the Saviour; we praise thee, O our God.

Ant. to Ben. Holy Mary, * succour the unhappy, help the faint-hearted, comfort the mourners, pray for the people, entreat for the clergy, intercede for the consecrated women: may all perceive thy help, who celebrate thy wonderful Motherhood.

II EVENSONG

As at I Evensong, except:
Ant. to Magn. Thy Motherhood, * O Virgin who bearest God, hath given tidings of joy to the whole world; for from thee hath arisen the sun of righteousness, Christ our God.

October 12
ST WILFRID, B.C.
Double

Common, p. 201.

Collect

O GOD, who by reason of the singular merits of thy blessed Bishop Saint Wilfrid, didst cause to shine forth in him many wondrous works: we beseech thee mercifully to grant; that like as we have learnt from his teaching to seek earnestly after all things heavenly, so we may at all times be defended by his intercession. Through.

Evensong of following, commem. of preceding.

October 13
ST EDWARD, K.C.
Double of II class

Common, p. 201.

Collect

O GOD, who didst bestow upon thy blessed Confessor King Edward the crown of everlasting glory: grant us, we pray thee; so to venerate him on earth, that we may be found worthy to reign with him in heaven. Through.

October 15
ST TERESA, V.
Double

As in Common, p. 205, except:

MATTINS

Hymn (872)

THIS is that ever-blessèd day
Whereon, upborne like whitest dove,
Teresa's dedicated soul
Soared to the hallowed courts above.

Eager she heard the Bridegroom's voice:
'Come, sister, come from Carmel's height;
Come to the marriage of the Lamb;
Come to thy crown of glory bright.'

O Jesu, Spouse of Virgin souls,
Thy name all heavenly orders praise,
And celebrate in bridal song
Thine honour unto endless days. Amen.

Collect

GRACIOUSLY hear us, O God of our salvation: that like as we do honour thy blessed Virgin Teresa in a joyful festival, so we, being fed by the sustenance of her heavenly doctrine, may learn to follow her example in godliness and charity. Through.

EVENSONG

Hymn (873)

THY father's house thou dost forsake,
Thy King, Teresa, to proclaim;
To heathen lands the Christ to bring,
Or else to suffer for his Name.

But for thee waits another death,
Another and a dearer smart,
The spear-point of the love divine
Is buried deep within thy heart.

Victim of charity, still pray
That love be kindled in us all,
And for the peoples intercede
Lest they to fires undying fall.

Praise to the Father and the Son,
And to the Comforter be praise;
Glory be thine, Blest Trinity,
Both now and unto endless days. Amen.

October 17
(1) ST ETHELDREDA, V.
Double

Common, p. 205.

Collect

O GOD, who makest us glad with the yearly festival of blessed Etheldreda thy Virgin: mercifully grant; that as we are enlightened by the pattern of her purity, so we may ever feel the succour of her merits. Through.

(2) ST MARGARET MARY, V.
Double

Common, p. 205.

Collect

O LORD Jesu Christ, who unto thy holy Virgin Margaret Mary didst in a wondrous manner reveal the unsearchable riches of thy Heart: grant unto us, loving thee above all things for thy sake; that we may after her example and through her merits find in that same Heart an everlasting dwelling-place: Who livest.

Evensong of morrow, commem. of preceding.

October 18
ST LUKE THE EVANGELIST
Double of II class

All from the Common, p. 194, except:

Collect

ALMIGHTY God, who callest Luke the physician, whose praise is in the Gospel, to be an Evangelist and physician of the soul: may it please thee; that by the wholesome medicines of the doctrine delivered by him, all the diseases of our souls may be healed. Through the merits of thy Son Jesus Christ our Lord, who liveth.

October 19
ST FRIDESWIDE, V.
Double

Common, p. 205.

Collect

ALMIGHTY and everlasting God, who art the author of virtue and lover of purity: grant, we beseech thee; that as by the chastity of her life thy holy Virgin Frideswide was well-pleasing unto thee, so we may be commended unto thee by her merits. Through.

October 24
ST RAPHAEL THE ARCHANGEL

Greater double

MATTINS

Invit. The Lord the King of Archangels: * O come, let us worship him.

Ant. 1 The Angel Raphael * was sent to Tobias and Sara, to heal them both.

2 The Angel * came in unto Tobias, and saluted him, and said: Joy be ever with thee.

3 Bless ye the God of heaven, * and praise him before all that live, because he hath shewed his mercy towards you.

(**4** Peace be unto you, * fear not: bless ye God, and sing unto him.)

Hymn (859)

THE Father's pardon from above
O Christ, bestow; thy servants spare;
And bending from thy throne of love,
Regard the blessèd Virgin's prayer.

Be ever nigh, Archangel pure,
Whose name proclaims God's healing blest;
Bring to the ailing body cure,
And solace to the mind distressed.

Bright Angels, happy evermore,
Who in your circles nine ascend,
As ye have guarded us before,
So may ye still our steps defend.

So may the realms of faith be blest,
So unbelief be chased away,
Till all within one fold find rest,
Secure beneath one Shepherd's sway.

To God the Father glory be,
Praise to the Saviour, Christ our Lord,
Praise, Holy Spirit, unto thee;
And may God's Angels be our ward. Amen.

℣. Even before the Angels will I sing praise unto thee, O my God. ℟. I will worship toward thy holy temple, and praise thy name.

Ant. to Ben. I am Raphael the Angel, * who stand before the Lord: therefore bless ye God, and tell of all his wonderful works, alleluia.

Collect

O GOD, who didst give blessed Raphael the Archangel unto thy servant Tobias to accompany him on his journey: grant also unto us thy servants to be ever defended by his succour and strengthened by his might. Through.

EVENSONG

Antiphons to Psalms as at Mattins.

Hymn (242, vv. 1, 4-6)

CHRIST, the fair glory of the holy Angels,
Thou who hast made us, thou who o'er us rulest,
Grant of thy mercy unto us thy servants
Steps up to heaven.

Send thy Archangel, Raphael, the restorer
Of the misguided ways of men who wander,
Who at thy bidding strengthens soul and body
With thine anointing.

May the blest Mother of our God and Saviour,
May the assembly of the Saints in glory,
May the celestial company of Angels
Ever assist us.

Father almighty, Son and Holy Spirit,
God ever blessèd, be thou our preserver;
Thine is the glory which the Angels worship
Veiling their faces. Amen.

℣. An Angel stood at the altar of the temple. ℟. Having a golden censer in his hand.
Ant. to Magn. O prince most glorious, * Archangel Raphael, be mindful of us: ever pray for us, here and everywhere, unto the Son of God.

October 25

SS CRISPIN AND CRISPINIAN, MM.

Commemoration

Ant. The hairs of your head are all numbered: fear not, ye are of more value than many sparrows.
℣. Let the Saints be joyful in glory. ℟. Let them rejoice in their beds.

Collect

O GOD, who dost vouchsafe unto us thy servants to keep the heavenly birthday of blessed Crispin and Crispinian thy holy Martyrs: mercifully grant; that as we here do celebrate their memory in a joyful festival, so we may be partakers in their perpetual fellowship in heaven. Through.

PROPER OF SAINTS

Last Sunday in October
OUR LORD JESUS CHRIST THE KING
Double of I class

I EVENSONG

Ant. 1 Thy name shall be called * the Peace of God, and thy throne shall be established for ever and ever.
2 His kingdom * is an everlasting kingdom, and all kings shall obey him and do him service.
3 Behold a Man, the Day-star * is his name: he shall sit and have dominion, and shall speak peace unto the Gentiles.
4 The Lord * is our judge, the Lord is our lawgiver, the Lord is our King; he will save us.
5 I have given thee * for a light to the Gentiles, that thou mayest be my salvation unto the end of the earth.

I Lesson Isa. 33.2-22.
(As at Evensong on Advent IV)

Hymn (818)

O CHRIST, to endless ages Lord,
O King, in every land adored,
The Judge of all mankind thou art,
The searcher of each mind and heart.

Though sinners still in rage defy
Thy governance, O Lord most high,
The Church to-day exulting sings
Thy glorious reign, O King of kings.

O Christ, O gracious Prince of peace,
Bid their rebellious clamour cease;
Bring to thy fold thy scattered sheep,
And all in quiet safety keep.

For this thy piercèd hands were spread,
For this thy precious Blood was shed,
For this the spear-thrust opened wide
The fountain of thy sacred side.

For this, 'neath forms of bread and wine
Lies hid that saving power divine,
Whereby thou ever dost impart
The mercy of thy sacred Heart.

Let all earth's rulers now acclaim
The glories of thy royal name;
Thee all who teach or judge confess,
And arts and laws thy truth express.

May kings to serve thee dedicate
The emblems of their royal state;
And every land and homestead be

Blest by thy gracious sovereignty.

All glory, Lord, to thee whose sway
The sceptres of the world obey;
Whom with the Father we adore,
And Holy Ghost, for evermore. Amen.

℣. All power is given unto me.
℟. In heaven and in earth.
Ant. to Magn. The Lord God shall give * unto him the throne of his father David: and he shall reign over the house of Jacob for ever, and of his kingdom there shall be no end, alleluia.

II Lesson   Matt. 28.16-end.
(As at Evensong on Trinity Sunday)

Collect

ALMIGHTY and everlasting God, who hast exalted thy beloved Son to be King over all worlds, and hast willed in him to make all things new: mercifully grant; that the kindreds of the earth, which now are wounded and estranged by sin, may speedily be brought under his gracious sovereignty: Who liveth.

Commem. of the Sunday.

MATTINS

Invit. Jesus Christ, the King of kings: * O come, let us worship him.
Ant. 1 The God of heaven * shall set up a kingdom, which shall break in pieces and consume all these kingdoms; and it shall stand for ever.
2 The Lord hath given him * dominion and glory and a kingdom; that all peoples, nations, and languages should serve him.
3 Living waters * shall go out from Jerusalem, and the Lord shall be King over all the earth.
4 He shall be great * even unto the ends of the earth; and this man shall be the peace.
5 The nation and kingdom * that will not serve thee shall perish; yea, those nations shall be utterly wasted.

I Lesson   Isa. 10.33-11.9.
(As at Evensong on Advent II).

II Lesson   Col. 1.1-20.
(As at Mattins on Christmas I)

Hymn (819)

UNFURLED the glorious banners fly,
Forth goes the Christ in triumph high;
Come, peoples all, with homage meet
The universal King to greet.

No ravage from his rule proceeds,
No terror to his triumph leads;
But on the Cross uplifted high
In love he draws all mankind nigh.

Lord, ever blest that land shall be
That dedicates itself to thee,
Whose folk with heart and hand have striven

To keep the laws that thou hast given.

Within its walls is peace, and there
No shouts of conflict rend the air;
There is no discord, no alarm,
That blessèd land no ill can harm.

There faith is kept, there Christian youth
Is fair with purity and truth,
The marriage-bond due honour holds,
And Christian grace the home enfolds.

O Christ, most gracious King, we pray,
Speed thou the coming of that day
When every land to thee its King
Shall its devoted treasure bring.

All glory, Lord, to thee whose sway
The sceptres of the world obey;
Whom with the Father we adore,
And Holy Ghost, for evermore. Amen.

℣. Of the increase of his government. ℟. And of his peace there shall be no end.

Ant. to Ben. Unto God and his Father * hath he made us to be a kingdom; who is the first-begotten of the dead, and the Prince of the kings of the earth, alleluia.

Commem. of the Sunday.

II EVENSONG

As at I Evensong, except:
I Lesson   Dan. 7.9-10, 13-14.
(As at II Evensong of Ascension Day)
℣. Of the increase of his government. ℟. And of his peace there shall be no end.
Ant. to Magn. He hath on his vesture * and on his thigh a name written: King of kings and Lord of lords; to him be glory and dominion for ever and ever.
II Lesson   Rev. 19.1-16.
(As at Evensong on Saturday before Advent)
Commem. of the Sunday.

October 28
SS SIMON AND JUDE, APOSTLES
Double of II class

All as in Common.

Collect

O ALMIGHTY God, who hast built thy Church upon the foundation of the Apostles and Prophets, Jesus Christ himself being the head cornerstone: grant us so to be joined together in spirit by their doctrine, that we may be made an holy temple, acceptable unto thee. Through the same.

Athanasian Creed.

November 1
ALL SAINTS
Double of I class
I EVENSONG

Ant. 1 I beheld a great multitude * which no man could number, out of every nation, standing before the throne.
2 And all the Angels * stood round about the throne, and fell before the throne on their faces, and worshipped God.
3 Thou hast redeemed us * by thy blood, O Lord our God, out of every kindred, and tongue, and people, and nation; and hast made us unto our God a kingdom.
4 Bless ye the Lord, * all ye his chosen: keep a day of gladness, and sing praise unto him.
5 All his Saints * shall praise him; even the children of Israel, even the people that serveth him; such honour have all his Saints.

Hymn (874)

THE Father's pardon from above,
O Christ, bestow; thy servants spare;
And bending from thy throne of love
Regard the blessed Virgin's prayer.

Bright Angels, happy evermore,
Who in your circles nine ascend,
As ye have guarded us before,
So may ye still our steps defend.

While Prophets and Apostles high
Forgiveness for our sins entreat,
Lord, hear thy servants as they cry,
And spare us at thy judgement-seat.

In purple clad, the Martyr-band,
Confessors too, a shining train,
All call us to our native land,
From this our exile, back again.

Ye choirs of Virgins, wise and chaste,
O may we share your seats on high,
With Hermits, who from deserts waste
Were called to mansions in the sky.

So may the realms of faith be blest,
So unbelief be chased away,
Till all within one fold find rest,
Secure beneath one Shepherd's sway.

To God the Father glory be,
And to his Sole-begotten Son,
And glory, Holy Ghost, to thee,
While everlasting ages run. Amen.

℣. Be glad, O ye righteous, and rejoice in the Lord. ℟. And be joyful, all ye that are true of heart.

Ant. to Magn. Angels, * Archangels, Thrones and Dominations, Principalities and Powers, heavenly Virtues, Cherubim and Seraphim, Patriarchs and Prophets, holy Doctors of the law, Apostles, all Martyrs of Christ, holy Confessors, Virgins of the Lord, Hermits and all Saints, intercede for us.

Collect

O ALMIGHTY God, who hast knit together thine elect in one communion and fellowship, in the mystical body of thy Son Christ our Lord: grant us grace so to follow thy blessed Saints in all virtuous and godly living, that we may come to those unspeakable joys which thou hast prepared for them that unfeignedly love thee. Through the same.

MATTINS

Invit. The Lord, the King of kings, O come let us worship him: * For he is the crown of all the Saints.

Hymn (249)

O SAVIOUR Jesu, not alone
We plead for help before thy throne;
Thy Mother's love shall aid our prayer
To win for us that healing care.

For souls defaulting supplicate
All orders of the Angel state,
The Patriarchs in line to thee,
The Prophets' goodly company.

For souls in guilt ensnarèd pray
The Baptist, herald of thy way,
The wielder of the heavenly keys,
The apostolic witnesses.

For souls polluted intercede
Thy Martyrs, hallowed in their deed,
Confessors high in priestly power,
And they who have the virgin dower.

Let all who served thy Church below,
And now thy heavenly freedom know,

Give heed to help our lingering strife,
And claim for us the crown of life.

* To God the Father, God the Son,
And God the Spirit, Three in One,
All honour, praise, and glory be
From age to age eternally. Amen.

℣. Let the Saints be joyful in glory. ℟. Let them rejoice in their beds.

Ant. to Ben. The glorious company * of the Apostles praise thee; the goodly fellowship of the Prophets praise thee; the noble army of Martyrs praise thee; and all the Saints and elect with one voice acknowledge thee, O blessed Trinity, one God.

II EVENSONG

As at I. Evensong, except:
℣. Let the Saints be joyful in glory. ℟. Let them rejoice in their beds.
Ant. to Magn. O how glorious is the kingdom, * wherein all the Saints rejoice with Christ, and clothed in white robes follow the Lamb whithersoever he goeth!

November 2
(or when that is a Sunday, November 3)
ALL SOULS' DAY
Double

All as in Common, p. 215.

Collect

O GOD, the Creator and Redeemer of all thy faithful people; grant unto the souls of thy servants and handmaids the forgiveness of all their sins; that as they have ever desired thy merciful pardon, so by the supplications of their brethren they may receive the same: Who livest.

November 6
ST LEONARD, ABBOT
Commemoration

Ant. Well done, good and faithful servant, because thou hast been faithful over a few things, I will make thee ruler over many things, saith the Lord.

℣. The Lord guided the righteous in right paths. ℟. And shewed him the kingdom of God.

Collect

GRANT, we beseech thee, O Lord, that the prayers of thy holy Abbot Saint Leonard may commend us unto thee: that we, who have no power of ourselves to help ourselves, may by his advocacy be aided in thy sight. Through.

November 11
ST MARTIN, B.C.
Double

MATTINS

Invit. Let us praise our God * For the testimony of blessed Martin.

Ant. 1 Lord, if thy people still have need of me, I do not refuse the labour: thy will be done.

2 With eyes and hands * ever lifted unto heaven, with dauntless spirit he ceased not from prayer, alleluia.

3 Martin * is received with joy in Abraham's bosom; Martin, here poor and lowly, entereth heaven rich, and is honoured by heavenly hymns.

Hymn as in Common, p. 203.

℣. The Lord guided the righteous in right paths. ℟. And shewed him the kingdom of God.

Ant. to Ben. O blessed Martin, * whose righteous soul possesseth Paradise; whereat the Angels triumph, the Archangels are joyful, the choir of Saints bids thee welcome, the Virgins' company inviteth: Do thou abide with us for ever.

Collect

O LORD God, who seest that we put not our trust in any thing that we do: mercifully grant; that by the intercession of blessed Martin thy Confessor and Bishop we may be defended against all adversity. Through.

EVENSONG

Antiphons to Psalms as at Mattins. Hymn as in Common, p. 202.

℣. The Lord guided the righteous in right paths. ℟. And shewed him the kingdom of God.

Ant. to Magn. O blessed Bishop, * who with all his soul loved Christ the King, and had no fear of the governance of earthly dominion! O most holy soul, which although it departed not by reason of the persecutor's sword, yet lost not the palm of martyrdom!

November 13
ST BRITIUS, B.C.
Commemoration

Ant. Well done, good and faithful servant, because thou hast been faithful over a few things, I will make thee ruler over many things, saith the Lord. ℣. The Lord guided the righteous in right paths. ℟. And shewed him the kingdom of God.

Collect

GRANT, we beseech thee, almighty God: that we devoutly observing the festival of blessed Britius thy Confessor and Bishop, may advance in true godliness, and attain unto everlasting salvation. Through.

November 15
ST ALBERT THE GREAT, B.C.D.
Double

Common, p. 201.

Collect

O GOD, who in thy Doctor and Bishop Saint Albert didst cause the light of faith to overcome the wisdom of this world: grant we beseech thee; so to follow his doctrine in holy life, that we may attain unto the perfect light of heaven. Through.

At Mattins, Commem. of St Machutus, B.C., as above for St Britius.

November 16
ST EDMUND, B.C.
Double

Common, p. 201.

Collect

O GOD, who by the providence of thine abundant bounty didst adorn thy Church with the merits of the wondrous life of blessed Edmund thy Confessor and Bishop, and gladden her with his glorious miracles: mercifully grant to us thy servants; that by his example we may learn to amend our lives, and by his intercession may be defended against all adversities. Through.

November 17
ST HUGH, B.C.
Double

Common, p. 201.

Collect

O GOD, who didst wondrously adorn blessed Hugh thy Confessor and Bishop with pre-eminent merits and glorious miracles: mercifully grant; that his example may be profitable unto us for our advancement, and his godliness for our enlightenment. Through.

November 19
ST ELISABETH, WIDOW
Double

Common, p. 207.

Collect

MERCIFUL Lord, we pray thee to pour the bright beams of thy grace into our hearts: that by the glorious prayers of thy blessed Saint Elisabeth, we may learn to despise all worldly prosperity, and ever to rejoice in all heavenly consolation. Through.

November 20
ST EDMUND, K.M.
Double

Common, p. 197.

Collect

O GOD of unspeakable mercy, who didst give thy blessed Saint King Edmund grace to overcome the enemy by dying for thy name: mercifully grant to us thy servants; that by his intercession we may be found worthy to conquer and subdue the temptations of our ancient adversary. Through.

November 22
ST CECILY, V.M.
Double

Common, p. 205.

Collect

O GOD, who makest us glad with this yearly festival of blessed Cecily the Virgin and Martyr: grant, we beseech thee; that as we do venerate her in our outward office, so we may follow the example of her godly conversation. Through.

November 23
ST CLEMENT, B.M.
Double

Common, p. 197.

Collect

O GOD, who makest us glad with the yearly festival of blessed Clement thy Martyr and Bishop: mercifully grant; that as we now observe his heavenly birthday, so we may imitate his constancy in suffering for thy sake. Through.

November 24
ST JOHN OF THE CROSS, C.D.
Double

Common, p. 201.

Collect

O GOD, who didst give to thy blessed Confessor and Doctor Saint John grace to shew forth a singular love of perfect self-denial and of carrying thy Cross: grant, we beseech thee; that we, cleaving stedfastly to his pattern, may attain to everlasting glory. Through.

November 25
ST CATHERINE, V.M.
Double

Common, p. 205.

Collect

O GOD, who on mount Sinai didst give the law to Moses, and didst mystically there bestow the body of blessed Catherine thy Virgin and Martyr: grant, we beseech thee; that by her intercession we may be brought unto that mountain which is Christ: Who liveth.

COMMON OF SAINTS

In Eastertide (except when a special Common is provided) **Alleluia** is added to the Invitatory, Antiphons, ℣℣. & ℟℟. of the Common.

COMMON OF APOSTLES

Out of Eastertide
I EVENSONG

Ant. 1 This is my commandment, * that ye love one another, as I have loved you.

2 Greater love * hath no man than this, that a man lay down his life for his friends.

3 Ye are my friends, * if ye do whatsoever I command you, saith the Lord.

4 Blessed are the peace-makers, * blessed are the pure in heart: for they shall see God.

5 In your patience * ye shall possess your souls.

Hymn (176)

LET the round world with songs rejoice;
Let heaven return the joyful voice;
All mindful of the Apostles' fame,
Let heaven and earth their praise proclaim.

Ye servants who once bore the light
Of Gospel truth o'er heathen night,
Still may your work that light impart,
To glad your eyes and cheer your heart.

O God, by whom to them was given
The key that shuts and opens heaven,
Our chains unbind, our loss repair,
And grant us grace to enter there;

For at thy will they preached the word
Which cured disease, which health conferred;
O may that healing power once more
Our souls to grace and health restore:

That when thy Son again shall come,
And speak the world's unerring doom,
He may with them pronounce us blest,
And place us in thy endless rest.

* To thee, O Father; Son, to thee;
To thee, blest Spirit, glory be;
So was it aye for ages past,
So shall through endless ages last. Amen.

℣. Their sound is gone out into all lands. ℟. And their words into the ends of the world.

Ant. to Magn. For they shall deliver you up * to the councils, and they will scourge you in their synagogues, and ye shall be brought before governors and kings for my sake, for a testimony against them and the Gentiles.

MATTINS

Invit. The Lord, the King of Apostles: * O come, let us worship him.
Antiphons to Psalms, and hymn, as at I Evensong.
℣. They declared the work of God. ℟. And wisely considered of his doings.
Ant. to Ben. Ye which have forsaken all * and followed me, shall receive an hundredfold, and shall inherit everlasting life.

II EVENSONG

Ant. 1 The Lord sware * and will not repent: Thou art a priest for ever.
2 The Lord shall set him * with the princes of his people.
3 Thou, O Lord, hast broken * my bonds in sunder: unto thee will I offer the sacrifice of praise.
4 They went on their way * weeping and bearing forth good seed.
5 Their governance * is exceeding stedfast, and thy friends are held in highest honour, O God.
Hymn as at I Evensong.
℣. They declared the work of God. ℟. And wisely considered of his doings.
Ant. to Magn. Be ye valiant * in the warfare, and fight against the old serpent: and ye shall receive an everlasting kingdom.

COMMON OF APOSTLES AND MARTYRS

In Eastertide

I EVENSONG

Ant. 1 Thy Saints, O Lord, * shall blossom as a lily, alleluia: and as the odour of balsam shall they be before thee, alleluia.
2 In the heavenly kingdom * the blessed have their dwelling-place, alleluia: and their rest for ever and ever, alleluia.
3 Within the veil * thy Saints, O Lord, do cry continually, alleluia, alleluia, alleluia.
4 O ye spirits and souls * of the righteous, sing a hymn to our God, alleluia, alleluia.
5 The righteous shall shine * like the sun in the sight of God, alleluia.

For Apostles:

Hymn (123, v. 4; 124, Pt. i)

THE sad Apostles mourn him slain,
Nor hope to see their Lord again;
Their Lord, whom rebel thralls defy,
Arraign, accuse and doom to die.

COMMON OF SAINTS

His cheering message from the grave
An Angel to the women gave:
'Full soon your Master ye shall see,
He goes before to Galilee.'

But while with flying steps they press
To bear the news, all eagerness,
Their Lord, the living Lord, they meet,
And prostrate fall to kiss his feet.

So when his mourning followers heard
The tidings of that faithful word
Quick went they forth to Galilee,
Their loved and lost once more to see.

Maker of all, to thee we pray,
Fulfil in us thy joy to-day;
When death assails, grant, Lord, that we
May share thy Paschal victory.

* To thee who, dead, again dost live,
All glory, Lord, thy people give;
All glory, as is ever meet,
To Father and to Paraclete.
Amen.

For one Martyr:
O God, thy soldiers' crown and guard, p. 196.

For Many Martyrs:
O glorious King of Martyr hosts, p. 200.
℣. O ye Saints and righteous, rejoice in the Lord, alleluia.
℟. God hath chosen you for his own inheritance, alleluia.
Ant. to Magn. Light perpetual * shall shine upon thy Saints, O Lord, and an ageless eternity, alleluia.
Collects for one or many Martyrs as on pp. 198 and 200.

MATTINS

For Apostles: Invit. The Lord, the King of Apostles: * O come, let us worship him, alleluia.
For Martyrs: Invit. Let the Saints be joyful in the Lord: * Alleluia.
Antiphons to Psalms as at I Evensong.
For Apostles:

Hymn (124, Pt. ii)

ON that fair day of Paschal joy
The sunshine was without alloy,
When to their very eyes restored
They looked upon the risen Lord.

The wounds before their eyes displayed
They see in living light arrayed,
And that they see they testify
In open witness fearlessly.

O Christ, the King of gentleness,
Our several hearts do thou possess,
That we may render all our days
Thy meed of thankfulness and praise.

Maker of all, to thee we pray
Fulfil in us thy joy to-day;
When death assails, grant, Lord that we
May share thy Paschal victory.

* To thee who, dead, again dost live,
All glory, Lord, thy people give;
All glory, as is ever meet,
To Father and to Paraclete. Amen.

For one Martyr:

Martyr of God, whose strength was steeled, p. 198.

For many Martyrs:

O glorious King of Martyr hosts, p. 200.

℣. Right dear in the sight of the Lord, alleluia. ℟. Is the death of his Saints, alleluia.

Ant. to Ben. Daughters of Jerusalem, * come forth, and behold the Martyrs with the diadems wherewith the Lord hath crowned them in the day of solemnity and rejoicing, alleluia, alleluia.

II EVENSONG

As at I Evensong, except:

℣. Right dear in the sight of the Lord, alleluia. ℟. Is the death of his Saints, alleluia.

Ant. to Magn. O ye Saints and righteous, * rejoice in the Lord, alleluia: God hath chosen you for his own inheritance, alleluia.

COMMON OF ONE MARTYR
Outside Eastertide
I EVENSONG

Ant. 1 Whosoever shall confess me * before men, him will I confess also before my Father.
2 He that followeth me * shall not walk in darkness, but shall have the light of life.
3 Whosoever serveth me, * let him follow me: and where I am, there shall also my servant be.
4 If any man serve me, * he shall be honoured of my Father which is in heaven, saith the Lord.
5 Father, I will * that where I am, there also shall my servant be.

Hymn (181)

O GOD, thy soldiers' crown and guard,
And their exceeding great reward,
From all transgressions set us free,
Who sing thy Martyr's victory.

The pleasures of the world be spurned,
From sin's pernicious lures he turned;
He knew their joys imbued with gall,
And thus he gained thy heavenly hall.

For thee through many a woe he ran,
In many a fight he played the man;

COMMON OF SAINTS

For thee his blood he dared to pour,
And thence hath joy for evermore.

We therefore pray thee, full of love,
Regard us from thy throne above;
On this thy Martyr's triumph day
Wash every stain of sin away.

* O Christ, most loving King, to thee
With God the Father, glory be;
Like glory, as is ever meet,
To God the holy Paraclete. Amen.

℣. Thou hast crowned him with glory and honour, O Lord.
℟. Thou makest him to have dominion of the works of thy hands.

Ant. to Magn. This Saint * contended for the law of his God even unto death, and feared not the words of the ungodly: for he was founded on a strong rock.

Collect

1 For a Martyr Bishop

ALMIGHTY God, mercifully look upon our infirmities: that whereas we are sore afflicted by the burden of our sins; the effectual prayers of blessed N. thy Martyr and Bishop may be our succour and defence. Through.

2 For the Same

O GOD, who makest us glad with the yearly festival of Saint N. thy Martyr and Bishop, mercifully grant; that as we now observe his heavenly birthday, so we may likewise rejoice in his protection. Through.

3 For a Martyr not a Bishop

GRANT, we beseech thee, almighty God, that as we celebrate the heavenly birthday of blessed N. thy Martyr, so by his prayers we may be established in the love of thy holy name. Through.

4 For the Same

GRANT, we beseech thee, almighty God: that by the prayers of blessed N. thy holy Martyr, we may be delivered from all adversities which may happen to the body, and from all evil thoughts which may assault and hurt the soul. Through.

MATTINS

Invit. The Lord, the King of Martyrs: * O come, let us worship him.
Antiphons to Psalms as at I Evensong.

Hymn (180)

MARTYR of God, whose strength was steeled
To follow close God's only Son,
Well didst thou brave the battlefield,
And well thy heavenly bliss was won!

Now join thy prayers with ours, who pray

COMMON OF SAINTS

That God may pardon us and bless;
For prayer keeps evil's plague away,
And draws from life its weariness.

* All praise to God the Father be,
All praise to thee, eternal Son;
All praise, O Holy Ghost, to thee,
While never-ending ages run. Amen.

Long, long ago, were loosed the chains
That held thy body once in thrall;
For us how many a bond remains!
O love of God, release us all.

℣. The righteous shall flourish like a palm tree. ℞. And shall spread abroad like a cedar in Libanus.

Ant. to Ben. He that hateth * his life in this world, shall keep it unto life eternal.

II EVENSONG

As at I. Evensong, except:
℣. The righteous shall flourish like a palm tree. ℞. And shall spread abroad like a cedar in Libanus.

Ant. to Magn. If any man will come after me, * saith the Lord, let him deny himself, and take up his cross, and follow me.

COMMON OF MANY MARTYRS

Outside Eastertide
I EVENSONG

Ant. 1 How great the torments * that all the Saints endured, that they might come in peace to the palm of martyrdom!
2 Bearing their palms * the Saints attained to the kingdom and received from the Lord's hand their crown of glory.
3 The bodies of the Saints * are buried in peace; and their name liveth for evermore.
4 O ye Martyrs of the Lord, * bless ye the Lord for evermore.
5 O ye choirs of Martyrs, * praise ye the Lord in heaven.

Hymn (182)

THE merits of the Saints,
Blessèd for evermore,
Their love that never faints,
The toils they bravely bore;
For these the Church to-day
Pours forth her joyous lay:
These victors win the noblest bay.

They, whom this world of ill,
While it yet held, abhorred;
Its withering flowers, that still
They spurned with one accord:
They knew them short-lived all,
And followed at thy call,
King Jesu, to thy heavenly hall.

Like sheep their blood they poured,
And without groan or tear
They bent before the sword

For that their King most dear:
Their souls, serenely blest,
In patience they possessed,
And looked in hope towards
  their rest.

What tongue may here declare,
Fancy or thought descry,
The joys thou dost prepare
For these thy Saints on high!
Empurpled in the flood
Of their victorious blood,
They won the laurel from their
  God.

To thee, O Lord most high,
One in three Persons still,
To pardon us we cry,
And to preserve from ill;
Here give thy servants peace,
Hereafter glad release,
And pleasures that shall never
  cease. Amen.

℣. Be glad, O ye righteous, and rejoice in the Lord. ℟. And be joyful, all ye that are true of heart.

Ant. to Magn. For theirs is the kingdom * of heaven, who despised the life of the world, and attained unto the rewards of the kingdom, and washed their robes in the blood of the Lamb.

Collect

1 For Many Martyr Bishops

DEFEND, O Lord, we beseech thee, thy servants who this day celebrate the memory of blessed N. and N. thy martyred Bishops: and grant; that by their meritorious supplication we may ever be aided in thy sight. Through.

2 For Martyrs not Bishops

O GOD, who dost vouchsafe unto us thy servants to keep the heavenly birthday of blessed N. and N. thy holy Martyrs: mercifully grant; that as we here do celebrate their memory in a joyful festival, so we may be partakers in their perpetual fellowship in heaven. Through.

3 For the same

O GOD, who makest us glad with the yearly festival of thy Martyrs N. and N.: grant, we beseech thee; that as we do rejoice in their merits, so we may be enkindled to follow them in all virtuous and godly living. Through.

MATTINS

Invit. The Lord, the King of Martyrs: * O come, let us worship him.

Antiphons to Psalms as at I Evensong.

Hymn (183)

O GLORIOUS King of Martyr hosts,

Thou crown that each Confessor boasts,
Who leadest to celestial day
The Saints who cast earth's joys away;

Thine ear in mercy, Saviour, lend,
While unto thee our prayers ascend;

COMMON OF SAINTS

And as we count their triumphs won,
Forgive the sins that we have done.

Martyrs in thee their triumphs gain,
Confessors grace from thee obtain;
We sinners humbly seek to thee,
From sin's offence to set us free.

* All laud to God the Father be,
All praise, eternal Son, to thee;
All glory, as is ever meet,
To God the holy Paraclete.
Amen.

℣. Let the Saints be joyful in glory. ℟. Let them rejoice in their beds.
Ant. to Ben. The hairs of your head * are all numbered: fear not, ye are of more value than many sparrows.

II EVENSONG

Ant. 1 These are the Saints * who gave their bodies up for the covenant of God, and have washed their robes in the blood of the Lamb.
2 The Saints through faith * subdued kingdoms, wrought righteousness, obtained promises.
3 The strength of the Saints * shall be renewed as eagles: they shall flourish like the lily in the city of the Lord.
4 God shall wipe away * all tears from the eyes of the Saints: and now there shall be no more sorrow, nor crying, neither shall there be any more pain: for the former things are passed away.
5 In the heavenly kingdom * is the dwelling-place of the Saints, and their rest for evermore.
Hymn as at I Evensong.
℣. Let the Saints be joyful in glory. ℟. Let them rejoice in their beds.
Ant. to Magn. In the heavenly kingdom * the souls of the Saints are rejoicing, who followed the footsteps of Christ their Master: and since for love of him they freely poured forth their life-blood, therefore with Christ they reign for ever and ever.

COMMON OF A CONFESSOR
I EVENSONG

Antiphons to Psalms: for a Bishop:
1 Behold a great priest, * who in his days pleased God, and was found righteous.
2 There was none found * like unto him, to keep the law of the most High.
3 Therefore with an oath * the Lord made him to increase among the people.
4 O ye priests of God, * bless ye the Lord: O ye servants of the Lord, sing a hymn to our God.
5 Good and faithful servant, *

enter thou into the joy of thy Lord.

Antiphons to Psalms: for a Confessor not a Bishop:

1 Lord, thou deliveredst * unto me five talents: behold, I have gained beside them five talents more.
2 Well done, good and faithful servant, * because thou hast been faithful over a few things, enter thou into the joy of thy Lord.
3 He is a faithful and wise servant, * whom his Lord hath made ruler over his household.
4 Blessed is that servant * whom his Lord, when he cometh and knocketh at the door, shall find watching.
5 Good and faithful servant, * enter thou into the joy of thy Lord.

Hymn (188)

HE whose confession God of old accepted,
Whom through the ages all now hold in honour,
Gaining his guerdon, this day came to enter
Heaven's high portal.

God-fearing, righteous, pure of mind and body,
Holy and humble, thus did all men find him;
While, through his members, to the life immortal
Mortal life called him.

Thus to the weary, from the life enshrinèd,
Potent in virtue, flowed humane compassion;
Sick and sore laden, howsoever burdened,
There they found healing.

So now in chorus, giving God the glory,
Raise we our anthem gladly in his honour,
That in fair kinship we may all be sharers
Here and hereafter.

Honour and glory, power and salvation,
Be in the highest unto him that reigneth
Changeless in heaven, over earthly changes,
Triune, eternal. Amen.

℣. The Lord loved him and adorned him. ℟. He clothed him with a robe of glory.

For a Bishop

Ant. to Magn. High priest and Bishop, * mighty in virtues, good shepherd of the people, pray for us unto the Lord.

1 Collect

GRANT, we beseech thee, almighty God: that we devoutly observing the festival of blessed N. thy Confessor and Bishop, may advance in true godliness, and attain unto everlasting salvation. Through.

2 Another Collect

WE beseech thee, O Lord, graciously to hear the prayers which we offer unto thee on this feast of Saint N. thy Confessor and Bishop: that like as he was found worthy to

COMMON OF SAINTS

do thee faithful service; so by the merits of his intercession we may be delivered from the chastisement we have deserved. Through.

For a Doctor

Ant. to Magn. O teacher most excellent, * O light of holy Church, O blessed N., lover of the divine law, intercede for us unto the Son of God.

3 Collect

O GOD, by whose providence Saint N. was sent to guide thy people in the way of everlasting salvation: grant, we beseech thee; that as we have learned of him the doctrine of life on earth, so we may be found worthy to have him for our advocate in heaven. Through.

For a Confessor not a Bishop

Ant. to Magn. I will liken him * unto a wise man, which built his house upon a rock.

4 Collect

O GOD, who for the remembrance of blessed N. thy Confessor dost cause us to rejoice in a yearly festival: mercifully grant; that as we now observe his heavenly birthday, so we may follow him in all virtuous and godly living. Through.

5 Another Collect

ASSIST us mercifully, O Lord, in these our supplications which we make before thee on the feast of thy holy Confessor Saint N.: that we who put not our trust in our own righteousness may be succoured by the prayers of him that found favour in thy sight. Through.

6 Collect for an Abbot

GRANT, we beseech thee, O Lord, that the prayers of thy holy Abbot Saint N. may commend us unto thee: that we, who have no power of ourselves to help ourselves, may by his advocacy be aided in thy sight. Through.

MATTINS

Invit. The Lord, the King of Confessors: * O come, let us worship him.
Antiphons to Psalms as at I Evensong.
For a Bishop:

Hymn (189)

O THOU whose all-redeeming might

Crowns every chief in faith's good fight:
On this commemoration day
Hear us, good Jesu, while we pray.

In faithful strife for thy dear name
Thy servant won the saintly fame

Which pious hearts with praise revere
In constant memory year by year.

Earth's fleeting joys he counted nought,
For higher, truer joys he sought,
And now, with Angels round thy throne,
Unfading treasures are his own.

O grant that we, most gracious God,
May follow in the steps he trod;
And, freed from every stain of sin,
As he hath won may also win.

* To thee, O Christ, our loving King,
All glory, praise and thanks we bring;
Whom with the Father we adore,
And Holy Ghost for evermore. Amen.

For a Confessor not a Bishop:

Hymn (876)

O JESU, crown above the sky,
Thou everlasting truth most high,
Who dost to thy Confessor give
Rewards with those that ever live.

Thy supplicating people spare;
O may we, holpen by his prayer,
Remission of our sins obtain,
And freedom from each binding chain.

Again the circling year hath brought
The blessèd day, with gladness fraught,
Whereon thy Saint from flesh set free
With joy ascended up to thee.

All earthly objects of desire
To him were but as filthy mire;
He deemed them with defilement soiled,
And so for things eternal toiled.

Thee, Christ, his King, most kind and blest,
With constant heart he still confessed;
And thus the crafty foe he beat,
And trampled Satan 'neath his feet.

How firm his faith and power of love!
Constant did his confession prove;
He oft was found in fast and prayer,
And now the heavenly feast doth share.

Lord Jesu, full of love and grace,
We humbly fall before thy face,
And for thy servant's sake, we pray,
Hearken, and wash our sins away.

* All praise to God the Father be,
All praise, eternal Son, to thee,
Whom with the Spirit we adore
For ever and for evermore. Amen.

℣. The Lord guided the righteous in right paths. ℟. And shewed him the kingdom of God.

Ant. to Ben. Well done, good and faithful servant, * because thou hast been faithful over a few things, I will make thee ruler over many things, saith the Lord.

II EVENSONG

As at I Evensong, except:

℣. The Lord guided the righteous in right paths. ℟ And shewed him the kingdom of God.

For a Bishop

Ant. to Magn. The Lord loved him * and adorned him: he clothed him with a robe of glory, and at the gates of paradise he crowned him.

For a Doctor

Ant. to Magn. O teacher most excellent, * O light of holy Church, O blessed N., lover of the divine law, intercede for us unto the Son of God.

For a Confessor not a Bishop

Ant. to Magn. This man, the world despising, * and earthly things renouncing, gaining the victory, laid up treasures in heaven by word and deed.

COMMON OF VIRGINS

I EVENSONG

Ant. 1 This is a wise Virgin, * and one of the number of the prudent.
2 This is a wise Virgin, * whom the Lord found watching.
3 This is she who was free * from defilement: who will have her reward in the honour paid by holy souls.
4 Come, my chosen one, * and I will set thee on my throne.
5 This is she who is fair * among the daughters of Jerusalem.

Hymn (192)

JESU, the Virgins' crown, do thou
Accept us as in prayer we bow;
Born of that Virgin whom alone
The Mother and the Maid we own.

Amongst the lilies thou dost feed,
With Virgin choirs accompanied:
With glory decked, the spotless brides
Whose bridal gifts thy love provides.

They, wheresoe'er thy footsteps bend
With hymns and praises still attend;
In blessèd troops they follow thee,
With dance and song and melody.

We pray thee therefore to bestow
Upon our senses here below
Thy grace, that so we may endure

From taint of all corruption pure.

* All laud to God the Father be,
All praise, eternal Son, to thee;
All glory, as is ever meet,
To God the holy Paraclete. Amen.

For one Virgin

℣. In thy grace and in thy beauty go forth. ℟. Ride prosperously and reign.

Ant. to Magn. Come, thou Bride of Christ, * receive the crown which the Lord hath prepared for thee for ever.

Collect

1 For a Virgin Martyr

O GOD, who among the manifold works of thine almighty power hast bestowed even upon the weakness of women strength to win the victory of martyrdom: grant, we beseech thee; that we who on this day recall the heavenly birth of Saint N. thy Virgin and Martyr, may so follow in her footsteps, that we may likewise attain unto thee. Through.

2 For the same

GRANT, O Lord, that as thy blessed Virgin and Martyr Saint N. by the merits of her chastity and godliness of conversation did ever walk acceptably in thy sight: so she may at all times effectually intercede for our forgiveness. Through.

3 For a Virgin not a Martyr

GRACIOUSLY hear us, O God of our salvation: that like as we do honour thy blessed Virgin N. in a joyful festival, so we may learn to follow her example in godliness and charity. Through.

4 For Many Virgin Martyrs

℣. The Virgins shall be brought after her to the King. ℟. Her fellows shall be brought unto thee.

Ant. to Magn. O ye wise Virgins, * take up your lamps, the Bridegroom cometh; go ye out to meet him.

Collect

GRANT, we beseech thee, O Lord our God, that we thy servants may never cease to venerate thy blessed Saints N. and N., who triumphed in a glorious martyrdom: and although we cannot worthily extol their virtue, yet we beseech thee to accept the worship we render in their honour. Through.

MATTINS

Invit. The Lord, the King of Virgins:* O come, let us worship him.

Antiphons to Psalms, and hymn, as at I Evensong.

For many Virgin Martyrs, ℣. & ℟., and Ant. as at I Evensong.

For one Virgin

℣. Full of grace are thy lips. ℟. Because God hath blessed thee for ever.

Ant. to Ben. The kingdom of heaven * is likened unto a merchant-man seeking goodly

COMMON OF SAINTS

pearls: who, when he had found one pearl of great price, went and sold all that he had, and bought it.

II EVENSONG

As at I Evensong, except:

For one Virgin

℣. Full of grace are thy lips.
℟. Because God hath blessed thee for ever.

Ant. to Magn. Come, thou Bride of Christ, * receive the crown which the Lord hath prepared for thee for ever.

COMMON OF HOLY WOMEN

I EVENSONG

Ant. 1 While the King * sitteth at his table, my spikenard sendeth forth the smell thereof.
2 We will run after thee * because of the savour of thy good ointments: greatly do the virgins love thee.
3 Lo, the winter is past, * the rains are over and gone: rise up, my love, and come away.
4 Come, my chosen one, * and I will set thee on my throne.
5 This is she who is fair * among the daughters of Jerusalem.

Hymn (193)

THE praises of that Saint we sing,
To whom all lands their tribute bring,
Who with indomitable heart
Bore throughout life true woman's part.

Restraining every froward sense
By gentle bonds of abstinence,
With prayer her hungry soul she fed,
And thus to heavenly joys hath sped.

King Christ, from whom all virtue springs,
Who only doest wondrous things,
As now to thee she kneels in prayer,
In mercy our petitions hear.

* All praise to God the Father be,
All praise, eternal Son, to thee;
Whom with the Father we adore,
For ever and for evermore. Amen.

For one Holy Woman

℣. In thy grace and in thy beauty go forth. ℟. Rise prosperously and reign.
Ant. to Magn. The kingdom of heaven * is likened unto a merchant-man seeking goodly pearls: who, when he had found one pearl of great price, went and sold all that he had, and bought it.

Collect

1 For a Martyr

O GOD, who among the manifold works of thine almighty power hast bestowed even upon the weakness of women strength to win the victory of martyrdom: grant, we beseech thee; that we who on this day recall the heavenly birth of Saint N. thy Martyr, may so follow in her footsteps, that we may likewise attain unto thee. Through.

2 For one neither Virgin nor Martyr

GRACIOUSLY hear us, O God of our salvation: that like as we do honour thy blessed Saint N. in a joyful festival, so we may learn to follow her example in godliness and charity. Through.

For Many Martyrs

℣. Thou hast crowned them with glory and honour, O Lord. ℟. Thou hast made them to have dominion of the works of thy hands.

Ant. to Magn. For theirs is the kingdom * of heaven, who despised the life of the world, and attained unto the rewards of the kingdom, and washed their robes in the blood of the Lamb.

3 Collect

GRANT, we beseech thee, O Lord our God, that we thy servants may never cease to venerate thy blessed Saints N. and N., who triumphed in a glorious martyrdom: and although we cannot worthily extol their virtue, yet we beseech thee to accept the worship we render in their honour. Through.

MATTINS

Invit. Let us praise our God: * Whom blessed N. (and N.) confessed.

Antiphons to Psalms, and hymn, as at I Evensong.

For many Martyrs, ℣. & ℟., and Ant. as at I Evensong.

For one Holy Woman

℣. Full of grace are thy lips. ℟. Because God hath blessed thee for ever.

Ant. to Ben. Give her * of the fruit of her hands, and let her own works praise her in the gates.

II EVENSONG

As at I Evensong, except:

For one Holy Woman

℣. Full of grace are thy lips. ℟. Because God hath blessed thee for ever.

Ant. to Magn. She stretched out her hand * to the poor, yea, she reacheth forth her hands to the needy, and eateth not the bread of idleness.

COMMON OF THE DEDICATION OF A CHURCH

I EVENSONG

Psalms of day (or 24, 84, 134).
Ant. 1 Holiness becometh thine house, * O Lord, for ever and ever.
2 My house * shall be called the house of prayer.
3 This is the house of the Lord, * most firmly builded, it is well founded upon a strong rock.
4 Firmly established * is the Lord's house, on a sure foundation.
5 All thy walls * are precious stones, and the towers of Jerusalem are builded with jewels.

I Lesson   I Kings 6.1-14. (As at Mattins on Monday after Trinity I)

Hymn (169)

BLESSÈD city, heavenly Salem,
Vision dear of peace and love,
Who, of living stones upbuilded,
Art the joy of heaven above,
And with Angel cohorts circled,
As a bride to earth dost move.

From celestial realms descending,
Bridal glory round her shed,
To his presence, decked with jewels,
By her Lord shall she be led:
All her streets and all her bulwarks
Of pure gold are fashionèd.

Bright with pearls her portals glitter,
They are open evermore;
And by virtue of his merits
Thither faithful souls may soar,
Who for Christ's dear sake in this world
Pain and tribulation bore.

Many a blow and biting sculpture
Fashioned well those stones elect,
In their places now compacted
By the heavenly architect,
Who therewith hath willed for ever
That his palace should be decked.

Laud and honour to the Father,
Laud and honour to the Son,
Laud and honour to the Spirit;
Ever Three and ever One;
Consubstantial, co-eternal,
While unending ages run. Amen.

℣. This is the house of the Lord, most firmly builded.
℟. It is well founded upon a strong rock.

Ant. to Magn. The Lord hath hallowed * his tabernacle: this is the house of the Lord, wherein men may call upon his name; whereof it is written: My name shall be there, saith the Lord.

COMMON OF SAINTS

II Lesson I Peter 1.22- 2.10.
(As at Mattins on Trinity XVIII)

Collect

O GOD, who in a yearly remembrance dost renew to us the day of the hallowing of this thy holy temple, and dost suffer us continually to draw near in safety unto thy holy mysteries: mercifully hear the prayers of thy people, and grant; that whosoever entereth this house to ask thy blessing may rejoice in obtaining all that he desireth. Through.

MATTINS

Invit. Holiness becometh the house of God: * Therein let us worship Christ her Bridegroom.

Psalms of day (or 48, 122), with antiphons as at I Evensong.

I Lesson I Chron. 29.10-end.
(As at Mattins on Friday after Trinity IV)
II Lesson John 10, 22-end.
(As at Mattins on Monday after Lent V)

Hymn (170)

CHRIST is made the sure foundation,
And the precious corner-stone,
Who, the two walls underlying,
Bound in each, binds both in one,
Holy Sion's help for ever,
And her confidence alone.

All that dedicated city,
Dearly loved by God on high,
In exultant jubilation
Pours perpetual melody,
God the One, and God the Trinal,
Singing everlastingly.

To this temple, where we call thee,
Come, O Lord of hosts, to-day;
With thy wonted loving-kindness
Hear thy people as they pray;
And thy fullest benediction
Shed within its walls for aye.

Here vouchsafe to all thy servants
What they supplicate to gain;
Here to have and hold for ever
Those good things their prayers obtain,
And hereafter in thy glory
With thy blessed ones to reign.

Laud and honour to the Father,
Laud and honour to the Son,
Laud and honour to the Spirit:
Ever Three and ever One;
Consubstantial, co-eternal,
While unending ages run.
   Amen.

℣. This is the house of the Lord, most firmly builded.
℟. It is well founded upon a strong rock.

Ant. to Ben. Zacchaeus, * make haste and come down, for to-day I must abide at thy house: and he made haste and came down, and received him joyfully into his house. This day is salvation come to this house from the Lord.

COMMON OF SAINTS 211

II EVENSONG

As at I Evensong, except:
Psalms of day (or 132, 133, 134),
with antiphons as at I Evensong.
I Lesson   Gen. 28.10-end.
(As at Evensong on Lent II)
℣. Holiness becometh thine house, O Lord. ℟. For ever and ever.

Ant. to Magn. O how dreadful * is this place: truly this is none other than the house of God and the gate of heaven.

II Lesson   Rev. 21.9- 22.5.
(As at Evensong on Advent III)

COMMON OF THE BLESSED VIRGIN MARY

I EVENSONG

Ant. 1 While the King * sitteth at his table, my spikenard sendeth forth the smell thereof.
2 His left hand * is under my head, and his right hand doth embrace me.
3 I am black * but comely, O ye daughters of Jerusalem; therefore the King hath loved me, and brought me into his chambers.
4 Lo, the winter is past, * the rains are over and gone: rise up, my love, and come away.
5 How fair * and how pleasant art thou for delights, O holy Mother of God.

Hymn (213)
The first verse is sung kneeling.

HAIL, O Star that pointest
Towards the port of heaven;
Thou to whom as Maiden
God for Son was given.

When the salutation
Gabriel had spoken,

Peace was shed upon us,
Eva's bonds were broken.

Bound by Satan's fetters,
Health and vision needing,
God will aid and light us
At thy gentle pleading.

Jesu's tender Mother,
Make thy supplication
Unto him who chose thee
At his Incarnation;

That, O matchless Maiden,
Passing meek and lowly,
Thy dear Son may make us
Blameless, chaste and holy.

So, as now we journey,
Aid our weak endeavour,
Till we gaze on Jesus,
And rejoice for ever.

Father, Son, and Spirit,
Three in One confessing,
Give we equal glory,
Equal praise and blessing.
Amen.

℣. Vouchsafe to receive my praises, O hallowed Virgin. ℟. Strengthen me to resist all thine enemies.

Ant. to Magn. Holy Mary, * succour the unhappy, help the faint-hearted, comfort the mourners, pray for the people, entreat for the clergy, intercede for the consecrated women: may all perceive thy help, who celebrate thy holy festival.

Collect

O LORD God almighty, we beseech thee to keep us thy servants both outwardly in our bodies and inwardly in our souls: and that at the glorious intercession of blessed Mary ever Virgin we may be delivered from our present sorrows, and attain in the end to everlasting joys. Through.

MATTINS

Invit. Holy Mary, Virgin Mother of God: * Intercede for us.

Antiphons to Psalms as at I Evensong.

Hymn (215)

O GLORIOUS Maid, exalted far
Beyond the light of burning star,
From him who made thee thou hast won
Grace to be Mother of his Son.

That which was lost in hapless Eve
Thy holy Scion did retrieve:
The tear-worn sons of Adam's race
Through thee have seen the heavenly place.

Thou wast the gate of heaven's high Lord,
The door through which the light hath poured;
Christians rejoice, for through a Maid
To all mankind is life conveyed.

All honour, laud and glory be,
O Jesu, Virgin-born, to thee;
All glory, as is ever meet,
To Father and to Paraclete.
Amen.

℣. Full of grace are thy lips. ℟. Because God hath blessed thee for ever.

Ant. to Ben. Blessed art thou, * O Mary, who hast believed; there shall be performed in thee the things which were told thee from the Lord.

II EVENSONG

As at I Evensong, except:
Ant. to Magn. All generations * shall call me blessed, for God hath regarded his lowly handmaiden.

COMMON OF SAINTS

OFFICE OF ST MARY ON SATURDAY
Simple
MATTINS

Invit. Hail, Mary, full of grace: * The Lord is with thee. (E.T. Alleluia.)
Psalms of the day with their antiphons as in the monthly course.

Hymn (215)

O GLORIOUS Maid, exalted far
Beyond the light of burning star,
From him who made thee thou hast won
Grace to be Mother of his Son.

That which was lost in hapless Eve
Thy holy Scion did retrieve;
The tear-worn sons of Adam's race
Through thee have seen the heavenly place.

Thou wast the gate of heaven's high Lord,
The door through which the light hath poured;
Christians, rejoice, for through a Maid
To all mankind is life conveyed.

All honour, laud and glory be,
O Jesu, Virgin-born, to thee;
All glory, as is ever meet,
To Father and to Paraclete. Amen.

℣. Blessed art thou among women. (E.T. Alleluia.) ℟. And blessed is the fruit of thy womb. (E.T. Alleluia.)

Antiphon to Benedictus

1. From January 14 to February 1:

A great and wondrous mystery * is made known to us this day: a new thing is wrought in nature; God is made man: that which he was he remaineth, and that which he was not he assumeth, suffering neither confusion nor yet division.

2. In Eastertide:

Joy to thee, * O Queen of heaven, alleluia; he whom thou wast meet to bear, alleluia, as he promised hath arisen, alleluia: pour for us to God thy prayer, alleluia.

3. Through the year (except Advent and Lent):

O blessed Mother of God, Mary * ever Virgin, temple of the Lord, shrine of the Holy Ghost, without a peer thou hast been pleasing unto our Lord Jesus Christ: pray for the people, entreat for the clergy, intercede for the consecrated women.

Collect

1. From January 14 to February 1:

O GOD, who by the childbearing of a pure Virgin hast bestowed upon all mankind the rewards of everlasting life: grant, we beseech thee; that we may know the succour of her intercession, through whom we have been found worthy to receive the author of life, even Jesus Christ thy Son our Lord: Who liveth.

2. At Other Times:

O LORD God almighty, we beseech thee to keep us thy servants both outwardly in our bodies and inwardly in our souls: and that at the glorious intercession of blessed Mary ever Virgin we may be delivered from our present sorrows, and attain in the end to everlasting joys. Through.

OFFICE OF THE DEAD

Instead of Glory be to the Father, there is said at the end of Psalms and Canticles:

Rest eternal * grant unto them, O Lord.
And let light perpetual * shine upon them.

MATTINS

Invit. The King to whom all things live: * O come let us worship him.
Ant. 1 Make thy way plain, * O Lord, before my face. Ps. 5.
2 Turn thee, * O Lord, and deliver my soul: for in death no man remembereth thee. Ps. 6.
3 Lest he devour my soul * like a lion, and tear it in pieces, while there is none to help. Ps. 7.

I Lesson Wis. 4.7-end.
(As at Evensong on Tuesday before Advent)
Ant. From the gate of hell * deliver my soul, O Lord.

The Song of Hezekiah
Isa. 38.10-20.

I SAID: In the cutting off of my days * I shall go down to the gates of the grave.
I am deprived of the residue of my years. * I said: I shall not see the Lord, even the Lord, in the land of the living.
I shall behold man no more, * with the inhabitants of the world.
Mine age is departed, and is removed from me, * as a shepherd's tent.
I have cut off like a weaver my life: * he will cut me off with pining sickness;
From day even to night * wilt thou make an end of me.
I reckoned till morning, that, as a lion, so will he break all my bones: * from day even to night wilt thou make an end of me;
Like a crane, or a swallow, so did I chatter, * I did mourn as a dove;
Mine eyes fail with looking upward: * O Lord, I am oppressed, undertake for me.
What shall I say? He hath both spoken unto me, and himself hath done it. * I shall go softly all my years in the bitterness of my soul.
O Lord, by these things men live, and in all these things is the life of my spirit, * so wilt thou recover me, and make me to live.
Behold, for peace I had great bitterness: but thou hast in love for my soul delivered it from the pit of corruption: * for thou hast cast all my sins behind thy back.
For the grave cannot praise thee, death cannot celebrate thee: * they that go down into the pit cannot hope for thy truth.
The Lord was ready to save me: * therefore will we sing my songs to the stringed instruments all the days of our life in the house of the Lord.
Rest eternal * grant unto them, O Lord.

And let light perpetual * shine upon them.
Ant. From the gate of hell * deliver my soul, O Lord.

II Lesson   I Cor. 15.35-end. (As at Mattins on Easter II)
℣. I heard a voice from heaven, saying unto me. ℟. Blessed are the dead which die in the Lord.
Ant. to Ben. I am * the resurrection and the life: he that believeth in me, though he were dead, yet shall he live; and whosoever liveth and believeth in me, shall never die.

Then is said kneeling:

Our Father, silently until:
℣. And lead us not into temptation. ℟. But deliver us from evil.

The following Psalm is not said on the day of death or burial, nor when the Office is said under the double rite.

Psalm 130

OUT of the deep have I called unto thee, O Lord: * Lord, hear my voice.

O let thine ears consider well * the voice of my complaint.

If thou, Lord, wilt be extreme to mark what is done amiss: * O Lord, who may abide it?

For there is mercy with thee: * therefore shalt thou be feared.

I look for the Lord; my soul doth wait for him: * in his word is my trust.

My soul fleeth unto the Lord * before the morning watch, I say before the morning watch.

O Israel, trust in the Lord, for with the Lord there is mercy: * and with him is plenteous redemption.

And he shall redeem Israel * from all his sins.

Rest eternal * grant unto them, O Lord.

And let light perpetual * shine upon them.
℣. From the gate of hell.
℟. Deliver *his soul*, O Lord.
℣. May *he* rest in peace.
℟. Amen.
℣. The Lord be with you.
℟. And with thy spirit.

Let us pray.

1   Collect
Day of Burial

ABSOLVE, we beseech thee, O Lord, the soul of thy servant (handmaid) N., that being dead unto the world *he* may live unto thee: and whatsoever *he* hath done amiss in *his* earthly life through the frailty of the flesh, do thou in the pitifulness of thy great goodness pardon and purge away. Through.

2 On the 3rd, 7th and 30th days after burial

WE beseech thee, O Lord, that the soul of thy servant (handmaid) N., whose body *three* days since we did commit unto the ground, may be made partaker of the fellowship of thine elect; and that thou wouldest pour upon *him* the continual dew of thy mercy. Through.

3 On the Anniversary

O GOD, to whom alone belongeth the forgiveness of sins: grant, we pray thee, to the souls of thy *servants (and handmaidens)*, the anniversary of whose burial we now commemorate, to find a place of refreshing, and the blessedness of thy rest, and to enjoy the glory of everlasting light. Through.

4 For a Bishop or Priest

O GOD, who didst cause thy servant, N. for whom we pray, to enjoy the office of *bishop (priest)* after the order of thine Apostles: grant unto him, we beseech thee; finally to rejoice in the company of those thy Saints in heaven whose ministry he did sometime share on earth. Through.

5 For a Man Departed

INCLINE thine ear, O Lord, unto the prayers wherewith we humbly entreat thy mercy: that the soul of thy servant N., which thou hast bidden to depart this life, may by thee be set in the abode of peace and light, and made partaker of the eternal fellowship of thine elect. Through.

6 For a Woman Departed

WE beseech thee, O Lord, of thy loving kindness to have mercy on the soul of thine handmaiden N.: that being purged from all defilements of our mortal nature, she may be restored to the portion of everlasting felicity. Through.

7 For Brethren, Kinsfolk and Benefactors

The second Collect under 9 below.

8 For Father and Mother

O GOD, who didst command thy people, saying, Honour thy father and thy mother: of thy loving kindness have mercy on the *souls of my father and mother*, and forgive *them* all *their* sins; and *I* humbly pray thee that thou wouldest grant unto *me* to behold *their faces* in the glory of everlasting felicity. Through.

9 In the Office of the Dead through the Year

O GOD, who didst cause thy servants, for whom we pray, to enjoy the dignity of the priesthood, and some to be bishops after the order of thine Apostles: grant unto them, we beseech thee, finally to rejoice in the company of those thy Saints in heaven whose ministry they did sometime share on earth. Through.

O GOD, who desirest not the death of a sinner, but rather that all mankind should be saved: we beseech thee mercifully to grant that the brethren, kinsfolk and benefactors of our congregation who have passed out of this world, may by the intercession of blessed Mary ever Virgin and of all thy Saints come to enjoy with them everlasting blessedness.

O GOD, the Creator and Redeemer of all thy faithful people: grant unto the souls of thy servants and handmaids the remission of all their sins: that as they have ever desired thy merciful pardon, so by the supplications of their brethren they may receive the same: Who livest.

℣. Rest eternal grant unto them, O Lord. ℟. And let light perpetual shine upon them.
℣. May they rest in peace. ℟. Amen.

EVENSONG

Ant. 1 I will walk * before the Lord in the land of the living. Ps. 116.
2 Woe is me, O Lord, * that I am constrained to dwell with Mesech. Ps. 120.
3 The Lord shall preserve thee * from all evil: yea, it is even he that shall keep thy soul. Ps. 121.
4 If what is done amiss * thou wilt be extreme to mark, O Lord: O Lord, who may abide it? Ps. 130.
5 Despise not, * O Lord, the works of thine own hands. Ps. 138.

I Lesson   Job 19.21-27. (As at Evensong on Easter Eve)
℣. I heard a voice from heaven saying unto me. ℟. Blessed are the dead which die in the Lord.

Ant. to Magn. All * that the Father hath given me shall come to me: and him that cometh unto me, I will in no wise cast out.

II Lesson   I Thess. 4.13-end. (As at Evensong on Thursday in Easter Week)

Nunc Dimittis is said without antiphon.
Then is said kneeling:
Our Father, silently until:
℣. And lead us not into temptation. ℟. But deliver us from evil.

The following Psalm is not said on the day of death or burial, nor when the Office is said under the double rite.

Psalm 146

PRAISE the Lord, O my soul; while I live will I praise the Lord: * yea, as long as I have any being, I will sing praises unto my God.

O put not your trust in princes, nor in any child of man: * for there is no help in them.

For when the breath of man goeth forth he shall turn again to his earth, * and then all his thoughts perish.

Blessed is he that hath the God of Jacob for his help, * and whose hope is in the Lord his God.

Who made heaven and earth, the sea, and all that therein is: * who keepeth his promise for ever;

Who helpeth them to right that suffer wrong: * who feedeth the hungry.

The Lord looseth men out of prison: * the Lord giveth sight to the blind.

The Lord helpeth them that

OFFICE OF THE DEAD

are fallen: * the Lord careth for the righteous.

The Lord careth for the strangers; he defendeth the fatherless and widow, * as for the way of the ungodly, he turneth it upside down.

The Lord thy God, O Sion, shall be King for evermore, * and throughout all generations.

Rest eternal * grant unto them, O Lord.

And let light perpetual * shine upon them.

℣. From the gate of hell.
℟. Deliver *his soul*, O Lord.
℣. May *he* rest in peace.
℟. Amen.
℣. O Lord, hear my prayer.
℟. And let my cry come unto thee.
℣. The Lord be with you.
℟. And with thy spirit.
Let us pray.

Collect and conclusion as at Mattins.

THE LITANY

O GOD the Father, of heaven, have mercy upon us miserable sinners.
O God the Father, of heaven, have mercy upon us miserable sinners.
O God the Son, Redeemer of the world, have mercy upon us miserable sinners.
O God the Son, Redeemer of the world, have mercy upon us miserable sinners.
O God the Holy Ghost, proceeding from the Father and the Son, have mercy upon us miserable sinners.
O God the Holy Ghost, proceeding from the Father and the Son, have mercy upon us miserable sinners.
O holy, blessed and glorious Trinity, three Persons and one God, have mercy upon us miserable sinners.
O holy, blessed and glorious Trinity, three Persons and one God, have mercy upon us miserable sinners.
Remember not, Lord, our offences, nor the offences of our forefathers; neither take thou vengeance of our sins: spare us, good Lord, whom thou hast redeemed with thy most precious blood, and be not angry with us for ever.
Spare us, good Lord.
From all evil and mischief; from sin, from the crafts and assaults of the devil; from thy wrath, and from everlasting damnation.
Good Lord, deliver us.
From all blindness of heart; from pride, vain-glory and hypocrisy; from envy, hatred and malice, and all uncharitableness,
From fornication, and all other deadly sin; and from all the deceits of the world, the flesh, and the devil,
From lightning and tempest; from plague, pestilence, and famine; from battle and murder, and from sudden death,
From all sedition, privy conspiracy, and rebellion; from all false doctrine, heresy, and schism; from hardness of heart, and contempt of thy Word and Commandment,
By the mystery of thy holy Incarnation; by thy holy nativity and circumcision; by thy baptism, fasting, and temptation,
By thine agony and bloody sweat; by thy cross and passion; by thy precious death and burial; by thy glorious resurrection and ascension; and by the coming of the Holy Ghost,
In all time of our tribulation; in all time of our wealth; in the hour of death, and in the day of judgement,
We sinners do beseech thee to hear us, O Lord God; and that it may please thee to rule and govern thy holy Church universal in the right way;
We beseech thee to hear us, good Lord.
That it may please thee to keep and strengthen in the true worshipping of thee, in righteousness and holiness of life, thy

servant Elizabeth, our most gracious Queen and Governor.

That it may please thee to rule her heart in thy faith, fear, and love, and that she may evermore have affiance in thee, and ever seek thy honour and glory;

That it may please thee to be her defender and keeper, giving her the victory over all her enemies;

That it may please thee to bless and preserve Elizabeth the Queen Mother, Philip Duke of Edinburgh, Charles Duke of Cornwall, and all the Royal Family;

That it may please thee to illuminate all bishops, priests and deacons, with true knowledge and understanding of thy Word; and that both by their preaching and living they may set it forth, and shew it accordingly;

That it may please thee to endue the Lords of the Council, and all the nobility, with grace, wisdom and understanding;

That it may please thee to bless and keep the magistrates, giving them grace to execute justice, and to maintain truth;

That it may please thee to bless and keep all thy people;

That it may please thee to give to all nations unity, peace and concord;

That it may please thee to give us an heart to love and dread thee, and diligently to live after thy commandments;

That it may please thee to give to all thy people increase of grace to hear meekly thy Word, and to receive it with pure affection, and to bring forth the fruits of the Spirit;

That it may please thee to bring into the way of truth all such as have erred, and are deceived;

That it may please thee to strengthen such as do stand; and to comfort and help the weak-hearted; and to raise up them that fall; and finally to beat down Satan under our feet;

That it may please thee to succour, help, and comfort, all that are in danger, necessity, and tribulation;

That it may please thee to preserve all that travel by land or by water, all women labouring of child, all sick persons, and young children; and to shew thy pity upon all prisoners and captives;

That it may please thee to defend, and provide for, the fatherless children, and widows, and all that are desolate and oppressed;

That it may please thee to have mercy upon all men;

That it may please thee to forgive our enemies, persecutors, and slanderers, and to turn their hearts;

That it may please thee to give and preserve to our use the kindly fruits of the earth, so as in due time we may enjoy them;

That it may please thee to give us true repentance; to forgive us all our sins, negligences, and ignorances; and to endue us with the grace of thy Holy Spirit to amend our lives according to thy holy Word;

Son of God, we beseech thee to hear us.
Son of God, we beseech thee to hear us.
O Lamb of God, that takest away the sins of the world;
Grant us thy peace.
O Lamb of God, that takest away the sins of the world;
Have mercy upon us.
O Christ, hear us.
O Christ, hear us.
Lord, have mercy upon us.
Lord, have mercy upon us.
Christ, have mercy upon us.
Christ, have mercy upon us.
Lord, have mercy upon us.
Lord, have mercy upon us.
Our Father . . . but deliver us from evil. Amen.

℣. O Lord, deal not with us after our sins. ℟. Neither reward us after our iniquities.

Let us pray.

O GOD, merciful Father, that despisest not the sighing of a contrite heart, nor the desire of such as be sorrowful: mercifully assist our prayers that we make before thee in all our troubles and adversities, whensoever they oppress us; and graciously hear us, that those evils, which the craft or subtlety of the devil or man worketh against us be brought to nought; and by the providence of thy goodness they may be dispersed; that we thy servants, being hurt by no persecutions, may evermore give thanks unto thee in thy holy Church. Through Jesus Christ our Lord.

O Lord, arise, help us, and deliver us for thy name's sake.
O God, we have heard with our ears, and our fathers have declared unto us: the noble works that thou didst in their days, and in the old time before them.
O Lord, arise, help us, and deliver us for thine honour.
℣. Glory be to the Father, and to the Son, and to the Holy Ghost. ℟. As it was in the beginning is now, and ever shall be, world without end. Amen.
℣. From our enemies defend us, O Christ. ℟. Graciously look upon our afflictions.
℣. Pitifully behold the sorrows of our hearts. ℟. Mercifully forgive the sins of thy people.
℣. Favourably with mercy hear our prayers. ℟. O Son of David, have mercy upon us.
℣. Both now and ever vouchsafe to hear us, O Christ. ℟. Graciously hear us, O Christ; graciously hear us, O Lord Christ.
℣. O Lord, let thy mercy be shewed upon us. ℟. As we do put our trust in thee.

Let us pray.

WE humbly beseech thee, O Father, mercifully to look upon our infirmities; and for the glory of thy name turn from us all those evils that we most righteously have deserved; and grant, that in all our troubles we may put our whole trust and confidence in thy mercy and, evermore serve thee in holiness and pureness of living, to thy honour and glory; through our only Mediator and Advocate, Jesus Christ our Lord. ℟. Amen.

ALMIGHTY God, who hast given us grace at this time with one accord to make our common supplications unto thee; and dost promise, that when two or three are gathered together in thy name, thou wilt grant their requests; fulfil now, O Lord, the desires and petitions of thy servants, as may be most expedient for them; granting us in this world knowledge of thy truth, and in the world to come life everlasting. ℟. Amen.

The grace of our Lord Jesus Christ, and the love of God, and the fellowship of the Holy Ghost, be with us all evermore. ℟. Amen.

ORDER OF COMMENDING A SOUL

SHORT LITANY

KYRIE, eleison.
Christe, eleison.
Kyrie, eleison.
Holy Mary, *pray for him* (*her*).
All ye holy Angels and Archangels,
Holy Abel,
All ye choir of the Righteous,
Holy Abraham,
Holy John Baptist,
Holy Joseph,
All ye holy Patriarchs and Prophets,
Holy Peter,
Holy Paul,
Holy Andrew,
Holy John,
All ye holy Apostles and Evangelists,
All ye holy Disciples of the Lord,
All ye holy Innocents,
Holy Stephen,
Holy Lawrence,
All ye holy Martyrs,
Holy Silvester,
Holy Gregory,
Holy Augustine,
All ye holy Bishops and Confessors,
Holy Benedict,
Holy Francis,
Holy Camillus,
Holy John of God,
All ye holy Monks and Hermits,
Holy Mary Magdalene,
Holy Lucy,
All ye holy Virgins and Widows,
All ye Saints of God, *intercede for him.*
Be thou merciful, *good Lord, spare him.*
Be thou merciful, *good Lord, deliver him.*
From thy wrath,
From the peril of death,
From an evil death,
From the pains of hell,
From all evil,
From the power of the devil,
By thy nativity,
By thy cross and passion,
By thy death and burial,
By thy glorious resurrection,
By thy wonderful ascension,
By the grace of the Holy Ghost the Comforter,
In the day of judgement,
Kyrie, eleison. Christe, eleison. Kyrie, eleison.

Prayer

GO forth, Christian soul, out of this world, in the name of God, the Father almighty, who created thee; in the name of Jesus Christ, the Son of the living God, who suffered for thee; in the name of the Holy Ghost, who was poured forth upon thee; in the name of the glorious and holy Mother of God, the Virgin Mary; in the name of blessed Joseph, the illustrious Spouse of that same Virgin; in the name of Angels and Archangels; in the name of Thrones and Dominations; in the name of Principalities and Powers; in the name of Cherubim and Seraphim; in the name of Patriarchs and Prophets; in the name of the holy Apostles and Evangelists; in the name of the holy Martyrs and Confessors; in the name of the holy Monks and Hermits; in the name of the holy Virgins, and of all the Saints of God; may thine abode this day be in peace, and thy dwelling-place in holy Sion. Through the same Christ our Lord. ℟. Amen.

Another Prayer of Commendation

O ALMIGHTY God, with whom do live the spirits of just men made perfect, after they are delivered from their earthly prisons; we humbly commend the soul of this thy servant, our dear *brother* into thy hands, as into the hands of a faithful Creator, and most merciful Saviour; most humbly beseeching thee that it may be precious in thy sight. Wash it, we pray thee, in the blood of that immaculate Lamb, that was slain to take away the sins of the world; that whatsoever defilements it may have contracted in the midst of this miserable and naughty world, through the lusts of the flesh, or the wiles of Satan, being purged and done away, it may be presented pure and without spot before thee. And teach us who survive, in this and other like daily spectacles of mortality, to see how frail and uncertain our own condition is; and so to number our days, that we may seriously apply our hearts to that holy and heavenly wisdom, whilst we live here, which may in the end bring us to life everlasting, through the merits of Jesus Christ thine only Son our Lord. ℟. Amen.

At the Expiry

Jesus, Jesus, Jesus.
Into thy hands, O Lord, I commend my spirit.

After the Death
Respond

℟. Come to *his* aid, ye Saints of God; come forth to meet *him*, ye Angels of the Lord, * Receive *his* soul, * Offer it also in the sight of the Most High. ℣. May Christ receive thee, who hath called thee, and may the Angels lead thee to Abraham's bosom. ℟. Receive *his* soul, * Offer it also in the sight of the Most High. ℣. Rest eternal grant unto *him*, O Lord: and let light perpetual shine upon *him*. * Offer it also in the sight of the Most High.

Kyrie, eleison. Christie, eleison.
  Kyrie, eleison.
Our Father.
℣. And lead us not into temptation. ℟. But deliver us from evil.
℣. From the gate of hell.
℟. Deliver *his* soul, O Lord.
℣. May *he* rest in peace.
℟. Amen.
℣. O Lord, hear my prayer.
℟. And let my cry come unto thee.
℣. The Lord be with you.
℟. And with thy spirit.

Let us pray.

WE commend unto thee, O Lord, the soul of thy servant (handmaid) N., that being dead unto the world, *he* may live unto thee; and whatsoever *he* hath done amiss through the frailty of our human nature, do thou in the pitifulness of thy great goodness pardon and purge away. Through Christ our Lord. ℟. Amen.

ITINERARY

If the journey is to be made alone, the following is said in the singular number; if with others, as printed.

Ant. Into the way.

Benedictus

BLESSED be the Lord God of Israel, * for he hath visited, and redeemed his people;

And hath raised up a mighty salvation for us * in the house of his servant David;

As he spake by the mouth of his holy Prophets, * which have been since the world began:

That we should be saved from our enemies, * and from the hands of all that hate us;

To perform the mercy promised to our forefathers, * and to remember his holy covenant;

To perform the oath which he sware to our forefather Abraham, * that he would give us,

That we, being delivered out of the hands of our enemies, * might serve him without fear.

In holiness and righteousness before him * all the days of our life.

And thou, child, shalt be called the Prophet of the Highest, * for thou shalt go before the face of the Lord to prepare his ways,

To give knowledge of salvation unto his people * for the remission of their sins,

Through the tender mercy of our God, * whereby the Dayspring from on high hath visited us,

To give light to them that sit in darkness and in the shadow of death, * and to guide our feet into the way of peace.

Glory be to the Father.

Ant. Into the way of peace and prosperity direct us, almighty and merciful Lord, and may the Angel Raphael go with us on our journey; that we may return to our homes in peace, safety and joy.

Kyrie, eleison. Christe, eleison. Kyrie, eleison.
Our Father, *silently until:*
℣. And lead us not into temptation. ℟. But deliver us from evil.
℣. O Lord, save thy servants. ℟. Who put their trust in thee.
℣. Be unto us, O Lord, a tower of strength. ℟. From the face of our enemy.
℣. Let the enemy have no occasion against us. ℟. Nor the son of wickedness approach to hurt us.
℣. Blessed be the Lord daily. ℟. And may the God of our salvation make our journey prosperous.
℣. Shew us thy ways, O Lord. ℟. And teach us thy paths.

℣. O that our ways were made so direct. ℟. That we might keep thy statutes.
℣. The crooked ways shall be made straight. ℟ And the rough places plain.
℣. God shall give his Angels charge concerning thee. ℟. To keep thee in all thy ways.
℣. O Lord, hear my prayer. ℟. And let my cry come unto thee.
℣. The Lord be with you. ℟. And with thy spirit.

Let us pray.

O GOD, who didst cause the children of Israel to go dryshod through the midst of the sea, and who by the leading of a star didst guide the Wise Men on their way to thee: grant us, we beseech thee; a prosperous journey and a quiet time; that, attended by thy holy Angel, we may now safely reach the place whither we are going, and at last come to the haven of eternal salvation.

O GOD, who didst lead thy servant Abraham out of Ur of the Chaldees, and preserve him unhurt throughout all the paths of his pilgrimage: we beseech thee; that thou wouldest vouchsafe to guard us thy servants: be unto us, O Lord, a support in setting out, a solace on the way, a shadow in the heat, a shelter from rain and cold, a chariot in weariness, a protection in danger, a staff in slippery places, a harbour in shipwreck; that by thy guidance we may happily reach the place whither we go, and at length come safely home.

ASSIST us mercifully, O Lord, in these our supplications and prayers, and dispose the way of thy servants towards the attainment of everlasting salvation; that among all the changes and chances of this mortal life, we may ever be defended by thy most gracious and ready help.

GRANT, we beseech thee, almighty God: that thy family may walk in the way of salvation; and by following the counsels of blessed John the Forerunner, may come in safety unto him whom he foretold, even Jesus Christ thy Son, our Lord: Who liveth and reigneth with thee in the unity of the Holy Ghost, ever one God, world without end. ℟. Amen.

℣. Let us go forth in peace. ℟. In the name of the Lord. Amen.

PRAYERS BEFORE AND AFTER MASS
PREPARATION FOR MASS

Ant. Remember not, * Lord, our offences, nor the offences of our forefathers, neither take thou vengeance of our sins. (E.T. Alleluia.)

Psalm 84

O HOW amiable are thy dwellings, * thou Lord of hosts!

My soul hath a desire and longing to enter into the courts of the Lord: * my heart and my flesh rejoice in the living God.

Yea, the sparrow hath found her an house, and the swallow a nest where she may lay her young: * even thy altars, O Lord of hosts, my King and my God.

Blessed are they that dwell in thy house, * they will be alway praising thee.

Blessed is the man whose strength is in thee, * in whose heart are thy ways.

Who going through the vale of misery use it for a well: * and the pools are filled with water.

They will go from strength to strength: * and unto the God of gods appeareth every one of them in Sion.

O Lord God of hosts, hear my prayer: * hearken, O God of Jacob.

Behold, O God our defender, * and look upon the face of thine Anointed.

For one day in thy courts * is better than a thousand.

I had rather be a door-keeper in the house of my God, * than to dwell in the tents of ungodliness.

For the Lord God is a light and defence: * the Lord shall give grace and worship, and no good thing shall he withhold from them that live a godly life.

O Lord of hosts, * blessed is the man that putteth his trust in thee.

Psalm 85

LORD, thou art become gracious unto thy land: * thou hast turned away the captivity of Jacob.

Thou hast forgiven the offence of thy people, * and covered all their sins.

Thou hast taken away all thy displeasure, * and turned thyself from thy wrathful indignation.

Turn us then, O God our Saviour, * and let thine anger cease from us.

Wilt thou be displeased at us for ever, * and wilt thou stretch out thy wrath from one generation to another?

Wilt thou not turn again, and quicken us, * that thy people may rejoice in thee?

Shew us thy mercy, O Lord, * and grant us thy salvation.

I will hearken what the Lord God will say concerning me: * for he shall speak peace unto his people, and to his saints, that they turn not again.

For his salvation is nigh them that fear him: * that glory may dwell in our land.

Mercy and truth are met together, * righteousness and peace have kissed each other.

Truth shall flourish out of the earth, * and righteousness hath looked down from heaven.

Yea, the Lord shall shew loving-kindness, * and our land shall give her increase.

Righteousness shall go before him, * and he shall direct his going in the way.

Psalm 86

BOW down thine ear, O Lord, and hear me, * for I am poor, and in misery.

Preserve thou my soul, for I am holy: * my God, save thy servant that putteth his trust in thee.

Be merciful unto me, O Lord, * for I will call daily upon thee.

Comfort the soul of thy servant, * for unto thee, O Lord, do I lift up my soul.

For thou, Lord, art good and gracious * and of great mercy unto all them that call upon thee.

Give ear, Lord, unto my prayer, * and ponder the voice of my humble desires.

In the time of my trouble I will call upon thee, * for thou hearest me.

Among the gods there is none like unto thee, O Lord: * there is not one that can do as thou doest.

All nations whom thou hast made shall come and worship thee, O Lord, * and shall glorify thy name.

For thou art great, and doest wondrous things: * thou art God alone.

Teach me thy way, O Lord, and I will walk in thy truth: * O knit my heart unto thee, that I may fear thy name.

I will thank thee, O Lord my God, with all my heart, * and will praise thy name for evermore.

For great is thy mercy toward me, * and they hast delivered my soul from the nethermost hell.

O God, the proud are risen against me, * and the congregations of naughty men have sought after my soul, and have not set thee before their eyes.

But thou, O Lord God, art full of compassion and mercy, * long-suffering, plenteous in goodness and truth.

O turn thee then unto me, and have mercy upon me: * give thy strength unto thy servant, and help the son of thine handmaid.

Shew some token upon me for good, that they who hate me may see it, and be ashamed, * because thou, Lord, hast holpen me, and comforted me.

Psalm 116, v. 10

I BELIEVED, and therefore will I speak; but I was sore troubled: * I said in my haste, 'All men are liars'.

What reward shall I give unto the Lord * for all the benefits that he hath done unto me?

I will receive the cup of salvation, * and call upon the name of the Lord.

I will pay my vows in the presence of all his people: * right dear in the sight of the Lord is the death of his saints.

Behold, O Lord, how that I am thy servant, * I am thy servant, and the son of thine handmaid; thou hast broken my bonds in sunder.

I will offer to thee the sacrifice of thanksgiving, * and will call upon the name of the Lord.

I will pay my vows unto the Lord, in the sight of all his people, * in the courts of the Lord's house, even in the midst of thee, O Jerusalem, Praise the Lord.

Psalm 130

OUT of the deep have I called unto thee, O Lord, * Lord hear my voice.

O let thine ears consider well * the voice of my complaint.

If thou, Lord, wilt be extreme to mark what is done amiss, * O Lord, who may abide it?

For there is mercy with thee: * therefore shalt thou be feared.

I look for the Lord; my soul doth wait for him: * in his word is my trust.

My soul fleeth unto the Lord * before the morning watch, I say, before the morning watch.

O Israel, trust in the Lord, for with the Lord there is mercy, * and with him is plenteous redemption.

And he shall redeem Israel * from all his sins.

Ant. Remember not, Lord, our offences, nor the offences of our forefathers, neither take thou vengeance of our sins. (E.T. Alleluia.)

Kyrie, eleison. Christe, eleison. Kyrie, eleison.

Our Father.

℣. And lead us not into temptation. ℟. But deliver us from evil.

℣. I said: Lord, be merciful unto me. ℟. Heal my soul, for I have sinned against thee.

℣. Turn thee again, O Lord, at the last. ℟. And be gracious unto thy servants.

℣. Let thy mercy, O Lord, be shewed upon us. ℟. As we do put our trust in thee.

℣. Let thy priests be clothed with righteousness. ℟. And thy Saints sing with joyfulness.

℣. Cleanse thou me, O Lord, from my secret faults. ℟. And keep thy servant from presumptuous sins.

℣. O Lord, hear my prayer. ℟. And let my cry come unto thee.

℣. The Lord be with you. ℟. And with thy spirit.

Let us pray.

MOST gracious God, incline thy merciful ears unto our prayers, and enlighten our hearts with the grace of the Holy Ghost, that we may worthily celebrate thy holy mysteries, and love thee with an everlasting love.

ALMIGHTY God, unto whom all hearts be open, all desires known, and from whom no secrets are hid: cleanse the thoughts of our hearts by the inspiration of thy Holy Spirit, that we may perfectly love thee, and worthily magnify thy holy name.

KINDLE, O Lord, our hearts and minds with the fire of thy Holy Spirit: that we may serve thee in chastity of body, and please thee in purity of soul.

MAY the Comforter, who proceedeth from thee, we beseech thee, O Lord, enlighten our minds: and lead us, as thy Son hath promised, into all truth.

O LORD, we beseech thee, may the power of the Holy Ghost be with us, and most mercifully cleanse and purge our hearts, and defend us from all adversities.

GOD, who didst teach the hearts of thy faithful people, by the sending to them the light of thy holy Spirit: grant us by the same Spirit to have a right judgement in all things, and evermore to rejoice in his holy comfort.

CLEANSE our consciences, we beseech thee, O Lord, by thy visitation: that thy Son, our Lord Jesus Christ, when he cometh, may find in us a mansion prepared for himself: Who liveth and reigneth with thee in the unity of the Holy Spirit, ever one God, world without end. ℟. Amen.

PRAYER OF ST AMBROSE

Sunday

O GREAT High Priest and true Bishop, Jesu Christ, who didst offer thyself to God the Father a pure and spotless Victim upon the altar of the Cross for us miserable sinners, and who didst give us thy Flesh to eat and thy Blood to drink, and didst ordain this mystery in the power of thy Holy Spirit, saying: As oft as ye shall do this, do it in remembrance of me: I pray thee, by the same thy Blood, the great price of our redemption, I pray thee by that wonderful and unspeakable charity, wherewith thou deignedst so to love us, miserable and unworthy, as to wash us from our sins in thine own Blood. Teach me, thine unworthy servant, whom thou hast vouchsafed, among thine other gifts, to call to thy priestly service, not for any merits of mine, but by the condescension of thy lovingkindness alone; teach me, I beseech thee, by thy Holy Spirit, to treat so great a mystery with that reverence and honour, that devotion and fear, which is due and fitting. Make me through thy grace always so to believe and understand, to conceive and firmly to hold, to think and to speak, as shall please thee and be good for my soul. Let thy good Spirit enter my heart, and there be heard without utterance, and without the sound of words speak all truth. For thy mysteries are exceeding deep, and hid beneath a sacred veil. For thy great mercy's sake grant me to celebrate thy holy mysteries with a clean heart, and a pure mind. Free my heart from all defiling and unholy, from all vain and hurtful thoughts. Defend me with the loving and faithful guard and most mighty protection of thy blessed Angels, that the enemies of all good may go away ashamed. By the virtue of this great mystery, and by the hand of thy holy Angel, drive far from me and from all thy servants the obstinate spirit of pride and vain-glory, of envy and blasphemy, of fornication and uncleanness, of doubting and mistrust. Let them be confounded that persecute us, let them perish that make haste to destroy us.

Monday

KING of Virgins and lover of chastity and innocence, extinguish in my body, by the heavenly dew of thy blessing, the fuel of evil desire, that so a calm purity of body and soul may remain in me. Mortify in my members the urgings of the flesh, and all wrongful emotions, and grant me true and abiding chastity, with thy other gifts, which are truly pleasing unto thee; that I may be able with chaste body and pure heart to offer unto thee the sacrifice of praise. For with what contrition of heart and flow of tears, with what reverence and awe, with what chastity of body and purity of soul should that divine and heavenly sacrifice be celebrated, wherein thy Flesh is indeed received and thy Blood indeed is drunk; wherein the lowest and the highest, things earthly and things heavenly, are joined together; where is present the company of thy holy Angels; where in a wonderful and unspeakable way thou thyself are appointed both sacrifice and priest.

Tuesday

WHO can worthily celebrate this sacrifice, unless thou, O God almighty, makest him worthy to offer it? I know, O Lord, yea, truly do I know, and confess it to thy loving-kindness, that I am not worthy to approach so great a mystery, by reason of my grievous sins and my manifold negligences. But I know, and truly believe with my whole heart, and confess with my mouth, that thou canst make me worthy, who alone canst make him clean that is conceived of sinful stock, and sinners to be righteous and holy. By this thine almighty power, I pray thee, O my God, that thou wouldest grant to me, a sinner, to celebrate this sacrifice with fear and trembling, with purity of heart and a fount of tears, with spiritual gladness and heavenly joy. May my mind feel the sweetness of thy most blessed presence, and the guard of thy holy Angels, keeping watch about me.

Wednesday

I THEN, O Lord, mindful of thy venerable passion, draw near unto thine altar, sinner though I am, to offer unto thee the sacrifice which thou hast instituted and commanded to be offered in remembrance of thee, for our salvation. Accept it, I beseech thee, O God most High, for thy holy Church, and for the people that thou hast purchased with thine own Blood. And because thou hast willed to set me a sinner between thee and this thy people, although thou dost not perceive in me any testimony of good works, yet do thou not refuse the service committed unto me by thine own ordinance; nor do thou let the price of their salvation fail through my unworthiness, since for them thou hast deigned to be the saving Victim and their Redemption. Moreover I bring before thee, O Lord, if thou wilt vouchsafe to look down in mercy, the tribulations of the peoples, the perils of the nations, the sorrowful sighing of the prisoners, the miseries of the orphans, the needs of travellers, the helplessness of the weak, the despair of them that are sick, the weakness of the aged, the aspirations of the young, the vows of virgins, and the lamentations of widows.

Thursday

FOR thou hast mercy upon all, O Lord, and hatest nothing that thou hast made. Remember whereof we are made: forasmuch as thou art our Father, thou art our God, be not angry with us exceedingly, nor shut thou up the multitude of thy tender mercies towards us. For we do not pour forth our supplications before thy face trusting in our own righteousness, but in thy manifold mercies. Take away from us our inquities, and mercifully kindle in us the fire of thy Holy Spirit. Take away the stony heart out of our flesh, and give us a heart of flesh, a heart to love and cherish thee, to delight in thee, to follow thee and enjoy thee. We implore, O Lord, thy mercy, that thou wouldest vouchsafe to look with a favourable countenance upon this thy family, paying due service to the honour of thy sacred name; and, that the desires of none may be in vain, do thou thyself inspire our prayers, that they may be such as thou in thy mercy dost delight to hear and answer.

Friday

WE pray thee also, O Lord, holy Father, for the souls of the faithful departed, that this great sacrament of thy love may be to them salvation and health, joy and refreshment. O Lord my God, grant them this day greatly and abundantly to feast on thee the living Bread, who camest down from heaven and gavest life for the world; on thy holy and blessed Flesh, who art the Lamb without spot, that takest away the sins of the world; on the Flesh that was taken of the womb of the blessed Virgin Mary and conceived by the Holy Ghost; and on that fountain of mercy, which, by the soldier's lance, was opened in thy most sacred side: that they may thereby be nourished and satisfied, refreshed and comforted; and may rejoice in thy praise and glory. I pray thy clemency, O Lord, that the fulness of thy blessing and the hallowing of thy Godhead may come down on the bread to be offered unto thee. May the unseen majesty of thy Holy Spirit, passing all comprehension, come down on it, as of old it came down on the offerings of the fathers; so that it may make our oblations thy Body and Blood, and teach us so to assist at thy mysteries with purity of heart and tears of devotion, with reverence and awe, that thou mayest with grace and favour receive the sacrifice at my hands, for the salvation of all thy people, living and departed.

Saturday

I PRAY thee also, O Lord, by the same most holy mystery of thy Body and Blood, whereby in thy Church we are daily given food and drink, and are washed and sanctified and are made partakers of the one supreme divinity. Grant me thy holy virtues, that being filled thereby I may with a good conscience go unto thine altar, so that these heavenly sacraments may become my salvation and life. For with thine own holy and blessed lips thou hast said: The bread that I will give is my Flesh, for the life of the world; I am the living Bread which came down from heaven; if any man eat of this Bread, he shall live for ever. O Bread most sweet, heal thou the palate of my heart, that I may perceive the tenderness of thy love. Heal it of every sickness, that I may perceive no other sweetness than thyself. O Bread most fair, having every delight and every taste, that ever refreshest us and never failest, may my heart feed on thee, and may my inmost soul be filled with the sweetness of thy savour. On thee the Angels feed and are satisfied; on thee may man feed in his pilgrimage, according to his measure, that being refreshed with such food for his journey, he may not faint by the way. O holy Bread, living Bread, purest Bread, who didst come down from heaven, and givest life unto the world, come into my heart, and cleanse it from every defilement of flesh and spirit. Enter into my soul, heal and cleanse me within and without. Be thou the defence and abiding salvation of my soul and body. Drive from me all the snares of the enemy, let them be driven far from the presence of thy might, that being both outwardly and inwardly guarded by thee, I may by a straight course attain to thy kingdom; where no more in mysteries, as in this present time, but face to face we shall see thee; when thou shalt have delivered up the kingdom to God, even the Father, and thou, God, shalt be all in all. For then shalt thou wondrously satisfy me with thyself, so that I shall never hunger nor thirst any more: Who with the same God the Father and the Holy Ghost livest and reignest, world without end. Amen.

Prayer of St Thomas Aquinas

ALMIGHTY and everlasting God, behold I come to the Sacrament of thine only-begotten Son, our Lord Jesus Christ; I come as one sick unto the physician of life, as one unclean to the fountain of thy loving-kindness, as one blind to the light of eternal brightness, as one poor and needy to the Lord of heaven and earth. I implore therefore the abundance of thine infinite goodness, that thou wouldest vouchsafe to heal my sickness, to wash my foulness, to enlighten my blindness, to enrich my poverty and to clothe my nakedness; that I may receive him who is the Bread of Angels, the King of kings and Lord of lords, with such reverence and humility, such contrition and devotion, such purity and faith, such a right purpose and intention, as is expedient for the salvation of my soul. Grant me, I beseech thee, to receive not only the Sacrament of the Lord's Body and Blood, but also the effect and virtue of the Sacrament. O most gracious God, grant me so to receive the Body of thy Son, our Lord Jesus Christ, that he took of the Virgin Mary, that I may be incorporated in his mystical Body, and ever reckoned among its members. O most loving Father, grant that as I purpose to receive thy beloved Son now in this earthly pilgrimage, when he is veiled from our sight, so at last I may behold him with unveiled face: Who liveth and reigneth with thee, in the unity of the Holy Ghost, ever one God, world without end. Amen.

Declaration of Intention before Mass

I DESIRE to celebrate the Mass, and consecrate the Body and Blood of our Lord Jesus Christ, according to the rites of the Catholic Church, to the praise of almighty God and of all the court of heaven, for my own salvation and that of all the Church militant, for all who have commended themselves to my prayers in general or in particular, and for the good estate of the Catholic Church. Amen.

THANKSGIVING AFTER MASS

Ant. Let us sing * the song of the three holy children, which they sang as they blessed the Lord in the burning fiery furnace. (E.T. Alleluia.)

Song of the Three Children

O ALL ye works of the Lord, bless ye the Lord: * praise him and magnify him for ever.

O ye Angels of the Lord, bless ye the Lord: * O ye heavens, bless ye the Lord.

O ye waters that be above the firmament, bless ye the Lord: * O all ye powers of the Lord, bless ye the Lord.

O ye sun and moon, bless ye the Lord: * O ye stars of heaven, bless ye the Lord.

O ye showers and dew, bless ye the Lord: * O ye winds of God, bless ye the Lord.

O ye fire and heat, bless ye the Lord: * O ye winter and summer, bless ye the Lord.

O ye dews and frosts, bless ye the Lord: * O ye frost and cold, bless ye the Lord.

O ye ice and snow, bless ye the Lord: * O ye nights and days, bless ye the Lord.

O ye light and darkness, bless ye the Lord: * O ye lightnings and clouds, bless ye the Lord.

O let the earth bless the Lord: * yea, let it praise him, and magnify him for ever.

O ye mountains and hills, bless ye the Lord: * O all ye green things upon the earth, bless ye the Lord.

O ye wells, bless ye the Lord: * O ye seas and floods, bless ye the Lord.

O ye whales, and all that move in the waters, bless ye the Lord; * O all ye fowls of the air, bless ye the Lord.

O all ye beasts and cattle, bless ye the Lord: * O ye children of men, bless ye the Lord.

O let Israel bless the Lord: * praise him, and magnify him for ever.

O ye priests of the Lord, bless ye the Lord: * O ye servants of the Lord, bless ye the Lord.

O ye spirits and souls of the righteous, bless ye the Lord: * O ye holy and humble men of heart, bless ye the Lord.

O Ananias, Azarias, and Misael, bless ye the Lord: * praise him and magnify him for ever.

Let us bless the Father, and the Son, with the Holy Ghost: * let us praise him and magnify him for ever.

Blessed art thou, O Lord, in the firmament of heaven: * and worthy to be praised, and glorious, and magnified for ever.

Psalm 150

O PRAISE God in his holiness; * praise him in the firmament of his power.

Praise him in his noble acts, * praise him according to his excellent greatness.

Praise him in the sound of the trumpet, * praise him upon the lute and harp.

Praise him in the cymbals and dances, * praise him upon the strings and pipe.

Praise him upon the well-tuned cymbals, * praise him upon the loud cymbals.

Let every thing that hath breath * praise the Lord.

Glory be.

Ant. Let us sing the song of the three holy children, which they sang as they blessed the Lord in the burning fiery furnace. (E.T. Alleluia.)

Kyrie, eleison. Christe, eleison. Kyrie, eleison.

Our Father.

℣. And lead us not into temptation. ℟. But deliver us from evil.

℣. All thy works praise thee, O Lord. ℟. And thy Saints give thanks unto thee.

℣. Let the Saints be joyful in glory. ℟. Let them rejoice in their beds.

℣. Not unto us, O Lord, not unto us. ℟. But unto thy name give the praise.

℣. O Lord, hear my prayer. ℟. And let my cry come unto thee.

℣. The Lord be with you. ℟. And with thy spirit.

Let us pray

O GOD, who for the three holy children didst assuage the flames of fire: mercifully grant that the flames of sin may not kindle upon us thy servants.

PREVENT us, O Lord, in all our doings with thy most gracious favour, and further us with thy continual help: that in all our works begun, continued, and ended in thee, we may glorify thy holy name, and finally by thy mercy obtain everlasting life.

GRANT us, we beseech thee, almighty God: to quench the flames of our temptations; even as thou didst enable thy blessed servant Lawrence to overcome the fires of his torments. Through Christ our Lord. ℟. Amen.

A Prayer of St Thomas Aquinas

I GIVE thanks to thee, O holy Lord, almighty Father, everlasting God, who hast deigned, not for any merit of mine, but only out of the goodness of thy mercy, to feed me, a sinner, thine unworthy servant, with the precious Body and Blood of thy Son, our Lord Jesus Christ; and I pray thee that this holy Communion may not bring upon me guilt unto my condemnation, but that it may be a saving intercession for my pardon. May it be to me as the armour of faith and the shield of good will. May it avail to deliver me from all my sins, to destroy in me all evil desires and wantonness, to increase in me charity and patience, humility and obedience, and every virtue; may it give me a sure defence against the wiles of all my enemies, visible and invisible; a perfect quieting of all my impulses, whether of soul or of body; a firm adherence to thee, the only true God; and a blessed end to my whole life. And I pray thee that thou wouldest vouchsafe to bring me, although I am a sinner, unto that heavenly feast where thou, with thy Son and the Holy Ghost, art to thy Saints true light, full satisfaction, everlasting joy, endless happiness and perfect felicity. Through the same Christ, our Lord. Amen.

APPENDIX

LITANY OF THE MOST HOLY NAME OF JESUS

KYRIE, eleison.
Christe, eleison.
Kyrie, eleison.
Jesu, hear us.
Jesu, graciously hear us.
O God the Father, of heaven, *have mercy upon us.*
O God the Son, Redeemer of the world,
O God the Holy Ghost,
Holy Trinity, one God,
Jesu, Son of the living God,
Jesu, splendour of the Father,
Jesu, brightness of the everlasting light,
Jesu, king of glory,
Jesu, sun of righteousness,
Jesu, Child of the Virgin Mary,
Jesu most lovable,
Jesu most wonderful,
Jesu, mighty God,
Jesu, father of the world to come,
Jesu, angel of great counsel,
Jesu most powerful,
Jesu most patient,
Jesu most obedient,
Jesu, meek and lowly of heart,
Jesu, lover of chastity,
Jesu, who lovest us,
Jesu, God of peace,
Jesu, author of life,
Jesu, pattern of virtues,
Jesu, zealous lover of souls,
Jesu, our God,
Jesu, our refuge,
Jesu, father of the poor,
Jesu, treasure of the faithful,
Jesu, good Shepherd,
Jesu, true light,
Jesu, eternal wisdom,
Jesu, infinite goodness,
Jesu, our way and our life,
Jesu, joy of Angels,
Jesu, king of Patriarchs,
Jesu, master of Apostles,
Jesu, teacher of Evangelists,
Jesu, strength of Martyrs,
Jesu, light of Confessors,
Jesu, purity of Virgins,
Jesu, crown of all Saints,
Be thou merciful, *spare us, Jesu.*
Be thou merciful, *graciously hear us, Jesu.*
From all evil, *Jesu, deliver us.*
From all sin,
From thy wrath,
From the snares of the devil,
From the spirit of uncleanness,
From everlasting death,
From the neglect of thine inspirations,
By the mystery of thy holy Incarnation,
By thy nativity,
By thine infancy,
By thy most divine life,
By thy labours,
By thine agony and passion,
By thy Cross and dereliction,
By thy weariness,
By thy death and burial,
By thy resurrection,
By thine ascension,
By thine institution of the most holy Eucharist,
By thy joys,
By thy glory,
O Lamb of God, that takest away the sins of the world, *spare us, O Jesu.*
O Lamb of God, that takest away the sins of the world, *graciously hear us, O Jesu.*
O Lamb of God, that takest

away the sins of the world, *have mercy upon us, O Jesu.*
Jesu, hear us.
Jesu, graciously hear us.

Let us pray.

O LORD Jesu Christ, who hast said: Ask, and ye shall receive; seek, and ye shall find; knock, and it shall be opened unto you: we beseech thee, that unto us who ask thou wouldest give such a measure of thy divine love, that in every thought and word and deed we may show forth our love for thee, and offer thee unceasing praise.

O LORD, who never failest to help and govern them whom thou dost bring up in thy stedfast fear and love: keep us, we beseech thee, under the protection of thy good providence, and make us to have a perpetual fear and love of thy holy Name: Who livest and reignest, world without end. R₇. Amen.

LITANY OF THE MOST SACRED HEART OF JESUS

KYRIE, eleison.
Christe, eleison.
Kyrie, eleison.
O Christ, hear us.
O Christ, graciously hear us.
O God the Father, of heaven, *have mercy upon us.*
O God the Son, Redeemer of the world,
O God the Holy Ghost,
Holy Trinity, one God,
Heart of Jesus, the Son of the eternal Father,
Heart of Jesus, formed by the Holy Ghost in the Virgin Mother's womb,
Heart of Jesus, united in substance with the Word of God,
Heart of Jesus, of an infinite majesty,
Heart of Jesus, holy temple of God,
Heart of Jesus, tabernacle of the most high,
Heart of Jesus, house of God and gate of heaven,
Heart of Jesus, glowing furnace of charity,
Heart of Jesus, treasury of righteousness and love,
Heart of Jesus, full of love and goodness,
Heart of Jesus, abyss of all virtues,
Heart of Jesus, most worthy of all praise,
Heart of Jesus, king and centre of all hearts,
Heart of Jesus, wherein are all the treasures of wisdom and knowledge,
Heart of Jesus, wherein dwelleth all the fulness of the Godhead,
Heart of Jesus, in which the Father is well pleased,
Heart of Jesus, of whose fulness we·have all received,
Heart of Jesus, desire of the eternal hills,
Heart of Jesus, long-suffering and of great mercy,
Heart of Jesus, bountiful to all that call upon thee,
Heart of Jesus, fount of life and holiness,

Heart of Jesus, propitiation for our sins,
Heart of Jesus, overwhelmed with reproaches,
Heart of Jesus, bruised for our iniquities,
Heart of Jesus, made obedient even unto death,
Heart of Jesus, pierced by the spear,
Heart of Jesus, fountain of all consolation,
Heart of Jesus, our life and resurrection,
Heart of Jesus, our peace and atonement,
Heart of Jesus, victim of our sins,
Heart of Jesus, salvation of them that put their trust in thee,
Heart of Jesus, hope of them that die in thee,
Heart of Jesus, delight of all the Saints,
O Lamb of God, that takest away the sins of the world, *spare us, O Lord.*
O Lamb of God, that takest away the sins of the world, *graciously hear us, O Lord.*
O Lamb of God, that takest away the sins of the world, *have mercy upon us.*

℣. Jesu, meek and lowly of Heart. ℟. Make our hearts like unto thy Heart.

Let us pray.

ALMIGHTY and everlasting God, look upon the Heart of thy well-beloved Son, and upon the offering of praise and atonement that he maketh unto thee in the name of sinners; and forasmuch as we implore thy loving-kindness, do thou mercifully grant us pardon in the name of the same thy Son Jesus Christ: Who liveth and reigneth with thee in the unity of the Holy Ghost, ever one God, world without end. ℟. Amen.

LITANY OF THE BLESSED VIRGIN MARY

KYRIE, eleison.
Christe, eleison.
Kyrie, eleison.
O God the Father, of heaven, *have mercy upon us.*
O God the Son, Redeemer of the world,
O God the Holy Ghost,
Holy Trinity, one God,
Holy Mary, *pray for us.*
Holy Mother of God,
Holy Virgin of Virgins,
Mother of Christ,
Mother of divine grace,
Mother most pure,
Mother most chaste,
Mother inviolate,
Mother undefiled,
Mother most lovable,
Mother most wonderful,
Mother of good counsel,
Mother of the Creator,
Mother of the Saviour,
Virgin most prudent,
Virgin most venerable,
Virgin most renowned,
Virgin most mighty,
Virgin most merciful,
Virgin most faithful,
Mirror of righteousness,

Seat of wisdom,
Cause of our joy,
Spiritual vessel,
Vessel of honour,
Wondrous vessel of devotion,
Mystical rose,
Tower of David,
Tower of ivory,
House of gold,
Ark of the covenant,
Gate of heaven,
Star of the morning,
Health of the sick,
Refuge of sinners,
Consoler of the afflicted,
Help of Christians,
Queen of Angels,
Queen of Patriarchs,
Queen of Prophets,
Queen of Apostles,
Queen of Martyrs,
Queen of Confessors,
Queen of Virgins,
Queen of all Saints,
Queen conceived without original sin,
Queen taken up into heaven,
Queen of the most holy Rosary,
Queen of peace,
O Lamb of God, that takest away the sins of the world, *spare us, O Lord.*
O Lamb of god, that takest away the sins of the world, *graciously hear us, O Lord.*
O Lamb of God, that takest away the sins of the world, *have mercy upon us, O Lord.*

℣. Pray for us, O holy Mother of God. ℟. That we may be made worthy of the promises of Christ.

Let us pray.

GRANT, we beseech thee, O Lord God; that we thy servants may ever enjoy health of mind and of body: and at the glorious intercession of blessed Mary ever Virgin, may be delivered from the sorrows of this present world, and rejoice in everlasting happiness in the world to come. Through Christ our Lord. ℟. Amen.

SHORT FORMS
For use in emergency

Baptism

N. I baptize thee in the name of the Father, and of the Son, and of the Holy Ghost. Amen.

If there is doubt whether the child is alive:
If thou art living, I baptize thee in the name of the Father, and of the Son, and of the Holy Ghost. Amen.

Absolution

Our Lord Jesus Christ, who hath left power to his Church to absolve all sinners who truly repent and believe in him, of his great mercy forgive thee thine offences: and by his authority committed unto me,

I absolve thee from all thy sins, in the name of the Father, and of the Son, and of the Holy Ghost. Amen.

In extreme urgency, the first paragraph may be omitted.

Holy Unction

By this holy Unction may the Lord pardon thee whatsoever thou hast done amiss. Amen.

If there is doubt whether the person is still alive.

If thou art living, by this holy Unction may the Lord pardon thee whatsoever thou hast done amiss. Amen.

ANTIPHONS TO THE PSALMS

In Eastertide, the Psalms are said under one antiphon: Alleluia, * alleluia, alleluia. Through the rest of the year they are as below.

DAY 1   MATTINS

1 Blessed is the man * who doth exercise himself in the law of the Lord. Ps. 1.
2 Serve the Lord * in fear: and rejoice unto him with reverence. Ps. 2.
3 Arise, * O Lord, and help me, O my God. Ps. 3.
4 Have mercy * upon me, O Lord, and hearken unto my prayer. Ps. 4.
5 O hearken thou * unto the voice of my calling, my King and my God. Ps. 5.

DAY 1   EVENSONG

1 Save me, * O Lord, for thy mercy's sake. Ps. 6.
2 I will give thanks * unto the Lord, according to his righteousness. Ps. 7.
3 How excellent * is thy name, O Lord, in all the world. Ps. 8.

DAY 2   MATTINS

1 Thou art set in the throne, * that judgest right. Ps. 9.
2 Arise, * O Lord God, and lift up thine hand. Ps. 10.
3 The righteous Lord * loveth righteousness. Ps. 11.

DAY 2   EVENSONG

1 Thou, O Lord, * shalt keep us: thou shalt preserve us for ever. Ps. 12.

2 Consider, and hear me, * O Lord my God. Ps. 13.
3 The Lord looked down * from heaven upon the children of men. Ps. 14.

DAY 3   MATTINS

1 He that doeth the thing that is right * shall rest upon thy holy hill, O Lord. Ps. 15.
2 My goods are nothing * unto thee; in thee have I trusted; preserve me, O my God. Ps. 16.
3 Incline thine ear, * O Lord, unto me, and hearken unto my words. Ps. 17.

DAY 3   EVENSONG

1 I will love thee, * O Lord, my strength. Ps. 18.

DAY 4   MATTINS

1 The law of the Lord * is an undefiled law; the testimony of the Lord is sure. Ps. 19.
2 The Lord hear thee, * in the day of trouble. Ps. 20.
3 The king shall rejoice * in thy strength, O Lord. Ps. 21.

DAY 4   EVENSONG

1 Go not from me, * O Lord, for trouble is hard at hand: and there is none to help me. Ps. 22.
2 The Lord shall feed me * in a green pasture. Ps. 23.

DAY 5   MATTINS

1 He that hath clean hands * and a pure heart, shall ascend into the hill of the Lord. Ps. 24.
2 My God, * in thee have I put my trust; O let me not be confounded. Ps. 25.

I

3 Thy loving-kindness, * O Lord, is ever before mine eyes, and I will walk in thy truth. Ps. 26.

DAY 5   EVENSONG

1 My light * and my salvation is the Lord. Ps. 27.
2 O give thy blessing * unto thine inheritance. Ps. 28.
3 It is the glorious God * that maketh the thunder: give the Lord the honour due unto his name. Ps. 29.

DAY 6   MATTINS

1 I will magnify thee, * O Lord, for thou hast set me up. Ps. 30.
2 O Lord, deliver me * in thy righteousness. Ps. 31.

DAY 6   EVENSONG

1 Be glad, O ye righteous, * and be joyful, all ye that are true of heart. Ps. 32.
2 The counsel of the Lord * shall endure for ever. Ps. 33.
3 The Angel of the Lord * tarrieth round about them that fear him, and delivereth them. Ps. 34.

DAY 7   MATTINS

1 Fight thou, O Lord, * against them that fight against me. Ps. 35.
2 Thy mercy, O Lord, * reachest unto the heavens. Ps. 36.

DAY 7   EVENSONG

1 Grieve not thyself * at him whose way doth prosper, that doeth after evil counsels. Ps. 37.

DAY 8   MATTINS

1 Put me not to rebuke, * in thine anger, O Lord. Ps. 38.
2 Take, O Lord, * thy plague away from me. Ps. 39.
3 The Lord hath regarded me, * and hearkened unto my prayer. Ps. 40.

DAY 8   EVENSONG

1 Thou upholdest me, O Lord, * and shalt set me before thy face. Ps. 41.
2 I will thank him * which is the help of my countenance, and my God. Ps. 42.
3 Defend my cause, * O God, against the ungodly people. Ps. 43.

DAY 9   MATTINS

1 Thou hast saved us, * O Lord, and we will praise thy name for ever. Ps. 44.
2 Thou art fairer * than the children of men, full of grace are thy lips. Ps. 45.
3 A very present help in trouble * is our God. Ps. 46.

DAY 9   EVENSONG

1 O sing unto God * with the voice of melody. Ps. 47.
2 Great is the Lord, * and highly to be praised in the city of our God. Ps. 48.
3 My mouth shall speak * of wisdom, and my heart shall muse of understanding. Ps. 49.

DAY 10   MATTINS

1 The Lord, * even the most mighty God, hath spoken. Ps. 50.
2 Thou shalt be pleased with

ANTIPHONS TO THE PSALMS

the sacrifice * of righteousness upon thine altar, O Lord. Ps. 51.

3 The goodness of God * endureth yet daily. Ps. 52.

DAY 10   EVENSONG

1 The Lord will deliver * his people out of captivity. Ps. 53.

2 God is my helper: * the Lord doth uphold my soul. Ps. 54.

3 Take heed unto me, * O Lord, and hear me. Ps. 55.

DAY 11   MATTINS

1 In God have I put my trust, * I will not be afraid what man can do unto me. Ps. 56.

2 Set up thyself, O God, * above the heavens, and thy glory above all the earth. Ps. 57.

3 Judge the thing that is right, * O ye sons of men. Ps. 58.

DAY 11   EVENSONG

1 O my God, shew me thy goodness plenteously. Ps. 59.

2 Be thou, O Lord, * our help in troubles. Ps. 60.

3 Thou hast given an heritage, * O Lord, unto those that fear thy name. Ps. 61.

DAY 12   MATTINS

1 In God is my health, * and my glory: and in God is my trust. Ps. 62.

2 As long as I live, * I will magnify thee, O Lord: and lift up my hands in thy name. Ps. 63.

3 The righteousness shall rejoice * in the Lord, and put his trust in him. Ps. 64.

DAY 12   EVENSONG

1 Thou, O God, * art praised in Sion. Ps. 65.

2 Behold the works of the Lord, * and make the voice of his praise to be heard. Ps. 66.

3 Shew the light of thy countenance, * O Lord, upon us. Ps. 67.

DAY 13   MATTINS

1 Let God arise * and let his enemies be scattered. Ps. 68.

DAY 13   EVENSONG

1 Save me, O God, * for the waters are come in, even unto my soul. Ps. 69.

2 Be thou my helper, * and my redeemer, O Lord. Ps. 70.

DAY 14   MATTINS

1 Be thou, O Lord, * my strong hold, my defence and castle. Ps. 71.

2 His name shall endure * for ever and ever. Ps. 72.

DAY 14   EVENSONG

1 Truly God is loving * unto Israel, even unto such as are of a clean heart. Ps. 73.

2 O think upon thy congregation, * O Lord, whom thou hast purchased of old. Ps. 74.

DAY 15   MATTINS

1 We will call * upon thy name, O Lord: thy wondrous works will we declare. Ps. 75.

2 The Lord's name * is great in Israel. Ps. 76.

3 I will cry unto God * with my voice: for God hath not forgotten to be gracious. Ps. 77.

DAY 15 EVENSONG
1 God hath made a covenant * with Jacob, and given Israel a law. Ps. 78.

DAY 16 MATTINS
1 Help us, * O God of our salvation: and be merciful unto our sins. Ps. 79.
2 Stir up thy strength, * O Lord, and come and help us. Ps. 80.
3 I am the Lord * thy God, O Israel, who brought thee out of the land of Egypt. Ps. 81.

DAY 16 EVENSONG
1 Thou shalt take all heathen * to thine inheritance, O Lord. Ps. 82.
2 Refrain not thyself, * O God, for they that hate thee have lift up their head. Ps. 83.
3 Blessed are they * that dwell in thy house, O Lord. Ps. 84.
4 Lord, thou art become gracious, * unto thy land: thou hast forgiven the offence of thy people. Ps. 85.

DAY 17 MATTINS
1 I will thank thee, * O Lord my God, with all my heart. Ps. 86.
2 Very excellent things * are spoken of thee, thou city of God. Ps. 87.
3 Let my prayer, * Lord, enter into thy presence. Ps. 88.

DAY 17 EVENSONG
1 Mercy and truth * shall go before thy face, O Lord. Ps. 89.

DAY 18 MATTINS
1 Lord, thou hast been our refuge * from one generation to another. Ps. 90.
2 God shall give his Angels * charge over thee to keep thee in all thy ways. Ps. 91.
3 O Lord, * how glorious are thy works. Ps. 92.

DAY 18 EVENSONG
1 The Lord is King * and hath put on glorious apparel. Ps. 93.
2 Arise, O Lord, * thou Judge of the world: and reward the proud after their deserving. Ps. 94.

DAY 19 MATTINS
1 O sing unto the Lord, * and praise his name. Ps. 96.
2 The Lord is King, * the earth may be glad thereof. Ps. 97.

DAY 19 EVENSONG
1 O shew yourselves joyful * before the Lord the King. Ps. 98.
2 O magnify * the Lord our God, and worship him upon his holy hill. Ps. 99.
3 O be joyful * in the Lord, all ye lands. Ps. 100.
4 Unto thee, O Lord, * will I sing; O let me have understanding in the way of godliness. Ps. 101.

DAY 20 MATTINS
1 Let my crying, * O Lord, come unto thee: hide not thy face from me. Ps. 102.
2 The merciful goodness * of the Lord endureth for ever and his kingdom ruleth over all. Ps. 103.

ANTIPHONS TO THE PSALMS

DAY 20   EVENSONG
1 O Lord my God, * thou art become exceeding glorious. Ps. 104.

DAY 21   MATTINS
1 The Lord our God * hath been alway mindful of his covenant. Ps. 105.

DAY 21   EVENSONG
1 The Lord helped them * for his name's sake. Ps. 106.

DAY 22   MATTINS
1 They cried unto the Lord, * and he delivered them from their distress. Ps. 107.

DAY 22   EVENSONG
1 Thy mercy, O Lord, * is great than the heavens. Ps. 108.
2 O God, hold not thy tongue * for they have compassed me about with words of hatred. Ps. 109.

DAY 23   MATTINS
1 The Lord said * unto my Lord: Sit thou on my right hand. Ps. 110.
2 The works of the Lord are great, * sought out of all them that have pleasure therein. Ps. 111.
3 He that feareth the Lord * hath great delight in his commandments. Ps. 112.
4 Blessed be the name of the Lord * for ever and ever.

DAY 23   EVENSONG
1 Tremble, thou earth * at the presence of the Lord. Ps. 114.
2 As for our God, * he is in heaven: he hath done whatsoever pleased him. Ps. 115.

DAY 24   MATTINS
1 The Lord hath inclined * his ear unto me. Ps. 116.
2 O praise the Lord, * all ye heathen. Ps. 117.
3 Thou art my God, * and I will thank thee: thou art my God, and I will praise thee. Ps. 118.

DAY 24   EVENSONG
1 Blessed are those that walk * in the law of the Lord. Ps. 119, v. 1.
2 With my lips * have I been telling of all the judgements of thy mouth. Ps. 119, v. 9.
3 Open thou mine eyes, O Lord, * that I may see the wondrous things of thy law. Ps. 119, v. 17.
4 Make me to understand * the way of thy commandments, O Lord. Ps. 119, v. 25.

DAY 25   MATTINS
1 Make me, O Lord, * to go in the path of thy commandments. Ps. 119, v. 33.
2 My delight shall be * in thy commandments, O Lord. Ps. 119, v. 41.
3 I remembered * thine everlasting judgements, O Lord, and received comfort. Ps. 119, v. 49.
4 I am a companion * of all them that keep thy commandments. Ps. 119, v. 57.
5 Thou art good and gracious: * teach me thy statutes, O Lord. Ps. 119, v. 65.

ANTIPHONS TO THE PSALMS

DAY 25   EVENSONG
1 I know, O Lord, * that thy judgements are right. Ps. 119, v. 73.
2 Quicken me, * after thy loving-kindness, O Lord. Ps. 119, v. 81.
3 I am thine; * save me, O Lord. Ps. 119, v. 89.
4 Through thy commandments * I get understanding, O Lord. Ps. 119, v. 97.

DAY 26   MATTINS
1 Thy testimonies, O Lord, * have I claimed as mine heritage. Ps. 119, v. 105.
2 O stablish me * according to thy word, that I may live. Ps. 119, v. 113.
3 O deal with thy servant * according unto thy loving mercy Lord. Ps. 119, v. 121.
4 Shew the light of thy countenance, * O Lord, upon thy servant. Ps. 119, v. 129.
5 Look thou upon me, * O my God, and be merciful unto me. Ps. 119, v. 137.

DAY 26   EVENSONG
1 Hear my voice, O Lord, * according to thy loving kindness. Ps. 119, v. 145.
2 Thy word, O Lord, * is true from everlasting. Ps. 119, v. 153.
3 Great is the peace * that they have who love thy law, O God. Ps. 119, v. 161.
4 O let my soul live, * and it shall praise thee, O Lord. Ps. 119, v. 169.

DAY 27   MATTINS
1 I called upon the Lord, * and he heard me. Ps. 120.
2 My help cometh * from the Lord, who hath made heaven and earth. Ps. 121.
3 I was glad * because of the things that they said unto me. Ps. 122.
4 O thou that dwellest in the heavens, * have mercy upon us. Ps. 123.
5 Our help standeth * in the name of the Lord. Ps. 124.
6 The Lord standeth round about * his people, from this time forth for evermore. Ps. 125.

DAY 27   EVENSONG
1 The Lord hath done great things * for us, we were made like unto them that dream. Ps. 126.
2 The Lord build * us an house, and keep the city. Ps. 127
3 Blessed are all they * that fear the Lord. Ps. 128.
4 Let them be confounded, * as many as have evil will at Sion. Ps. 129.
5 Out of the deep * have I called unto thee, O Lord. Ps. 130.
6 Lord, * I am not highminded. Ps. 131.

DAY 28   MATTINS
1 The Lord hath chosen Sion * to be an habitation for himself. Ps. 132.
2 Behold how good * and joyful a thing it is, brethren, to dwell together in unity. Ps. 133.
3 Praise the Lord, * all ye his servants. Ps. 134.
4 O praise the name * of the Lord, ye that stand in the house of the Lord. Ps. 135.

ANTIPHONS TO THE PSALMS

DAY 28 — EVENSONG

1 O give thanks unto the Lord, * for his mercy endureth for ever. Ps. 136.
2 Let my tongue cling * to the roof of my mouth, if I prefer not Jerusalem in my mirth. Ps. 137.
3 I will praise thy name, * O Lord, because of thy loving-kindness and truth. Ps. 138.

DAY 29 — MATTINS

1 O Lord, * thou hast searched me out and known me. Ps. 139.
2 Leave me not, * O Lord, thou strength of my health. Ps. 140.
3 Lord, I call upon thee, * haste thee unto me. Ps. 141.

DAY 29 — EVENSONG

1 Bring my soul * out of prison, that I may give thanks unto thy name. Ps. 142.
2 Deliver me * from mine enemies, O Lord, for I flee unto thee. Ps. 143.

DAYS 30 & 31 — MATTINS

1 Blessed by the Lord, * my castle and my deliverer. Ps. 144.
2 Great is the Lord, * and marvellous worthy to be praised there is no end of his greatness. Ps. 145.
3 While I live * will I praise my God. Ps. 146.

DAYS 30 & 31 — EVENSONG

1 It is a joyful thing * to be thankful unto our God. Ps. 147.
2 O praise the Lord * of heaven. Ps. 148.
3 Let the children of Sion * be joyful in their King. Ps. 149.
4 Let everything that hath breath * praise the Lord. Ps. 150

THE PSALMS OF DAVID.

THE PSALMS OF DAVID.

THE FIRST DAY.

Morning Prayer

PSALM I. *Beatus vir, qui non abiit &c.*

BLESSED is the man that hath not walked in the counsel of the ungodly, nor stood in the way of sinners : and hath not sat in the seat of the scornful.

2 But his delight is in the law of the Lord : and in his law will he exercise himself day and night.

3 And he shall be like a tree planted by the water-side : that will bring forth his fruit in due season.

4 His leaf also shall not wither : and look, whatsoever he doeth, it shall prosper.

5 As for the ungodly, it is not so with them : but they are like the chaff, which the wind scattereth away from the face of the earth.

6 Therefore the ungodly shall not be able to stand in the judgement : neither the sinners in the congregation of the righteous.

7 But the Lord knoweth the way of the righteous : and the way of the ungodly shall perish.

PSALM II. *Quare fremuerunt gentes?*

WHY do the heathen so furiously rage together : and why do the people imagine a vain thing?

2 The kings of the earth stand up, and the rulers take counsel together : against the Lord, and against his Anointed.

3 Let us break their bonds asunder : and cast away their cords from us.

4 He that dwelleth in heaven shall laugh them to scorn : the Lord shall have them in derision.

5 Then shall he speak unto them in his wrath : and vex them in his sore displeasure.

6 Yet have I set my King : upon my holy hill of Sion.

7 I will preach the law, whereof the Lord hath said unto me : Thou art my Son, this day have I begotten thee.

8 Desire of me, and I shall give thee the heathen for thine inheritance : and the utmost parts of the earth for thy possession.

9 Thou shalt bruise them with a rod of iron : and break them in pieces like a potter's vessel.

10 Be wise now therefore, O ye kings : be learned, ye that are judges of the earth.

11 Serve the Lord in fear : and rejoice unto him with reverence.

12 Kiss the Son, lest he be angry, and so ye perish from the right way : if his wrath be kindled, (yea, but a little,) blessed are all they that put their trust in him.

PSALM III. *Domine, quid multiplicati?*

LORD, how are they increased that trouble me : many are they that rise against me.

2 Many one there be that say of my soul : There is no help for him in his God.

3 But thou, O Lord, art my defender : thou art my worship, and the lifter up of my head.

4 I did call upon the Lord with my voice : and he heard me out of his holy hill.

5 I laid me down and slept, and rose up again : for the Lord sustained me.

6 I will not be afraid for ten thousands of the people : that have set themselves against me round about.

7 Up, Lord, and help me, O my God : for thou smitest all mine enemies upon the cheek-bone; thou hast broken the teeth of the ungodly.

8 Salvation belongeth unto the Lord : and thy blessing is upon thy people.

PSALM IV. *Cum invocarem.*

HEAR me when I call, O God of my righteousness : thou hast set me at liberty when I was in trouble; have mercy upon me, and hearken unto my prayer.

2 O ye sons of men, how long will ye blaspheme mine honour : and have such pleasure in vanity, and seek after leasing?

3 Know this also, that the Lord hath chosen to himself the man that is godly : when I call upon the Lord, he will hear me.

4 Stand in awe, and sin not : commune with your own heart, and in your chamber, and be still.

5 Offer the sacrifice of righteousness : and put your trust in the Lord.

6 There be many that say : Who will shew us any good?

7 Lord, lift thou up : the light of thy countenance upon us.

8 Thou hast put gladness in my heart : since the time that their corn, and wine, and oil, increased.

9 I will lay me down in peace, and take my rest : for it is thou, Lord, only, that makest me dwell in safety.

PSALM V. *Verba mea auribus.*

PONDER my words, O Lord : consider my meditation.

2 O hearken thou unto the voice of my calling, my King, and my God : for unto thee will I make my prayer.

3 My voice shalt thou hear betimes, O Lord : early in the morning will I direct my prayer unto thee, and will look up.

4 For thou art the God that hast no pleasure in wickedness : neither shall any evil dwell with thee.

5 Such as be foolish shall not stand in thy sight : for thou hatest all them that work vanity.

6 Thou shalt destroy them that speak leasing : the Lord will abhor both the blood-thirsty and deceitful man.

7 But as for me, I will come into thine house, even upon the multitude of thy mercy : and in thy fear will I worship toward thy holy temple.

8 Lead me, O Lord, in thy righteousness, because of mine enemies : make thy way plain before my face.

9 For there is no faithfulness in his mouth : their inward parts are very wickedness.

10 Their throat is an open sepulchre : they flatter with their tongue.

11 Destroy thou them, O God; let them perish through their own imaginations : cast them out in the multitude of their ungodliness; for they have rebelled against thee.

12 And let all them that put their trust in thee rejoice : they shall ever be giving of thanks, because thou defendest them; they that love thy Name shall be joyful in thee;

13 For thou, Lord, wilt give thy blessing unto the righteous : and with thy favourable kindness wilt thou defend him as with a shield.

Evening Prayer

PSALM VI. *Domine, ne in furore.*

O LORD, rebuke me not in thine indignation : neither chasten me in thy displeasure.

2 Have mercy upon me, O Lord, for I am weak : O Lord, heal me, for my bones are vexed.

3 My soul also is sore troubled : but, Lord, how long wilt thou punish me?

4 Turn thee, O Lord, and deli-

ver my soul : O save me for thy mercy's sake.

5 For in death no man remembereth thee : and who will give thee thanks in the pit?

6 I am weary of my groaning; every night wash I my bed : and water my couch with my tears.

7 My beauty is gone for very trouble : and worn away because of all mine enemies.

8 Away from me, all ye that work vanity : for the Lord hath heard the voice of my weeping.

9 The Lord hath heard my petition : the Lord will receive my prayer.

10 All mine enemies shall be confounded, and sore vexed : they shall be turned back, and put to shame suddenly.

PSALM VII. *Domine, Deus meus.*

O LORD my God, in thee have I put my trust : save me from all them that persecute me, and deliver me;

2 Lest he devour my soul, like a lion, and tear it in pieces : while there is none to help.

3 O Lord my God, if I have done any such thing : or if there be any wickedness in my hands;

4 If I have rewarded evil unto him that dealt friendly with me : yea, I have delivered him that without any cause is mine enemy;

5 Then let mine enemy persecute my soul, and take me : yea, let him tread my life down upon the earth, and lay mine honour in the dust.

6 Stand up, O Lord, in thy wrath, and lift up thyself, because of the indignation of mine enemies : arise up for me in the judgement that thou hast commanded.

7 And so shall the congregation of the people come about thee : for their sakes therefore lift up thyself again.

8 The Lord shall judge the people; give sentence with me, O Lord : according to my righteousness, and according to the innocency that is in me.

9 O let the wickedness of the ungodly come to an end : but guide thou the just.

10 For the righteous God : trieth the very hearts and reins.

11 My help cometh of God : who preserveth them that are true of heart.

12 God is a righteous Judge, strong, and patient : and God is provoked every day.

13 If a man will not turn, he will whet his sword : he hath bent his bow, and made it ready.

14 He hath prepared for him the instruments of death : he ordaineth his arrows against the persecutors.

15 Behold, he travaileth with mischief : he hath conceived sorrow, and brought forth ungodliness.

16 He hath graven and digged up a pit : and is fallen himself into the destruction that he made for other.

17 For his travail shall come upon his own head : and his wickedness shall fall on his own pate.

18 I will give thanks unto the Lord, according to his righteousness : and I will praise the Name of the Lord most High.

PSALM VIII. *Domine, Dominus noster.*

O LORD our Governor, how excellent is thy Name in all the world : thou that hast set thy glory above the heavens!

2 Out of the mouth of very babes and sucklings hast thou ordained strength, because of thine enemies : that thou mightest still the enemy, and the avenger.

3 For I will consider thy heavens, even the works of thy fingers : the moon and the stars, which thou hast ordained.

4 What is man, that thou art mindful of him : and the son of man, that thou visitest him?

5 Thou madest him lower than

the angels : to crown him with glory and worship.

6 Thou makest him to have dominion of the works of thy hands : and thou hast put all things in subjection under his feet;

7 All sheep and oxen : yea, and the beasts of the field;

8 The fowls of the air, and the fishes of the sea : and whatsoever walketh through the paths of the seas.

9 O Lord our Governor : how excellent is thy Name in all the world!

Morning Prayer

PSALM IX. *Confitebor tibi.*

I WILL give thanks unto thee, O Lord, with my whole heart : I will speak of all thy marvellous works.

2 I will be glad and rejoice in thee : yea, my songs will I make of thy Name, O thou most Highest.

3 While mine enemies are driven back : they shall fall and perish at thy presence.

4 For thou hast maintained my right and my cause : thou art set in the throne that judgest right.

5 Thou hast rebuked the heathen, and destroyed the ungodly : thou hast put out their name for ever and ever.

6 O thou enemy, destructions are come to a perpetual end : even as the cities which thou hast destroyed; their memorial is perished with them.

7 But the Lord shall endure for ever : he hath also prepared his seat for judgement.

8 For he shall judge the world in righteousness : and minister true judgement unto the people.

9 The Lord also will be a defence for the oppressed : even a refuge in due time of trouble.

10 And they that know thy Name will put their trust in thee : for thou, Lord, hast never failed them that seek thee.

11 O praise the Lord which dwelleth in Sion : shew the people of his doings.

12 For, when he maketh inquisition for blood, he remembereth them : and forgetteth not the complaint of the poor.

13 Have mercy upon me, O Lord; consider the trouble which I suffer of them that hate me : thou that liftest me up from the gates of death.

14 That I may shew all thy praises within the ports of the daughter of Sion : I will rejoice in thy salvation.

15 The heathen are sunk down in the pit that they made : in the same net which they hid privily, is their foot taken.

16 The Lord is known to execute judgement : the ungodly is trapped in the work of his own hands.

17 The wicked shall be turned into hell : and all the people that forget God.

18 For the poor shall not alway be forgotten : the patient abiding of the meek shall not perish for ever.

19 Up, Lord, and let not man have the upper hand : let the heathen be judged in thy sight.

20 Put them in fear, O Lord : that the heathen may know themselves to be but men.

PSALM X. *Ut quid, Domine?*

WHY standest thou so far off, O Lord : and hidest thy face in the needful time of trouble?

2 The ungodly for his own lust doth persecute the poor : let them be taken in the crafty wiliness that they have imagined.

3 For the ungodly hath made boast of his own heart's desire : and speaketh good of the covetous, whom God abhorreth.

4 The ungodly is so proud, that he careth not for God : neither is God in all his thoughts.

5 His ways are alway grievous :

thy judgements are far above out of his sight, and therefore defieth he all his enemies.

6 For he hath said in his heart, Tush, I shall never be cast down : there shall no harm happen unto me.

7 His mouth is full of cursing, deceit, and fraud : under his tongue is ungodliness and vanity.

8 He sitteth lurking in the thievish corners of the streets : and privily in his lurking dens doth he murder the innocent; his eyes are set against the poor.

9 For he lieth waiting secretly, even as a lion lurketh he in his den : that he may ravish the poor.

10 He doth ravish the poor : when he getteth him into his net.

11 He falleth down, and humbleth himself : that the congregation of the poor may fall into the hands of his captains.

12 He hath said in his heart, Tush, God hath forgotten : he hideth away his face, and he will never see it.

13 Arise, O Lord God, and lift up thine hand : forget not the poor.

14 Wherefore should the wicked blaspheme God : while he doth say in his heart, Tush, thou God carest not for it.

15 Surely thou hast seen it : for thou beholdest ungodliness and wrong.

16 That thou mayest take the matter into thine hand : the poor committeth himself unto thee; for thou art the helper of the friendless.

17 Break thou the power of the ungodly and malicious : take away his ungodliness, and thou shalt find none.

18 The Lord is King for ever and ever : and the heathen are perished out of the land.

19 Lord, thou hast heard the desire of the poor : thou preparest their heart, and thine ear hearkeneth thereto;

20 To help the fatherless and poor unto their right : that the man of the earth be no more exalted against them.

PSALM XI. *In Domino confido.*

IN the Lord put I my trust : how say ye then to my soul, that she should flee as a bird unto the hill?

2 For lo, the ungodly bend their bow, and make ready their arrows within the quiver : that they may privily shoot at them which are true of heart.

3 For the foundations will be cast down : and what hath the righteous done?

4 The Lord is in his holy temple : the Lord's seat is in heaven.

5 His eyes consider the poor : and his eye-lids try the children of men.

6 The Lord alloweth the righteous : but the ungodly, and him that delighteth in wickedness doth his soul abhor.

7 Upon the ungodly he shall rain snares, fire and brimstone, storm and tempest : this shall be their portion to drink.

8 For the righteous Lord loveth righteousness : his countenance will behold the thing that is just.

Evening Prayer

PSALM XII. *Salvum me fac.*

HELP me, Lord, for there is not one godly man left : for the faithful are minished from among the children of men.

2 They talk of vanity every one with his neighbour : they do but flatter with their lips, and dissemble in their double heart.

3 The Lord shall root out all deceitful lips : and the tongue that speaketh proud things;

4 Which have said, With our tongue will we prevail : we are they that ought to speak, who is lord over us?

5 Now for the comfortless troubles' sake of the needy : and because of the deep sighing of the poor,

6 I will up, saith the Lord : and will help every one from him that swelleth against him, and will set him at rest.

7 The words of the Lord are pure words : even as the silver, which from the earth is tried, and purified seven times in the fire.

8 Thou shalt keep them, O Lord : thou shalt preserve him from this generation for ever.

9 The ungodly walk on every side : when they are exalted, the children of men are put to rebuke.

PSALM XIII. *Usque quo, Domine?*

HOW long wilt thou forget me, O Lord, for ever : how long wilt thou hide thy face from me?

2 How long shall I seek counsel in my soul, and be so vexed in my heart : how long shall mine enemies triumph over me?

3 Consider, and hear me, O Lord my God : lighten mine eyes, that I sleep not in death.

4 Lest mine enemy say, I have prevailed against him : for if I be cast down, they that trouble me will rejoice at it.

5 But my trust is in thy mercy : and my heart is joyful in thy salvation.

6 I will sing of the Lord, because he hath dealt so lovingly with me : yea, I will praise the Name of the Lord most Highest.

PSALM XIV. *Dixit insipiens.*

THE fool hath said in his heart : There is no God.

2 They are corrupt, and become abominable in their doings : there is none that doeth good, no not one.

3 The Lord looked down from heaven upon the children of men : to see if there were any that would understand, and seek after God.

4 But they are all gone out of the way, they are altogether become abominable : there is none that doeth good, no not one.

5 Their throat is an open sepulchre, with their tongues have they deceived : the poison of asps is under their lips.

6 Their mouth is full of cursing and bitterness : their feet are swift to shed blood.

7 Destruction and unhappiness is in their ways, and the way of peace have they not known : there is no fear of God before their eyes.

8 Have they no knowledge, that they are all such workers of mischief : eating up my people as it were bread, and call not upon the Lord?

9 There were they brought in great fear, even where no fear was : for God is in the generation of the righteous.

10 As for you, ye have made a mock at the counsel of the poor : because he putteth his trust in the Lord.

11 Who shall give salvation unto Israel out of Sion? When the Lord turneth the captivity of his people : then shall Jacob rejoice, and Israel shall be glad.

Morning Prayer

PSALM XV. *Domine, quis habitabit?*

LORD, who shall dwell in thy tabernacle : or who shall rest upon thy holy hill?

2 Even he, that leadeth an uncorrupt life : and doeth the thing which is right, and speaketh the truth from his heart.

3 He that hath used no deceit in his tongue, nor done evil to his neighbour : and hath not slandered his neighbour.

4 He that setteth not by himself, but is lowly in his own eyes : and maketh much of them that fear the Lord.

5 He that sweareth unto his neighbour, and disappointeth him not : though it were to his own hindrance.

6 He that hath not given his money upon usury : nor taken reward against the innocent.

7 Whoso doeth these things : shall never fall.

PSALM XVI. *Conserva me, Domine.*

PRESERVE me, O God : for in thee have I put my trust.

2 O my soul, thou hast said unto the Lord : Thou art my God, my goods are nothing unto thee.

3 All my delight is upon the saints, that are in the earth : and upon such as excel in virtue.

4 But they that run after another god : shall have great trouble.

5 Their drink-offerings of blood will I not offer : neither make mention of their names within my lips.

6 The Lord himself is the portion of mine inheritance, and of my cup : thou shalt maintain my lot.

7 The lot is fallen unto me in a fair ground : yea, I have a goodly heritage.

8 I will thank the Lord for giving me warning : my reins also chasten me in the night-season.

9 I have set God always before me : for he is on my right hand, therefore I shall not fall.

10 Wherefore my heart was glad, and my glory rejoiced : my flesh also shall rest in hope.

11 For why? thou shalt not leave my soul in hell : neither shalt thou suffer thy Holy One to see corruption.

12 Thou shalt shew me the path of life; in thy presence is the fulness of joy : and at thy right hand there is pleasure for evermore.

PSALM XVII. *Exaudi, Domine.*

HEAR the right, O Lord, consider my complaint : and hearken unto my prayer, that goeth not out of feigned lips.

2 Let my sentence come forth from thy presence : and let thine eyes look upon the thing that is equal.

3 Thou hast proved and visited mine heart in the night-season; thou hast tried me, and shalt find no wickedness in me : for I am utterly purposed that my mouth shall not offend.

4 Because of men's works, that are done against the words of thy lips : I have kept me from the ways of the destroyer.

5 O hold thou up my goings in thy paths : that my footsteps slip not.

6 I have called upon thee, O God, for thou shalt hear me incline thine ear to me, and hearken unto my words.

7 Shew thy marvellous loving-kindness, thou that art the Saviour of them which put their trust in thee : from such as resist thy right hand.

8 Keep me as the apple of an eye : hide me under the shadow of thy wings,

9 From the ungodly that trouble me : mine enemies compass me round about to take away my soul.

10 They are inclosed in their own fat : and their mouth speaketh proud things.

11 They lie waiting in our way on every side : turning their eyes down to the ground;

12 Like as a lion that is greedy of his prey : and as it were a lion's whelp, lurking in secret places.

13 Up, Lord, disappoint him, and cast him down : deliver my soul from the ungodly, which is a sword of thine;

14 From the men of thy hand, O Lord, from the men, I say, and from the evil world : which have their portion in this life, whose bellies thou fillest with thy hid treasure.

15 They have children at their desire : and leave the rest of their substance for their babes.

16 But as for me, I will behold thy presence in righteousness : and when I awake up after thy likeness, I shall be satisfied with it.

THE PSALMS.

Evening Prayer

PSALM XVIII. *Diligam te, Domine.*

1 I WILL love thee, O Lord, my strength; the Lord is my stony rock, and my defence: my Saviour, my God, and my might, in whom I will trust, my buckler, the horn also of my salvation, and my refuge.

2 I will call upon the Lord, which is worthy to be praised: so shall I be safe from mine enemies.

3 The sorrows of death compassed me: and the overflowings of ungodliness made me afraid.

4 The pains of hell came about me: the snares of death overtook me.

5 In my trouble I will call upon the Lord: and complain unto my God.

6 So shall he hear my voice out of his holy temple: and my complaint shall come before him, it shall enter even into his ears.

7 The earth trembled and quaked: the very foundations also of the hills shook, and were removed, because he was wroth.

8 There went a smoke out in his presence: and a consuming fire out of his mouth, so that coals were kindled at it.

9 He bowed the heavens also, and came down: and it was dark under his feet.

10 He rode upon the cherubims, and did fly: he came flying upon the wings of the wind.

11 He made darkness his secret place: his pavilion round about him with dark water, and thick clouds to cover him.

12 At the brightness of his presence his clouds removed: hailstones, and coals of fire.

13 The Lord also thundered out of heaven, and the Highest gave his thunder: hail-stones, and coals of fire.

14 He sent out his arrows, and scattered them: he cast forth lightnings, and destroyed them.

15 The springs of waters were seen, and the foundations of the round world were discovered, at thy chiding, O Lord: at the blasting of the breath of thy displeasure.

16 He shall send down from on high to fetch me: and shall take me out of many waters.

17 He shall deliver me from my strongest enemy, and from them which hate me: for they are too mighty for me.

18 They prevented me in the day of my trouble: but the Lord was my upholder.

19 He brought me forth also into a place of liberty: he brought me forth, even because he had a favour unto me.

20 The Lord shall reward me after my righteous dealing: according to the cleanness of my hands shall he recompense me.

21 Because I have kept the ways of the Lord: and have not forsaken my God, as the wicked doth.

22 For I have an eye unto all his laws: and will not cast out his commandments from me.

23 I was also uncorrupt before him: and eschewed mine own wickedness.

24 Therefore shall the Lord reward me after my righteous dealing: and according unto the cleanness of my hands in his eye-sight.

25 With the holy thou shalt be holy: and with a perfect man thou shalt be perfect.

26 With the clean thou shalt be clean: and with the froward thou shalt learn frowardness.

27 For thou shalt save the people that are in adversity: and shalt bring down the high looks of the proud.

28 Thou also shalt light my candle: the Lord my God shall make my darkness to be light.

29 For in thee I shall discomfit an host of men: and with the help of my God I shall leap over the wall.

30 The way of God is an undefiled way : the word of the Lord also is tried in the fire; he is the defender of all them that put their trust in him.

31 For who is God, but the Lord : or who hath any strength, except our God?

32 It is God, that girdeth me with strength of war : and maketh my way perfect.

33 He maketh my feet like harts' feet : and setteth me up on high.

34 He teacheth mine hands to fight : and mine arms shall break even a bow of steel.

35 Thou hast given me the defence of thy salvation : thy right hand also shall hold me up, and thy loving correction shall make me great.

36 Thou shalt make room enough under me for to go : that my footsteps shall not slide.

37 I will follow upon mine enemies, and overtake them : neither will I turn again till I have destroyed them.

38 I will smite them, that they shall not be able to stand : but fall under my feet.

39 Thou hast girded me with strength unto the battle : thou shalt throw down mine enemies under me.

40 Thou hast made mine enemies also to turn their backs upon me : and I shall destroy them that hate me.

41 They shall cry, but there shall be none to help them : yea, even unto the Lord shall they cry, but he shall not hear them.

42 I will beat them as small as the dust before the wind : I will cast them out as the clay in the streets.

43 Thou shalt deliver me from the strivings of the people : and thou shalt make me the head of the heathen.

44 A people whom I have not known : shall serve me.

45 As soon as they hear of me, they shall obey me : but the strange children shall dissemble with me.

46 The strange children shall fail : and be afraid out of their prisons.

47 The Lord liveth, and blessed be my strong helper : and praised be the God of my salvation.

48 Even the God that seeth that I be avenged : and subdueth the people unto me.

49 It is he that delivereth me from my cruel enemies, and setteth me up above mine adversaries : thou shalt rid me from the wicked man.

50 For this cause will I give thanks unto thee, O Lord, among the Gentiles : and sing praises unto thy Name.

51 Great prosperity giveth he unto his King : and sheweth loving-kindness unto David his Anointed, and unto his seed for evermore.

Morning Prayer

PSALM XIX. *Cœli enarrant.*

THE heavens declare the glory of God : and the firmament sheweth his handy-work.

2 One day telleth another : and one night certifieth another.

3 There is neither speech nor language : but their voices are heard among them.

4 Their sound is gone out into all lands : and their words into the ends of the world.

5 In them hath he set a tabernacle for the sun : which cometh forth as a bridegroom out of his chamber, and rejoiceth as a giant to run his course.

6 It goeth forth from the uttermost part of the heaven, and runneth about unto the end of it again : and there is nothing hid from the heat thereof.

7 The law of the Lord is an undefiled law, converting the soul :

the testimony of the Lord is sure, and giveth wisdom unto the simple.

8 The statutes of the Lord are right, and rejoice the heart : the commandment of the Lord is pure, and giveth light unto the eyes.

9 The fear of the Lord is clean, and endureth for ever : the judgements of the Lord are true, and righteous altogether.

10 More to be desired are they than gold, yea, than much fine gold : sweeter also than honey, and the honey-comb.

11 Moreover, by them is thy servant taught : and in keeping of them there is great reward.

12 Who can tell how oft he offendeth : O cleanse thou me from my secret faults.

13 Keep thy servant also from presumptuous sins, lest they get the dominion over me : so shall I be undefiled, and innocent from the great offence.

14 Let the words of my mouth, and the meditation of my heart : be alway acceptable in thy sight,

15 O Lord : my strength, and my redeemer.

PSALM XX. *Exaudiat te Dominus.*

THE Lord hear thee in the day of trouble : the Name of the God of Jacob defend thee;

2 Send thee help from the sanctuary : and strengthen thee out of Sion;

3 Remember all thy offerings : and accept thy burnt-sacrifice;

4 Grant thee thy heart's desire : and fulfil all thy mind.

5 We will rejoice in thy salvation, and triumph in the Name of the Lord our God : the Lord perform all thy petitions.

6 Now know I, that the Lord helpeth his Anointed, and will hear him from his holy heaven : even with the wholesome strength of his right hand.

7 Some put their trust in chariots, and some in horses : but we will remember the Name of the Lord our God.

8 They are brought down, and fallen : but we are risen, and stand upright.

9 Save, Lord, and hear us, O King of heaven : when we call upon thee.

PSALM XXI. *Domine, in virtute tua.*

THE King shall rejoice in thy strength, O Lord : exceeding glad shall he be of thy salvation.

2 Thou hast given him his heart's desire : and hast not denied him the request of his lips.

3 For thou shalt prevent him with the blessings of goodness : and shalt set a crown of pure gold upon his head.

4 He asked life of thee, and thou gavest him a long life : even for ever and ever.

5 His honour is great in thy salvation : glory and great worship shalt thou lay upon him.

6 For thou shalt give him everlasting felicity : and make him glad with the joy of thy countenance.

7 And why? because the King putteth his trust in the Lord : and in the mercy of the most Highest he shall not miscarry.

8 All thine enemies shall feel thy hand : thy right hand shall find out them that hate thee.

9 Thou shalt make them like a fiery oven in time of thy wrath : the Lord shall destroy them in his displeasure, and the fire shall consume them.

10 Their fruit shalt thou root out of the earth : and their seed from among the children of men.

11 For they intended mischief against thee : and imagined such a device as they are not able to perform.

12 Therefore shalt thou put them to flight : and the strings of thy bow shalt thou make ready against the face of them.

13 Be thou exalted, Lord, in thine own strength : so will we sing, and praise thy power.

Evening Prayer
PSALM XXII. *Deus, Deus meus.*

MY God, my God, look upon me; why hast thou forsaken me : and art so far from my health, and from the words of my complaint?

2 O my God, I cry in the day-time, but thou hearest not : and in the night-season also I take no rest.

3 And thou continuest holy : O thou worship of Israel.

4 Our fathers hoped in thee : they trusted in thee, and thou didst deliver them.

5 They called upon thee, and were holpen : they put their trust in thee, and were not confounded.

6 But as for me, I am a worm, and no man : a very scorn of men, and the out-cast of the people.

7 All they that see me laugh me to scorn : they shoot out their lips, and shake their heads, saying,

8 He trusted in God, that he would deliver him : let him deliver him, if he will have him.

9 But thou art he that took me out of my mother's womb : thou wast my hope, when I hanged yet upon my mother's breasts.

10 I have been left unto thee ever since I was born : thou art my God even from my mother's womb.

11 O go not from me, for trouble is hard at hand : and there is none to help me.

12 Many oxen are come about me : fat bulls of Basan close me in on every side.

13 They gape upon me with their mouths : as it were a ramping and a roaring lion.

14 I am poured out like water, and all my bones are out of joint : my heart also in the midst of my body is even like melting wax.

15 My strength is dried up like a potsherd, and my tongue cleaveth to my gums : and thou shalt bring me into the dust of death.

16 For many dogs are come about me : and the council of the wicked layeth siege against me.

17 They pierced my hands and my feet; I may tell all my bones : they stand staring and looking upon me.

18 They part my garments among them : and cast lots upon my vesture.

19 But be not thou far from me, O Lord : thou art my succour, haste thee to help me.

20 Deliver my soul from the sword : my darling from the power of the dog.

21 Save me from the lion's mouth : thou hast heard me also from among the horns of the unicorns.

22 I will declare thy Name unto my brethren : in the midst of the congregation will I praise thee.

23 O praise the Lord, ye that fear him : magnify him, all ye of the seed of Jacob, and fear him, all ye seed of Israel;

24 For he hath not despised, nor abhorred, the low estate of the poor : he hath not hid his face from him, but when he called unto him he heard him.

25 My praise is of thee in the great congregation : my vows will I perform in the sight of them that fear him.

26 The poor shall eat, and be satisfied : they that seek after the Lord shall praise him; your heart shall live for ever.

27 All the ends of the world shall remember themselves, and be turned unto the Lord : and all the kindreds of the nations shall worship before him.

28 For the kingdom is the Lord's : and he is the Governor among the people.

29 All such as be fat upon earth : have eaten, and worshipped.

30 All they that go down into the dust shall kneel before him : and no man hath quickened his own soul.

31 My seed shall serve him : they shall be counted unto the Lord for a generation.

32 They shall come, and the heavens shall declare his righteousness : unto a people that shall be born, whom the Lord hath made.

PSALM XXIII. *Dominus regit me.*

THE Lord is my shepherd : therefore can I lack nothing.

2 He shall feed me in a green pasture : and lead me forth beside the waters of comfort.

3 He shall convert my soul : and bring me forth in the paths of righteousness, for his Name's sake.

4 Yea, though I walk through the valley of the shadow of death, I will fear no evil : for thou art with me; thy rod and thy staff comfort me.

5 Thou shalt prepare a table before me against them that trouble me : thou hast anointed my head with oil, and my cup shall be full.

6 But thy loving-kindness and mercy shall follow me all the days of my life : and I will dwell in the house of the Lord for ever.

Morning Prayer
PSALM XXIV. *Domini est terra.*

THE earth is the Lord's, and all that therein is : the compass of the world, and they that dwell therein.

2 For he hath founded it upon the seas : and prepared it upon the floods.

3 Who shall ascend into the hill of the Lord : or who shall rise up in his holy place?

4 Even he that hath clean hands, and a pure heart : and that hath not lift up his mind unto vanity, nor sworn to deceive his neighbour.

5 He shall receive the blessing from the Lord : and righteousness from the God of his salvation.

6 This is the generation of them that seek him : even of them that seek thy face, O Jacob.

7 Lift up your heads, O ye gates, and be ye lift up, ye everlasting doors : and the King of glory shall come in.

8 Who is the King of glory : it is the Lord strong and mighty, even the Lord mighty in battle.

9 Lift up your heads, O ye gates, and be ye lift up, ye everlasting doors : and the King of glory shall come in.

10 Who is the King of glory : even the Lord of hosts, he is the King of glory.

PSALM XXV. *Ad te, Domine, levavi.*

UNTO thee, O Lord, will I lift up my soul; my God, I have put my trust in thee : O let me not be confounded, neither let mine enemies triumph over me.

2 For all they that hope in thee shall not be ashamed : but such as transgress without a cause shall be put to confusion.

3 Shew me thy ways, O Lord : and teach me thy paths.

4 Lead me forth in thy truth, and learn me : for thou art the God of my salvation; in thee hath been my hope all the day long.

5 Call to remembrance, O Lord, thy tender mercies : and thy loving-kindnesses, which have been ever of old.

6 O remember not the sins and offences of my youth : but according to thy mercy think thou upon me, O Lord, for thy goodness.

7 Gracious and righteous is the Lord : therefore will he teach sinners in the way.

8 Them that are meek shall he guide in judgement : and such as

Day 5. THE PSALMS. *Day 5.*

are gentle, them shall he learn his way.

9 All the paths of the Lord are mercy and truth : unto such as keep his covenant, and his testimonies.

10 For thy Name's sake, O Lord : be merciful unto my sin, for it is great.

11 What man is he, that feareth the Lord : him shall he teach in the way that he shall choose.

12 His soul shall dwell at ease : and his seed shall inherit the land.

13 The secret of the Lord is among them that fear him : and he will shew them his covenant.

14 Mine eyes are ever looking unto the Lord : for he shall pluck my feet out of the net.

15 Turn thee unto me, and have mercy upon me : for I am desolate, and in misery.

16 The sorrows of my heart are enlarged : O bring thou me out of my troubles.

17 Look upon my adversity and misery : and forgive me all my sin.

18 Consider mine enemies, how many they are : and they bear a tyrannous hate against me.

19 O keep my soul, and deliver me : let me not be confounded, for I have put my trust in thee.

20 Let perfectness and righteous dealing wait upon me : for my hope hath been in thee.

21 Deliver Israel, O God : out of all his troubles.

PSALM XXVI. *Judica me, Domine.*

BE thou my Judge, O Lord, for I have walked innocently : my trust hath been also in the Lord, therefore shall I not fall.

2 Examine me, O Lord, and prove me : try out my reins and my heart.

3 For thy loving-kindness is ever before mine eyes : and I will walk in thy truth.

4 I have not dwelt with vain persons : neither will I have fellowship with the deceitful.

5 I have hated the congregation of the wicked : and will not sit among the ungodly.

6 I will wash my hands in innocency, O Lord : and so will I go to thine altar;

7 That I may shew the voice of thanksgiving : and tell of all thy wondrous works.

8 Lord, I have loved the habitation of thy house : and the place where thine honour dwelleth.

9 O shut not up my soul with the sinners : nor my life with the blood-thirsty;

10 In whose hands is wickedness : and their right hand is full of gifts.

11 But as for me, I will walk innocently : O deliver me, and be merciful unto me.

12 My foot standeth right : I will praise the Lord in the congregations.

Evening Prayer

PSALM XXVII. *Dominus illuminatio.*

THE Lord is my light, and my salvation; whom then shall I fear : the Lord is the strength of my life; of whom then shall I be afraid?

2 When the wicked, even mine enemies, and my foes, came upon me to eat up my flesh : they stumbled and fell.

3 Though an host of men were laid against me, yet shall not my heart be afraid : and though there rose up war against me, yet will I put my trust in him.

4 One thing have I desired of the Lord, which I will require : even that I may dwell in the house of the Lord all the days of my life, to behold the fair beauty of the Lord, and to visit his temple.

5 For in the time of trouble he shall hide me in his tabernacle : yea, in the secret place of his dwelling shall he hide me, and set me up upon a rock of stone.

6 And now shall he lift up mine head : above mine enemies round about me.

7 Therefore will I offer in his dwelling an oblation with great gladness : I will sing, and speak praises unto the Lord.

8 Hearken unto my voice, O Lord, when I cry unto thee : have mercy upon me, and hear me.

9 My heart hath talked of thee, Seek ye my face : Thy face, Lord, will I seek.

10 O hide not thou thy face from me : nor cast thy servant away in displeasure.

11 Thou hast been my succour : leave me not, neither forsake me, O God of my salvation.

12 When my father and my mother forsake me : the Lord taketh me up.

13 Teach me thy way, O Lord : and lead me in the right way, because of mine enemies.

14 Deliver me not over into the will of mine adversaries : for there are false witnesses risen up against me, and such as speak wrong.

15 I should utterly have fainted : but that I believe verily to see the goodness of the Lord in the land of the living.

16 O tarry thou the Lord's leisure : be strong, and he shall comfort thine heart; and put thou thy trust in the Lord.

PSALM XXVIII. *Ad te, Domine.*

UNTO thee will I cry, O Lord my strength : think no scorn of me ; lest, if thou make as though thou hearest not, I become like them that go down into the pit.

2 Hear the voice of my humble petitions, when I cry unto thee : when I hold up my hands towards the mercy-seat of thy holy temple.

3 O pluck me not away, neither destroy me with the ungodly and wicked doers : which speak friendly to their neighbours, but imagine mischief in their hearts.

4 Reward them according to their deeds : and according to the wickedness of their own inventions.

5 Recompense them after the work of their hands : pay them that they have deserved.

6 For they regard not in their mind the works of the Lord, nor the operation of his hands : therefore shall he break them down, and not build them up.

7 Praised be the Lord : for he hath heard the voice of my humble petitions.

8 The Lord is my strength, and my shield; my heart hath trusted in him, and I am helped : therefore my heart danceth for joy, and in my song will I praise him.

9 The Lord is my strength : and he is the wholesome defence of his Anointed.

10 O save thy people, and give thy blessing unto thine inheritance : feed them, and set them up for ever.

PSALM XXIX. *Afferte Domino.*

BRING unto the Lord, O ye mighty, bring young rams unto the Lord : ascribe unto the Lord worship and strength.

2 Give the Lord the honour due unto his Name : worship the Lord with holy worship.

3 It is the Lord, that commandeth the waters : it is the glorious God, that maketh the thunder.

4 It is the Lord, that ruleth the sea; the voice of the Lord is mighty in operation : the voice of the Lord is a glorious voice.

5 The voice of the Lord breaketh the cedar-trees : yea, the Lord breaketh the cedars of Libanus.

6 He maketh them also to skip like a calf : Libanus also, and Sirion, like a young unicorn.

7 The voice of the Lord divideth the flames of fire ; the voice of the Lord shaketh the wilderness : yea, the Lord shaketh the wilderness of Cades.

8 The voice of the Lord maketh the hinds to bring forth young, and discovereth the thick bushes : in his temple doth every man speak of his honour.

9 The Lord sitteth above the water-flood : and the Lord remaineth a King for ever.

10 The Lord shall give strength unto his people : the Lord shall give his people the blessing of peace.

Morning Prayer

PSALM XXX. *Exaltabo te, Domine.*

I WILL magnify thee, O Lord, for thou hast set me up : and not made my foes to triumph over me.

2 O Lord my God, I cried unto thee : and thou hast healed me.

3 Thou, Lord, hast brought my soul out of hell : thou hast kept my life from them that go down to the pit.

4 Sing praises unto the Lord, O ye saints of his : and give thanks unto him for a remembrance of his holiness.

5 For his wrath endureth but the twinkling of an eye, and in his pleasure is life : heaviness may endure for a night, but joy cometh in the morning.

6 And in my prosperity I said, I shall never be removed : thou, Lord, of thy goodness hast made my hill so strong.

7 Thou didst turn thy face from me : and I was troubled.

8 Then cried I unto thee, O Lord : and gat me to my Lord right humbly.

9 What profit is there in my blood : when I go down to the pit?

10 Shall the dust give thanks unto thee : or shall it declare thy truth?

11 Hear, O Lord, and have mercy upon me : Lord, be thou my helper.

12 Thou hast turned my heaviness into joy : thou hast put off my sackcloth, and girded me with gladness.

13 Therefore shall every good man sing of thy praise without ceasing : O my God, I will give thanks unto thee for ever.

PSALM XXXI. *In te, Domine, speravi.*

IN thee, O Lord, have I put my trust : let me never be put to confusion, deliver me in thy righteousness.

2 Bow down thine ear to me : make haste to deliver me.

3 And be thou my strong rock, and house of defence : that thou mayest save me.

4 For thou art my strong rock, and my castle : be thou also my guide, and lead me for thy Name's sake.

5 Draw me out of the net, that they have laid privily for me : for thou art my strength.

6 Into thy hands I commend my spirit : for thou hast redeemed me, O Lord, thou God of truth.

7 I have hated them that hold of superstitious vanities : and my trust hath been in the Lord.

8 I will be glad, and rejoice in thy mercy : for thou hast considered my trouble, and hast known my soul in adversities.

9 Thou hast not shut me up into the hand of the enemy : but hast set my feet in a large room.

10 Have mercy upon me, O Lord, for I am in trouble : and mine eye is consumed for very heaviness; yea, my soul and my body.

11 For my life is waxen old with heaviness : and my years with mourning.

12 My strength faileth me, because of mine iniquity : and my bones are consumed.

13 I became a reproof among all mine enemies, but especially among my neighbours : and they of mine acquaintance were afraid of me; and they that did see

me without conveyed themselves from me.

14 I am clean forgotten, as a dead man out of mind : I am become like a broken vessel.

15 For I have heard the blasphemy of the multitude : and fear is on every side, while they conspire together against me, and take their counsel to take away my life.

16 But my hope hath been in thee, O Lord : I have said, Thou art my God.

17 My time is in thy hand ; deliver me from the hand of mine enemies : and from them that persecute me.

18 Shew thy servant the light of thy countenance : and save me for thy mercy's sake.

19 Let me not be confounded, O Lord, for I have called upon thee : let the ungodly be put to confusion, and be put to silence in the grave.

20 Let the lying lips be put to silence : which cruelly, disdainfully, and despitefully, speak against the righteous.

21 O how plentiful is thy goodness, which thou hast laid up for them that fear thee : and that thou hast prepared for them that put their trust in thee, even before the sons of men !

22 Thou shalt hide them privily by thine own presence from the provoking of all men : thou shalt keep them secretly in thy tabernacle from the strife of tongues.

23 Thanks be to the Lord : for he hath shewed me marvellous great kindness in a strong city.

24 And when I made haste, I said : I am cast out of the sight of thine eyes.

25 Nevertheless, thou heardest the voice of my prayer : when I cried unto thee.

26 O love the Lord, all ye his saints : for the Lord preserveth them that are faithful, and plenteously rewardeth the proud doer.

27 Be strong, and he shall establish your heart : all ye that put your trust in the Lord.

Evening Prayer

PSALM XXXII. *Beati, quorum.*

BLESSED is he whose unrighteousness is forgiven : and whose sin is covered.

2 Blessed is the man unto whom the Lord imputeth no sin : and in whose spirit there is no guile.

3 For while I held my tongue : my bones consumed away through my daily complaining.

4 For thy hand is heavy upon me day and night : and my moisture is like the drought in summer.

5 I will acknowledge my sin unto thee : and mine unrighteousness have I not hid.

6 I said, I will confess my sins unto the Lord : and so thou forgavest the wickedness of my sin.

7 For this shall every one that is godly make his prayer unto thee, in a time when thou mayest be found : but in the great waterfloods they shall not come nigh him.

8 Thou art a place to hide me in, thou shalt preserve me from trouble : thou shalt compass me about with songs of deliverance.

9 I will inform thee, and teach thee in the way wherein thou shalt go : and I will guide thee with mine eye.

10 Be ye not like to horse and mule, which have no understanding : whose mouths must be held with bit and bridle, lest they fall upon thee.

11 Great plagues remain for the ungodly : but whoso putteth his trust in the Lord, mercy embraceth him on every side.

12 Be glad, O ye righteous, and rejoice in the Lord : and be joyful, all ye that are true of heart.

PSALM XXXIII. *Exultate, justi.*

REJOICE in the Lord, O ye righteous : for it becometh well the just to be thankful.

2 Praise the Lord with harp : sing praises unto him with the lute, and instrument of ten strings.
3 Sing unto the Lord a new song : sing praises lustily unto him with a good courage.
4 For the word of the Lord is true : and all his works are faithful.
5 He loveth righteousness and judgement : the earth is full of the goodness of the Lord.
6 By the word of the Lord were the heavens made : and all the hosts of them by the breath of his mouth.
7 He gathereth the waters of the sea together, as it were upon an heap : and layeth up the deep, as in a treasure-house.
8 Let all the earth fear the Lord : stand in awe of him, all ye that dwell in the world.
9 For he spake, and it was done : he commanded, and it stood fast.
10 The Lord bringeth the counsel of the heathen to nought : and maketh the devices of the people to be of none effect, and casteth out the counsels of princes.
11 The counsel of the Lord shall endure for ever : and the thoughts of his heart from generation to generation.
12 Blessed are the people, whose God is the Lord Jehovah : and blessed are the folk, that he hath chosen to him to be his inheritance.
13 The Lord looked down from heaven, and beheld all the children of men : from the habitation of his dwelling he considereth all them that dwell on the earth.
14 He fashioneth all the hearts of them : and understandeth all their works.
15 There is no king that can be saved by the multitude of an host : neither is any mighty man delivered by much strength.
16 A horse is counted but a vain thing to save a man : neither shall he deliver any man by his great strength.
17 Behold, the eye of the Lord is upon them that fear him : and upon them that put their trust in his mercy;
18 To deliver their soul from death : and to feed them in the time of dearth.
19 Our soul hath patiently tarried for the Lord : for he is our help, and our shield.
20 For our heart shall rejoice in him : because we have hoped in his holy Name.
21 Let thy merciful kindness, O Lord, be upon us : like as we do put our trust in thee.

PSALM XXXIV. *Benedicam Domino.*

I WILL alway give thanks unto the Lord : his praise shall ever be in my mouth.
2 My soul shall make her boast in the Lord : the humble shall hear thereof, and be glad.
3 O praise the Lord with me : and let us magnify his Name together.
4 I sought the Lord, and he heard me : yea, he delivered me out of all my fear.
5 They had an eye unto him, and were lightened : and their faces were not ashamed.
6 Lo, the poor crieth, and the Lord heareth him : yea, and saveth him out of all his troubles.
7 The angel of the Lord tarrieth round about them that fear him : and delivereth them.
8 O taste, and see, how gracious the Lord is : blessed is the man that trusteth in him.
9 O fear the Lord, ye that are his saints : for they that fear him lack nothing.
10 The lions do lack, and suffer hunger : but they who seek the Lord shall want no manner of thing that is good.
11 Come, ye children, and hearken unto me : I will teach you the fear of the Lord.

12 What man is he that lusteth to live : and would fain see good days?

13 Keep thy tongue from evil : and thy lips, that they speak no guile.

14 Eschew evil, and do good : seek peace, and ensue it.

15 The eyes of the Lord are over the righteous : and his ears are open unto their prayers.

16 The countenance of the Lord is against them that do evil : to root out the remembrance of them from the earth.

17 The righteous cry, and the Lord heareth them : and delivereth them out of all their troubles.

18 The Lord is nigh unto them that are of a contrite heart : and will save such as be of an humble spirit.

19 Great are the troubles of the righteous : but the Lord delivereth him out of all.

20 He keepeth all his bones : so that not one of them is broken.

21 But misfortune shall slay the ungodly : and they that hate the righteous shall be desolate.

22 The Lord delivereth the souls of his servants : and all they that put their trust in him shall not be destitute.

Morning Prayer

PSALM XXXV. *Judica, Domine.*

PLEAD thou my cause, O Lord, with them that strive with me : and fight thou against them that fight against me.

2 Lay hand upon the shield and buckler : and stand up to help me.

3 Bring forth the spear, and stop the way against them that persecute me : say unto my soul, I am thy salvation.

4 Let them be confounded, and put to shame, that seek after my soul : let them be turned back, and brought to confusion, that imagine mischief for me.

5 Let them be as the dust before the wind : and the angel of the Lord scattering them.

6 Let their way be dark and slippery : and let the angel of the Lord persecute them.

7 For they have privily laid their net to destroy me without a cause : yea, even without a cause have they made a pit for my soul.

8 Let a sudden destruction come upon him unawares, and his net, that he hath laid privily, catch himself : that he may fall into his own mischief.

9 And, my soul, be joyful in the Lord : it shall rejoice in his salvation.

10 All my bones shall say, Lord, who is like unto thee, who deliverest the poor from him that is too strong for him : yea, the poor, and him that is in misery, from him that spoileth him?

11 False witnesses did rise up : they laid to my charge things that I knew not.

12 They rewarded me evil for good : to the great discomfort of my soul.

13 Nevertheless, when they were sick, I put on sackcloth, and humbled my soul with fasting : and my prayer shall turn into mine own bosom.

14 I behaved myself as though it had been my friend, or my brother : I went heavily, as one that mourneth for his mother.

15 But in mine adversity they rejoiced, and gathered themselves together : yea, the very abjects came together against me unawares, making mouths at me, and ceased not.

16 With the flatterers were busy mockers : who gnashed upon me with their teeth.

17 Lord, how long wilt thou look upon this : O deliver my soul from the calamities which they bring on me, and my darling from the lions.

18 So will I give thee thanks in the great congregation : I will praise thee among much people.
19 O let not them that are mine enemies triumph over me ungodly : neither let them wink with their eyes that hate me without a cause.
20 And why? their communing is not for peace : but they imagine deceitful words against them that are quiet in the land.
21 They gaped upon me with their mouths, and said : Fie on thee, fie on thee, we saw it with our eyes.
22 This thou hast seen, O Lord : hold not thy tongue then, go not far from me, O Lord.
23 Awake, and stand up to judge my quarrel : avenge thou my cause, my God, and my Lord.
24 Judge me, O Lord my God, according to thy righteousness : and let them not triumph over me.
25 Let them not say in their hearts, There, there, so would we have it : neither let them say, We have devoured him.
26 Let them be put to confusion and shame together, that rejoice at my trouble : let them be clothed with rebuke and dishonour, that boast themselves against me.
27 Let them be glad and rejoice, that favour my righteous dealing : yea, let them say alway, Blessed be the Lord, who hath pleasure in the prosperity of his servant.
28 And as for my tongue, it shall be talking of thy righteousness : and of thy praise all the day long.

PSALM XXXVI. *Dixit injustus.*

M Y heart sheweth me the wickedness of the ungodly : that there is no fear of God before his eyes.
2 For he flattereth himself in his own sight : until his abominable sin be found out.
3 The words of his mouth are unrighteous, and full of deceit : he hath left off to behave himself wisely, and to do good.
4 He imagineth mischief upon his bed, and hath set himself in no good way : neither doth he abhor any thing that is evil.
5 Thy mercy, O Lord, reacheth unto the heavens : and thy faithfulness unto the clouds.
6 Thy righteousness standeth like the strong mountains : thy judgements are like the great deep.
7 Thou, Lord, shalt save both man and beast ; How excellent is thy mercy, O God : and the children of men shall put their trust under the shadow of thy wings.
8 They shall be satisfied with the plenteousness of thy house : and thou shalt give them drink of thy pleasures, as out of the river.
9 For with thee is the well of life : and in thy light shall we see light.
10 O continue forth thy lovingkindness unto them that know thee : and thy righteousness unto them that are true of heart.
11 O let not the foot of pride come against me : and let not the hand of the ungodly cast me down.
12 There are they fallen, all that work wickedness : they are cast down, and shall not be able to stand.

Evening Prayer

PSALM XXXVII. *Noli æmulari.*

F RET not thyself because of the ungodly : neither be thou envious against the evil doers.
2 For they shall soon be cut down like the grass : and be withered even as the green herb.
3 Put thou thy trust in the Lord, and be doing good : dwell in the land, and verily thou shalt be fed.
4 Delight thou in the Lord : and he shall give thee thy heart's desire.

5 Commit thy way unto the Lord, and put thy trust in him : and he shall bring it to pass.

6 He shall make thy righteousness as clear as the light : and thy just dealing as the noon-day.

7 Hold thee still in the Lord, and abide patiently upon him : but grieve not thyself at him, whose way doth prosper, against the man that doeth after evil counsels.

8 Leave off from wrath, and let go displeasure : fret not thyself, else shalt thou be moved to do evil.

9 Wicked doers shall be rooted out : and they that patiently abide the Lord, those shall inherit the land.

10 Yet a little while, and the ungodly shall be clean gone : thou shalt look after his place, and he shall be away.

11 But the meek-spirited shall possess the earth : and shall be refreshed in the multitude of peace.

12 The ungodly seeketh counsel against the just : and gnasheth upon him with his teeth.

13 The Lord shall laugh him to scorn : for he hath seen that his day is coming.

14 The ungodly have drawn out the sword, and have bent their bow : to cast down the poor and needy, and to slay such as are of a right conversation.

15 Their sword shall go through their own heart : and their bow shall be broken.

16 A small thing that the righteous hath : is better than great riches of the ungodly.

17 For the arms of the ungodly shall be broken : and the Lord upholdeth the righteous.

18 The Lord knoweth the days of the godly : and their inheritance shall endure for ever.

19 They shall not be confounded in the perilous time : and in the days of dearth they shall have enough.

20 As for the ungodly, they shall perish; and the enemies of the Lord shall consume as the fat of lambs : yea, even as the smoke, shall they consume away.

21 The ungodly borroweth, and payeth not again : but the righteous is merciful, and liberal.

22 Such as are blessed of God shall possess the land : and they that are cursed of him shall be rooted out.

23 The Lord ordereth a good man's going : and maketh his way acceptable to himself.

24 Though he fall, he shall not be cast away : for the Lord upholdeth him with his hand.

25 I have been young, and now am old : and yet saw I never the righteous forsaken, nor his seed begging their bread.

26 The righteous is ever merciful, and lendeth : and his seed is blessed.

27 Flee from evil, and do the thing that is good : and dwell for evermore.

28 For the Lord loveth the thing that is right : he forsaketh not his that be godly, but they are preserved for ever.

29 The unrighteous shall be punished : as for the seed of the ungodly, it shall be rooted out.

30 The righteous shall inherit the land : and dwell therein for ever.

31 The mouth of the righteous is exercised in wisdom : and his tongue will be talking of judgement.

32 The law of his God is in his heart : and his goings shall not slide.

33 The ungodly seeth the righteous : and seeketh occasion to slay him.

34 The Lord will not leave him in his hand : nor condemn him when he is judged.

35 Hope thou in the Lord, and keep his way, and he shall promote thee, that thou shalt possess

the land : when the ungodly shall perish, thou shalt see it.

36 I myself have seen the ungodly in great power : and flourishing like a green bay-tree.

37 I went by, and lo, he was gone : I sought him, but his place could no where be found.

38 Keep innocency, and take heed unto the thing that is right : for that shall bring a man peace at the last.

39 As for the transgressors, they shall perish together : and the end of the ungodly is, they shall be rooted out at the last.

40 But the salvation of the righteous cometh of the Lord : who is also their strength in the time of trouble.

41 And the Lord shall stand by them, and save them : he shall deliver them from the ungodly, and shall save them, because they put their trust in him.

Morning Prayer

PSALM XXXVIII. *Domine, ne in furore.*

PUT me not to rebuke, O Lord, in thine anger : neither chasten me in thy heavy displeasure.

2 For thine arrows stick fast in me : and thy hand presseth me sore.

3 There is no health in my flesh, because of thy displeasure : neither is there any rest in my bones, by reason of my sin.

4 For my wickednesses are gone over my head : and are like a sore burden, too heavy for me to bear.

5 My wounds stink, and are corrupt : through my foolishness.

6 I am brought into so great trouble and misery : that I go mourning all the day long.

7 For my loins are filled with a sore disease : and there is no whole part in my body.

8 I am feeble, and sore smitten : I have roared for the very disquietness of my heart.

9 Lord, thou knowest all my desire : and my groaning is not hid from thee.

10 My heart panteth, my strength hath failed me : and the sight of mine eyes is gone from me.

11 My lovers and my neighbours did stand looking upon my trouble : and my kinsmen stood afar off.

12 They also that sought after my life laid snares for me : and they that went about to do me evil talked of wickedness, and imagined deceit all the day long.

13 As for me, I was like a deaf man, and heard not : and as one that is dumb, who doth not open his mouth.

14 I became even as a man that heareth not : and in whose mouth are no reproofs.

15 For in thee, O Lord, have I put my trust : thou shalt answer for me, O Lord my God.

16 I have required that they, even mine enemies, should not triumph over me : for when my foot slipped, they rejoiced greatly against me.

17 And I, truly, am set in the plague : and my heaviness is ever in my sight.

18 For I will confess my wickedness : and be sorry for my sin.

19 But mine enemies live, and are mighty : and they that hate me wrongfully are many in number.

20 They also that reward evil for good are against me : because I follow the thing that good is.

21 Forsake me not, O Lord my God : be not thou far from me.

22 Haste thee to help me : O Lord God of my salvation.

PSALM XXXIX. *Dixi, custodiam.*

I SAID, I will take heed to my ways : that I offend not in my tongue.

2 I will keep my mouth as it were with a bridle : while the ungodly is in my sight.

3 I held my tongue, and spake

nothing : I kept silence, yea, even from good words; but it was pain and grief to me.

4 My heart was hot within me, and while I was thus musing the fire kindled : and at the last I spake with my tongue;

5 Lord, let me know mine end, and the number of my days : that I may be certified how long I have to live.

6 Behold, thou hast made my days as it were a span long : and mine age is even as nothing in respect of thee; and verily every man living is altogether vanity.

7 For man walketh in a vain shadow, and disquieteth himself in vain : he heapeth up riches, and cannot tell who shall gather them.

8 And now, Lord, what is my hope : truly my hope is even in thee.

9 Deliver me from all mine offences : and make me not a rebuke unto the foolish.

10 I became dumb, and opened not my mouth : for it was thy doing.

11 Take thy plague away from me : I am even consumed by the means of thy heavy hand.

12 When thou with rebukes dost chasten man for sin, thou makest his beauty to consume away, like as it were a moth fretting a garment : every man therefore is but vanity.

13 Hear my prayer, O Lord, and with thine ears consider my calling : hold not thy peace at my tears.

14 For I am a stranger with thee : and a sojourner, as all my fathers were.

15 O spare me a little, that I may recover my strength : before I go hence, and be no more seen.

PSALM XL. *Expectans expectavi.*

I WAITED patiently for the Lord : and he inclined unto me, and heard my calling.

2 He brought me also out of the horrible pit, out of the mire and clay : and set my feet upon the rock, and ordered my goings.

3 And he hath put a new song in my mouth : even a thanksgiving unto our God.

4 Many shall see it, and fear : and shall put their trust in the Lord.

5 Blessed is the man that hath set his hope in the Lord : and turned not unto the proud, and to such as go about with lies.

6 O Lord my God, great are the wondrous works which thou hast done, like as be also thy thoughts which are to us-ward : and yet there is no man that ordereth them unto thee.

7 If I should declare them, and speak of them : they should be more than I am able to express.

8 Sacrifice, and meat-offering, thou wouldest not : but mine ears hast thou opened.

9 Burnt-offerings, and sacrifice for sin, hast thou not required : then said I, Lo, I come,

10 In the volume of the book it is written of me, that I should fulfil thy will, O my God : I am content to do it; yea, thy law is within my heart.

11 I have declared thy righteousness in the great congregation : lo, I will not refrain my lips, O Lord, and that thou knowest.

12 I have not hid thy righteousness within my heart : my talk hath been of thy truth, and of thy salvation.

13 I have not kept back thy loving mercy and truth : from the great congregation.

14 Withdraw not thou thy mercy from me, O Lord : let thy loving-kindness and thy truth alway preserve me.

15 For innumerable troubles are come about me; my sins have taken such hold upon me that I am not able to look up : yea, they are more in number than

the hairs of my head, and my heart hath failed me.

16 O Lord, let it be thy pleasure to deliver me : make haste, O Lord, to help me.

17 Let them be ashamed, and confounded together, that seek after my soul to destroy it : let them be driven backward, and put to rebuke, that wish me evil.

18 Let them be desolate, and rewarded with shame : that say unto me, Fie upon thee, fie upon thee.

19 Let all those that seek thee be joyful and glad in thee : and let such as love thy salvation say alway, The Lord be praised.

20 As for me, I am poor and needy : but the Lord careth for me.

21 Thou art my helper and redeemer : make no long tarrying, O my God.

Evening Prayer

PSALM XLI. *Beatus qui intelligit.*

BLESSED is he that considereth the poor and needy : the Lord shall deliver him in the time of trouble.

2 The Lord preserve him, and keep him alive, that he may be blessed upon earth : and deliver not thou him into the will of his enemies.

3 The Lord comfort him, when he lieth sick upon his bed : make thou all his bed in his sickness.

4 I said, Lord, be merciful unto me : heal my soul, for I have sinned against thee.

5 Mine enemies speak evil of me : When shall he die, and his name perish?

6 And if he come to see me, he speaketh vanity : and his heart conceiveth falsehood within himself, and when he cometh forth he telleth it.

7 All mine enemies whisper together against me : even against me do they imagine this evil.

8 Let the sentence of guiltiness proceed against him : and now that he lieth, let him rise up no more.

9 Yea, even mine own familiar friend, whom I trusted : who did also eat of my bread, hath laid great wait for me.

10 But be thou merciful unto me, O Lord : raise thou me up again, and I shall reward them.

11 By this I know thou favourest me : that mine enemy doth not triumph against me.

12 And when I am in my health, thou upholdest me : and shalt set me before thy face for ever.

13 Blessed be the Lord God of Israel : world without end. Amen.

PSALM XLII. *Quemadmodum.*

LIKE as the hart desireth the water-brooks : so longeth my soul after thee, O God.

2 My soul is athirst for God, yea, even for the living God : when shall I come to appear before the presence of God?

3 My tears have been my meat day and night : while they daily say unto me, Where is now thy God?

4 Now when I think thereupon, I pour out my heart by myself : for I went with the multitude, and brought them forth into the house of God;

5 In the voice of praise and thanksgiving : among such as keep holy-day.

6 Why art thou so full of heaviness, O my soul : and why art thou so disquieted within me?

7 Put thy trust in God : for I will yet give him thanks for the help of his countenance.

8 My God, my soul is vexed within me : therefore will I remember thee concerning the land of Jordan, and the little hill of Hermon.

9 One deep calleth another, because of the noise of the water-

pipes : all thy waves and storms are gone over me.

10 The Lord hath granted his loving-kindness in the day-time : and in the night-season did I sing of him, and made my prayer unto the God of my life.

11 I will say unto the God of my strength, Why hast thou forgotten me : why go I thus heavily, while the enemy oppresseth me?

12 My bones are smitten asunder as with a sword : while mine enemies that trouble me cast me in the teeth;

13 Namely, while they say daily unto me : Where is now thy God?

14 Why art thou so vexed, O my soul : and why art thou so disquieted within me?

15 O put thy trust in God : for I will yet thank him, which is the help of my countenance, and my God.

PSALM XLIII. *Judica me, Deus.*

GIVE sentence with me, O God, and defend my cause against the ungodly people : O deliver me from the deceitful and wicked man.

2 For thou art the God of my strength, why hast thou put me from thee : and why go I so heavily, while the enemy oppresseth me?

3 O send out thy light and thy truth, that they may lead me : and bring me unto thy holy hill, and to thy dwelling.

4 And that I may go unto the altar of God, even unto the God of my joy and gladness : and upon the harp will I give thanks unto thee, O God, my God.

5 Why art thou so heavy, O my soul : and why art thou so disquieted within me?

6 O put thy trust in God : for I will yet give him thanks, which is the help of my countenance, and my God.

Morning Prayer

PSALM XLIV. *Deus, auribus.*

WE have heard with our ears, O God, our fathers have told us : what thou hast done in their time of old;

2 How thou hast driven out the heathen with thy hand, and planted them in : how thou hast destroyed the nations, and cast them out.

3 For they gat not the land in possession through their own sword : neither was it their own arm that helped them;

4 But thy right hand, and thine arm, and the light of thy countenance : because thou hadst a favour unto them.

5 Thou art my King, O God : send help unto Jacob.

6 Through thee will we overthrow our enemies : and in thy Name will we tread them under, that rise up against us.

7 For I will not trust in my bow : it is not my sword that shall help me;

8 But it is thou that savest us from our enemies : and puttest them to confusion that hate us.

9 We make our boast of God all day long : and will praise thy Name for ever.

10 But now thou art far off, and puttest us to confusion : and goest not forth with our armies.

11 Thou makest us to turn our backs upon our enemies : so that they which hate us spoil our goods.

12 Thou lettest us be eaten up like sheep : and hast scattered us among the heathen.

13 Thou sellest thy people for nought : and takest no money for them.

14 Thou makest us to be rebuked of our neighbours : to be laughed to scorn, and had in derision of them that are round about us.

15 Thou makest us to be a by-

word among the heathen : and that the people shake their heads at us.

16 My confusion is daily before me : and the shame of my face hath covered me;

17 For the voice of the slanderer and blasphemer : for the enemy and avenger.

18 And though all this be come upon us, yet do we not forget thee : nor behave ourselves frowardly in thy covenant.

19 Our heart is not turned back : neither our steps gone out of thy way;

20 No, not when thou hast smitten us into the place of dragons : and covered us with the shadow of death.

21 If we have forgotten the Name of our God, and holden up our hands to any strange god : shall not God search it out? for he knoweth the very secrets of the heart.

22 For thy sake also are we killed all the day long : and are counted as sheep appointed to be slain.

23 Up, Lord, why sleepest thou : awake, and be not absent from us for ever.

24 Wherefore hidest thou thy face : and forgettest our misery and trouble?

25 For our soul is brought low, even unto the dust : our belly cleaveth unto the ground.

26 Arise, and help us : and deliver us for thy mercy's sake.

PSALM XLV. *Eructavit cor meum.*

MY heart is inditing of a good matter : I speak of the things which I have made unto the King.

2 My tongue is the pen : of a ready writer.

3 Thou art fairer than the children of men : full of grace are thy lips, because God hath blessed thee for ever.

4 Gird thee with thy sword upon thy thigh, O thou most Mighty : according to thy worship and renown.

5 Good luck have thou with thine honour : ride on, because of the word of truth, of meekness, and righteousness; and thy right hand shall teach thee terrible things.

6 Thy arrows are very sharp, and the people shall be subdued unto thee : even in the midst among the King's enemies.

7 Thy seat, O God, endureth for ever : the sceptre of thy kingdom is a right sceptre.

8 Thou hast loved righteousness, and hated iniquity : wherefore God, even thy God, hath anointed thee with the oil of gladness above thy fellows.

9 All thy garments smell of myrrh, aloes, and cassia : out of the ivory palaces, whereby they have made thee glad.

10 Kings' daughters were among thy honourable women : upon thy right hand did stand the queen in a vesture of gold, wrought about with divers colours.

11 Hearken, O daughter, and consider, incline thine ear : forget also thine own people, and thy father's house.

12 So shall the King have pleasure in thy beauty : for he is thy Lord God, and worship thou him.

13 And the daughter of Tyre shall be there with a gift : like as the rich also among the people shall make their supplication before thee.

14 The King's daughter is all glorious within : her clothing is of wrought gold.

15 She shall be brought unto the King in raiment of needlework : the virgins that be her fellows shall bear her company, and shall be brought unto thee.

16 With joy and gladness shall they be brought : and shall enter into the King's palace.

17 Instead of thy fathers thou shalt have children : whom thou mayest make princes in all lands.

18 I will remember thy Name from one generation to another : therefore shall the people give thanks unto thee, world without end.

PSALM XLVI. *Deus noster refugium.*

GOD is our hope and strength : a very present help in trouble.

2 Therefore will we not fear, though the earth be moved : and though the hills be carried into the midst of the sea.

3 Though the waters thereof rage and swell : and though the mountains shake at the tempest of the same.

4 The rivers of the flood thereof shall make glad the city of God : the holy place of the tabernacle of the most Highest.

5 God is in the midst of her, therefore shall she not be removed : God shall help her, and that right early.

6 The heathen make much ado, and the kingdoms are moved : but God hath shewed his voice, and the earth shall melt away.

7 The Lord of hosts is with us : the God of Jacob is our refuge.

8 O come hither, and behold the works of the Lord : what destruction he hath brought upon the earth.

9 He maketh wars to cease in all the world : he breaketh the bow, and knappeth the spear in sunder, and burneth the chariots in the fire.

10 Be still then, and know that I am God : I will be exalted among the heathen, and I will be exalted in the earth.

11 The Lord of hosts is with us : the God of Jacob is our refuge.

Evening Prayer

PSALM XLVII. *Omnes gentes, plaudite.*

O CLAP your hands together, all ye people : O sing unto God with the voice of melody.

2 For the Lord is high, and to be feared : he is the great King upon all the earth.

3 He shall subdue the people under us : and the nations under our feet.

4 He shall choose out an heritage for us : even the worship of Jacob, whom he loved.

5 God is gone up with a merry noise : and the Lord with the sound of the trump.

6 O sing praises, sing praises unto our God : O sing praises, sing praises unto our King.

7 For God is the King of all the earth : sing ye praises with understanding.

8 God reigneth over the heathen : God sitteth upon his holy seat.

9 The princes of the people are joined unto the people of the God of Abraham : for God, which is very high exalted, doth defend the earth, as it were with a shield.

PSALM XLVIII. *Magnus Dominus.*

GREAT is the Lord, and highly to be praised : in the city of our God. even upon his holy hill.

2 The hill of Sion is a fair place, and the joy of the whole earth : upon the north-side lieth the city of the great King; God is well known in her palaces as a sure refuge.

3 For lo, the kings of the earth : are gathered, and gone by together.

4 They marvelled to see such things : they were astonished, and suddenly cast down.

5 Fear came there upon them, and sorrow : as upon a woman in her travail.

6 Thou shalt break the ships of the sea : through the east-wind.

7 Like as we have heard, so have we seen in the city of the Lord of hosts, in the city of our God : God upholdeth the same for ever.

8 We wait for thy loving-kindness, O God : in the midst of thy temple.
9 O God, according to thy Name, so is thy praise unto the world's end : thy right hand is full of righteousness.
10 Let the mount Sion rejoice, and the daughters of Judah be glad : because of thy judgements.
11 Walk about Sion, and go round about her : and tell the towers thereof.
12 Mark well her bulwarks, set up her houses : that ye may tell them that come after.
13 For this God is our God for ever and ever : he shall be our guide unto death.

PSALM XLIX. *Audite hæc, omnes.*

O HEAR ye this, all ye people : ponder it with your ears, all ye that dwell in the world;
2 High and low, rich and poor : one with another.
3 My mouth shall speak of wisdom : and my heart shall muse of understanding.
4 I will incline mine ear to the parable : and shew my dark speech upon the harp.
5 Wherefore should I fear in the days of wickedness : and when the wickedness of my heels compasseth me round about?
6 There be some that put their trust in their goods : and boast themselves in the multitude of their riches.
7 But no man may deliver his brother : nor make agreement unto God for him;
8 For it cost more to redeem their souls : so that he must let that alone for ever;
9 Yea, though he live long : and see not the grave.
10 For he seeth that wise men also die, and perish together : as well as the ignorant and foolish, and leave their riches for other.
11 And yet they think that their houses shall continue for ever : and that their dwelling-places shall endure from one generation to another; and call the lands after their own names.
12 Nevertheless, man will not abide in honour : seeing he may be compared unto the beasts that perish; this is the way of them.
13 This is their foolishness : and their posterity praise their saying.
14 They lie in the hell like sheep, death gnaweth upon them, and the righteous shall have domination over them in the morning : their beauty shall consume in the sepulchre out of their dwelling.
15 But God hath delivered my soul from the place of hell : for he shall receive me.
16 Be not thou afraid, though one be made rich : or if the glory of his house be increased;
17 For he shall carry nothing away with him when he dieth : neither shall his pomp follow him.
18 For while he lived, he counted himself an happy man : and so long as thou doest well unto thyself, men will speak good of thee.
19 He shall follow the generation of his fathers : and shall never see light.
20 Man being in honour hath no understanding : but is compared unto the beasts that perish.

Morning Prayer

PSALM L. *Deus deorum.*

THE Lord, even the most mighty God, hath spoken : and called the world, from the rising up of the sun, unto the going down thereof.
2 Out of Sion hath God appeared : in perfect beauty.
3 Our God shall come, and shall not keep silence : there shall go before him a consuming fire, and a mighty tempest shall be stirred up round about him.
4 He shall call the heaven from

above : and the earth, that he may judge his people.

5 Gather my saints together unto me : those that have made a covenant with me with sacrifice.

6 And the heaven shall declare his righteousness : for God is Judge himself.

7 Hear, O my people, and I will speak : I myself will testify against thee, O Israel; for I am God, even thy God.

8 I will not reprove thee because of thy sacrifices, or for thy burnt-offerings : because they were not alway before me.

9 I will take no bullock out of thine house : nor he-goat out of thy folds.

10 For all the beasts of the forest are mine : and so are the cattle upon a thousand hills.

11 I know all the fowls upon the mountains : and the wild beasts of the field are in my sight.

12 If I be hungry, I will not tell thee : for the whole world is mine, and all that is therein.

13 Thinkest thou that I will eat bulls' flesh : and drink the blood of goats?

14 Offer unto God thanksgiving : and pay thy vows unto the most Highest.

15 And call upon me in the time of trouble : so will I hear thee, and thou shalt praise me.

16 But unto the ungodly said God : Why dost thou preach my laws, and takest my covenant in thy mouth;

17 Whereas thou hatest to be reformed : and hast cast my words behind thee?

18 When thou sawest a thief, thou consentedst unto him : and hast been partaker with the adulterers.

19 Thou hast let thy mouth speak wickedness : and with thy tongue thou hast set forth deceit.

20 Thou satest, and spakest against thy brother : yea, and hast slandered thine own mother's son.

21 These things hast thou done, and I held my tongue, and thou thoughtest wickedly, that I am even such a one as thyself : but I will reprove thee, and set before thee the things that thou hast done.

22 O consider this, ye that forget God : lest I pluck you away, and there be none to deliver you.

23 Whoso offereth me thanks and praise, he honoureth me : and to him that ordereth his conversation right will I shew the salvation of God.

PSALM LI. *Miserere mei, Deus.*

HAVE mercy upon me, O God, after thy great goodness : according to the multitude of thy mercies do away mine offences.

2 Wash me throughly from my wickedness : and cleanse me from my sin.

3 For I acknowledge my faults : and my sin is ever before me.

4 Against thee only have I sinned, and done this evil in thy sight : that thou mightest be justified in thy saying, and clear when thou art judged.

5 Behold, I was shapen in wickedness : and in sin hath my mother conceived me.

6 But lo, thou requirest truth in the inward parts : and shalt make me to understand wisdom secretly.

7 Thou shalt purge me with hyssop, and I shall be clean : thou shalt wash me, and I shall be whiter than snow.

8 Thou shalt make me hear of joy and gladness : that the bones which thou hast broken may rejoice.

9 Turn thy face from my sins : and put out all my misdeeds.

10 Make me a clean heart, O God : and renew a right spirit within me.

11 Cast me not away from thy presence : and take not thy holy Spirit from me.

12 O give me the comfort of thy help again : and stablish me with thy free Spirit.

13 Then shall I teach thy ways unto the wicked : and sinners shall be converted unto thee.

14 Deliver me from blood-guiltiness, O God, thou that art the God of my health : and my tongue shall sing of thy righteousness.

15 Thou shalt open my lips, O Lord : and my mouth shall shew thy praise.

16 For thou desirest no sacrifice, else would I give it thee : but thou delightest not in burnt-offerings.

17 The sacrifice of God is a troubled spirit : a broken and contrite heart, O God, shalt thou not despise.

18 O be favourable and gracious unto Sion : build thou the walls of Jerusalem.

19 Then shalt thou be pleased with the sacrifice of righteousness, with the burnt-offerings and oblations : then shall they offer young bullocks upon thine altar.

PSALM LII. *Quid gloriaris?*

WHY boastest thou thyself, thou tyrant : that thou canst do mischief;

2 Whereas the goodness of God : endureth yet daily?

3 Thy tongue imagineth wickedness : and with lies thou cuttest like a sharp razor.

4 Thou hast loved unrighteousness more than goodness : and to talk of lies more than righteousness.

5 Thou hast loved to speak all words that may do hurt : O thou false tongue.

6 Therefore shall God destroy thee for ever : he shall take thee, and pluck thee out of thy dwelling, and root thee out of the land of the living.

7 The righteous also shall see this, and fear : and shall laugh him to scorn;

8 Lo, this is the man that took not God for his strength : but trusted unto the multitude of his riches, and strengthened himself in his wickedness.

9 As for me, I am like a green olive-tree in the house of God : my trust is in the tender mercy of God for ever and ever.

10 I will always give thanks unto thee for that thou hast done : and I will hope in thy Name, for thy saints like it well.

Evening Prayer

PSALM LIII. *Dixit insipiens.*

THE foolish body hath said in his heart : There is no God.

2 Corrupt are they, and become abominable in their wickedness : there is none that doeth good.

3 God looked down from heaven upon the children of men : to see if there were any, that would understand, and seek after God.

4 But they are all gone out of the way, they are altogether become abominable : there is also none that doeth good, no not one.

5 Are not they without understanding that work wickedness : eating up my people as if they would eat bread? they have not called upon God.

6 They were afraid where no fear was : for God hath broken the bones of him that besieged thee; thou hast put them to confusion, because God hath despised them.

7 Oh, that the salvation were given unto Israel out of Sion : Oh, that the Lord would deliver his people out of captivity!

8 Then should Jacob rejoice : and Israel should be right glad.

PSALM LIV. *Deus, in nomine.*

SAVE me, O God, for thy Name's sake : and avenge me in thy strength.

2 Hear my prayer, O God : and hearken unto the words of my mouth.

3 For strangers are risen up

against me : and tyrants, which have not God before their eyes, seek after my soul.

4 Behold, God is my helper : the Lord is with them that uphold my soul.

5 He shall reward evil unto mine enemies : destroy thou them in thy truth.

6 An offering of a free heart will I give thee, and praise thy Name, O Lord : because it is so comfortable.

7 For he hath delivered me out of all my trouble : and mine eye hath seen his desire upon mine enemies.

PSALM LV. *Exaudi, Deus.*

HEAR my prayer, O God : and hide not thyself from my petition.

2 Take heed unto me, and hear me : how I mourn in my prayer, and am vexed.

3 The enemy crieth so, and the ungodly cometh on so fast : for they are minded to do me some mischief; so maliciously are they set against me.

4 My heart is disquieted within me : and the fear of death is fallen upon me.

5 Fearfulness and trembling are come upon me : and an horrible dread hath overwhelmed me.

6 And I said, O that I had wings like a dove : for then would I flee away, and be at rest.

7 Lo, then would I get me away far off : and remain in the wilderness.

8 I would make haste to escape : because of the stormy wind and tempest.

9 Destroy their tongues, O Lord, and divide them : for I have spied unrighteousness and strife in the city.

10 Day and night they go about within the walls thereof : mischief also and sorrow are in the midst of it.

11 Wickedness is therein : deceit and guile go not out of their streets.

12 For it is not an open enemy, that hath done me this dishonour : for then I could have borne it.

13 Neither was it mine adversary, that did magnify himself against me : for then peradventure I would have hid myself from him.

14 But it was even thou, my companion : my guide, and mine own familiar friend.

15 We took sweet counsel together : and walked in the house of God as friends.

16 Let death come hastily upon them, and let them go down quick into hell : for wickedness is in their dwellings, and among them.

17 As for me, I will call upon God : and the Lord shall save me.

18 In the evening, and morning, and at noon-day will I pray, and that instantly : and he shall hear my voice.

19 It is he that hath delivered my soul in peace from the battle that was against me : for there were many with me.

20 Yea, even God, that endureth for ever, shall hear me, and bring them down : for they will not turn, nor fear God.

21 He laid his hands upon such as be at peace with him : and he brake his covenant.

22 The words of his mouth were softer than butter, having war in his heart : his words were smoother than oil, and yet be they very swords.

23 O cast thy burden upon the Lord, and he shall nourish thee : and shall not suffer the righteous to fall for ever.

24 And as for them : thou, O God, shalt bring them into the pit of destruction.

25 The blood-thirsty and deceitful men shall not live out half their days : nevertheless, my trust shall be in thee, O Lord.

Morning Prayer

PSALM LVI. *Miserere mei, Deus.*

BE merciful unto me, O God, for man goeth about to devour me : he is daily fighting, and troubling me.

2 Mine enemies are daily in hand to swallow me up : for they be many that fight against me, O thou most Highest.

3 Nevertheless, though I am sometime afraid : yet put I my trust in thee.

4 I will praise God, because of his word : I have put my trust in God, and will not fear what flesh can do unto me.

5 They daily mistake my words : all that they imagine is to do me evil.

6 They hold all together, and keep themselves close : and mark my steps, when they lay wait for my soul.

7 Shall they escape for their wickedness : thou, O God, in thy displeasure shalt cast them down.

8 Thou tellest my flittings ; put my tears into thy bottle : are not these things noted in thy book?

9 Whensoever I call upon thee, then shall mine enemies be put to flight : this I know ; for God is on my side.

10 In God's word will I rejoice : in the Lord's word will I comfort me.

11 Yea, in God have I put my trust : I will not be afraid what man can do unto me.

12 Unto thee, O God, will I pay my vows : unto thee will I give thanks.

13 For thou hast delivered my soul from death, and my feet from falling : that I may walk before God in the light of the living.

PSALM LVII. *Miserere mei, Deus.*

BE merciful unto me, O God, be merciful unto me, for my soul trusteth in thee : and under the shadow of thy wings shall be my refuge, until this tyranny be over-past.

2 I will call unto the most high God : even unto the God that shall perform the cause which I have in hand.

3 He shall send from heaven : and save me from the reproof of him that would eat me up.

4 God shall send forth his mercy and truth : my soul is among lions.

5 And I lie even among the children of men, that are set on fire : whose teeth are spears and arrows, and their tongue a sharp sword.

6 Set up thyself, O God, above the heavens : and thy glory above all the earth.

7 They have laid a net for my feet, and pressed down my soul : they have digged a pit before me, and are fallen into the midst of it themselves.

8 My heart is fixed, O God, my heart is fixed : I will sing, and give praise.

9 Awake up, my glory ; awake, lute and harp : I myself will awake right early.

10 I will give thanks unto thee, O Lord, among the people : and I will sing unto thee among the nations.

11 For the greatness of thy mercy reacheth unto the heavens : and thy truth unto the clouds.

12 Set up thyself, O God, above the heavens : and thy glory above all the earth.

PSALM LVIII. *Si vere utique.*

ARE your minds set upon righteousness, O ye congregation : and do ye judge the thing that is right, O ye sons of men?

2 Yea, ye imagine mischief in your heart upon the earth : and your hands deal with wickedness.

3 The ungodly are froward, even from their mother's womb : as soon as they are born, they go astray, and speak lies.

4 They are as venomous as the poison of a serpent : even like the deaf adder that stoppeth her ears ;
5 Which refuseth to hear the voice of the charmer : charm he never so wisely.
6 Break their teeth, O God, in their mouths; smite the jaw-bones of the lions, O Lord : let them fall away like water that runneth apace ; and when they shoot their arrows let them be rooted out.
7 Let them consume away like a snail, and be like the untimely fruit of a woman : and let them not see the sun.
8 Or ever your pots be made hot with thorns : so let indignation vex him, even as a thing that is raw.
9 The righteous shall rejoice when he seeth the vengeance : he shall wash his footsteps in the blood of the ungodly.
10 So that a man shall say, Verily there is a reward for the righteous : doubtless there is a God that judgeth the earth.

Evening Prayer

PSALM LIX. *Eripe me de inimicis.*

DELIVER me from mine enemies, O God : defend me from them that rise up against me.
2 O deliver me from the wicked doers : and save me from the blood-thirsty men.
3 For lo, they lie waiting for my soul : the mighty men are gathered against me, without any offence or fault of me, O Lord.
4 They run and prepare themselves without my fault : arise thou therefore to help me, and behold.
5 Stand up, O Lord God of hosts, thou God of Israel, to visit all the heathen : and be not merciful unto them that offend of malicious wickedness.
6 They go to and fro in the evening : they grin like a dog, and run about through the city.
7 Behold, they speak with their mouth, and swords are in their lips : for who doth hear?
8 But thou, O Lord, shalt have them in derision : and thou shalt laugh all the heathen to scorn.
9 My strength will I ascribe unto thee : for thou art the God of my refuge.
10 God sheweth me his goodness plenteously : and God shall let me see my desire upon mine enemies.
11 Slay them not, lest my people forget it : but scatter them abroad among the people, and put them down, O Lord, our defence.
12 For the sin of their mouth, and for the words of their lips, they shall be taken in their pride : and why? their preaching is of cursing and lies.
13 Consume them in thy wrath, consume them, that they may perish : and know that it is God that ruleth in Jacob, and unto the ends of the world.
14 And in the evening they will return : grin like a dog, and will go about the city.
15 They will run here and there for meat : and grudge if they be not satisfied.
16 As for me, I will sing of thy power, and will praise thy mercy betimes in the morning : for thou hast been my defence and refuge in the day of my trouble.
17 Unto thee, O my strength, will I sing : for thou, O God, art my refuge, and my merciful God.

PSALM LX. *Deus, repulisti nos.*

O GOD, thou hast cast us out, and scattered us abroad : thou hast also been displeased; O turn thee unto us again.
2 Thou hast moved the land, and divided it : heal the sores thereof, for it shaketh.
3 Thou hast shewed thy people

heavy things : thou hast given us a drink of deadly wine.

4 Thou hast given a token for such as fear thee : that they may triumph because of the truth.

5 Therefore were thy beloved delivered : help me with thy right hand, and hear me.

6 God hath spoken in his holiness, I will rejoice, and divide Sichem : and mete out the valley of Succoth.

7 Gilead is mine, and Manasses is mine : Ephraim also is the strength of my head; Judah is my law-giver;

8 Moab is my wash-pot; over Edom will I cast out my shoe : Philistia, be thou glad of me.

9 Who will lead me into the strong city : who will bring me into Edom?

10 Hast not thou cast us out, O God : wilt not thou, O God, go out with our hosts?

11 O be thou our help in trouble : for vain is the help of man.

12 Through God will we do great acts : for it is he that shall tread down our enemies.

PSALM LXI. *Exaudi, Deus.*

HEAR my crying, O God : give ear unto my prayer.

2 From the ends of the earth will I call upon thee : when my heart is in heaviness.

3 O set me up upon the rock that is higher than I : for thou hast been my hope, and a strong tower for me against the enemy.

4 I will dwell in thy tabernacle for ever : and my trust shall be under the covering of thy wings.

5 For thou, O Lord, hast heard my desires : and hast given an heritage unto those that fear thy Name.

6 Thou shalt grant the King a long life : that his years may endure throughout all generations.

7 He shall dwell before God for ever : O prepare thy loving mercy and faithfulness, that they may preserve him.

8 So will I alway sing praise unto thy Name : that I may daily perform my vows.

Morning Prayer
PSALM LXII. *Nonne Deo?*

MY soul truly waiteth still upon God : for of him cometh my salvation.

2 He verily is my strength and my salvation : he is my defence, so that I shall not greatly fall.

3 How long will ye imagine mischief against every man : ye shall be slain all the sort of you; yea, as a tottering wall shall ye be, and like a broken hedge.

4 Their device is only how to put him out whom God will exalt : their delight is in lies; they give good words with their mouth, but curse with their heart.

5 Nevertheless, my soul, wait thou still upon God : for my hope is in him.

6 He truly is my strength and my salvation : he is my defence, so that I shall not fall.

7 In God is my health, and my glory : the rock of my might, and in God is my trust.

8 O put your trust in him alway, ye people : pour out your hearts before him, for God is our hope.

9 As for the children of men, they are but vanity : the children of men are deceitful upon the weights, they are altogether lighter than vanity itself.

10 O trust not in wrong and robbery, give not yourselves unto vanity : if riches increase, set not your heart upon them.

11 God spake once, and twice I have also heard the same : that power belongeth unto God;

12 And that thou, Lord, art merciful : for thou rewardest every man according to his work.

THE PSALMS.

PSALM LXIII. *Deus, Deus meus.*

O GOD, thou art my God : early will I seek thee.

2 My soul thirsteth for thee, my flesh also longeth after thee : in a barren and dry land where no water is.

3 Thus have I looked for thee in holiness : that I might behold thy power and glory.

4 For thy loving-kindness is better than the life itself : my lips shall praise thee.

5 As long as I live will I magnify thee on this manner : and lift up my hands in thy Name.

6 My soul shall be satisfied, even as it were with marrow and fatness : when my mouth praiseth thee with joyful lips.

7 Have I not remembered thee in my bed : and thought upon thee when I was waking?

8 Because thou hast been my helper : therefore under the shadow of thy wings will I rejoice.

9 My soul hangeth upon thee : thy right hand hath upholden me.

10 These also that seek the hurt of my soul : they shall go under the earth.

11 Let them fall upon the edge of the sword : that they may be a portion for foxes.

12 But the King shall rejoice in God; all they also that swear by him shall be commended : for the mouth of them that speak lies shall be stopped.

PSALM LXIV. *Exaudi, Deus.*

HEAR my voice, O God, in my prayer : preserve my life from fear of the enemy.

2 Hide me from the gathering together of the froward : and from the insurrection of wicked doers;

3 Who have whet their tongue like a sword : and shoot out their arrows, even bitter words;

4 That they may privily shoot at him that is perfect : suddenly do they hit him, and fear not.

5 They encourage themselves in mischief : and commune among themselves how they may lay snares, and say, that no man shall see them.

6 They imagine wickedness, and practise it : that they keep secret among themselves, every man in the deep of his heart.

7 But God shall suddenly shoot at them with a swift arrow : that they shall be wounded.

8 Yea, their own tongues shall make them fall : insomuch that whoso seeth them shall laugh them to scorn.

9 And all men that see it shall say, This hath God done : for they shall perceive that it is his work.

10 The righteous shall rejoice in the Lord, and put his trust in him : and all they that are true of heart shall be glad.

Evening Prayer

PSALM LXV. *Te decet hymnus.*

THOU O God, art praised in Sion : and unto thee shall the vow be performed in Jerusalem.

2 Thou that hearest the prayer : unto thee shall all flesh come.

3 My misdeeds prevail against me : O be thou merciful unto our sins.

4 Blessed is the man, whom thou choosest, and receivest unto thee : he shall dwell in thy court, and shall be satisfied with the pleasures of thy house, even of thy holy temple.

5 Thou shalt shew us wonderful things in thy righteousness, O God of our salvation : thou that art the hope of all the ends of the earth, and of them that remain in the broad sea.

6 Who in his strength setteth fast the mountains : and is girded about with power.

7 Who stilleth the raging of the sea : and the noise of his waves, and the madness of the people.

8 They also that dwell in the uttermost parts of the earth shall

Day 12. THE PSALMS. *Day* 12.

be afraid at thy tokens : thou that makest the outgoings of the morning and evening to praise thee.

9 Thou visitest the earth, and blessest it : thou makest it very plenteous.

10 The river of God is full of water : thou preparest their corn, for so thou providest for the earth.

11 Thou waterest her furrows, thou sendest rain into the little valleys thereof : thou makest it soft with the drops of rain, and blessest the increase of it.

12 Thou crownest the year with thy goodness : and thy clouds drop fatness.

13 They shall drop upon the dwellings of the wilderness : and the little hills shall rejoice on every side.

14 The folds shall be full of sheep : the valleys also shall stand so thick with corn, that they shall laugh and sing.

PSALM LXVI. *Jubilate Deo.*

O BE joyful in God, all ye lands : sing praises unto the honour of his Name, make his praise to be glorious.

2 Say unto God, O how wonderful art thou in thy works : through the greatness of thy power shall thine enemies be found liars unto thee.

3 For all the world shall worship thee : sing of thee, and praise thy Name.

4 O come hither, and behold the works of God : how wonderful he is in his doing toward the children of men.

5 He turned the sea into dry land : so that they went through the water on foot; there did we rejoice thereof.

6 He ruleth with his power for ever; his eyes behold the people : and such as will not believe shall not be able to exalt themselves.

7 O praise our God, ye people : and make the voice of his praise to be heard;

8 Who holdeth our soul in life : and suffereth not our feet to slip.

9 For thou, O God, hast proved us : thou also hast tried us, like as silver is tried.

10 Thou broughtest us into the snare : and laidest trouble upon our loins.

11 Thou sufferedst men to ride over our heads : we went through fire and water, and thou broughtest us out into a wealthy place.

12 I will go into thine house with burnt-offerings : and will pay thee my vows, which I promised with my lips, and spake with my mouth, when I was in trouble.

13 I will offer unto thee fat burnt-sacrifices, with the incense of rams : I will offer bullocks and goats.

14 O come hither, and hearken, all ye that fear God : and I will tell you what he hath done for my soul.

15 I called unto him with my mouth : and gave him praises with my tongue.

16 If I incline unto wickedness with mine heart : the Lord will not hear me.

17 But God hath heard me : and considered the voice of my prayer.

18 Praised be God who hath not cast out my prayer : nor turned his mercy from me.

PSALM LXVII. *Deus misereatur.*

G OD be merciful unto us, and bless us : and shew us the light of his countenance, and be merciful unto us;

2 That thy way may be known upon earth : thy saving health among all nations.

3 Let the people praise thee, O God : yea, let all the people praise thee.

4 O let the nations rejoice and be glad : for thou shalt judge the folk righteously, and govern the nations upon earth.

5 Let the people praise thee, O God : let all the people praise thee.

6 Then shall the earth bring forth her increase : and God, even our own God, shall give us his blessing.

7 God shall bless us : and all the ends of the world shall fear him.

Morning Prayer
PSALM LXVIII. *Exurgat Deus.*

LET God arise, and let his enemies be scattered : let them also that hate him flee before him.

2 Like as the smoke vanisheth, so shalt thou drive them away : and like as wax melteth at the fire, so let the ungodly perish at the presence of God.

3 But let the righteous be glad and rejoice before God : let them also be merry and joyful.

4 O sing unto God, and sing praises unto his Name : magnify him that rideth upon the heavens, as it were upon an horse; praise him in his Name JAH, and rejoice before him.

5 He is a Father of the fatherless, and defendeth the cause of the widows : even God in his holy habitation.

6 He is the God that maketh men to be of one mind in an house, and bringeth the prisoners out of captivity : but letteth the runagates continue in scarceness.

7 O God, when thou wentest forth before the people : when thou wentest through the wilderness,

8 The earth shook, and the heavens dropped at the presence of God : even as Sinai also was moved at the presence of God, who is the God of Israel.

9 Thou, O God, sentest a gracious rain upon thine inheritance : and refreshedst it when it was weary.

10 Thy congregation shall dwell therein : for thou, O God, hast of thy goodness prepared for the poor.

11 The Lord gave the word : great was the company of the preachers.

12 Kings with their armies did flee, and were discomfited : and they of the household divided the spoil.

13 Though ye have lien among the pots, yet shall ye be as the wings of a dove : that is covered with silver wings, and her feathers like gold.

14 When the Almighty scattered kings for their sake : then were they as white as snow in Salmon.

15 As the hill of Basan, so is God's hill : even an high hill, as the hill of Basan.

16 Why hop ye so, ye high hills? this is God's hill, in the which it pleaseth him to dwell : yea, the Lord will abide in it for ever.

17 The chariots of God are twenty thousand, even thousands of angels : and the Lord is among them, as in the holy place of Sinai.

18 Thou art gone up on high, thou hast led captivity captive, and received gifts for men : yea, even for thine enemies, that the Lord God might dwell among them.

19 Praised be the Lord daily : even the God who helpeth us, and poureth his benefits upon us.

20 He is our God, even the God of whom cometh salvation : God is the Lord, by whom we escape death.

21 God shall wound the head of his enemies : and the hairy scalp of such a one as goeth on still in his wickedness.

22 The Lord hath said, I will bring my people again, as I did from Basan : mine own will I bring again, as I did sometime from the deep of the sea.

23 That thy foot may be dipped in the blood of thine enemies : and that the tongue of thy dogs may be red through the same.
24 It is well seen, O God, how thou goest : how thou, my God and King, goest in the sanctuary.
25 The singers go before, the minstrels follow after : in the midst are the damsels playing with the timbrels.
26 Give thanks, O Israel, unto God the Lord in the congregations : from the ground of the heart.
27 There is little Benjamin their ruler, and the princes of Judah their counsel : the princes of Zabulon, and the princes of Nephthali.
28 Thy God hath sent forth strength for thee : stablish the thing, O God, that thou hast wrought in us,
29 For thy temple's sake at Jerusalem : so shall kings bring presents unto thee.
30 When the company of the spear-men, and multitude of the mighty are scattered abroad among the beasts of the people, so that they humbly bring pieces of silver : and when he hath scattered the people that delight in war;
31 Then shall the princes come out of Egypt : the Morians' land shall soon stretch out her hands unto God.
32 Sing unto God, O ye kingdoms of the earth : O sing praises unto the Lord;
33 Who sitteth in the heavens over all from the beginning : lo, he doth send out his voice, yea, and that a mighty voice.
34 Ascribe ye the power to God over Israel : his worship, and strength is in the clouds.
35 O God, wonderful art thou in thy holy places : even the God of Israel; he will give strength and power unto his people; blessed be God.

Evening Prayer

PSALM LXIX. *Salvum me fac.*

SAVE me, O God : for the waters are come in, even unto my soul.
2 I stick fast in the deep mire, where no ground is : I am come into deep waters, so that the floods run over me.
3 I am weary of crying ; my throat is dry : my sight faileth me for waiting so long upon my God.
4 They that hate me without a cause are more than the hairs of my head : they that are mine enemies, and would destroy me guiltless, are mighty.
5 I paid them the things that I never took : God, thou knowest my simpleness, and my faults are not hid from thee.
6 Let not them that trust in thee, O Lord God of hosts, be ashamed for my cause : let not those that seek thee be confounded through me, O Lord God of Israel.
7 And why? for thy sake have I suffered reproof : shame hath covered my face.
8 I am become a stranger unto my brethren : even an alien unto my mother's children.
9 For the zeal of thine house hath even eaten me : and the rebukes of them that rebuked thee are fallen upon me.
10 I wept, and chastened myself with fasting : and that was turned to my reproof.
11 I put on sackcloth also : and they jested upon me.
12 They that sit in the gate speak against me : and the drunkards make songs upon me.
13 But, Lord, I make my prayer unto thee : in an acceptable time.
14 Hear me, O God, in the multitude of thy mercy : even in the truth of thy salvation.
15 Take me out of the mire, that I sink not : O let me be

delivered from them that hate me, and out of the deep waters.

16 Let not the water-flood drown me, neither let the deep swallow me up : and let not the pit shut her mouth upon me.

17 Hear me, O Lord, for thy loving-kindness is comfortable : turn thee unto me according to the multitude of thy mercies.

18 And hide not thy face from thy servant, for I am in trouble : O haste thee, and hear me.

19 Draw nigh unto my soul, and save it : O deliver me, because of mine enemies.

20 Thou hast known my reproof, my shame, and my dishonour : mine adversaries are all in thy sight.

21 Thy rebuke hath broken my heart; I am full of heaviness : I looked for some to have pity on me, but there was no man, neither found I any to comfort me.

22 They gave me gall to eat : and when I was thirsty they gave me vinegar to drink.

23 Let their table be made a snare to take themselves withal : and let the things that should have been for their wealth be unto them an occasion of falling.

24 Let their eyes be blinded, that they see not : and ever bow thou down their backs.

25 Pour out thine indignation upon them : and let thy wrathful displeasure take hold of them.

26 Let their habitation be void : and no man to dwell in their tents.

27 For they persecute him whom thou hast smitten : and they talk how they may vex them whom thou hast wounded.

28 Let them fall from one wickedness to another : and not come into thy righteousness.

29 Let them be wiped out of the book of the living : and not be written among the righteous.

30 As for me, when I am poor and in heaviness : thy help, O God, shall lift me up.

31 I will praise the Name of God with a song : and magnify it with thanksgiving.

32 This also shall please the Lord : better than a bullock that hath horns and hoofs.

33 The humble shall consider this, and be glad : seek ye after God, and your soul shall live.

34 For the Lord heareth the poor : and despiseth not his prisoners.

35 Let heaven and earth praise him : the sea, and all that moveth therein.

36 For God will save Sion, and build the cities of Judah : that men may dwell there, and have it in possession.

37 The posterity also of his servants shall inherit it : and they that love his Name shall dwell therein.

PSALM LXX. *Deus in adjutorium.*

HASTE thee, O God, to deliver me : make haste to help me, O Lord.

2 Let them be ashamed and confounded that seek after my soul: let them be turned backward and put to confusion that wish me evil.

3 Let them for their reward be soon brought to shame : that cry over me, There, there.

4 But let all those that seek thee be joyful and glad in thee : and let all such as delight in thy salvation say alway, The Lord be praised.

5 As for me, I am poor and in misery : haste thee unto me, O God.

6 Thou art my helper, and my redeemer : O Lord, make no long tarrying.

Morning Prayer

PSALM LXXI. *In te, Domine, speravi.*

IN thee, O Lord, have I put my trust, let me never be put to confusion : but rid me, and deliver me, in thy righteousness; incline thine ear unto me, and save me.

2 Be thou my strong hold, whereunto I may alway resort : thou hast promised to help me, for thou art my house of defence, and my castle.

3 Deliver me, O my God, out of the hand of the ungodly : out of the hand of the unrighteous and cruel man.

4 For thou, O Lord God, art the thing that I long for : thou art my hope, even from my youth.

5 Through thee have I been holden up ever since I was born : thou art he that took me out of my mother's womb; my praise shall be always of thee.

6 I am become as it were a monster unto many : but my sure trust is in thee.

7 O let my mouth be filled with thy praise : that I may sing of thy glory and honour all the day long.

8 Cast me not away in the time of age : forsake me not when my strength faileth me.

9 For mine enemies speak against me, and they that lay wait for my soul take their counsel together, saying : God hath forsaken him; persecute him, and take him, for there is none to deliver him.

10 Go not far from me, O God : my God, haste thee to help me.

11 Let them be confounded and perish that are against my soul : let them be covered with shame and dishonour that seek to do me evil.

12 As for me, I will patiently abide alway : and will praise thee more and more.

13 My mouth shall daily speak of thy righteousness and salvation : for I know no end thereof.

14 I will go forth in the strength of the Lord God : and will make mention of thy righteousness only.

15 Thou, O God, hast taught me from my youth up until now : therefore will I tell of thy wondrous works.

16 Forsake me not, O God, in mine old age, when I am gray-headed : until I have shewed thy strength unto this generation, and thy power to all them that are yet for to come.

17 Thy righteousness, O God, is very high : and great things are they that thou hast done; O God, who is like unto thee?

18 O what great troubles and adversities hast thou shewed me! and yet didst thou turn and refresh me : yea, and broughtest me from the deep of the earth again.

19 Thou hast brought me to great honour : and comforted me on every side.

20 Therefore will I praise thee and thy faithfulness, O God, playing upon an instrument of musick : unto thee will I sing upon the harp, O thou Holy One of Israel.

21 My lips will be fain when I sing unto thee : and so will my soul whom thou hast delivered.

22 My tongue also shall talk of thy righteousness all the day long : for they are confounded and brought unto shame that seek to do me evil.

PSALM LXXII. *Deus, judicium.*

GIVE the King thy judgements, O God : and thy righteousness unto the King's son.

2 Then shall he judge thy people according unto right : and defend the poor.

3 The mountains also shall bring peace : and the little hills righteousness unto the people.

4 He shall keep the simple folk by their right : defend the children of the poor, and punish the wrong doer.

5 They shall fear thee, as long as the sun and moon endureth : from one generation to another.

6 He shall come down like the rain into a fleece of wool : even as the drops that water the earth.

7 In his time shall the righteous flourish : yea, and abundance of

peace, so long as the moon endureth.

8 His dominion shall be also from the one sea to the other : and from the flood unto the world's end.

9 They that dwell in the wilderness shall kneel before him : his enemies shall lick the dust.

10 The kings of Tharsis and of the isles shall give presents : the kings of Arabia and Saba shall bring gifts.

11 All kings shall fall down before him : all nations shall do him service.

12 For he shall deliver the poor when he crieth : the needy also, and him that hath no helper.

13 He shall be favourable to the simple and needy : and shall preserve the souls of the poor.

14 He shall deliver their souls from falsehood and wrong : and dear shall their blood be in his sight.

15 He shall live, and unto him shall be given of the gold of Arabia : prayer shall be made ever unto him, and daily shall he be praised.

16 There shall be an heap of corn in the earth, high upon the hills : his fruit shall shake like Libanus, and shall be green in the city like grass upon the earth.

17 His Name shall endure for ever; his Name shall remain under the sun among the posterities : which shall be blessed through him; and all the heathen shall praise him.

18 Blessed be the Lord God, even the God of Israel : which only doeth wondrous things;

19 And blessed be the Name of his Majesty for ever : and all the earth shall be filled with his Majesty. Amen, Amen.

Evening Prayer

PSALM LXXIII. *Quam bonus Israel!*

TRULY God is loving unto Israel : even unto such as are of a clean heart.

2 Nevertheless, my feet were almost gone : my treadings had well-nigh slipt.

3 And why? I was grieved at the wicked : I do also see the ungodly in such prosperity.

4 For they are in no peril of death : but are lusty and strong.

5 They come in no misfortune like other folk : neither are they plagued like other men.

6 And this is the cause that they are so holden with pride ; and overwhelmed with cruelty.

7 Their eyes swell with fatness : and they do even what they lust.

8 They corrupt other, and speak of wicked blasphemy : their talking is against the most High.

9 For they stretch forth their mouth unto the heaven : and their tongue goeth through the world.

10 Therefore fall the people unto them : and thereout suck they no small advantage.

11 Tush, say they, how should God perceive it : is there knowledge in the most High?

12 Lo, these are the ungodly, these prosper in the world, and these have riches in possession : and I said, Then have I cleansed my heart in vain, and washed mine hands in innocency.

13 All the day long have I been punished : and chastened every morning.

14 Yea, and I had almost said even as they : but lo, then I should have condemned the generation of thy children.

15 Then thought I to understand this : but it was too hard for me,

16 Until I went into the sanctuary of God : then understood I the end of these men;

17 Namely, how thou dost set them in slippery places : and castest them down, and destroyest them.

18 Oh, how suddenly do they consume : perish, and come to a fearful end!

19 Yea, even like as a dream when one awaketh: so shalt thou make their image to vanish out of the city.
20 Thus my heart was grieved: and it went even through my reins.
21 So foolish was I, and ignorant: even as it were a beast before thee.
22 Nevertheless, I am alway by thee: for thou hast holden me by my right hand.
23 Thou shalt guide me with thy counsel: and after that receive me with glory.
24 Whom have I in heaven but thee: and there is none upon earth that I desire in comparison of thee.
25 My flesh and my heart faileth: but God is the strength of my heart, and my portion for ever.
26 For lo, they that forsake thee shall perish: thou hast destroyed all them that commit fornication against thee.
27 But it is good for me to hold me fast by God, to put my trust in the Lord God: and to speak of all thy works in the gates of the daughter of Sion.

PSALM LXXIV. *Ut quid Deus?*

O GOD, wherefore art thou absent from us so long: why is thy wrath so hot against the sheep of thy pasture?
2 O think upon thy congregation: whom thou hast purchased, and redeemed of old.
3 Think upon the tribe of thine inheritance: and mount Sion, wherein thou hast dwelt.
4 Lift up thy feet, that thou mayest utterly destroy every enemy: which hath done evil in thy sanctuary.
5 Thine adversaries roar in the midst of thy congregations: and set up their banners for tokens.
6 He that hewed timber afore out of the thick trees: was known to bring it to an excellent work.
7 But now they break down all the carved work thereof: with axes and hammers.
8 They have set fire upon thy holy places: and have defiled the dwelling-place of thy Name, even unto the ground.
9 Yea, they said in their hearts, Let us make havock of them altogether: thus have they burnt up all the houses of God in the land.
10 We see not our tokens, there is not one prophet more: no, not one is there among us, that understandeth any more.
11 O God, how long shall the adversary do this dishonour: how long shall the enemy blaspheme thy Name, for ever?
12 Why withdrawest thou thy hand: why pluckest thou not thy right hand out of thy bosom to consume the enemy?
13 For God is my King of old: the help that is done upon earth he doeth it himself.
14 Thou didst divide the sea through thy power: thou brakest the heads of the dragons in the waters.
15 Thou smotest the heads of Leviathan in pieces: and gavest him to be meat for the people in the wilderness.
16 Thou broughtest out fountains and waters out of the hard rocks: thou driedst up mighty waters.
17 The day is thine, and the night is thine: thou hast prepared the light and the sun.
18 Thou hast set all the borders of the earth: thou hast made summer and winter.
19 Remember this, O Lord, how the enemy hath rebuked: and how the foolish people hath blasphemed thy Name.
20 O deliver not the soul of thy turtle-dove unto the multitude of the enemies: and forget not the congregation of the poor for ever.
21 Look upon the covenant :

for all the earth is full of darkness, and cruel habitations.

22 O let not the simple go away ashamed : but let the poor and needy give praise unto thy Name.

23 Arise, O God, maintain thine own cause : remember how the foolish man blasphemeth thee daily.

24 Forget not the voice of thine enemies : the presumption of them that hate thee increaseth evermore and more.

Morning Prayer

PSALM LXXV. *Confitebimur tibi.*

UNTO thee, O God, do we give thanks : yea, unto thee do we give thanks.

2 Thy Name also is so nigh : and that do thy wondrous works declare.

3 When I receive the congregation : I shall judge according unto right.

4 The earth is weak, and all the inhabiters thereof : I bear up the pillars of it.

5 I said unto the fools, Deal not so madly : and to the ungodly, Set not up your horn.

6 Set not up your horn on high : and speak not with a stiff neck.

7 For promotion cometh neither from the east, nor from the west : nor yet from the south.

8 And why? God is the Judge : he putteth down one, and setteth up another.

9 For in the hand of the Lord there is a cup, and the wine is red : it is full mixed, and he poureth out of the same.

10 As for the dregs thereof : all the ungodly of the earth shall drink them, and suck them out.

11 But I will talk of the God of Jacob : and praise him for ever.

12 All the horns of the ungodly also will I break : and the horns of the righteous shall be exalted.

PSALM LXXVI. *Notus in Judæa.*

IN Jewry is God known : his Name is great in Israel.

2 At Salem is his tabernacle : and his dwelling in Sion.

3 There brake he the arrows of the bow : the shield, the sword, and the battle.

4 Thou art of more honour and might : than the hills of the robbers.

5 The proud are robbed, they have slept their sleep : and all the men whose hands were mighty have found nothing.

6 At thy rebuke, O God of Jacob : both the chariot and horse are fallen.

7 Thou, even thou art to be feared : and who may stand in thy sight when thou art angry?

8 Thou didst cause thy judgement to be heard from heaven : the earth trembled, and was still,

9 When God arose to judgement : and to help all the meek upon earth.

10 The fierceness of man shall turn to thy praise : and the fierceness of them shalt thou refrain.

11 Promise unto the Lord your God, and keep it, all ye that are round about him : bring presents unto him that ought to be feared.

12 He shall refrain the spirit of princes : and is wonderful among the kings of the earth.

PSALM LXXVII.
Voce mea ad Dominum.

I WILL cry unto God with my voice : even unto God will I cry with my voice, and he shall hearken unto me.

2 In the time of my trouble I sought the Lord : my sore ran, and ceased not in the night-season; my soul refused comfort.

3 When I am in heaviness, I will think upon God : when my heart is vexed, I will complain.

4 Thou holdest mine eyes wak-

Day 15.   THE PSALMS.   Day 15.

ing : I am so feeble, that I cannot speak.

5 I have considered the days of old : and the years that are past.

6 I call to remembrance my song : and in the night I commune with mine own heart, and search out my spirits.

7 Will the Lord absent himself for ever : and will he be no more intreated?

8 Is his mercy clean gone for ever : and is his promise come utterly to an end for evermore?

9 Hath God forgotten to be gracious : and will he shut up his loving-kindness in displeasure?

10 And I said, It is mine own infirmity : but I will remember the years of the right hand of the most Highest.

11 I will remember the works of the Lord : and call to mind thy wonders of old time.

12 I will think also of all thy works : and my talking shall be of thy doings.

13 Thy way, O God, is holy : who is so great a God as our God?

14 Thou art the God that doeth wonders : and hast declared thy power among the people.

15 Thou hast mightily delivered thy people : even the sons of Jacob and Joseph.

16 The waters saw thee, O God, the waters saw thee, and were afraid : the depths also were troubled.

17 The clouds poured out water, the air thundered : and thine arrows went abroad.

18 The voice of thy thunder was heard round about : the lightnings shone upon the ground; the earth was moved, and shook withal.

19 Thy way is in the sea, and thy paths in the great waters : and thy footsteps are not known.

20 Thou leddest thy people like sheep : by the hand of Moses and Aaron.

Evening Prayer

PSALM LXXVIII. *Attendite, popule.*

HEAR my law, O my people : incline your ears unto the words of my mouth.

2 I will open my mouth in a parable : I will declare hard sentences of old;

3 Which we have heard and known : and such as our fathers have told us;

4 That we should not hide them from the children of the generations to come : but to shew the honour of the Lord, his mighty and wonderful works that he hath done.

5 He made a covenant with Jacob, and gave Israel a law : which he commanded our forefathers to teach their children;

6 That their posterity might know it : and the children which were yet unborn;

7 To the intent that when they came up : they might shew their children the same;

8 That they might put their trust in God : and not to forget the works of God, but to keep his commandments;

9 And not to be as their forefathers, a faithless and stubborn generation : a generation that set not their heart aright, and whose spirit cleaveth not stedfastly unto God;

10 Like as the children of Ephraim : who being harnessed, and carrying bows, turned themselves back in the day of battle.

11 They kept not the covenant of God : and would not walk in his law;

12 But forgat what he had done : and the wonderful works that he had shewed for them.

13 Marvellous things did he in the sight of our forefathers, in the land of Egypt : even in the field of Zoan.

14 He divided the sea, and let them go through : he made the waters to stand on an heap.

15 In the day-time also he led them with a cloud : and all the night through with a light of fire.

16 He clave the hard rocks in the wilderness : and gave them drink thereof, as it had been out of the great depth.

17 He brought waters out of the stony rock : so that it gushed out like the rivers.

18 Yet for all this they sinned more against him : and provoked the most Highest in the wilderness.

19 They tempted God in their hearts : and required meat for their lust.

20 They spake against God also, saying : Shall God prepare a table in the wilderness?

21 He smote the stony rock indeed, that the water gushed out, and the streams flowed withal : but can he give bread also, or provide flesh for his people?

22 When the Lord heard this, he was wroth : so the fire was kindled in Jacob, and there came up heavy displeasure against Israel;

23 Because they believed not in God : and put not their trust in his help.

24 So he commanded the clouds above : and opened the doors of heaven.

25 He rained down manna also upon them for to eat : and gave them food from heaven.

26 So man did eat angels' food : for he sent them meat enough.

27 He caused the east-wind to blow under heaven : and through his power he brought in the south-west-wind.

28 He rained flesh upon them as thick as dust : and feathered fowls like as the sand of the sea.

29 He let it fall among their tents : even round about their habitation.

30 So they did eat, and were well filled; for he gave them their own desire : they were not disappointed of their lust.

31 But while the meat was yet in their mouths, the heavy wrath of God came upon them, and slew the wealthiest of them : yea, and smote down the chosen men that were in Israel.

32 But for all this they sinned yet more : and believed not his wondrous works.

33 Therefore their days did he consume in vanity : and their years in trouble.

34 When he slew them, they sought him : and turned them early, and enquired after God.

35 And they remembered that God was their strength : and that the high God was their redeemer.

36 Nevertheless, they did but flatter him with their mouth : and dissembled with him in their tongue.

37 For their heart was not whole with him : neither continued they stedfast in his covenant.

38 But he was so merciful, that he forgave their misdeeds : and destroyed them not.

39 Yea, many a time turned he his wrath away : and would not suffer his whole displeasure to arise.

40 For he considered that they were but flesh : and that they were even a wind that passeth away, and cometh not again.

41 Many a time did they provoke him in the wilderness : and grieved him in the desert.

42 They turned back, and tempted God : and moved the Holy One in Israel.

43 They thought not of his hand : and of the day when he delivered them from the hand of the enemy;

44 How he had wrought his miracles in Egypt : and his wonders in the field of Zoan.

45 He turned their waters into blood : so that they might not drink of the rivers.

THE PSALMS.

46 He sent lice among them, and devoured them up : and frogs to destroy them.
47 He gave their fruit unto the caterpillar : and their labour unto the grasshopper.
48 He destroyed their vines with hail-stones : and their mulberry-trees with the frost.
49 He smote their cattle also with hail-stones : and their flocks with hot thunder-bolts.
50 He cast upon them the furiousness of his wrath, anger, displeasure, and trouble : and sent evil angels among them.
51 He made a way to his indignation, and spared not their soul from death : but gave their life over to the pestilence;
52 And smote all the first-born in Egypt : the most principal and mightiest in the dwellings of Ham.
53 But as for his own people, he led them forth like sheep : and carried them in the wilderness like a flock.
54 He brought them out safely, that they should not fear : and overwhelmed their enemies with the sea.
55 And brought them within the borders of his sanctuary : even to his mountain which he purchased with his right hand.
56 He cast out the heathen also before them : caused their land to be divided among them for an heritage, and made the tribes of Israel to dwell in their tents.
57 So they tempted, and displeased the most high God : and kept not his testimonies;
58 But turned their backs, and fell away like their forefathers : starting aside like a broken bow.
59 For they grieved him with their hill-altars : and provoked him to displeasure with their images.
60 When God heard this, he was wroth : and took sore displeasure at Israel.

61 So that he forsook the tabernacle in Silo : even the tent that he had pitched among men.
62 He delivered their power into captivity : and their beauty into the enemy's hand.
63 He gave his people over also unto the sword : and was wroth with his inheritance.
64 The fire consumed their young men : and their maidens were not given to marriage.
65 Their priests were slain with the sword : and there were no widows to make lamentation.
66 So the Lord awaked as one out of sleep : and like a giant refreshed with wine.
67 He smote his enemies in the hinder parts : and put them to a perpetual shame.
68 He refused the tabernacle of Joseph : and chose not the tribe of Ephraim;
69 But chose the tribe of Judah : even the hill of Sion which he loved.
70 And there he built his temple on high : and laid the foundation of it like the ground which he hath made continually.
71 He chose David also his servant : and took him away from the sheep-folds.
72 As he was following the ewes great with young ones he took him : that he might feed Jacob his people, and Israel his inheritance.
73 So he fed them with a faithful and true heart : and ruled them prudently with all his power.

Morning Prayer
PSALM LXXIX. *Deus, venerunt.*

O GOD, the heathen are come into thine inheritance : thy holy temple have they defiled, and made Jerusalem an heap of stones.
2 The dead bodies of thy servants have they given to be meat unto the fowls of the air : and the

flesh of thy saints unto the beasts of the land.

3 Their blood have they shed like water on every side of Jerusalem : and there was no man to bury them.

4 We are become an open shame to our enemies : a very scorn and derision unto them that are round about us.

5 Lord, how long wilt thou be angry : shall thy jealousy burn like fire for ever?

6 Pour out thine indignation upon the heathen that have not known thee : and upon the kingdoms that have not called upon thy Name.

7 For they have devoured Jacob : and laid waste his dwellingplace.

8 O remember not our old sins, but have mercy upon us, and that soon : for we are come to great misery.

9 Help us, O God of our salvation, for the glory of thy Name : O deliver us, and be merciful unto our sins, for thy Name's sake.

10 Wherefore do the heathen say : Where is now their God?

11 O let the vengeance of thy servants' blood that is shed : be openly shewed upon the heathen in our sight.

12 O let the sorrowful sighing of the prisoners come before thee : according to the greatness of thy power, preserve thou those that are appointed to die.

13 And for the blasphemy wherewith our neighbours have blasphemed thee : reward thou them, O Lord, seven-fold into their bosom.

14 So we, that are thy people, and sheep of thy pasture, shall give thee thanks for ever : and will alway be shewing forth thy praise from generation to generation.

PSALM LXXX. *Qui regis Israel.*

HEAR, O thou Shepherd of Israel, thou that leadest Joseph like a sheep : shew thyself also, thou that sittest upon the cherubims.

2 Before Ephraim, Benjamin, and Manasses : stir up thy strength, and come, and help us.

3 Turn us again, O God : shew the light of thy countenance, and we shall be whole.

4 O Lord God of hosts : how long wilt thou be angry with thy people that prayeth?

5 Thou feedest them with the bread of tears : and givest them plenteousness of tears to drink.

6 Thou hast made us a very strife unto our neighbours : and our enemies laugh us to scorn.

7 Turn us again, thou God of hosts : shew the light of thy countenance, and we shall be whole.

8 Thou hast brought a vine out of Egypt : thou hast cast out the heathen, and planted it.

9 Thou madest room for it : and when it had taken root it filled the land.

10 The hills were covered with the shadow of it : and the boughs thereof were like the goodly cedar-trees.

11 She stretched out her branches unto the sea : and her boughs unto the river.

12 Why hast thou then broken down her hedge : that all they that go by pluck off her grapes?

13 The wild boar out of the wood doth root it up : and the wild beasts of the field devour it.

14 Turn thee again, thou God of hosts, look down from heaven : behold, and visit this vine;

15 And the place of the vineyard that thy right hand hath planted : and the branch that thou madest so strong for thyself.

16 It is burnt with fire, and cut down : and they shall perish at the rebuke of thy countenance.

17 Let thy hand be upon the man of thy right hand : and upon the son of man, whom thou madest so strong for thine own self.

18 And so will not we go back from thee : O let us live, and we shall call upon thy Name.

19 Turn us again, O Lord God of hosts : shew the light of thy countenance, and we shall be whole.

PSALM LXXXI. *Exultate Deo.*

SING we merrily unto God our strength : make a cheerful noise unto the God of Jacob.

2 Take the psalm, bring hither the tabret : the merry harp with the lute.

3 Blow up the trumpet in the new-moon : even in the time appointed, and upon our solemn feast-day.

4 For this was made a statute for Israel : and a law of the God of Jacob.

5 This he ordained in Joseph for a testimony : when he came out of the land of Egypt, and had heard a strange language.

6 I eased his shoulder from the burden : and his hands were delivered from making the pots.

7 Thou calledst upon me in troubles, and I delivered thee : and heard thee what time as the storm fell upon thee.

8 I proved thee also : at the waters of strife.

9 Hear, O my people, and I will assure thee, O Israel : if thou wilt hearken unto me,

10 There shall no strange god be in thee : neither shalt thou worship any other god.

11 I am the Lord thy God, who brought thee out of the land of Egypt : open thy mouth wide, and I shall fill it.

12 But my people would not hear my voice : and Israel would not obey me.

13 So I gave them up unto their own hearts' lusts : and let them follow their own imaginations.

14 O that my people would have hearkened unto me : for if Israel had walked in my ways,

15 I should soon have put down their enemies : and turned my hand against their adversaries.

16 The haters of the Lord should have been found liars : but their time should have endured for ever.

17 He should have fed them also with the finest wheat-flour : and with honey out of the stony rock should I have satisfied thee.

Evening Prayer

PSALM LXXXII. *Deus stetit.*

GOD standeth in the congregation of princes : he is a Judge among gods.

2 How long will ye give wrong judgement : and accept the persons of the ungodly?

3 Defend the poor and fatherless : see that such as are in need and necessity have right.

4 Deliver the out-cast and poor : save them from the hand of the ungodly.

5 They will not be learned nor understand, but walk on still in darkness : all the foundations of the earth are out of course.

6 I have said, Ye are gods : and ye are all the children of the most Highest.

7 But ye shall die like men : and fall like one of the princes.

8 Arise, O God, and judge thou the earth : for thou shalt take all heathen to thine inheritance.

PSALM LXXXIII. *Deus, quis similis?*

HOLD not thy tongue, O God, keep not still silence : refrain not thyself, O God.

2 For lo, thine enemies make a murmuring : and they that hate thee have lift up their head.

3 They have imagined craftily against thy people : and taken counsel against thy secret ones.

4 They have said, Come, and let us root them out, that they be no more a people : and that the name of Israel may be no more in remembrance.

5 For they have cast their heads together with one consent : and are confederate against thee;

6 The tabernacles of the Edomites, and the Ismaelites : the Moabites, and Hagarens;

7 Gebal, and Ammon, and Amalek : the Philistines, with them that dwell at Tyre.

8 Assur also is joined with them : and have holpen the children of Lot.

9 But do thou to them as unto the Madianites : unto Sisera, and unto Jabin at the brook of Kison;

10 Who perished at En-dor : and became as the dung of the earth.

11 Make them and their princes like Oreb and Zeb : yea, make all their princes like as Zeba and Salmana;

12 Who say, Let us take to ourselves : the houses of God in possession.

13 O my God, make them like unto a wheel : and as the stubble before the wind;

14 Like as the fire that burneth up the wood : and as the flame that consumeth the mountains.

15 Persecute them even so with thy tempest : and make them afraid with thy storm.

16 Make their faces ashamed, O Lord : that they may seek thy Name.

17 Let them be confounded and vexed ever more and more : let them be put to shame, and perish.

18 And they shall know that thou, whose Name is Jehovah : art only the most Highest over all the earth.

PSALM LXXXIV. *Quam dilecta!*

O HOW amiable are thy dwellings : thou Lord of hosts!

2 My soul hath a desire and longing to enter into the courts of the Lord : my heart and my flesh rejoice in the living God.

3 Yea, the sparrow hath found her an house, and the swallow a nest where she may lay her young : even thy altars, O Lord of hosts, my King and my God.

4 Blessed are they that dwell in thy house : they will be alway praising thee.

5 Blessed is the man whose strength is in thee : in whose heart are thy ways.

6 Who going through the vale of misery use it for a well : and the pools are filled with water.

7 They will go from strength to strength : and unto the God of gods appeareth every one of them in Sion.

8 O Lord God of hosts, hear my prayer : hearken, O God of Jacob.

9 Behold, O God our defender : and look upon the face of thine Anointed.

10 For one day in thy courts : is better than a thousand.

11 I had rather be a door-keeper in the house of my God : than to dwell in the tents of ungodliness.

12 For the Lord God is a light and defence : the Lord will give grace and worship, and no good thing shall he withhold from them that live a godly life.

13 O Lord God of hosts : blessed is the man that putteth his trust in thee.

PSALM LXXXV. *Benedixisti, Domine.*

LORD, thou art become gracious unto thy land : thou hast turned away the captivity of Jacob.

2 Thou hast forgiven the offence of thy people : and covered all their sins.

3 Thou hast taken away all thy displeasure : and turned thyself from thy wrathful indignation.

4 Turn us then, O God our Saviour : and let thine anger cease from us.

5 Wilt thou be displeased at us for ever : and wilt thou stretch out thy wrath from one generation to another?

6 Wilt thou not turn again, and quicken us : that thy people may rejoice in thee?

7 Shew us thy mercy, O Lord : and grant us thy salvation.

8 I will hearken what the Lord God will say concerning me : for he shall speak peace unto his people, and to his saints, that they turn not again.

9 For his salvation is nigh them that fear him : that glory may dwell in our land.

10 Mercy and truth are met together : righteousness and peace have kissed each other.

11 Truth shall flourish out of the earth : and righteousness hath looked down from heaven.

12 Yea, the Lord shall shew loving-kindness : and our land shall give her increase.

13 Righteousness shall go before him : and he shall direct his going in the way.

Morning Prayer

PSALM LXXXVI. *Inclina, Domine.*

BOW down thine ear, O Lord, and hear me : for I am poor, and in misery.

2 Preserve thou my soul, for I am holy : my God, save thy servant that putteth his trust in thee.

3 Be merciful unto me, O Lord : for I will call daily upon thee.

4 Comfort the soul of thy servant : for unto thee, O Lord, do I lift up my soul.

5 For thou, Lord, art good and gracious : and of great mercy unto all them that call upon thee.

6 Give ear, Lord, unto my prayer : and ponder the voice of my humble desires.

7 In the time of my trouble I will call upon thee : for thou hearest me.

8 Among the gods there is none like unto thee, O Lord : there is not one that can do as thou doest.

9 All nations whom thou hast made shall come and worship thee, O Lord : and shall glorify thy Name.

10 For thou art great, and doest wondrous things : thou art God alone.

11 Teach me thy way, O Lord, and I will walk in thy truth : O knit my heart unto thee, that I may fear thy Name.

12 I will thank thee, O Lord my God, with all my heart : and will praise thy Name for evermore.

13 For great is thy mercy toward me : and thou hast delivered my soul from the nethermost hell.

14 O God, the proud are risen against me : and the congregations of naughty men have sought after my soul, and have not set thee before their eyes.

15 But thou, O Lord God, art full of compassion and mercy : long-suffering, plenteous in goodness and truth.

16 O turn thee then unto me, and have mercy upon me : give thy strength unto thy servant, and help the son of thine handmaid.

17 Shew some token upon me for good, that they who hate me may see it, and be ashamed : because thou, Lord, hast holpen me, and comforted me.

PSALM LXXXVII. *Fundamenta ejus.*

HER foundations are upon the holy hills : the Lord loveth the gates of Sion more than all the dwellings of Jacob.

2 Very excellent things are spoken of thee : thou city of God.

3 I will think upon Rahab and Babylon : with them that know me.

4 Behold ye the Philistines also : and they of Tyre, with the Morians; lo, there was he born.

5 And of Sion it shall be reported that he was born in her : and the most High shall stablish her.

6 The Lord shall rehearse it when he writeth up the people : that he was born there.

7 The singers also and trumpeters shall he rehearse : All my fresh springs shall be in thee.

PSALM LXXXVIII. *Domine Deus.*

O LORD God of my salvation, I have cried day and night before thee : O let my prayer enter into thy presence, incline thine ear unto my calling.

2 For my soul is full of trouble : and my life draweth nigh unto hell.

3 I am counted as one of them that go down into the pit : and I have been even as a man that hath no strength.

4 Free among the dead, like unto them that are wounded, and lie in the grave : who are out of remembrance, and are cut away from thy hand.

5 Thou hast laid me in the lowest pit : in a place of darkness, and in the deep.

6 Thine indignation lieth hard upon me : and thou hast vexed me with all thy storms.

7 Thou hast put away mine acquaintance far from me : and made me to be abhorred of them.

8 I am so fast in prison : that I cannot get forth.

9 My sight faileth for very trouble : Lord, I have called daily upon thee, I have stretched forth my hands unto thee.

10 Dost thou shew wonders among the dead : or shall the dead rise up again, and praise thee?

11 Shall thy loving-kindness be shewed in the grave : or thy faithfulness in destruction?

12 Shall thy wondrous works be known in the dark : and thy righteousness in the land where all things are forgotten?

13 Unto thee have I cried, O Lord : and early shall my prayer come before thee.

14 Lord, why abhorrest thou my soul : and hidest thou thy face from me?

15 I am in misery, and like unto him that is at the point to die : even from my youth up thy terrors have I suffered with a troubled mind.

16 Thy wrathful displeasure goeth over me : and the fear of thee hath undone me.

17 They came round about me daily like water : and compassed me together on every side.

18 My lovers and friends hast thou put away from me : and hid mine acquaintance out of my sight.

Evening Prayer

PSALM LXXXIX. *Misericordias Domini.*

MY song shall be alway of the loving-kindness of the Lord : with my mouth will I ever be shewing thy truth from one generation to another.

2 For I have said, Mercy shall be set up for ever : thy truth shalt thou stablish in the heavens.

3 I have made a covenant with my chosen : I have sworn unto David my servant;

4 Thy seed will I stablish for ever : and set up thy throne from one generation to another.

5 O Lord, the very heavens shall praise thy wondrous works : and thy truth in the congregation of the saints.

6 For who is he among the clouds : that shall be compared unto the Lord?

7 And what is he among the gods : that shall be like unto the Lord?

8 God is very greatly to be feared in the council of the saints : and to be had in reverence of all them that are round about him.

9 O Lord God of hosts, who is like unto thee : thy truth, most mighty Lord, is on every side.

THE PSALMS.

10 Thou rulest the raging of the sea : thou stillest the waves thereof when they arise.

11 Thou hast subdued Egypt, and destroyed it : thou hast scattered thine enemies abroad with thy mighty arm.

12 The heavens are thine, the earth also is thine : thou hast laid the foundation of the round world, and all that therein is.

13 Thou hast made the north and the south : Tabor and Hermon shall rejoice in thy Name.

14 Thou hast a mighty arm : strong is thy hand, and high is thy right hand.

15 Righteousness and equity are the habitation of thy seat : mercy and truth shall go before thy face.

16 Blessed is the people, O Lord, that can rejoice in thee : they shall walk in the light of thy countenance.

17 Their delight shall be daily in thy Name : and in thy righteousness shall they make their boast.

18 For thou art the glory of their strength : and in thy lovingkindness thou shalt lift up our horns.

19 For the Lord is our defence : the Holy One of Israel is our King.

20 Thou spakest sometime in visions unto thy saints, and saidst : I have laid help upon one that is mighty ; I have exalted one chosen out of the people.

21 I have found David my servant : with my holy oil have I anointed him.

22 My hand shall hold him fast : and my arm shall strengthen him.

23 The enemy shall not be able to do him violence : the son of wickedness shall not hurt him.

24 I will smite down his foes before his face : and plague them that hate him.

25 My truth also and my mercy shall be with him : and in my Name shall his horn be exalted.

26 I will set his dominion also in the sea : and his right hand in the floods.

27 He shall call me, Thou art my Father : my God, and my strong salvation.

28 And I will make him my first-born : higher than the kings of the earth.

29 My mercy will I keep for him for evermore : and my covenant shall stand fast with him.

30 His seed also will I make to endure for ever : and his throne as the days of heaven.

31 But if his children forsake my law : and walk not in my judgements ;

32 If they break my statutes, and keep not my commandments : I will visit their offences with the rod, and their sin with scourges.

33 Nevertheless, my lovingkindness will I not utterly take from him : nor suffer my truth to fail.

34 My covenant will I not break, nor alter the thing that is gone out of my lips : I have sworn once by my holiness, that I will not fail David.

35 His seed shall endure for ever : and his seat is like as the sun before me.

36 He shall stand fast for evermore as the moon : and as the faithful witness in heaven.

37 But thou hast abhorred and forsaken thine Anointed : and art displeased at him.

38 Thou hast broken the covenant of thy servant : and cast his crown to the ground.

39 Thou hast overthrown all his hedges : and broken down his strong holds.

40 All they that go by spoil him : and he is become a reproach to his neighbours.

41 Thou hast set up the right hand of his enemies : and made all his adversaries to rejoice.

42 Thou hast taken away the edge of his sword : and givest him not victory in the battle.

43 Thou hast put out his glory : and cast his throne down to the ground.

44 The days of his youth hast thou shortened : and covered him with dishonour.

45 Lord, how long wilt thou hide thyself, for ever : and shall thy wrath burn like fire?

46 O remember how short my time is : wherefore hast thou made all men for nought?

47 What man is he that liveth, and shall not see death : and shall he deliver his soul from the hand of hell?

48 Lord, where are thy old loving-kindnesses : which thou swarest unto David in thy truth?

49 Remember, Lord, the rebuke that thy servants have : and how I do bear in my bosom the rebukes of many people;

50 Wherewith thine enemies have blasphemed thee, and slandered the footsteps of thine Anointed : Praised be the Lord for evermore. Amen, and Amen.

Morning Prayer
PSALM XC. *Domine, refugium.*

LORD, thou hast been our refuge : from one generation to another.

2 Before the mountains were brought forth, or ever the earth and the world were made : thou art God from everlasting, and world without end.

3 Thou turnest man to destruction : again thou sayest, Come again, ye children of men.

4 For a thousand years in thy sight are but as yesterday : seeing that is past as a watch in the night.

5 As soon as thou scatterest them they are even as a sleep : and fade away suddenly like the grass.

6 In the morning it is green, and groweth up : but in the evening it is cut down, dried up, and withered.

7 For we consume away in thy displeasure : and are afraid at thy wrathful indignation.

8 Thou hast set our misdeeds before thee : and our secret sins in the light of thy countenance.

9 For when thou art angry all our days are gone : we bring our years to an end, as it were a tale that is told.

10 The days of our age are threescore years and ten; and though men be so strong that they come to fourscore years : yet is their strength then but labour and sorrow; so soon passeth it away, and we are gone.

11 But who regardeth the power of thy wrath : for even thereafter as a man feareth, so is thy displeasure.

12 So teach us to number our days : that we may apply our hearts unto wisdom.

13 Turn thee again, O Lord, at the last : and be gracious unto thy servants.

14 O satisfy us with thy mercy, and that soon : so shall we rejoice and be glad all the days of our life.

15 Comfort us again now after the time that thou hast plagued us : and for the years wherein we have suffered adversity.

16 Shew thy servants thy work : and their children thy glory.

17 And the glorious Majesty of the Lord our God be upon us : prosper thou the work of our hands upon us, O prosper thou our handy-work.

PSALM XCI. *Qui habitat.*

WHOSO dwelleth under the defence of the most High : shall abide under the shadow of the Almighty.

2 I will say unto the Lord, Thou art my hope, and my strong hold : my God, in him will I trust.

3 For he shall deliver thee from the snare of the hunter : and from the noisome pestilence.

4 He shall defend thee under his wings, and thou shalt be safe under his feathers : his faithfulness and truth shall be thy shield and buckler.

5 Thou shalt not be afraid for any terror by night : nor for the arrow that flieth by day;

6 For the pestilence that walketh in darkness : nor for the sickness that destroyeth in the noon-day.

7 A thousand shall fall beside thee, and ten thousand at thy right hand : but it shall not come nigh thee.

8 Yea, with thine eyes shalt thou behold : and see the reward of the ungodly.

9 For thou, Lord, art my hope : thou hast set thine house of defence very high.

10 There shall no evil happen unto thee : neither shall any plague come nigh thy dwelling.

11 For he shall give his angels charge over thee : to keep thee in all thy ways.

12 They shall bear thee in their hands : that thou hurt not thy foot against a stone.

13 Thou shalt go upon the lion and adder : the young lion and the dragon shalt thou tread under thy feet.

14 Because he hath set his love upon me, therefore will I deliver him : I will set him up, because he hath known my Name.

15 He shall call upon me, and I will hear him : yea, I am with him in trouble; I will deliver him, and bring him to honour.

16 With long life will I satisfy him : and shew him my salvation.

PSALM XCII. *Bonum est confiteri.*

IT is a good thing to give thanks unto the Lord : and to sing praises unto thy Name, O most Highest:

2 To tell of thy loving-kindness early in the morning : and of thy truth in the night-season;

3 Upon an instrument of ten strings, and upon the lute : upon a loud instrument, and upon the harp.

4 For thou, Lord, hast made me glad through thy works : and I will rejoice in giving praise for the operations of thy hands.

5 O Lord, how glorious are thy works : thy thoughts are very deep.

6 An unwise man doth not well consider this : and a fool doth not understand it.

7 When the ungodly are green as the grass, and when all the workers of wickedness do flourish : then shall they be destroyed for ever; but thou, Lord, art the most Highest for evermore.

8 For lo, thine enemies, O Lord, lo, thine enemies shall perish : and all the workers of wickedness shall be destroyed.

9 But mine horn shall be exalted like the horn of an unicorn : for I am anointed with fresh oil.

10 Mine eye also shall see his lust of mine enemies : and mine ear shall hear his desire of the wicked that arise up against me.

11 The righteous shall flourish like a palm-tree : and shall spread abroad like a cedar in Libanus.

12 Such as are planted in the house of the Lord : shall flourish in the courts of the house of our God.

13 They also shall bring forth more fruit in their age : and shall be fat and well-liking.

14 That they may shew how true the Lord my strength is : and that there is no unrighteousness in him.

Evening Prayer

PSALM XCIII. *Dominus regnavit.*

THE Lord is King, and hath put on glorious apparel : the Lord hath put on his apparel, and girded himself with strength.

2 He hath made the round world so sure : that it cannot be moved.

3 Ever since the world began hath thy seat been prepared : thou art from everlasting.

4 The floods are risen, O Lord, the floods have lift up their voice : the floods lift up their waves.

5 The waves of the sea are mighty, and rage horribly : but yet the Lord, who dwelleth on high, is mightier.

6 Thy testimonies, O Lord, are very sure : holiness becometh thine house for ever.

PSALM XCIV. *Deus ultionum.*

O LORD God, to whom vengeance belongeth : thou God, to whom vengeance belongeth, shew thyself.

2 Arise, thou Judge of the world : and reward the proud after their deserving.

3 Lord, how long shall the ungodly : how long shall the ungodly triumph?

4 How long shall all wicked doers speak so disdainfully : and make such proud boasting?

5 They smite down thy people, O Lord : and trouble thine heritage.

6 They murder the widow, and the stranger : and put the fatherless to death.

7 And yet they say, Tush, the Lord shall not see : neither shall the God of Jacob regard it.

8 Take heed, ye unwise among the people : O ye fools, when will ye understand?

9 He that planted the ear, shall he not hear : or he that made the eye, shall he not see?

10 Or he that nurtureth the heathen : it is he that teacheth man knowledge, shall not he punish?

11 The Lord knoweth the thoughts of man : that they are but vain.

12 Blessed is the man whom thou chastenest, O Lord : and teachest him in thy law;

13 That thou mayest give him patience in time of adversity : until the pit be digged up for the ungodly.

14 For the Lord will not fail his people : neither will he forsake his inheritance;

15 Until righteousness turn again unto judgement : all such as are true in heart shall follow it.

16 Who will rise up with me against the wicked : or who will take my part against the evildoers?

17 If the Lord had not helped me : it had not failed but my soul had been put to silence.

18 But when I said, My foot hath slipt : thy mercy, O Lord, held me up.

19 In the multitude of the sorrows that I had in my heart : thy comforts have refreshed my soul.

20 Wilt thou have any thing to do with the stool of wickedness : which imagineth mischief as a law?

21 They gather them together against the soul of the righteous : and condemn the innocent blood.

22 But the Lord is my refuge : and my God is the strength of my confidence.

23 He shall recompense them their wickedness, and destroy them in their own malice : yea, the Lord our God shall destroy them.

Morning Prayer

PSALM XCV. *Venite, exultemus.*

O COME, let us sing unto the Lord : let us heartily rejoice in the strength of our salvation.

2 Let us come before his presence with thanksgiving : and shew ourselves glad in him with psalms.

3 For the Lord is a great God : and a great King above all gods.

4 In his hand are all the corners of the earth : and the strength of the hills is his also.

5 The sea is his, and he made it : and his hands prepared the dry land.

6 O come, let us worship and fall down : and kneel before the Lord our Maker.

7 For he is the Lord our God : and we are the people of his pasture, and the sheep of his hand.

8 To-day if ye will hear his voice, harden not your hearts : as in the provocation, and as in the day of temptation in the wilderness;

9 When your fathers tempted me : proved me, and saw my works.

10 Forty years long was I grieved with this generation, and said : It is a people that do err in their hearts, for they have not known my ways;

11 Unto whom I sware in my wrath : that they should not enter into my rest.

PSALM XCVI. *Cantate Domino.*

O SING unto the Lord a new song : sing unto the Lord, all the whole earth.

2 Sing unto the Lord, and praise his Name : be telling of his salvation from day to day.

3 Declare his honour unto the heathen : and his wonders unto all people.

4 For the Lord is great, and cannot worthily be praised : he is more to be feared than all gods.

5 As for all the gods of the heathen, they are but idols : but it is the Lord that made the heavens.

6 Glory and worship are before him : power and honour are in his sanctuary.

7 Ascribe unto the Lord, O ye kindreds of the people : ascribe unto the Lord worship and power.

8 Ascribe unto the Lord the honour due unto his Name : bring presents, and come into his courts.

9 O worship the Lord in the beauty of holiness : let the whole earth stand in awe of him.

10 Tell it out among the heathen that the Lord is King : and that it is he who hath made the round world so fast that it cannot be moved; and how that he shall judge the people righteously.

11 Let the heavens rejoice, and let the earth be glad : let the sea make a noise, and all that therein is.

12 Let the field be joyful, and all that is in it : then shall all the trees of the wood rejoice before the Lord.

13 For he cometh, for he cometh to judge the earth : and with righteousness to judge the world, and the people with his truth.

PSALM XCVII. *Dominus regnavit.*

THE Lord is King, the earth may be glad thereof : yea, the multitude of the isles may be glad thereof.

2 Clouds and darkness are round about him : righteousness and judgement are the habitation of his seat.

3 There shall go a fire before him : and burn up his enemies on every side.

4 His lightnings gave shine unto the world : the earth saw it, and was afraid.

5 The hills melted like wax at the presence of the Lord : at the presence of the Lord of the whole earth.

6 The heavens have declared his righteousness : and all the people have seen his glory.

7 Confounded be all they that worship carved images, and that delight in vain gods : worship him, all ye gods.

8 Sion heard of it, and rejoiced : and the daughters of Judah were glad, because of thy judgements, O Lord.

9 For thou, Lord, art higher than all that are in the earth : thou art exalted far above all gods.

Day 19. THE PSALMS. Day 19.

10 O ye that love the Lord, see that ye hate the thing which is evil: the Lord preserveth the souls of his saints; he shall deliver them from the hand of the ungodly.

11 There is sprung up a light for the righteous : and joyful gladness for such as are true-hearted.

12 Rejoice in the Lord, ye righteous : and give thanks for a remembrance of his holiness.

Evening Prayer

PSALM XCVIII. *Cantate Domino.*

O SING unto the Lord a new song : for he hath done marvellous things.

2 With his own right hand, and with his holy arm : hath he gotten himself the victory.

3 The Lord declared his salvation : his righteousness hath he openly shewed in the sight of the heathen.

4 He hath remembered his mercy and truth toward the house of Israel : and all the ends of the world have seen the salvation of our God.

5 Shew yourselves joyful unto the Lord, all ye lands : sing, rejoice, and give thanks.

6 Praise the Lord upon the harp : sing to the harp with a psalm of thanksgiving.

7 With trumpets also, and shawms : O shew yourselves joyful before the Lord the King.

8 Let the sea make a noise, and all that therein is : the round world, and they that dwell therein.

9 Let the floods clap their hands, and let the hills be joyful together before the Lord : for he is come to judge the earth.

10 With righteousness shall he judge the world : and the people with equity.

PSALM XCIX. *Dominus regnavit.*

THE Lord is King, be the people never so impatient : he sitteth between the cherubims, be the earth never so unquiet.

2 The Lord is great in Sion : and high above all people.

3 They shall give thanks unto thy Name : which is great, wonderful, and holy.

4 The King's power loveth judgement; thou hast prepared equity : thou hast executed judgement and righteousness in Jacob.

5 O magnify the Lord our God : and fall down before his footstool, for he is holy.

6 Moses and Aaron among his priests, and Samuel among such as call upon his Name : these called upon the Lord, and he heard them.

7 He spake unto them out of the cloudy pillar : for they kept his testimonies, and the law that he gave them.

8 Thou heardest them, O Lord our God : thou forgavest them, O God, and punishedst their own inventions.

9 O magnify the Lord our God, and worship him upon his holy hill : for the Lord our God is holy.

PSALM C. *Jubilate Deo.*

O BE joyful in the Lord, all ye lands : serve the Lord with gladness, and come before his presence with a song.

2 Be ye sure that the Lord he is God : it is he that hath made us, and not we ourselves; we are his people, and the sheep of his pasture.

3 O go your way into his gates with thanksgiving, and into his courts with praise : be thankful unto him, and speak good of his Name.

4 For the Lord is gracious, his mercy is everlasting : and his truth endureth from generation to generation.

PSALM CI. *Misericordiam et judicium.*

MY song shall be of mercy and judgement : unto thee, O Lord, will I sing.

2 O let me have understanding : in the way of godliness.
3 When wilt thou come unto me : I will walk in my house with a perfect heart.
4 I will take no wicked thing in hand; I hate the sins of unfaithfulness : there shall no such cleave unto me.
5 A froward heart shall depart from me : I will not know a wicked person.
6 Whoso privily slandereth his neighbour : him will I destroy.
7 Whoso hath also a proud look and high stomach : I will not suffer him.
8 Mine eyes look upon such as are faithful in the land : that they may dwell with me.
9 Whoso leadeth a godly life : he shall be my servant.
10 There shall no deceitful person dwell in my house : he that telleth lies shall not tarry in my sight.
11 I shall soon destroy all the ungodly that are in the land : that I may root out all wicked doers from the city of the Lord.

Morning Prayer

PSALM CII. *Domine, exaudi.*

HEAR my prayer, O Lord : and let my crying come unto thee.
2 Hide not thy face from me in the time of my trouble : incline thine ear unto me when I call; O hear me, and that right soon.
3 For my days are consumed away like smoke : and my bones are burnt up as it were a firebrand.
4 My heart is smitten down, and withered like grass : so that I forget to eat my bread.
5 For the voice of my groaning : my bones will scarce cleave to my flesh.
6 I am become like a pelican in the wilderness : and like an owl that is in the desert.
7 I have watched, and am even as it were a sparrow : that sitteth alone upon the house-top.
8 Mine enemies revile me all the day long : and they that are mad upon me are sworn together against me.
9 For I have eaten ashes as it were bread : and mingled my drink with weeping;
10 And that because of thine indignation and wrath : for thou hast taken me up, and cast me down.
11 My days are gone like a shadow : and I am withered like grass.
12 But, thou, O Lord, shalt endure for ever : and thy remembrance throughout all generations.
13 Thou shalt arise, and have mercy upon Sion : for it is time that thou have mercy upon her, yea, the time is come.
14 And why? thy servants think upon her stones : and it pitieth them to see her in the dust.
15 The heathen shall fear thy Name, O Lord : and all the kings of the earth thy Majesty;
16 When the Lord shall build up Sion : and when his glory shall appear;
17 When he turneth him unto the prayer of the poor destitute : and despiseth not their desire.
18 This shall be written for those that come after : and the people which shall be born shall praise the Lord.
19 For he hath looked down from his sanctuary : out of the heaven did the Lord behold the earth;
20 That he might hear the mournings of such as are in captivity : and deliver the children appointed unto death;
21 That they may declare the Name of the Lord in Sion : and his worship at Jerusalem;
22 When the people are gathered together : and the kingdoms also, to serve the Lord.

23 He brought down my strength in my journey: and shortened my days.

24 But I said, O my God, take me not away in the midst of mine age: as for thy years, they endure throughout all generations.

25 Thou, Lord, in the beginning hast laid the foundation of the earth: and the heavens are the work of thy hands.

26 They shall perish, but thou shalt endure: they all shall wax old as doth a garment;

27 And as a vesture shalt thou change them, and they shall be changed: but thou art the same, and thy years shall not fail.

28 The children of thy servants shall continue: and their seed shall stand fast in thy sight.

PSALM CIII. *Benedic, anima mea.*

PRAISE the Lord, O my soul: and all that is within me praise his holy Name.

2 Praise the Lord, O my soul: and forget not all his benefits;

3 Who forgiveth all thy sin: and healeth all thine infirmities;

4 Who saveth thy life from destruction: and crowneth thee with mercy and loving-kindness;

5 Who satisfieth thy mouth with good things: making thee young and lusty as an eagle.

6 The Lord executeth righteousness and judgement: for all them that are oppressed with wrong.

7 He shewed his ways unto Moses: his works unto the children of Israel.

8 The Lord is full of compassion and mercy: long-suffering, and of great goodness.

9 He will not alway be chiding: neither keepeth he his anger for ever.

10 He hath not dealt with us after our sins: nor rewarded us according to our wickednesses.

11 For look how high the heaven is in comparison of the earth: so great is his mercy also toward them that fear him.

12 Look how wide also the east is from the west: so far hath he set our sins from us.

13 Yea, like as a father pitieth his own children: even so is the Lord merciful unto them that fear him.

14 For he knoweth whereof we are made: he remembereth that we are but dust.

15 The days of man are but as grass: for he flourisheth as a flower of the field.

16 For as soon as the wind goeth over it, it is gone: and the place thereof shall know it no more.

17 But the merciful goodness of the Lord endureth for ever and ever upon them that fear him: and his righteousness upon children's children;

18 Even upon such as keep his covenant: and think upon his commandments to do them.

19 The Lord hath prepared his seat in heaven: and his kingdom ruleth over all.

20 O praise the Lord, ye angels of his, ye that excel in strength: ye that fulfil his commandment, and hearken unto the voice of his words.

21 O praise the Lord, all ye his hosts: ye servants of his that do his pleasure.

22 O speak good of the Lord, all ye works of his, in all places of his dominion: praise thou the Lord, O my soul.

Evening Prayer

PSALM CIV. *Benedic, anima mea.*

PRAISE the Lord, O my soul: O Lord my God, thou art become exceeding glorious; thou art clothed with majesty and honour.

2 Thou deckest thyself with light as it were with a garment: and spreadest out the heavens like a curtain.

3 Who layeth the beams of his chambers in the waters : and maketh the clouds his chariot, and walketh upon the wings of the wind.

4 He maketh his angels spirits : and his ministers a flaming fire.

5 He laid the foundations of the earth : that it never should move at any time.

6 Thou coveredst it with the deep like as with a garment : the waters stand in the hills.

7 At thy rebuke they flee : at the voice of thy thunder they are afraid.

8 They go up as high as the hills, and down to the valleys beneath : even unto the place which thou hast appointed for them.

9 Thou hast set them their bounds which they shall not pass : neither turn again to cover the earth.

10 He sendeth the springs into the rivers : which run among the hills.

11 All beasts of the field drink thereof : and the wild asses quench their thirst.

12 Beside them shall the fowls of the air have their habitation : and sing among the branches.

13 He watereth the hills from above : the earth is filled with the fruit of thy works.

14 He bringeth forth grass for the cattle : and green herb for the service of men;

15 That he may bring food out of the earth, and wine that maketh glad the heart of man : and oil to make him a cheerful countenance, and bread to strengthen man's heart.

16 The trees of the Lord also are full of sap : even the cedars of Libanus which he hath planted;

17 Wherein the birds make their nests : and the fir-trees are a dwelling for the stork.

18 The high hills are a refuge for the wild goats : and so are the stony rocks for the conies.

19 He appointed the moon for certain seasons : and the sun knoweth his going down.

20 Thou makest darkness that it may be night : wherein all the beasts of the forest do move.

21 The lions roaring after their prey : do seek their meat from God.

22 The sun ariseth, and they get them away together : and lay them down in their dens.

23 Man goeth forth to his work, and to his labour : until the evening.

24 O Lord, how manifold are thy works : in wisdom hast thou made them all; the earth is full of thy riches.

25 So is the great and wide sea also : wherein are things creeping innumerable, both small and great beasts.

26 There go the ships, and there is that Leviathan : whom thou hast made to take his pastime therein.

27 These wait all upon thee : that thou mayest give them meat in due season.

28 When thou givest it them they gather it : and when thou openest thy hand they are filled with good.

29 When thou hidest thy face they are troubled : when thou takest away their breath they die, and are turned again to their dust.

30 When thou lettest thy breath go forth they shall be made : and thou shalt renew the face of the earth.

31 The glorious Majesty of the Lord shall endure for ever : the Lord shall rejoice in his works.

32 The earth shall tremble at the look of him : if he do but touch the hills, they shall smoke.

33 I will sing unto the Lord as long as I live : I will praise my God while I have my being.

34 And so shall my words please him : my joy shall be in the Lord.

35 As for sinners, they shall be

consumed out of the earth, and the ungodly shall come to an end : praise thou the Lord, O my soul, praise the Lord.

Morning Prayer

PSALM CV. *Confitemini Domino.*

O GIVE thanks unto the Lord, and call upon his Name : tell the people what things he hath done.

2 O let your songs be of him, and praise him : and let your talking be of all his wondrous works.

3 Rejoice in his holy Name : let the heart of them rejoice that seek the Lord.

4 Seek the Lord and his strength : seek his face evermore.

5 Remember the marvellous works that he hath done : his wonders, and the judgements of his mouth,

6 O ye seed of Abraham his servant : ye children of Jacob his chosen.

7 He is the Lord our God : his judgements are in all the world.

8 He hath been alway mindful of his covenant and promise : that he made to a thousand generations;

9 Even the covenant that he made with Abraham : and the oath that he sware unto Isaac;

10 And appointed the same unto Jacob for a law : and to Israel for an everlasting testament;

11 Saying, Unto thee will I give the land of Canaan : the lot of your inheritance;

12 When there were yet but a few of them : and they strangers in the land;

13 What time as they went from one nation to another : from one kingdom to another people;

14 He suffered no man to do them wrong : but reproved even kings for their sakes;

15 Touch not mine Anointed : and do my prophets no harm.

16 Moreover, he called for a dearth upon the land : and destroyed all the provision of bread.

17 But he had sent a man before them : even Joseph, who was sold to be a bond-servant;

18 Whose feet they hurt in the stocks : the iron entered into his soul;

19 Until the time came that his cause was known : the word of the Lord tried him.

20 The king sent, and delivered him : the prince of the people let him go free.

21 He made him lord also of his house : and ruler of all his substance;

22 That he might inform his princes after his will : and teach his senators wisdom.

23 Israel also came into Egypt : and Jacob was a stranger in the land of Ham.

24 And he increased his people exceedingly : and made them stronger than their enemies;

25 Whose heart turned so, that they hated his people : and dealt untruly with his servants.

26 Then sent he Moses his servant : and Aaron whom he had chosen.

27 And these shewed his tokens among them : and wonders in the land of Ham.

28 He sent darkness, and it was dark : and they were not obedient unto his word.

29 He turned their waters into blood : and slew their fish.

30 Their land brought forth frogs : yea, even in their kings' chambers.

31 He spake the word, and there came all manner of flies : and lice in all their quarters.

32 He gave them hail-stones for rain : and flames of fire in their land.

33 He smote their vines also and fig-trees : and destroyed the trees that were in their coasts.

34 He spake the word, and the

grasshoppers came, and caterpillars innumerable : and did eat up all the grass in their land, and devoured the fruit of their ground.

35 He smote all the first-born in their land : even the chief of all their strength.

36 He brought them forth also with silver and gold : there was not one feeble person among their tribes.

37 Egypt was glad at their departing : for they were afraid of them.

38 He spread out a cloud to be a covering : and fire to give light in the night-season.

39 At their desire he brought quails : and he filled them with the bread of heaven.

40 He opened the rock of stone, and the waters flowed out : so that rivers ran in the dry places.

41 For why? he remembered his holy promise : and Abraham his servant.

42 And he brought forth his people with joy : and his chosen with gladness;

43 And gave them the lands of the heathen : and they took the labours of the people in possession;

44 That they might keep his statutes : and observe his laws.

Evening Prayer

PSALM CVI. *Confitemini Domino.*

O GIVE thanks unto the Lord, for he is gracious : and his mercy endureth for ever.

2 Who can express the noble acts of the Lord : or shew forth all his praise?

3 Blessed are they that alway keep judgement : and do righteousness.

4 Remember me, O Lord, according to the favour that thou bearest unto thy people : O visit me with thy salvation;

5 That I may see the felicity of thy chosen : and rejoice in the gladness of thy people, and give thanks with thine inheritance.

6 We have sinned with our fathers : we have done amiss, and dealt wickedly.

7 Our fathers regarded not thy wonders in Egypt, neither kept they thy great goodness in remembrance : but were disobedient at the sea, even at the Red sea.

8 Nevertheless, he helped them for his Name's sake : that he might make his power to be known.

9 He rebuked the Red sea also, and it was dried up : so he led them through the deep, as through a wilderness.

10 And he saved them from the adversary's hand : and delivered them from the hand of the enemy.

11 As for those that troubled them, the waters overwhelmed them : there was not one of them left.

12 Then believed they his words : and sang praise unto him.

13 But within a while they forgat his works : and would not abide his counsel.

14 But lust came upon them in the wilderness : and they tempted God in the desert.

15 And he gave them their desire : and sent leanness withal into their soul.

16 They angered Moses also in the tents : and Aaron the saint of the Lord.

17 So the earth opened, and swallowed up Dathan : and covered the congregation of Abiram.

18 And the fire was kindled in their company : the flame burnt up the ungodly.

19 They made a calf in Horeb : and worshipped the molten image.

20 Thus they turned their glory : into the similitude of a calf that eateth hay.

21 And they forgat God their Saviour : who had done so great things in Egypt;

22 Wondrous works in the land of Ham : and fearful things by the Red sea.

23 So he said, he would have destroyed them, had not Moses his chosen stood before him in the gap : to turn away his wrathful indignation, lest he should destroy them.
24 Yea, they thought scorn of that pleasant land : and gave no credence unto his word;
25 But murmured in their tents : and hearkened not unto the voice of the Lord.
26 Then lift he up his hand against them : to overthrow them in the wilderness;
27 To cast out their seed among the nations : and to scatter them in the lands.
28 They joined themselves unto Baal-peor : and ate the offerings of the dead.
29 Thus they provoked him to anger with their own inventions : and the plague was great among them.
30 Then stood up Phinees and prayed : and so the plague ceased.
31 And that was counted unto him for righteousness : among all posterities for evermore.
32 They angered him also at the waters of strife : so that he punished Moses for their sakes;
33 Because they provoked his spirit : so that he spake unadvisedly with his lips.
34 Neither destroyed they the heathen : as the Lord commanded them;
35 But were mingled among the heathen : and learned their works.
36 Insomuch that they worshipped their idols, which turned to their own decay : yea, they offered their sons and their daughters unto devils;
37 And shed innocent blood, even the blood of their sons and of their daughters : whom they offered unto the idols of Canaan; and the land was defiled with blood.

38 Thus were they stained with their own works : and went a whoring with their own inventions.
39 Therefore was the wrath of the Lord kindled against his people : insomuch that he abhorred his own inheritance.
40 And he gave them over into the hand of the heathen : and they that hated them were lords over them.
41 Their enemies oppressed them : and had them in subjection.
42 Many a time did he deliver them : but they rebelled against him with their own inventions, and were brought down in their wickedness.
43 Nevertheless, when he saw their adversity : he heard their complaint.
44 He thought upon his covenant, and pitied them, according unto the multitude of his mercies : yea, he made all those that led them away captive to pity them.
45 Deliver us, O Lord our God, and gather us from among the heathen : that we may give thanks unto thy holy Name, and make our boast of thy praise.
46 Blessed be the Lord God of Israel from everlasting, and world without end : and let all the people say, Amen.

Morning Prayer

PSALM CVII. *Confitemini Domino.*

O GIVE thanks unto the Lord, for he is gracious : and his mercy endureth for ever.
2 Let them give thanks whom the Lord hath redeemed : and delivered from the hand of the enemy;
3 And gathered them out of the lands, from the east, and from the west : from the north, and from the south.
4 They went astray in the

wilderness out of the way : and found no city to dwell in;

5 Hungry and thirsty : their soul fainted in them.

6 So they cried unto the Lord in their trouble : and he delivered them from their distress.

7 He led them forth by the right way : that they might go to the city where they dwelt.

8 O that men would therefore praise the Lord for his goodness : and declare the wonders that he doeth for the children of men!

9 For he satisfieth the empty soul : and filleth the hungry soul with goodness.

10 Such as sit in darkness, and in the shadow of death : being fast bound in misery and iron;

11 Because they rebelled against the words of the Lord : and lightly regarded the counsel of the most Highest;

12 He also brought down their heart through heaviness : they fell down, and there was none to help them.

13 So when they cried unto the Lord in their trouble : he delivered them out of their distress.

14 For he brought them out of darkness, and out of the shadow of death : and brake their bonds in sunder.

15 O that men would therefore praise the Lord for his goodness : and declare the wonders that he doeth for the children of men!

16 For he hath broken the gates of brass : and smitten the bars of iron in sunder.

17 Foolish men are plagued for their offence : and because of their wickedness.

18 Their soul abhorred all manner of meat : and they were even hard at death's door.

19 So when they cried unto the Lord in their trouble : he delivered them out of their distress.

20 He sent his word, and healed them : and they were saved from their destruction.

21 O that men would therefore praise the Lord for his goodness : and declare the wonders that he doeth for the children of men!

22 That they would offer unto him the sacrifice of thanksgiving : and tell out his works with gladness!

23 They that go down to the sea in ships : and occupy their business in great waters;

24 These men see the works of the Lord : and his wonders in the deep.

25 For at his word the stormy wind ariseth : which lifteth up the waves thereof.

26 They are carried up to the heaven, and down again to the deep : their soul melteth away because of the trouble.

27 They reel to and fro, and stagger like a drunken man : and are at their wit's end.

28 So when they cry unto the Lord in their trouble : he delivereth them out of their distress.

29 For he maketh the storm to cease : so that the waves thereof are still.

30 Then are they glad, because they are at rest : and so he bringeth them unto the haven where they would be.

31 O that men would therefore praise the Lord for his goodness : and declare the wonders that he doeth for the children of men!

32 That they would exalt him also in the congregation of the people : and praise him in the seat of the elders!

33 Who turneth the floods into a wilderness : and drieth up the water-springs.

34 A fruitful land maketh he barren : for the wickedness of them that dwell therein.

35 Again, he maketh the wilderness a standing water : and water-springs of a dry ground.

36 And there he setteth the hungry : that they may build them a city to dwell in;

37 That they may sow their land, and plant vineyards : to yield them fruits of increase.
38 He blesseth them, so that they multiply exceedingly : and suffereth not their cattle to decrease.
39 And again, when they are minished, and brought low : through oppression, through any plague, or trouble;
40 Though he suffer them to be evil intreated through tyrants : and let them wander out of the way in the wilderness;
41 Yet helpeth he the poor out of misery: and maketh him households like a flock of sheep.
42 The righteous will consider this, and rejoice : and the mouth of all wickedness shall be stopped.
43 Whoso is wise will ponder these things : and they shall understand the loving-kindness of the Lord.

Evening Prayer

PSALM CVIII. *Paratum cor meum.*

O GOD, my heart is ready, my heart is ready : I will sing and give praise with the best member that I have.
2 Awake, thou lute, and harp : I myself will awake right early.
3 I will give thanks unto thee, O Lord, among the people : I will sing praises unto thee among the nations.
4 For thy mercy is greater than the heavens : and thy truth reacheth unto the clouds.
5 Set up thyself, O God, above the heavens : and thy glory above all the earth.
6 That thy beloved may be delivered : let thy right hand save them, and hear thou me.
7 God hath spoken in his holiness : I will rejoice therefore, and divide Sichem, and mete out the valley of Succoth.
8 Gilead is mine, and Manasses is mine : Ephraim also is the strength of my head.
9 Judah is my law-giver, Moab is my wash-pot : over Edom will I cast out my shoe; upon Philistia will I triumph.
10 Who will lead me into the strong city : and who will bring me into Edom?
11 Hast not thou forsaken us, O God : and wilt not thou, O God, go forth with our hosts?
12 O help us against the enemy : for vain is the help of man.
13 Through God we shall do great acts : and it is he that shall tread down our enemies.

PSALM CIX. *Deus laudem.*

HOLD not thy tongue, O God of my praise : for the mouth of the ungodly, yea, the mouth of the deceitful is opened upon me.
2 And they have spoken against me with false tongues : they compassed me about also with words of hatred, and fought against me without a cause.
3 For the love that I had unto them, lo, they take now my contrary part : but I give myself unto prayer.
4 Thus have they rewarded me evil for good : and hatred for my good will.
5 Set thou an ungodly man to be ruler over him : and let Satan stand at his right hand.
6 When sentence is given upon him, let him be condemned : and let his prayer be turned into sin.
7 Let his days be few : and let another take his office.
8 Let his children be fatherless : and his wife a widow.
9 Let his children be vagabonds, and beg their bread : let them seek it also out of desolate places.
10 Let the extortioner consume all that he hath : and let the stranger spoil his labour.
11 Let there be no man to pity him : nor to have compassion upon his fatherless children.
12 Let his posterity be destroy-

Day 22. THE PSALMS. *Day* 23.

ed : and in the next generation let his name be clean put out.

13 Let the wickedness of his fathers be had in remembrance in the sight of the Lord : and let not the sin of his mother be done away.

14 Let them alway be before the Lord : that he may root out the memorial of them from off the earth;

15 And that, because his mind was not to do good : but persecuted the poor helpless man, that he might slay him that was vexed at the heart.

16 His delight was in cursing, and it shall happen unto him : he loved not blessing, therefore shall it be far from him.

17 He clothed himself with cursing, like as with a raiment : and it shall come into his bowels like water, and like oil into his bones.

18 Let it be unto him as the cloke that he hath upon him : and as the girdle that he is alway girded withal.

19 Let it thus happen from the Lord unto mine enemies : and to those that speak evil against my soul.

20 But deal thou with me, O Lord God, according unto thy Name : for sweet is thy mercy.

21 O deliver me, for I am helpless and poor : and my heart is wounded within me.

22 I go hence like the shadow that departeth : and am driven away as the grasshopper.

23 My knees are weak through fasting : my flesh is dried up for want of fatness.

24 I became also a reproach unto them : they that looked upon me shaked their heads.

25 Help me, O Lord my God : O save me according to thy mercy;

26 And they shall know, how that this is thy hand : and that thou, Lord, hast done it.

27 Though they curse, yet bless thou : and let them be confounded that rise up against me; but let thy servant rejoice.

28 Let mine adversaries be clothed with shame : and let them cover themselves with their own confusion, as with a cloke.

29 As for me, I will give great thanks unto the Lord with my mouth : and praise him among the multitude;

30 For he shall stand at the right hand of the poor : to save his soul from unrighteous judges.

Morning Prayer

PSALM CX. *Dixit Dominus.*

THE Lord said unto my Lord : Sit thou on my right hand, until I make thine enemies thy footstool.

2 The Lord shall send the rod of thy power out of Sion : be thou ruler, even in the midst among thine enemies.

3 In the day of thy power shall the people offer thee free-will offerings with an holy worship : the dew of thy birth is of the womb of the morning.

4 The Lord sware, and will not repent : Thou art a Priest for ever after the order of Melchisedech.

5 The Lord upon thy right hand : shall wound even kings in the day of his wrath.

6 He shall judge among the heathen; he shall fill the places with the dead bodies : and smite in sunder the heads over divers countries.

7 He shall drink of the brook in the way : therefore shall he lift up his head.

PSALM CXI. *Confitebor tibi.*

I WILL give thanks unto the Lord with my whole heart : secretly among the faithful, and in the congregation.

2 The works of the Lord are great : sought out of all them that have pleasure therein.

3 His work is worthy to be praised, and had in honour : and his righteousness endureth for ever.

4 The merciful and gracious Lord hath so done his marvellous works : that they ought to be had in remembrance.

5 He hath given meat unto them that fear him : he shall ever be mindful of his covenant.

6 He hath shewed his people the power of his works : that he may give them the heritage of the heathen.

7 The works of his hands are verity and judgement : all his commandments are true.

8 They stand fast for ever and ever : and are done in truth and equity.

9 He sent redemption unto his people : he hath commanded his covenant for ever; holy and reverend is his Name.

10 The fear of the Lord is the beginning of wisdom : a good understanding have all they that do thereafter; the praise of it endureth for ever.

PSALM CXII. *Beatus vir.*

BLESSED is the man that feareth the Lord : he hath great delight in his commandments.

2 His seed shall be mighty upon earth : the generation of the faithful shall be blessed.

3 Riches and plenteousness shall be in his house : and his righteousness endureth for ever.

4 Unto the godly there ariseth up light in the darkness : he is merciful, loving, and righteous.

5 A good man is merciful, and lendeth : and will guide his words with discretion.

6 For he shall never be moved : and the righteous shall be had in everlasting remembrance.

7 He will not be afraid of any evil tidings : for his heart standeth fast, and believeth in the Lord.

8 His heart is established, and will not shrink : until he see his desire upon his enemies.

9 He hath dispersed abroad, and given to the poor : and his righteousness remaineth for ever; his horn shall be exalted with honour.

10 The ungodly shall see it, and it shall grieve him : he shall gnash with his teeth, and consume away; the desire of the ungodly shall perish.

PSALM CXIII. *Laudate, pueri.*

PRAISE the Lord, ye servants : O praise the Name of the Lord.

2 Blessed be the Name of the Lord : from this time forth for evermore.

3 The Lord's Name is praised : from the rising up of the sun unto the going down of the same.

4 The Lord is high above all heathen : and his glory above the heavens.

5 Who is like unto the Lord our God, that hath his dwelling so high : and yet humbleth himself to behold the things that are in heaven and earth?

6 He taketh up the simple out of the dust : and lifteth the poor out of the mire;

7 That he may set him with the princes : even with the princes of his people.

8 He maketh the barren woman to keep house : and to be a joyful mother of children.

Evening Prayer

PSALM CXIV. *In exitu Israel.*

WHEN Israel came out of Egypt : and the house of Jacob from among the strange people,

2 Judah was his sanctuary : and Israel his dominion.

3 The sea saw that, and fled : Jordan was driven back.

4 The mountains skipped like

rams : and the little hills like young sheep.

5 What aileth thee, O thou sea, that thou fleddest : and thou Jordan, that thou wast driven back?

6 Ye mountains, that ye skipped like rams : and ye little hills, like young sheep?

7 Tremble, thou earth, at the presence of the Lord : at the presence of the God of Jacob;

8 Who turned the hard rock into a standing water : and the flint-stone into a springing well.

PSALM CXV. *Non nobis, Domine.*

NOT unto us, O Lord, not unto us, but unto thy Name give the praise : for thy loving mercy, and for thy truth's sake.

2 Wherefore shall the heathen say : Where is now their God?

3 As for our God, he is in heaven : he hath done whatsoever pleased him.

4 Their idols are silver and gold : even the work of men's hands.

5 They have mouths, and speak not : eyes have they, and see not.

6 They have ears, and hear not : noses have they, and smell not.

7 They have hands, and handle not; feet have they, and walk not : neither speak they through their throat.

8 They that make them are like unto them : and so are all such as put their trust in them.

9 But thou, house of Israel, trust thou in the Lord : he is their succour and defence.

10 Ye house of Aaron, put your trust in the Lord : he is their helper and defender.

11 Ye that fear the Lord, put your trust in the Lord : he is their helper and defender.

12 The Lord hath been mindful of us, and he shall bless us : even he shall bless the house of Israel, he shall bless the house of Aaron.

13 He shall bless them that fear the Lord : both small and great.

14 The Lord shall increase you more and more : you and your children.

15 Ye are the blessed of the Lord : who made heaven and earth.

16 All the whole heavens are the Lord's : the earth hath he given to the children of men.

17 The dead praise not thee, O Lord : neither all they that go down into silence.

18 But we will praise the Lord : from this time forth for evermore. Praise the Lord.

Morning Prayer

PSALM CXVI. *Dilexi, quoniam.*

I AM well pleased : that the Lord hath heard the voice of my prayer;

2 That he hath inclined his ear unto me : therefore will I call upon him as long as I live.

3 The snares of death compassed me round about : and the pains of hell gat hold upon me.

4 I shall find trouble and heaviness, and I will call upon the Name of the Lord : O Lord, I beseech thee, deliver my soul.

5 Gracious is the Lord, and righteous : yea, our God is merciful.

6 The Lord preserveth the simple : I was in misery, and he helped me.

7 Turn again then unto thy rest, O my soul : for the Lord hath rewarded thee.

8 And why? thou hast delivered my soul from death : mine eyes from tears, and my feet from falling.

9 I will walk before the Lord : in the land of the living.

10 I believed, and therefore will I speak; but I was sore troubled : I said in my haste, All men are liars.

C 3

11 What reward shall I give unto the Lord : for all the benefits that he hath done unto me?
12 I will receive the cup of salvation : and call upon the Name of the Lord.
13 I will pay my vows now in the presence of all his people : right dear in the sight of the Lord is the death of his saints.
14 Behold, O Lord, how that I am thy servant : I am thy servant, and the son of thine handmaid; thou hast broken my bonds in sunder.
15 I will offer to thee the sacrifice of thanksgiving : and will call upon the Name of the Lord.
16 I will pay my vows unto the Lord, in the sight of all his people : in the courts of the Lord's house, even in the midst of thee, O Jerusalem. Praise the Lord.

PSALM CXVII. *Laudate Dominum.*

O PRAISE the Lord, all ye heathen : praise him, all ye nations.
2 For his merciful kindness is ever more and more towards us : and the truth of the Lord endureth for ever. Praise the Lord.

PSALM CXVIII. *Confitemini Domino.*

O GIVE thanks unto the Lord, for he is gracious : because his mercy endureth for ever.
2 Let Israel now confess, that he is gracious : and that his mercy endureth for ever.
3 Let the house of Aaron now confess : that his mercy endureth for ever.
4 Yea, let them now that fear the Lord confess : that his mercy endureth for ever.
5 I called upon the Lord in trouble : and the Lord heard me at large.
6 The Lord is on my side : I will not fear what man doeth unto me.
7 The Lord taketh my part with them that help me : therefore shall I see my desire upon mine enemies.
8 It is better to trust in the Lord : than to put any confidence in man.
9 It is better to trust in the Lord : than to put any confidence in princes.
10 All nations compassed me round about : but in the Name of the Lord will I destroy them.
11 They kept me in on every side, they kept me in, I say, on every side : but in the Name of the Lord will I destroy them.
12 They came about me like bees, and are extinct even as the fire among the thorns : for in the Name of the Lord I will destroy them.
13 Thou hast thrust sore at me, that I might fall : but the Lord was my help.
14 The Lord is my strength, and my song : and is become my salvation.
15 The voice of joy and health is in the dwellings of the righteous : the right hand of the Lord bringeth mighty things to pass.
16 The right hand of the Lord hath the pre-eminence : the right hand of the Lord bringeth mighty things to pass.
17 I shall not die, but live : and declare the works of the Lord.
18 The Lord hath chastened and corrected me : but he hath not given me over unto death.
19 Open me the gates of righteousness : that I may go into them, and give thanks unto the Lord.
20 This is the gate of the Lord : the righteous shall enter into it.
21 I will thank thee, for thou hast heard me : and art become my salvation.
22 The same stone which the builders refused : is become the head-stone in the corner.
23 This is the Lord's doing : and it is marvellous in our eyes.
24 This is the day which the

Lord hath made : we will rejoice and be glad in it.

25 Help me now, O Lord : O Lord, send us now prosperity.

26 Blessed be he that cometh in the Name of the Lord : we have wished you good luck, ye that are of the house of the Lord.

27 God is the Lord who hath shewed us light : bind the sacrifice with cords, yea, even unto the horns of the altar.

28 Thou art my God, and I will thank thee : thou art my God, and I will praise thee.

29 O give thanks unto the Lord, for he is gracious : and his mercy endureth for ever.

Evening Prayer

PSALM CXIX. *Beati immaculati.*

BLESSED are those that are undefiled in the way : and walk in the law of the Lord.

2 Blessed are they that keep his testimonies : and seek him with their whole heart.

3 For they who do no wickedness : walk in his ways.

4 Thou hast charged : that we shall diligently keep thy commandments.

5 O that my ways were made so direct : that I might keep thy statutes !

6 So shall I not be confounded : while I have respect unto all thy commandments.

7 I will thank thee with an unfeigned heart : when I shall have learned the judgements of thy righteousness.

8 I will keep thy ceremonies : O forsake me not utterly.

In quo corriget?

WHEREWITHAL shall a young man cleanse his way : even by ruling himself after thy word.

10 With my whole heart have I sought thee : O let me not go wrong out of thy commandments.

11 Thy words have I hid within my heart : that I should not sin against thee.

12 Blessed art thou, O Lord : O teach me thy statutes.

13 With my lips have I been telling : of all the judgements of thy mouth.

14 I have had as great delight in the way of thy testimonies : as in all manner of riches.

15 I will talk of thy commandments : and have respect unto thy ways.

16 My delight shall be in thy statutes : and I will not forget thy word.

Retribue servo tuo.

O DO well unto thy servant : that I may live, and keep thy word.

18 Open thou mine eyes : that I may see the wondrous things of thy law.

19 I am a stranger upon earth : O hide not thy commandments from me.

20 My soul breaketh out for the very fervent desire : that it hath alway unto thy judgements.

21 Thou hast rebuked the proud : and cursed are they that do err from thy commandments.

22 O turn from me shame and rebuke : for I have kept thy testimonies.

23 Princes also did sit and speak against me : but thy servant is occupied in thy statutes.

24 For thy testimonies are my delight : and my counsellors.

Adhæsit pavimento.

MY soul cleaveth to the dust : O quicken thou me, according to thy word.

26 I have acknowledged my ways, and thou heardest me : O teach me thy statutes.

27 Make me to understand the way of thy commandments : and so shall I talk of thy wondrous works.

28 My soul melteth away for

very heaviness : comfort thou me according unto thy word.

29 Take from me the way of lying : and cause thou me to make much of thy law.

30 I have chosen the way of truth : and thy judgements have I laid before me.

31 I have stuck unto thy testimonies : O Lord, confound me not.

32 I will run the way of thy commandments : when thou hast set my heart at liberty.

Morning Prayer

Legem pone.

TEACH me, O Lord, the way of thy statutes : and I shall keep it unto the end.

34 Give me understanding, and I shall keep thy law : yea, I shall keep it with my whole heart.

35 Make me to go in the path of thy commandments : for therein is my desire.

36 Incline my heart unto thy testimonies : and not to covetousness.

37 O turn away mine eyes, lest they behold vanity : and quicken thou me in thy way.

38 O stablish thy word in thy servant : that I may fear thee.

39 Take away the rebuke that I am afraid of : for thy judgements are good.

40 Behold, my delight is in thy commandments : O quicken me in thy righteousness.

Et veniat super me.

LET thy loving mercy come also unto me, O Lord : even thy salvation, according unto thy word.

42 So shall I make answer unto my blasphemers : for my trust is in thy word.

43 O take not the word of thy truth utterly out of my mouth : for my hope is in thy judgements.

44 So shall I alway keep thy law : yea, for ever and ever.

45 And I will walk at liberty : for I seek thy commandments.

46 I will speak of thy testimonies also, even before kings : and will not be ashamed.

47 And my delight shall be in thy commandments : which I have loved.

48 My hands also will I lift up unto thy commandments, which I have loved : and my study shall be in thy statutes.

Memor esto servi tui.

O THINK upon thy servant, as concerning thy word : wherein thou hast caused me to put my trust.

50 The same is my comfort in my trouble : for thy word hath quickened me.

51 The proud have had me exceedingly in derision : yet have I not shrinked from thy law.

52 For I remembered thine everlasting judgements, O Lord : and received comfort.

53 I am horribly afraid : for the ungodly that forsake thy law.

54 Thy statutes have been my songs : in the house of my pilgrimage.

55 I have thought upon thy Name, O Lord, in the night-season : and have kept thy law.

56 This I had : because I kept thy commandments.

Portio mea, Domine.

THOU art my portion, O Lord : I have promised to keep thy law.

58 I made my humble petition in thy presence with my whole heart : O be merciful unto me, according to thy word.

59 I called mine own ways to remembrance : and turned my feet unto thy testimonies.

60 I made haste, and prolonged not the time : to keep thy commandments.

Day 25.   THE PSALMS.   *Day* 25.

61 The congregations of the ungodly have robbed me : but I have not forgotten thy law.

62 At midnight I will rise to give thanks unto thee : because of thy righteous judgements.

63 I am a companion of all them that fear thee : and keep thy commandments.

64 The earth, O Lord, is full of thy mercy : O teach me thy statutes.

Bonitatem fecisti.

O LORD, thou hast dealt graciously with thy servant : according unto thy word.

66 O learn me true understanding and knowledge : for I have believed thy commandments.

67 Before I was troubled, I went wrong : but now have I kept thy word.

68 Thou art good and gracious : O teach me thy statutes.

69 The proud have imagined a lie against me : but I will keep thy commandments with my whole heart.

70 Their heart is as fat as brawn : but my delight hath been in thy law.

71 It is good for me that I have been in trouble : that I may learn thy statutes.

72 The law of thy mouth is dearer unto me : than thousands of gold and silver.

Evening Prayer
Manus tuæ fecerunt me.

THY hands have made me and fashioned me : O give me understanding, that I may learn thy commandments.

74 They that fear thee will be glad when they see me : because I have put my trust in thy word.

75 I know, O Lord, that thy judgements are right : and that thou of very faithfulness hast caused me to be troubled.

76 O let thy merciful kindness be my comfort : according to thy word unto thy servant.

77 O let thy loving mercies come unto me, that I may live : for thy law is my delight.

78 Let the proud be confounded, for they go wickedly about to destroy me : but I will be occupied in thy commandments.

79 Let such as fear thee, and have known thy testimonies : be turned unto me.

80 O let my heart be sound in thy statutes : that I be not ashamed.

Defecit anima mea.

MY soul hath longed for thy salvation : and I have a good hope because of thy word.

82 Mine eyes long sore for thy word : saying, O when wilt thou comfort me?

83 For I am become like a bottle in the smoke : yet do I not forget thy statutes.

84 How many are the days of thy servant : when wilt thou be avenged of them that persecute me?

85 The proud have digged pits for me : which are not after thy law.

86 All thy commandments are true : they persecute me falsely; O be thou my help.

87 They had almost made an end of me upon earth : but I forsook not thy commandments.

88 O quicken me after thy loving-kindness : and so shall I keep the testimonies of thy mouth.

In æternum, Domine.

O LORD, thy word : endureth for ever in heaven.

90 Thy truth also remaineth from one generation to another : thou hast laid the foundation of the earth, and it abideth.

91 They continue this day according to thine ordinance : for all things serve thee.

92 If my delight had not been in thy law : I should have perished in my trouble.

93 I will never forget thy commandments : for with them thou hast quickened me.
94 I am thine, O save me : for I have sought thy commandments.
95 The ungodly laid wait for me to destroy me : but I will consider thy testimonies.
96 I see that all things come to an end : but thy commandment is exceeding broad.

Quomodo dilexi!
LORD, what love have I unto thy law : all the day long is my study in it.
98 Thou through thy commandments hast made me wiser than mine enemies : for they are ever with me.
99 I have more understanding than my teachers : for thy testimonies are my study.
100 I am wiser than the aged : because I keep thy commandments.
101 I have refrained my feet from every evil way : that I may keep thy word.
102 I have not shrunk from thy judgements : for thou teachest me.
103 O how sweet are thy words unto my throat : yea, sweeter than honey unto my mouth.
104 Through thy commandments I get understanding : therefore I hate all evil ways.

Morning Prayer

Lucerna pedibus meis.
THY word is a lantern unto my feet : and a light unto my paths.
106 I have sworn, and am stedfastly purposed : to keep thy righteous judgements.
107 I am troubled above measure : quicken me, O Lord, according to thy word.
108 Let the free-will offerings of my mouth please thee, O Lord : and teach me thy judgements.

109 My soul is alway in my hand : yet do I not forget thy law.
110 The ungodly have laid a snare for me : but yet I swerved not from thy commandments.
111 Thy testimonies have I claimed as mine heritage for ever : and why? they are the very joy of my heart.
112 I have applied my heart to fulfil thy statutes alway : even unto the end.

Iniquos odio habui.
I HATE them that imagine evil things : but thy law do I love.
114 Thou art my defence and shield : and my trust is in thy word.
115 Away from me, ye wicked : I will keep the commandments of my God.
116 O stablish me according to thy word, that I may live : and let me not be disappointed of my hope.
117 Hold thou me up, and I shall be safe : yea, my delight shall be ever in thy statutes.
118 Thou hast trodden down all them that depart from thy statutes : for they imagine but deceit.
119 Thou puttest away all the ungodly of the earth like dross : therefore I love thy testimonies.
120 My flesh trembleth for fear of thee : and I am afraid of thy judgements.

Feci judicium.
I DEAL with the thing that is lawful and right : O give me not over unto mine oppressors.
122 Make thou thy servant to delight in that which is good : that the proud do me no wrong.
123 Mine eyes are wasted away with looking for thy health : and for the word of thy righteousness.
124 O deal with thy servant according unto thy loving mercy : and teach me thy statutes.

125 I am thy servant, O grant me understanding : that I may know thy testimonies.
126 It is time for thee, Lord, to lay to thine hand : for they have destroyed thy law.
127 For I love thy commandments : above gold and precious stone.
128 Therefore hold I straight all thy commandments : and all false ways I utterly abhor.

Mirabilia.

THY testimonies are wonderful : therefore doth my soul keep them.
130 When thy word goeth forth : it giveth light and understanding unto the simple.
131 I opened my mouth, and drew in my breath : for my delight was in thy commandments.
132 O look thou upon me, and be merciful unto me : as thou usest to do unto those that love thy Name.
133 Order my steps in thy word : and so shall no wickedness have dominion over me.
134 O deliver me from the wrongful dealings of men : and so shall I keep thy commandments.
135 Shew the light of thy countenance upon thy servant : and teach me thy statutes.
136 Mine eyes gush out with water : because men keep not thy law.

Justus es, Domine.

RIGHTEOUS art thou, O Lord : and true is thy judgement.
138 The testimonies that thou hast commanded : are exceeding righteous and true.
139 My zeal hath even consumed me : because mine enemies have forgotten thy words.
140 Thy word is tried to the uttermost : and thy servant loveth it.
141 I am small, and of no reputation : yet do I not forget thy commandments.
142 Thy righteousness is an everlasting righteousness : and thy law is the truth.
143 Trouble and heaviness have taken hold upon me : yet is my delight in thy commandments.
144 The righteousness of thy testimonies is everlasting : O grant me understanding, and I shall live.

Evening Prayer

Clamavi in toto corde meo.

I CALL with my whole heart : hear me, O Lord, I will keep thy statutes.
146 Yea, even unto thee do I call : help me, and I shall keep thy testimonies.
147 Early in the morning do I cry unto thee : for in thy word is my trust.
148 Mine eyes prevent the night-watches : that I might be occupied in thy words.
149 Hear my voice, O Lord, according unto thy loving-kindness : quicken me, according as thou art wont.
150 They draw nigh that of malice persecute me : and are far from thy law.
151 Be thou nigh at hand, O Lord : for all thy commandments are true.
152 As concerning thy testimonies, I have known long since : that thou hast grounded them for ever.

Vide humilitatem.

O CONSIDER mine adversity, and deliver me : for I do not forget thy law.
154 Avenge thou my cause, and deliver me : quicken me, according to thy word.
155 Health is far from the ungodly : for they regard not thy statutes.
156 Great is thy mercy, O Lord : quicken me, as thou art wont.

157 Many there are that trouble me, and persecute me : yet do I not swerve from thy testimonies.
158 It grieveth me when I see the transgressors : because they keep not thy law.
159 Consider, O Lord, how I love thy commandments : O quicken me, according to thy loving-kindness.
160 Thy word is true from everlasting : all the judgements of thy righteousness endure for evermore.

Principes persecuti sunt.

PRINCES have persecuted me without a cause : but my heart standeth in awe of thy word.
162 I am as glad of thy word : as one that findeth great spoils.
163 As for lies, I hate and abhor them : but thy law do I love.
164 Seven times a day do I praise thee : because of thy righteous judgements.
165 Great is the peace that they have who love thy law : and they are not offended at it.
166 Lord, I have looked for thy saving health : and done after thy commandments.
167 My soul hath kept thy testimonies : and loved them exceedingly.
168 I have kept thy commandments and testimonies : for all my ways are before thee.

Appropinquet deprecatio.

LET my complaint come before thee, O Lord : give me understanding, according to thy word.
170 Let my supplication come before thee : deliver me, according to thy word.
171 My lips shall speak of thy praise : when thou hast taught me thy statutes.
172 Yea, my tongue shall sing of thy word : for all thy commandments are righteous.

173 Let thine hand help me : for I have chosen thy commandments.
174 I have longed for thy saving health, O Lord : and in thy law is my delight.
175 O let my soul live, and it shall praise thee : and thy judgements shall help me.
176 I have gone astray like a sheep that is lost : O seek thy servant, for I do not forget thy commandments.

Morning Prayer

PSALM CXX. *Ad Dominum.*

WHEN I was in trouble I called upon the Lord : and he heard me.
2 Deliver my soul, O Lord, from lying lips : and from a deceitful tongue.
3 What reward shall be given or done unto thee, thou false tongue : even mighty and sharp arrows, with hot burning coals.
4 Woe is me, that I am constrained to dwell with Mesech : and to have my habitation among the tents of Kedar.
5 My soul hath long dwelt among them : that are enemies unto peace.
6 I labour for peace, but when I speak unto them thereof : they make them ready to battle.

PSALM CXXI. *Levavi oculos.*

I WILL lift up mine eyes unto the hills : from whence cometh my help.
2 My help cometh even from the Lord : who hath made heaven and earth.
3 He will not suffer thy foot to be moved : and he that keepeth thee will not sleep.
4 Behold, he that keepeth Israel : shall neither slumber nor sleep.
5 The Lord himself is thy keeper : the Lord is thy defence upon thy right hand;
6 So that the sun shall not

burn thee by day : neither the moon by night.

7 The Lord shall preserve thee from all evil : yea, it is even he that shall keep thy soul.

8 The Lord shall preserve thy going out, and thy coming in : from this time forth for evermore.

PSALM CXXII. *Lætatus sum.*

I WAS glad when they said unto me : We will go into the house of the Lord.

2 Our feet shall stand in thy gates : O Jerusalem.

3 Jerusalem is built as a city : that is at unity in itself.

4 For thither the tribes go up, even the tribes of the Lord : to testify unto Israel, to give thanks unto the Name of the Lord.

5 For there is the seat of judgement : even the seat of the house of David.

6 O pray for the peace of Jerusalem : they shall prosper that love thee.

7 Peace be within thy walls : and plenteousness within thy palaces.

8 For my brethren and companions' sakes : I will wish thee prosperity.

9 Yea, because of the house of the Lord our God : I will seek to do thee good.

PSALM CXXIII.
Ad te levavi oculos meos.

UNTO thee lift I up mine eyes : O thou that dwellest in the heavens.

2 Behold, even as the eyes of servants look unto the hand of their masters, and as the eyes of a maiden unto the hand of her mistress : even so our eyes wait upon the Lord our God, until he have mercy upon us.

3 Have mercy upon us, O Lord, have mercy upon us : for we are utterly despised.

4 Our soul is filled with the scornful reproof of the wealthy : and with the despitefulness of the proud.

PSALM CXXIV. *Nisi quia Dominus.*

IF the Lord himself had not been on our side, now may Israel say : if the Lord himself had not been on our side, when men rose up against us;

2 They had swallowed us up quick : when they were so wrathfully displeased at us.

3 Yea, the waters had drowned us : and the stream had gone over our soul.

4 The deep waters of the proud : had gone even over our soul.

5 But praised be the Lord : who hath not given us over for a prey unto their teeth.

6 Our soul is escaped even as a bird out of the snare of the fowler : the snare is broken, and we are delivered.

7 Our help standeth in the Name of the Lord : who hath made heaven and earth.

PSALM CXXV. *Qui confidunt.*

THEY that put their trust in the Lord shall be even as the mount Sion : which may not be removed, but standeth fast for ever.

2 The hills stand about Jerusalem : even so standeth the Lord round about his people, from this time forth for evermore.

3 For the rod of the ungodly cometh not into the lot of the righteous : lest the righteous put their hand unto wickedness.

4 Do well, O Lord : unto those that are good and true of heart.

5 As for such as turn back unto their own wickedness : the Lord shall lead them forth with the evil-doers; but peace shall be upon Israel.

Evening Prayer

PSALM CXXVI. *In convertendo.*

WHEN the Lord turned again the captivity of Sion :

then were we like unto them that dream.

2 Then was our mouth filled with laughter : and our tongue with joy.

3 Then said they among the heathen : The Lord hath done great things for them.

4 Yea, the Lord hath done great things for us already : whereof we rejoice.

5 Turn our captivity, O Lord : as the rivers in the south.

6 They that sow in tears : shall reap in joy.

7 He that now goeth on his way weeping, and beareth forth good seed : shall doubtless come again with joy, and bring his sheaves with him.

PSALM CXXVII. *Nisi Dominus.*

EXCEPT the Lord build the house : their labour is but lost that build it.

2 Except the Lord keep the city : the watchman waketh but in vain.

3 It is but lost labour that ye haste to rise up early, and so late take rest, and eat the bread of carefulness : for so he giveth his beloved sleep.

4 Lo, children and the fruit of the womb : are an heritage and gift that cometh of the Lord.

5 Like as the arrows in the hand of the giant : even so are the young children.

6 Happy is the man that hath his quiver full of them : they shall not be ashamed when they speak with their enemies in the gate.

PSALM CXXVIII. *Beati omnes.*

BLESSED are all they that fear the Lord : and walk in his ways.

2 For thou shalt eat the labours of thine hands : O well is thee, and happy shalt thou be.

3 Thy wife shall be as the fruitful vine : upon the walls of thine house.

4 Thy children like the olive-branches : round about thy table.

5 Lo, thus shall the man be blessed : that feareth the Lord.

6 The Lord from out of Sion shall so bless thee : that thou shalt see Jerusalem in prosperity all thy life long.

7 Yea, that thou shalt see thy children's children : and peace upon Israel.

PSALM CXXIX. *Sæpe expugnaverunt.*

MANY a time have they fought against me from my youth up : may Israel now say.

2 Yea, many a time have they vexed me from my youth up : but they have not prevailed against me.

3 The plowers plowed upon my back : and made long furrows.

4 But the righteous Lord : hath hewn the snares of the ungodly in pieces.

5 Let them be confounded and turned backward : as many as have evil will at Sion.

6 Let them be even as the grass growing upon the house-tops : which withereth afore it be plucked up;

7 Whereof the mower filleth not his hand : neither he that bindeth up the sheaves his bosom.

8 So that they who go by say not so much as, The Lord prosper you : we wish you good luck in the Name of the Lord.

PSALM CXXX. *De profundis.*

OUT of the deep have I called unto thee, O Lord : Lord, hear my voice.

2 O let thine ears consider well : the voice of my complaint.

3 If thou, Lord, wilt be extreme to mark what is done amiss : O Lord, who may abide it?

4 For there is mercy with thee : therefore shalt thou be feared.

5 I look for the Lord; my soul doth wait for him : in his word is my trust.

6 My soul fleeteth unto the Lord : before the morning watch, I say, before the morning watch.
7 O Israel, trust in the Lord, for with the Lord there is mercy : and with him is plenteous redemption.
8 And he shall redeem Israel : from all his sins.

PSALM CXXXI. *Domine, non est.*

LORD, I am not high-minded : I have no proud looks.
2 I do not exercise myself in great matters : which are too high for me.
3 But I refrain my soul, and keep it low, like as a child that is weaned from his mother : yea, my soul is even as a weaned child.
4 O Israel, trust in the Lord : from this time forth for evermore.

Morning Prayer

PSALM CXXXII. *Memento, Domine.*

LORD, remember David : and all his trouble;
2 How he sware unto the Lord : and vowed a vow unto the Almighty God of Jacob;
3 I will not come within the tabernacle of mine house : nor climb up into my bed;
4 I will not suffer mine eyes to sleep, nor mine eye-lids to slumber : neither the temples of my head to take any rest;
5 Until I find out a place for the temple of the Lord : an habitation for the mighty God of Jacob.
6 Lo, we heard of the same at Ephrata : and found it in the wood.
7 We will go into his tabernacle : and fall low on our knees before his footstool.
8 Arise, O Lord, into thy resting-place : thou, and the ark of thy strength.
9 Let thy priests be clothed with righteousness : and let thy saints sing with joyfulness.
10 For thy servant David's sake : turn not away the presence of thine Anointed.
11 The Lord hath made a faithful oath unto David : and he shall not shrink from it;
12 Of the fruit of thy body : shall I set upon thy seat.
13 If thy children will keep my covenant, and my testimonies that I shall learn them : their children also shall sit upon thy seat for evermore.
14 For the Lord hath chosen Sion to be an habitation for himself : he hath longed for her.
15 This shall be my rest for ever : here will I dwell, for I have a delight therein.
16 I will bless her victuals with increase : and will satisfy her poor with bread.
17 I will deck her priests with health : and her saints shall rejoice and sing.
18 There shall I make the horn of David to flourish : I have ordained a lantern for mine Anointed.
19 As for his enemies, I shall clothe them with shame : but upon himself shall his crown flourish.

PSALM CXXXIII. *Ecce, quam bonum!*

BEHOLD, how good and joyful a thing it is : brethren, to dwell together in unity!
2 It is like the precious ointment upon the head, that ran down unto the beard : even unto Aaron's beard, and went down to the skirts of his clothing.
3 Like as the dew of Hermon : which fell upon the hill of Sion.
4 For there the Lord promised his blessing : and life for evermore.

PSALM CXXXIV. *Ecce nunc.*

BEHOLD now, praise the Lord : all ye servants of the Lord;
2 Ye that by night stand in the

house of the Lord : even in the courts of the house of our God.

3 Lift up your hands in the sanctuary : and praise the Lord.

4 The Lord that made heaven and earth : give thee blessing out of Sion.

PSALM CXXXV. *Laudate Nomen.*

O PRAISE the Lord, laud ye the Name of the Lord : praise it, O ye servants of the Lord;

2 Ye that stand in the house of the Lord : in the courts of the house of our God.

3 O praise the Lord, for the Lord is gracious : O sing praises unto his Name, for it is lovely.

4 For why? the Lord hath chosen Jacob unto himself : and Israel for his own possession.

5 For I know that the Lord is great : and that our Lord is above all gods.

6 Whatsoever the Lord pleased, that did he in heaven, and in earth : and in the sea, and in all deep places.

7 He bringeth forth the clouds from the ends of the world : and sendeth forth lightnings with the rain, bringing the winds out of his treasures.

8 He smote the first-born of Egypt : both of man and beast.

9 He hath sent tokens and wonders into the midst of thee, O thou land of Egypt : upon Pharaoh, and all his servants.

10 He smote divers nations : and slew mighty kings;

11 Sehon king of the Amorites, and Og the king of Basan : and all the kingdoms of Canaan;

12 And gave their land to be an heritage : even an heritage unto Israel his people.

13 Thy Name, O Lord, endureth for ever : so doth thy memorial, O Lord, from one generation to another.

14 For the Lord will avenge his people : and be gracious unto his servants.

15 As for the images of the heathen, they are but silver and gold : the work of men's hands.

16 They have mouths, and speak not : eyes have they, but they see not.

17 They have ears, and yet they hear not : neither is there any breath in their mouths.

18 They that make them are like unto them : and so are all they that put their trust in them.

19 Praise the Lord, ye house of Israel : praise the Lord, ye house of Aaron.

20 Praise the Lord, ye house of Levi : ye that fear the Lord, praise the Lord.

21 Praised be the Lord out of Sion : who dwelleth at Jerusalem.

Evening Prayer

PSALM CXXXVI. *Confitemini.*

O GIVE thanks unto the Lord, for he is gracious : and his mercy endureth for ever.

2 O give thanks unto the God of all gods : for his mercy endureth for ever.

3 O thank the Lord of all lords : for his mercy endureth for ever.

4 Who only doeth great wonders : for his mercy endureth for ever.

5 Who by his excellent wisdom made the heavens : for his mercy endureth for ever.

6 Who laid out the earth above the waters : for his mercy endureth for ever.

7 Who hath made great lights : for his mercy endureth for ever;

8 The sun to rule the day : for his mercy endureth for ever;

9 The moon and the stars to govern the night : for his mercy endureth for ever.

10 Who smote Egypt with their first-born : for his mercy endureth for ever;

11 And brought out Israel from among them : for his mercy endureth for ever;

12 With a mighty hand, and stretched out arm : for his mercy endureth for ever.

13 Who divided the Red sea in two parts : for his mercy endureth for ever;

14 And made Israel to go through the midst of it : for his mercy endureth for ever.

15 But as for Pharaoh and his host, he overthrew them in the Red sea : for his mercy endureth for ever.

16 Who led his people through the wilderness : for his mercy endureth for ever.

17 Who smote great kings : for his mercy endureth for ever;

18 Yea, and slew mighty kings : for his mercy endureth for ever;

19 Sehon king of the Amorites : for his mercy endureth for ever;

20 And Og the king of Basan : for his mercy endureth for ever;

21 And gave away their land for an heritage : for his mercy endureth for ever;

22 Even for an heritage unto Israel his servant : for his mercy endureth for ever.

23 Who remembered us when we were in trouble : for his mercy endureth for ever;

24 And hath delivered us from our enemies : for his mercy endureth for ever.

25 Who giveth food to all flesh : for his mercy endureth for ever.

26 O give thanks unto the God of heaven : for his mercy endureth for ever.

27 O give thanks unto the Lord of lords : for his mercy endureth for ever.

PSALM CXXXVII. *Super flumina.*

BY the waters of Babylon we sat down and wept : when we remembered thee, O Sion.

2 As for our harps, we hanged them up : upon the trees that are therein.

3 For they that led us away captive required of us then a song, and melody, in our heaviness : Sing us one of the songs of Sion.

4 How shall we sing the Lord's song : in a strange land?

5 If I forget thee, O Jerusalem : let my right hand forget her cunning.

6 If I do not remember thee, let my tongue cleave to the roof of my mouth : yea, if I prefer not Jerusalem in my mirth.

7 Remember the children of Edom, O Lord, in the day of Jerusalem : how they said, Down with it, down with it, even to the ground.

8 O daughter of Babylon, wasted with misery : yea, happy shall he be that rewardeth thee, as thou hast served us.

9 Blessed shall he be that taketh thy children : and throweth them against the stones.

PSALM CXXXVIII. *Confitebor tibi.*

I WILL give thanks unto thee, O Lord, with my whole heart : even before the gods will I sing praise unto thee.

2 I will worship toward thy holy temple, and praise thy Name, because of thy loving-kindness and truth : for thou hast magnified thy Name, and thy Word, above all things.

3 When I called upon thee, thou heardest me : and enduedst my soul with much strength.

4 All the kings of the earth shall praise thee, O Lord : for they have heard the words of thy mouth.

5 Yea, they shall sing in the ways of the Lord : that great is the glory of the Lord.

6 For though the Lord be high, yet hath he respect unto the lowly : as for the proud, he beholdeth them afar off.

7 Though I walk in the midst of trouble, yet shalt thou refresh me : thou shalt stretch

forth thy hand upon the furiousness of mine enemies, and thy right hand shall save me.

8 The Lord shall make good his loving-kindness toward me : yea, thy mercy, O Lord, endureth for ever; despise not then the works of thine own hands.

Morning Prayer

PSALM CXXXIX. *Domine, probasti.*

O LORD, thou hast searched me out, and known me : thou knowest my down-sitting, and mine up-rising; thou understandest my thoughts long before.

2 Thou art about my path, and about my bed : and spiest out all my ways.

3 For lo, there is not a word in my tongue : but thou, O Lord, knowest it altogether.

4 Thou hast fashioned me behind and before : and laid thine hand upon me.

5 Such knowledge is too wonderful and excellent for me : I cannot attain unto it.

6 Whither shall I go then from thy Spirit : or whither shall I go then from thy presence?

7 If I climb up into heaven, thou art there : if I go down to hell, thou art there also.

8 If I take the wings of the morning : and remain in the uttermost parts of the sea;

9 Even there also shall thy hand lead me : and thy right hand shall hold me.

10 If I say, Peradventure the darkness shall cover me : then shall my night be turned to day.

11 Yea, the darkness is no darkness with thee, but the night is as clear as the day : the darkness and light to thee are both alike.

12 For my reins are thine : thou hast covered me in my mother's womb.

13 I will give thanks unto thee, for I am fearfully and wonderfully made : marvellous are thy works, and that my soul knoweth right well.

14 My bones are not hid from thee : though I be made secretly, and fashioned beneath in the earth.

15 Thine eyes did see my substance, yet being imperfect : and in thy book were all my members written;

16 Which day by day were fashioned : when as yet there was none of them.

17 How dear are thy counsels unto me, O God : O how great is the sum of them!

18 If I tell them, they are more in number than the sand : when I wake up I am present with thee.

19 Wilt thou not slay the wicked, O God : depart from me, ye blood-thirsty men.

20 For they speak unrighteously against thee : and thine enemies take thy Name in vain.

21 Do not I hate them, O Lord, that hate thee : and am not I grieved with those that rise up against thee?

22 Yea, I hate them right sore : even as though they were mine enemies.

23 Try me, O God, and seek the ground of my heart : prove me, and examine my thoughts.

24 Look well if there be any way of wickedness in me : and lead me in the way everlasting.

PSALM CXL. *Eripe me, Domine.*

DELIVER me, O Lord, from the evil man : and preserve me from the wicked man.

2 Who imagine mischief in their hearts : and stir up strife all the day long.

3 They have sharpened their tongues like a serpent : adder's poison is under their lips.

4 Keep me, O Lord, from the

hands of the ungodly : preserve me from the wicked men, who are purposed to overthrow my goings.

5 The proud have laid a snare for me, and spread a net abroad with cords : yea, and set traps in my way.

6 I said unto the Lord, Thou art my God : hear the voice of my prayers, O Lord.

7 O Lord God, thou strength of my health : thou hast covered my head in the day of battle.

8 Let not the ungodly have his desire, O Lord : let not his mischievous imagination prosper, lest they be too proud.

9 Let the mischief of their own lips fall upon the head of them : that compass me about.

10 Let hot burning coals fall upon them : let them be cast into the fire, and into the pit, that they never rise up again.

11 A man full of words shall not prosper upon the earth : evil shall hunt the wicked person to overthrow him.

12 Sure I am that the Lord will avenge the poor : and maintain the cause of the helpless.

13 The righteous also shall give thanks unto thy Name : and the just shall continue in thy sight.

PSALM CXLI. *Domine, clamavi.*

LORD, I call upon thee, haste thee unto me : and consider my voice when I cry unto thee.

2 Let my prayer be set forth in thy sight as the incense : and let the lifting up of my hands be an evening sacrifice.

3 Set a watch, O Lord, before my mouth : and keep the door of my lips.

4 O let not mine heart be inclined to any evil thing : let me not be occupied in ungodly works with the men that work wickedness, lest I eat of such things as please them.

5 Let the righteous rather smite me friendly : and reprove me.

6 But let not their precious balms break my head : yea, I will pray yet against their wickedness.

7 Let their judges be overthrown in stony places : that they may hear my words, for they are sweet.

8 Our bones lie scattered before the pit : like as when one breaketh and heweth wood upon the earth.

9 But mine eyes look unto thee, O Lord God : in thee is my trust, O cast not out my soul.

10 Keep me from the snare that they have laid for me : and from the traps of the wicked doers.

11 Let the ungodly fall into their own nets together : and let me ever escape them.

Evening Prayer

PSALM CXLII. *Voce mea ad Dominum.*

I CRIED unto the Lord with my voice : yea, even unto the Lord did I make my supplication.

2 I poured out my complaints before him : and shewed him of my trouble.

3 When my spirit was in heaviness thou knewest my path : in the way wherein I walked have they privily laid a snare for me.

4 I looked also upon my right hand : and saw there was no man that would know me.

5 I had no place to flee unto : and no man cared for my soul.

6 I cried unto thee, O Lord, and said : Thou art my hope, and my portion in the land of the living.

7 Consider my complaint : for I am brought very low.

8 O deliver me from my persecutors : for they are too strong for me.

PSALM CXLIII. *Domine, exaudi.*

9 Bring my soul out of prison, that I may give thanks unto thy Name : which thing if thou wilt grant me, then shall the righteous resort unto my company.

PSALM CXLIII. *Domine, exaudi.*

HEAR my prayer, O Lord, and consider my desire : hearken unto me for thy truth and righteousness' sake.

2 And enter not into judgement with thy servant : for in thy sight shall no man living be justified.

3 For the enemy hath persecuted my soul; he hath smitten my life down to the ground : he hath laid me in the darkness, as the men that have been long dead.

4 Therefore is my spirit vexed within me : and my heart within me is desolate.

5 Yet do I remember the time past; I muse upon all thy works : yea, I exercise myself in the works of thy hands.

6 I stretch forth my hands unto thee : my soul gaspeth unto thee as a thirsty land.

7 Hear me, O Lord, and that soon, for my spirit waxeth faint : hide not thy face from me, lest I be like unto them that go down into the pit.

8 O let me hear thy lovingkindness betimes in the morning, for in thee is my trust : shew thou me the way that I should walk in, for I lift up my soul unto thee.

9 Deliver me, O Lord, from mine enemies : for I flee unto thee to hide me.

10 Teach me to do the thing that pleaseth thee, for thou art my God : let thy loving Spirit lead me forth into the land of righteousness.

11 Quicken me, O Lord, for thy Name's sake : and for thy righteousness' sake bring my soul out of trouble.

12 And of thy goodness slay mine enemies : and destroy all them that vex my soul; for I am thy servant.

Morning Prayer

PSALM CXLIV. *Benedictus Dominus.*

BLESSED be the Lord my strength : who teacheth my hands to war, and my fingers to fight;

2 My hope and my fortress, my castle and deliverer, my defender in whom I trust : who subdueth my people that is under me.

3 Lord, what is man, that thou hast such respect unto him : or the son of man, that thou so regardest him?

4 Man is like a thing of nought : his time passeth away like a shadow.

5 Bow thy heavens, O Lord, and come down : touch the mountains, and they shall smoke.

6 Cast forth thy lightning, and tear them : shoot out thine arrows, and consume them.

7 Send down thine hand from above : deliver me, and take me out of the great waters, from the hand of strange children;

8 Whose mouth talketh of vanity : and their right hand is a right hand of wickedness.

9 I will sing a new song unto thee, O God : and sing praises unto thee upon a ten-stringed lute.

10 Thou hast given victory unto kings : and hast delivered David thy servant from the peril of the sword.

11 Save me, and deliver me from the hand of strange children : whose mouth talketh of vanity, and their right hand is a right hand of iniquity.

12 That our sons may grow up as the young plants : and that our daughters may be as the polished corners of the temple.

13 That our garners may be full and plenteous with all manner of store : that our sheep may bring

forth thousands and ten thousands in our streets.

14 That our oxen may be strong to labour, that there be no decay : no leading into captivity, and no complaining in our streets.

15 Happy are the people that are in such a case : yea, blessed are the people who have the Lord for their God.

PSALM CXLV. *Exaltabo te, Deus.*

I WILL magnify thee, O God, my King : and I will praise thy Name for ever and ever.

2 Every day will I give thanks unto thee : and praise thy Name for ever and ever.

3 Great is the Lord, and marvellous worthy to be praised : there is no end of his greatness.

4 One generation shall praise thy works unto another : and declare thy power.

5 As for me, I will be talking of thy worship : thy glory, thy praise, and wondrous works;

6 So that men shall speak of the might of thy marvellous acts : and I will also tell of thy greatness.

7 The memorial of thine abundant kindness shall be shewed : and men shall sing of thy righteousness.

8 The Lord is gracious, and merciful : long-suffering, and of great goodness.

9 The Lord is loving unto every man : and his mercy is over all his works.

10 All thy works praise thee, O Lord : and thy saints give thanks unto thee.

11 They shew the glory of thy kingdom : and talk of thy power;

12 That thy power, thy glory, and mightiness of thy kingdom : might be known unto men.

13 Thy kingdom is an everlasting kingdom : and thy dominion endureth throughout all ages.

14 The Lord upholdeth all such as fall : and lifteth up all those that are down.

15 The eyes of all wait upon thee, O Lord : and thou givest them their meat in due season.

16 Thou openest thine hand : and fillest all things living with plenteousness.

17 The Lord is righteous in all his ways : and holy in all his works.

18 The Lord is nigh unto all them that call upon him : yea, all such as call upon him faithfully.

19 He will fulfil the desire of them that fear him : he also will hear their cry, and will help them.

20 The Lord preserveth all them that love him : but scattereth abroad all the ungodly.

21 My mouth shall speak the praise of the Lord : and let all flesh give thanks unto his holy Name for ever and ever.

PSALM CXLVI. *Lauda, anima mea.*

PRAISE the Lord, O my soul; while I live will I praise the Lord : yea, as long as I have any being, I will sing praises unto my God.

2 O put not your trust in princes, nor in any child of man : for there is no help in them.

3 For when the breath of man goeth forth he shall turn again to his earth : and then all his thoughts perish.

4 Blessed is he that hath the God of Jacob for his help : and whose hope is in the Lord his God;

5 Who made heaven and earth, the sea, and all that therein is : who keepeth his promise for ever;

6 Who helpeth them to right that suffer wrong : who feedeth the hungry.

7 The Lord looseth men out of prison : the Lord giveth sight to the blind.

8 The Lord helpeth them that

are fallen : the Lord careth for the righteous.

9 The Lord careth for the strangers; he defendeth the fatherless and widow : as for the way of the ungodly, he turneth it upside down.

10 The Lord thy God, O Sion, shall be King for evermore : and throughout all generations.

Evening Prayer

PSALM CXLVII. *Laudate Dominum.*

O PRAISE the Lord, for it is a good thing to sing praises unto our God : yea, a joyful and pleasant thing it is to be thankful.

2 The Lord doth build up Jerusalem : and gather together the out-casts of Israel.

3 He healeth those that are broken in heart : and giveth medicine to heal their sickness.

4 He telleth the number of the stars : and calleth them all by their names.

5 Great is our Lord, and great is his power : yea, and his wisdom is infinite.

6 The Lord setteth up the meek : and bringeth the ungodly down to the ground.

7 O sing unto the Lord with thanksgiving : sing praises upon the harp unto our God;

8 Who covereth the heaven with clouds, and prepareth rain for the earth : and maketh the grass to grow upon the mountains, and herb for the use of men;

9 Who giveth fodder unto the cattle : and feedeth the young ravens that call upon him.

10 He hath no pleasure in the strength of an horse : neither delighteth he in any man's legs.

11 But the Lord's delight is in them that fear him : and put their trust in his mercy.

12 Praise the Lord, O Jerusalem : praise thy God, O Sion.

13 For he hath made fast the bars of thy gates : and hath blessed thy children within thee.

14 He maketh peace in thy borders : and filleth thee with the flour of wheat.

15 He sendeth forth his commandment upon earth : and his word runneth very swiftly.

16 He giveth snow like wool : and scattereth the hoar-frost like ashes.

17 He casteth forth his ice like morsels : who is able to abide his frost?

18 He sendeth out his word, and melteth them : he bloweth with his wind, and the waters flow.

19 He sheweth his word unto Jacob : his statutes and ordinances unto Israel.

20 He hath not dealt so with any nation : neither have the heathen knowledge of his laws.

PSALM CXLVIII. *Laudate Dominum.*

O PRAISE the Lord of heaven : praise him in the height.

2 Praise him, all ye angels of his : praise him, all his host.

3 Praise him, sun and moon : praise him, all ye stars and light.

4 Praise him, all ye heavens : and ye waters that are above the heavens.

5 Let them praise the Name of the Lord : for he spake the word, and they were made; he commanded, and they were created.

6 He hath made them fast for ever and ever : he hath given them a law which shall not be broken.

7 Praise the Lord upon earth : ye dragons, and all deeps;

8 Fire and hail, snow and vapours : wind and storm, fulfilling his word;

9 Mountains and all hills : fruitful trees and all cedars;

10 Beasts and all cattle : worms and feathered fowls;

11 Kings of the earth and all

Day 30.   THE PSALMS.   Day 30.

people : princes and all judges of the world;

12 Young men and maidens, old men and children, praise the Name of the Lord : for his Name only is excellent, and his praise above heaven and earth.

13 He shall exalt the horn of his people; all his saints shall praise him : even the children of Israel, even the people that serveth him.

PSALM CXLIX. *Cantate Domino.*

O SING unto the Lord a new song : let the congregation of saints praise him.

2 Let Israel rejoice in him that made him : and let the children of Sion be joyful in their King.

3 Let them praise his Name in the dance : let them sing praises unto him with tabret and harp.

4 For the Lord hath pleasure in his people : and helpeth the meek-hearted.

5 Let the saints be joyful with glory : let them rejoice in their beds.

6 Let the praises of God be in their mouth : and a two-edged sword in their hands;

7 To be avenged of the heathen : and to rebuke the people;

8 To bind their kings in chains : and their nobles with links of iron.

9 That they may be avenged of them, as it is written : Such honour have all his saints.

PSALM CL. *Laudate Dominum.*

O PRAISE God in his holiness : praise him in the firmament of his power.

2 Praise him in his noble acts : praise him according to his excellent greatness.

3 Praise him in the sound of the trumpet : praise him upon the lute and harp.

4 Praise him in the cymbals and dances : praise him upon the strings and pipe.

5 Praise him upon the well-tuned cymbals : praise him upon the loud cymbals.

6 Let every thing that hath breath : praise the Lord.

Printed in the USA
CPSIA information can be obtained
at www.ICGtesting.com
CBHW050221171024
15986CB00004B/65